# Where to Watch Birds in Europe

With *Where to Watch Birds*, his first book, John Gooders scored an immediate success. He left a career as a teacher and lecturer at a college of education to become editor of the nine volume encyclopedia, *Birds of the World*. In 1970 he took two months off on a Churchill Fellowship to study migration through North Africa. Subsequently he launched his own magazine *World of Birds*, but left after a year to write television scripts for Anglia Television's *Survival* series and edit the company's house magazine, *The World of Survival*. He now devotes his time to full-time writing about birds and natural history. He lives in London, where his wife runs the wildlife photographic agency, Ardea. They have two children and a cottage in Sussex, where bird-watching and the family come first.

His *How to Watch Birds* and *Where to Watch Birds* are also published in Pan Books.

# John Gooders

in collaboration with Jeremy Brock

# Where to Watch Birds in Europe

**Pan Books** London and Sydney

First published 1970 as Where to Watch Birds in Britain and Europe
by André Deutsch Ltd
This edition published 1974 by André Deutsch Ltd
First published in paperback 1978 by Pan Books Ltd,
Cavaye Place, London SW10 9PG
© John Gooders 1970, 1974
ISBN 0 330 25315 8
Made and printed in Great Britain by
Richard Clay (The Chaucer Press) Ltd, Bungay, Suffolk

to Su

# Contents

# List of Maps

# List of Illustrations

# Acknowledgements

I am grateful to all of those bird-watchers who have entertained me with accounts of their travels, sent me details of their routes, parted with their favourite spots, and given me their most useful contacts. Many have read parts and chapters in draft and offered advice and criticism. I have corresponded with the leading ornithologists in many countries, and in some cases they have done my job by selecting the areas for inclusion and sending me all the details that I needed to write up the accounts. By and large they are listed under countries below. There are also a large number of other correspondents throughout Europe who have supplied details of one or more places that they know intimately. It has sometimes been surprising to receive details intended for publication of the exact whereabouts of rare or scarce species, in one case even down to a cross on a map for the nest site. I have used my discretion regarding the publication of the whereabouts of rare birds and in several cases have been deliberately vague. I have also felt free to use the literature, though in many cases it is out of date and cannot be relied upon. I have enjoyed the use of the Map Room of the British Museum, and the Bird Room and General Library of the British Museum of Natural History, to the staff of which I am extremely grateful. The tourist boards, cultural exchange organizations, and embassies of many countries have supplied useful travel and other information, and the AA have been of similar assistance.

Particular help has been received from:
Belgium – R. F. Verheyen
Bulgaria – B. L. Sage
Czechoslovakia – J. Boswall, I. Brdicka, Dr W. Černý
Denmark – Dr C. Smout
Faroes – R. G. Gibbs
Finland – D. Shepherd, A. J. Smith
France – P. Barruel
Germany – Dr H. Kramer, Dr R. S. Pfeifer, Dr W. Przygodda, W. Valk
Greece – A. D. Brewer, R. Hitchcock, M. E. Hodge, R. H. Wilson
Holland – J. F. Burton, R. Kettle, W. Valk
Hungary – L. A. Batten, Dr A. Keve
Ireland – W. Valk
Iceland – P. J. Sellar
Poland – Z. Głowacinski

Portugal – R. G. Gibbs, N. Gordon, R. O. Vincente
Romania – J. A. Burton
Switzerland – Sir H. F. I. Elliott
Sweden – R. Gyllin, Dr K. Curry-Lindahl
Turkey – R. Porter
Yugoslavia – E. J. Salholm, B. L. Sage, Professor I. Tutman
The following have supplied information and help in one form or another
from whole regions downwards:

J. Auburn, Dr E. K. Barth, G. Bergengren, N. Binsbergen, J. R. Brock,
C-I. Carlsson, A. Clarke, M. D. England, A. J. Gaston, M. Gauntlett,
C. Griffiths, N. Henson, Dr L. Hoffman, S. Hogstrom, Dr W. Keil, A. Knox,
Dr C. Konig, K. Paludan, N. O. Preuss, P. Lindberg, M. F. M. Meiklejohn,
D. J. Montier, B. Nau, P. J. Olney, U. Ottoson, W. Plomer, Dr G. Rudebeck,
L. Rydbeck, A. Stagen, A. G. Verrall, D. Wood.

Academy Travel, Animals Magazine, Bundesanstalt für Vegetationskunde
Naturschutz und Landschaftspflege, Deutscher Bund für Vogelschutz,
International Council for Bird Preservation, International Wildfowl
Research Bureau, Irish Society for the Protection of Birds, Naturfrednings-
radet (København), Ornitholidays, Polska Akademia Nank Zaklad
Ochrony Przyrody, Schweizerische Vogelwarte Sempach, Staatliche
Vogelschutzwarte für Baden-Württemberg, Staatliche Vogelschutzwarte
des Landes Nordrhein – Westfalen, University College of North Wales,
Iberian Expedition 1967, Vereniging Tot Behoud Van Natuurmonumenten
in Nederland, Vogelschutzwarte für Hessen Rheinland-Pfalz und Saarland,
Vogelwarte Radolfzell.

I have relied for translations on Mrs K. Lloyd in particular, and Miss S.
Brewer, Miss C. Mattsson, C. Svensgaard and Mrs W. Wisniowiecka. Mrs
D. Sculley has turned my much amended manuscript into an acceptable
typescript. Piers Burnett of the publishers, and Bruce Coleman have been
helpful at every stage that books pass through.

Finally my thanks are due to my collaborator, Jeremy Brock, who has been
responsible for collecting the material for a number of countries and has helped
at every stage in the work of producing this guide. Without his help it would
have been a far less useful book. Between us we have visited almost every
country in Europe, and travelled from the Varanger Fjord to southern Portugal, and Asiatic Turkey to Cape Wrath. We both agreed that each time we
started working on a country we immediately wanted to go to the places we
discovered and we hope that readers will feel the same.

Additional information on any area, and full details of any place not included would be most welcome for any future revisions. Following a similar
appeal in *Where to Watch Birds* details of large numbers of new places were
sent. With Europe I anticipate, and would welcome, a flood. An imitation in
note form of the method of treatment used in the book is ideal. Please send to
John Gooders, c/o André Deutsch Ltd, 105 Great Russell Street, London
WC1, United Kingdom.

# Preface

While it is interesting to keep a list of the birds seen in a back-garden it is more interesting and worthwhile to list the birds of a local park, neighbourhood, or county. So, the argument continues, it is even better to list the birds seen in a particular country and thus we have the Austrian List, British List, Czechoslovakian List, etc. If someone looks skywards long enough, say from a backyard in Solihull, he will sooner or later see a rough-legged buzzard, wild swans, and who knows what other rarities. All can be added to the list, but in what sense are they birds of a back-garden? And of what interest is it that if one puts in enough hours staring skywards and has the ability to identify what is seen, perseverance will be finally rewarded by a sight of birds that we know must pass over the district every so often anyway? The British List is a hallowed institution that by the luck of history and geography has a certain logic to it. But whereas that list notes the occurrence of birds on a group of offshore islands that form an entity, what of the Czech List, German List, or Polish List? The frontiers of these countries are drawn for political reasons, and have been redrawn at least twice this century with deletions and additions to the appropriate list. A rare bird could do a quick lap of Lake Constance and get itself added to the Austrian, German, and Swiss Lists in a matter of a few hours. Indeed, it seems quite possible that an American laughing gull did something similar by visiting Sweden in 1964, France in 1965, and Britain in 1966. The possibility of this bird(s) having been an escape merely adds to the hilarity of national lists.

Fortunately this insular approach is dying. The *Field Guide to the Birds of Britain and Europe* first published in 1954 and since translated into eleven foreign languages did more than anything else to break us of the absurd, but understandable, habit of considering as somehow rather different birds that have managed to stagger to our shores. Voous's *Atlas of European Birds* continued the trend in 1960, showing that Europe can and should be treated as a zoogeographic entity and not as a series of isolated politically limited pockets. Finally the successor to the *Handbook of British Birds*, Witherby's ornithologist's bible, is to be *The Birds of the Western Palearctic*, i.e. Europe. Of course, this does not go far enough. The Palearctic is a zoogeographic region, the Western Palearctic barely half a region. But it should bring ornithological unity to Europe, and together with *The Birds of the Soviet Union* (now in process of translation) covers the best part of the Palearctic.

There has been one further, and I believe important, influence on the European concept of bird-watching that is peculiar to Britain. Guy Mountfort's series of *Portraits*, the first of which *Portrait of a Wilderness* has been said to read like the *Field Guide* in narrative form, have opened the eyes of many of the younger generation to the wonderful birds around the Mediterranean basin and in south-eastern Europe. The well organized expeditions that were the basis of these books have been followed by other bird-watchers in more or less organized fashions, and finally by the young sleep-under-a-hedge hitch-hiking brigade. It is surprising what is being found by these travellers, most of whom do not send records of what they see to anyone, let alone for publication. Whilst working on this guide I have received details of Marmora's warblers at no less than seven places on the European mainland from one end of the Mediterranean to the other. Yet the textbooks say that Marmora's warbler is confined to islands and one site on the east coast of Spain.

*Where to Watch Birds in Britain and Europe* has been designed to cater for the needs of the ornitho-traveller on a European scale. Where, for instance, are the nearest great white herons to Malmö? The nearest white-winged black terns to Frankfurt? The most convenient white storks to Manchester? The easiest-to-find dotterels from Paris? Or the most accessible Alpine swifts from Amsterdam? Many have automatically sought the answers to these and other questions in the Camargue and the Coto Donãna and most have never heard of the Biebrzanskie marshes or the Obedska Bara.

This guide has the basic aim of opening the eyes of the would-be traveller to the possibilities of places he has never heard of, and perhaps persuading him to go. We know most of what there is at the Camargue, we do not know very much about the Gulf of Arta in Greece. We would like to know more. Many people prefer to know exactly where to go, and what they are going to see where, almost down to the last bush. For them there are griffon vultures at Ronda, masked shrikes at Avas gorge, and hundreds of others. To those who prefer to find their own birds in a good but comparatively unknown area, where they can make an original contribution to our knowledge, there are the marshes at Pyrgos, the lagoons of Languedoc, and the majority of the other places mentioned in the book. It must be borne in mind that ornithology outside a very few countries like Britain, Germany and Holland is very young and that there is nothing like the organization provided in this country by the British Trust for Ornithology, the Royal Society for the Protection of Birds, and the network of county and regional societies. In many countries detailed knowledge of distribution is scanty or even non-existent, and anyone who spends a bird-watching holiday in a confined area will often become the 'expert'. Nevertheless we have tried to meet the obvious needs of the traveller who wants to know where to go, when to go, what he will see, where he might stay, how to get there, where to obtain permits, and the state of knowledge. This book could have been twice its size. Indeed it is possible to produce a guide similar to my *Where to Watch Birds* (in England, Scotland, and Wales) for every country in Europe; such guides are already planned for Germany and Greece. Clearly, there is a need for a guide to almost every spot in a particular country for local inhabitants, but there is also a need for a holiday guide to the best spots in a whole sub-continent. No one wants to buy twenty guides to cover the whole of Europe.

In this book many of the best spots are often grouped together to form a holiday unit. Some smaller places, however, though far too restricted for a holiday just could not be resisted. Thus the user will find the southern part of the French Massif Central under the Gorges du Tarn, and Ringköbing Fjord in Danish Jutland given similar treatment. There is no justification for devoting the same attention to a lake as one does to a region save only that most bird-watchers would do the same.

The format is basically the same as *Where to Watch Birds* with a description of the birds and habitats of the area, a summary table of birds, and travel directions. Jargon and abbreviation have been eliminated as far as possible and what little there is needs no explanation. Maps vary so much from country to country that it is impracticable to give the equivalent Ordnance Survey number as was done in the British book. In the preparation we have used the cheap maps prepared for the various petrol companies, specialized 1:50,000 maps produced by the government of the country concerned, and everything between. We have found the Esso maps of individual countries most useful for general locations with GSGS 1:200,000 (British military maps) useful for countries not covered, and for areas with very low populations, like Lapland. The best advice, and what we did, is to consult Stanford, 12–14 Long Acre, London, WC2, when an area has been chosen. While distances are given in kilometres as almost all maps of continental countries use this unit, areas and heights are given in standard British units for ease of understanding. Access details are given including addresses for permits where necessary. 'Reserves', however, does not necessarily mean the same thing in each country. While permits are generally required here, access there is straightforward if not downright lax. 'Warden' too can mean anything from manager to vermin exterminator, and what counts as vermin in one country might be highly prized and protected in the next.

The names of birds are those in current English usage and follow the 1966 revised *Field Guide* except where it attempts to lead rather than follow. The name bearded reedling for instance, though far more appropriate, is not used by bird-watchers who stick firmly to bearded tit.

# Reading List

This bibliography is a selected list of general references that might be helpful to intending travellers and is not a record of works consulted in the preparation of this guide. The works cited are additional to those mentioned at the beginning of each chapter.

Davidson A. *A Bird-Watcher in Scandinavia* (1954)
Jorgensen H. I. *Nomina Avium Europaearum* (1958)
Mountfort G. *Portrait of a Wilderness* (1958)
Mountfort G. *Portrait of a River* (1962)
Peterson R. T., Mountfort G., Hollom P. A. D. *A Field Guide to the Birds of Britain and Europe* (1966)
Vaurie C. *The Birds of the Palearctic Fauna* (1959–1965)
Voous K. H. *Atlas of European Birds* (1960)

# Albania

Visitors to Albania must join one of the approved tourist parties and be sure not to partake in any independent activity like talking to natives. It seems unlikely that many birds would be seen on such a venture. There are several excellent wetland spots that would attract bird-watchers could they get at them.

# Austria

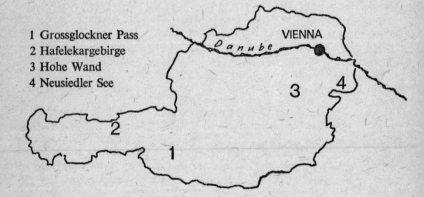

1 Grossglockner Pass
2 Hafelekargebirge
3 Hohe Wand
4 Neusiedler See

VIENNA

*Danube*

ÖSTERREICHISCHE VOGELWARTE NEUSIEDLERSEE,
Neusiedl-am-See, Burgenland.

READ: *Verzeichnis der Vögel Osterreichs* (1951) by K. Bauer and G. Rokitaskk (Neusieldl).

## GROSSGLOCKNER PASS

The Grossglockner is one of the major passes between Austria and Italy and is an excellent stopping place for magnificent views and high Alpine birds. There are a few chalets at the top and hordes of Alpine choughs loaf around the parked cars picking up discarded picnic scraps. Alpine accentors and snow finches are also easy to see here, and there are water pipits nearby. The odd griffon vulture is sometimes seen and the Tauern Mountains have seen the return of the lammergeier in recent years. Crag martins are found on the south side of the pass, and a stop should be made for citril finch *en route* to the top. These little birds haunt the upper edge of the pine forests and are not found at the top itself.

SUMMER: griffon vulture, Alpine chough, Alpine swift, crag martin, Alpine accentor, snow finch, citril finch, water pipit.

Leave Salzburg southwards on the E17 and turn left at Lofer on to route 168. At Bruck take route 107 southwards to Grossglockner. A fee is payable.

## HAFELEKARGEBIRGE

The Hafelekargebirge is a typical mountain area of the Austrian Tyrol rising to over 7,000 feet and resembles thousands of other such areas throughout the country. It has no rarities but is the haunt of the usual Alpine birds. There are, however, two factors in its favour. Firstly it lies immediately north of one of Austria's most popular resorts, Innsbruck; and secondly it can be reached by cable car. Undoubtedly the major attraction are the high Alpine birds that can be seen without effort. Alpine choughs in particular are present in large numbers feeding from the hands of visiting tourists and snapping up the crumbs at the mountain-top café. Walking westwards away from the crowds produces other high top species like snow finch and Alpine accentor. The coniferous woodland below holds nutcracker, buzzard, and black redstart, while the valley floor has red-backed shrike and whinchat. Overhead there are black kite and raven.

SUMMER: black kite, buzzard, nutcracker, red-backed shrike, raven, Alpine chough, Alpine accentor, whinchat, redstart, black redstart, snow finch.

Access to the top is by cable car from Innsbruck. For those who are fit and like walking, the descent through the forest will take five hours including excellent bird-watching *en route*.

## HOHE WAND

*Hohe Wand* in German means literally 'high wall', and that just about sums up
this spot to the west of Eisenstadt and 50 km south-west of Vienna. At this
point a high plateau plunges dramatically to the valley below and the spectacular scenery that results is a well-known tourist spot with a road to the top.
The forests are coniferous and hold nutcracker, crested tit, and capercaillie.
The rocky cliff itself has rock thrush and rock bunting and is a known haunt
of the rare wall creeper. Of course, most of the places where wall creepers
occur are spectacular, but there cannot be many more so than this.
   SUMMER: capercaillie, nutcracker, wall creeper, rock thrush, crested tit,
rock bunting, Bonelli's warbler.
   This is a good spot for a day trip, mostly on the E7 motorway, from Vienna,
or as a rest from the marshes of Neusiedl. Leave Eisenstadt westwards on
route 222 and watch out for signs to Hohe Wand after 8 km.

## NEUSIEDLER SEE

This huge inland lake is 25 km long and up to 7 km wide. It lies in Burgenland,
the extreme eastern province of Austria, which is geographically more akin to
neighbouring Hungary than to the rest of the country. Lake Neusiedl is the
only example of a steppe lake in Western Europe but even so overlaps the
Hungarian frontier to the south. The lake is nowhere deeper than six feet and
nearly half of its surface is covered with emergent vegetation, notably vast
reed beds which are in places 6 km wide. 280 species of birds have been recorded here. Amongst the most important breeding in the reedbelt are great
white heron (the colony of about 200 pairs is the largest in Western Europe)
spoonbill, and purple heron, though there are other attractions like greylag
goose, ferruginous duck, Savi's, moustached and great reed warblers, little
bittern and a variety of rails. Away from the reeds a wide variety of birds can
be found on the adjoining farmland and in the villages. Around the typical
village are serin, Syrian woodpecker, black redstart, barred and marsh
warblers, hoopoe, crested lark, and lesser grey shrike, with penduline tit,
golden oriole and aquatic warbler amongst the scrub where the reeds begin.
There are also numbers of avocet, and black-tailed godwit in appropriate
places, and twenty-five pairs of white stork breed in Rust. In autumn and
winter there are vast numbers of wildfowl on the lake including up to 100,000
geese mainly white-fronted and bean.
   To the east of Neusiedler See is the large vineyard area of Seewinkel with its
many small alkaline lakes, several with muddy margins. Variations in the
water level attract large numbers of migrant waders including Temminck's
stint and marsh sandpiper, and such species as Caspian tern, white-winged
black tern and Mediterranean gull. Amongst breeding birds are greylag
goose and black-necked grebe galore. Particular attention should be paid to
the Oberstinkersee, Lange Lacke, and Zicksee near Illmitz (not to be confused

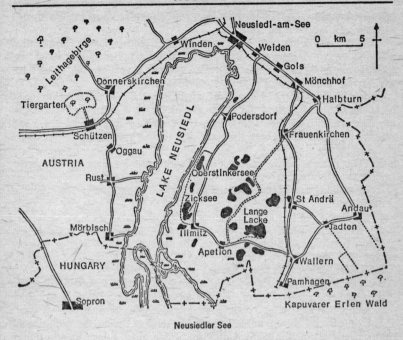

Neusiedler See

with a larger and more commercialized lake of the same name near St
Andrä).

South-east of Seewinkel is the Tadten Plain adjoining the Hungarian
border. This steppe country is intensively cultivated but still holds a few pairs
of great bustards as well as quail and black-tailed godwit. It is also visited by a
very interesting variety of raptors from the Hungarian forests to the south, but
these can best be seen south of Tadten near the border, soaring over the
Kapuvarer Erlen Wald which is actually in Hungary. Regularly noted raptors
include imperial, spotted, and lesser spotted eagles, all three harriers, hobby,
red-footed falcon, lesser kestrel, honey buzzard and goshawk. Black storks
also occasionally join them.

The Leithagebirge is a range of wooded hills north-west of Neusiedl that
holds lesser spotted eagle, goshawk, black stork, and roller amongst others.

SUMMER: black-necked grebe, red-necked grebe, greylag goose, ferruginous
duck, spoonbill, great white heron, purple heron, night heron, bittern, little
bittern, white stork, black stork, imperial eagle, spotted eagle, lesser spotted
eagle, marsh harrier, Montagu's harrier, hen harrier, red-footed falcon, lesser
kestrel, honey buzzard, goshawk, spotted crake, little crake, great bustard,
Kentish plover, black-tailed godwit, avocet, roller, Syrian woodpecker,
woodchat shrike, lesser grey shrike, Savi's warbler, moustached warbler,

great-reed warbler, aquatic warbler, river warbler, barred warbler, bluethroat penduline tit, bearded tit, serin.

AUTUMN: greylag goose, bean goose, duck, Kentish plover, black-tailed godwit, green sandpiper, wood sandpiper, marsh sandpiper, spotted redshank, greenshank, little stint, Temminck's stint, turnstone, ruff, avocet, black tern, white-winged black tern, Caspian tern, Mediterranean gull.

Neusiedl-am-See is the ideal centre for exploring the area and a vast range of birds can be found around the village and along the road that runs down to the lake shore. The Neusiedl single track railway line provides a good vantage point for views over the reed beds to north and south. Excursions should include:

1.  The village of Rust on the western shore, and *en route* the Tiergarten Park near Schützen if open.
2.  Seewinkel and particularly Oberstinkersee, Lange Lacke, and Zicksee near Illmitz.
3.  Tadten Plain to the south-east of Seekwinkel.
4.  Kapuvarer Erlen Wald; leave Tadten south-eastwards towards the Hungarian border. Stop in sight of the frontier and watch for soaring raptors.
5.  Leithagebirge hills north-west of Neusiedl-am-See.
6.  The Schönnbrunn Park near the centre of Vienna is worth visiting for grey-headed, green, Syrian, lesser-spotted, middle-spotted, and great spotted woodpeckers, and collared and red-breasted flycatchers.

There are hotels in Neusiedl-am-See and in some of the smaller villages, and camp sites at Rust, Illmitz, St Andrä, and Podersdorf. Leave Vienna south-eastwards on route 10 to Neusiedl.

# Belgium

1 Blankaart
2 Campine
3 Genk
4 Harchies

5 Hautes-Fagnes National Park
6 Kalmthout Heath
7 Yser Estuary
8 Zwin

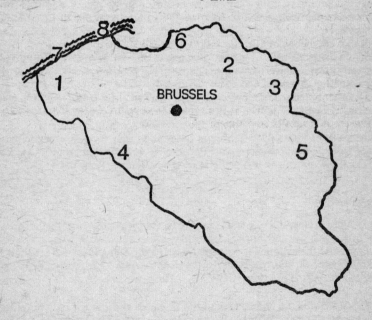

LES RÉSERVES NATURELLES ET ORNITHOLOGIQUES DE BELGIQUE,
31 rue Vautier, Bruxelles 4.

SECTION DE LA CONSERVATION DE LA NATURE ET DES RESERVES A L'IRSNB,
31 rue Vautier, Bruxelles 4.

READ: the IRSNB has published an eight volume work on Belgian birds (1934–
1951) by R. Verheyen. Each volume has a different title.


## BLANKAART

Blankaart lies in western Belgium to the south-west of Woumen which is
south of Diksmuide, and was declared a reserve covering 1,000 acres in 1959.
It lies on the marshy right bank of the River Yser and its centre consists of the
170 acre Lake Blankaart. A large part of the lake is covered with floating
reeds amounting to quite extensive reed beds in many places, and it is surrounded by permanent water meadows. These are the haunt of many birds
including black-tailed godwit. But it is the lake itself, and particularly the reed
beds that are the major attraction. Bittern and little bittern breed and all three
common harriers have done so, the marsh harrier regularly. Reed, and
probably great reed warblers breed and there is a good population of passage
and wintering duck and waders.

SUMMER: bittern, little bittern, marsh harrier, Montagu's harrier, hen
harrier, black-tailed godwit, reed warbler, great reed warbler.

Blankaart is on the west side of route 69 just south of which is Woumen
4 km south of Diksmuide. There are buses and trains from Diksmuide, and
buses from Ieper, Roeselare, and Poperinghe. Information from RNOB, De
Blankaart, Woumen, West-Flanders: or 31 rue Vautier, Bruxelles 4.


## CAMPINE

The Campine is an infertile sandy land, covered by extensive heathlands with
marshes, swamps, and bogs. Large areas are covered with woods, mainly
conifers, and the avifauna is particularly rich in breeding species. Three areas
are reserves of various types and they lie close together 35 km east of Antwerp
to the north of the motorway E39.

1.  **Snepkensvijver:** a typical area of the Campine and though only covering
fifty acres exhibits all of the landforms—heath, marsh and woodland. 16,000
pairs of black-headed gulls dominate the scene but there are a few pairs of
teal, curlew, water rail, and at least one pair of black woodpeckers. The
reserve is near Herentals.

SUMMER: teal, water rail, curlew, black-headed gull, black woodpecker.

Leave the E39 northwards at Bouwel. The reserve belongs to the RNOB and visitors should contact them at 31 rue Vautier, Bruxelles 4.

2.  **Zegge:** a slightly larger area covering 100 acres in the marshy valley of the Petite-Nèthe near Geel. This is a very varied area with dry heathland as well as bogs and swamps with scrub. It is the haunt of bittern, water rail, and spotted crake while black-tailed godwits are found in the meadows and bluethroats in the scrub. Migrants are predominantly duck.

SUMMER: bittern, water rail, spotted crake, black-tailed godwit, curlew, bluethroat.

Geel to the north is 14 km on from Herentals above. It is a small town with the Hotel Concordia and a camp site, and would be a good centre for exploring this area. The reserve is owned by the Société Royale de Zoologie d'Anvers, Koningin Astridplein, Antwerp, and is managed by the RNOB who appoint the warden Mr M. Verbruggen, Groene Wanderling 11, s'Gravenwezel, Antwerp.

3.  **Tikkebroeken:** the name given to the marshes of Kasterlee which are 9 km north of Geel on route 20. The reserve which covers 125 acres is situated on the marshes of the Rode Loop, a tiny tributary of the Petite-Nèthe. The vegetation is varied but dominated by the thick undergrowth and various berry-bearing trees. Small marshes, lakes, and meadows are also found, as are many acid loving flowering plants. 50 species breed here including water rail and bluethroat in the marshes, and long-eared owl and black woodpecker in the surrounding pines.

SUMMER: water rail, long-eared owl, black woodpecker, bluethroat.

The reserve is administered and partially owned by the De Wielewaal Ornithological Society. Kasterlee can be reached by 'bus from Geel, Turnhout, and Westerlo. Contact De Wielewaal, Mr F. Segers, Graatakker 13, Turnhout.

## GENK

Genk lies in the north-eastern corner of Belgium to the north of Liège near Hasselt. The area was declared a reserve in 1956 and now covers 550 acres. The main part is the marshy valley of Stiemerbeck bordering the plateau of the Campine. Here there are 20 lakes bordered by peat marshes with an extensive growth of reeds that are mainly the result of human activities. They are surrounded by vast heathlands. The area is unique in Belgium for the variety of flowers and holds 80 breeding species of birds. Outstanding amongst these are both bitterns, marsh harrier, and black tern. Purple herons sometimes breed as do whiskered terns. A good area for migrant waders and wildfowl.

SUMMER: bittern, little bittern, purple heron? pochard? marsh harrier, black tern, whiskered tern, nightjar.

Leave Hasselt, which is just by-passed by the E39, northwards on route 15. Turn right on to route 22 to Genk. There are buses. Contact RNOB, 31 rue Vautier, Bruxelles 4.

## HARCHIES

Harchies lies on the French border to the west of Mons in that rather uninspiring industrial area based on coal mining. The nature reserve here covers 750 acres of flooded mining subsidence which, like most other such areas, has given rise to shallow marshy lagoons and vast reed beds. It is not exactly everyone's idea of the joys of bird-watching but for those that do not mind the surroundings the birds here are really excellent. Bittern and little bittern both breed as do marsh harrier, and black-tailed godwit on the surrounding fields. Bluethroats haunt the tangled willows and the area is outstanding as the only site of Cetti's warbler in the country. This bird is, however, spreading north and will no doubt soon appear in other places.

SUMMER: great crested grebe, bittern, little bittern, marsh harrier, black-tailed godwit, bluethroat, Cetti's warbler.

The reserve is administered by the RNOB who appoint the warden P. Simon, Ferme de Graux, Gaurain-Ramecroix, Hainault. Harchies can be reached by train from Mons, or by road. Leave the E10 (route 22) northwards on to route 61. Turn left to Harchies after 11 km.

## HAUTES-FAGNES NATIONAL PARK

The High Fagnes National Park consists of part of the high plateau in the extreme east of Belgium near Liège together with the Baraque Michel (so-called because of a small hut built on that spot in 1808 by a villager of Jalhay who had lost his way in the snow). It covers 9,015 acres and is mainly known for its extraordinary peat deposits – in French 'fagnes' means moss-hags. Though of great interest geomorphologically, hydrologically, palaebotani-cally, etc., the wild scenery attracts crowds of visitors every year. Nevertheless it is a lonely plain at 2,000 feet bordered by thick woodland with red deer, roe deer, wild boar, and wolves until 1848, though recently forestry activity has menaced several of the more valuable sites. Buzzards breed and the red grouse is still an exciting and rare attraction to continental bird-watchers. During migration this is a principal resting place of cranes.

SUMMER: buzzard, curlew, red grouse.

PASSAGE: crane.

There are buses into the park from Verviers where there is a good range of hotels, and there are many camp sites in and around the Park.

## KALMTHOUT HEATH

Kalmthout was declared a reserve in its present form in 1964 covering 4,200 acres. It lies to the north of Antwerp near the Dutch border and is typical of the infertile Campine landscape. The open heaths are interrupted by areas of marsh, by open sand dunes, and by quite extensive areas of woodland. The proximity of the area to the massive feeding grounds of the huge Escaut,

Meuse, and Rhine delta is responsible for its wealth of breeding and migrating marsh birds. These include many duck like teal, garganey, and shelduck, waders including black-tailed godwit, and black terns. The pine woods that turn the area from a rather boring landscape into one reminiscent of parts of Scotland are the haunt of the magnificent black woodpecker, long-eared owl, black grouse, and hobby. Many species of duck and waders pass through on passage.

SUMMER: black-necked grebe, teal, garganey, pochard, shelduck, redshank, curlew, black-tailed godwit, black-headed gull, black tern, long-eared owl, black grouse, black woodpecker.

Leave Antwerp northwards on the E10 and fork left to Kalmthout at Maria-ter-Heide. There are trains and 'buses from Antwerp. Visitors intending to visit the reserve should contact Mr G. Huyskens (Conservateur), Dorpstraat 74, Stabroek, Antwerp.


## YSER ESTUARY

The Yser is not a long river and its estuary near Nieuwpoort is not large, especially when compared with the massive inlets to the north-east. It nevertheless remains one of the few areas of marsh between the Scheldt and the little estuaries of the Boulonnais and attracts a great many migrating waders that use this major coastal route. Part of the area is a reserve and this covers a cross section of the landforms including part of the Yser channel, the Lombardzijde creek, an area of brackish ditches, dykes and some large dunes. It is the only permanent site of *Beta maritima* in Belgium and holds many of the more interesting breeding birds of the area. These include little ringed and Kentish plovers, shelduck, avocet, and crested lark. Though birds like avocets are worth seeing any time this really is a better place during migration with little stint, curlew sandpiper, wood and green sandpipers, etc., all present in good numbers.

SUMMER: shelduck, little ringed plover, Kentish plover, oystercatcher, crested lark.

PASSAGE: duck, little stint, curlew sandpiper, wood sandpiper, green sandpiper, gulls, terns.

The estuary is easily reached from Nieuwpoort which has good train, tram, and 'bus services, or from Veurne, Diksmuide, and Ostend. For information about the reserve write to RNOB, De Blankaart, Woumen, West-Flanders. Accommodation at masses of hotels and camp sites along the coast.


## ZWIN

The Zwin reserve is one of the best known ornithological sites in Belgium. It lies on the Dutch border and indeed extends by some 60 acres across the frontier. This together with the 320 acres on the Belgian side is the centre of the reserve though there are restrictions covering some 3,750 acres in all. It was created in 1952 to protect the old saltings at the former mouth of the Zwin through which ships sailed to Bruges until the thirteenth century. It is flooded by the sea every year and has a characteristic flora including the very rare *Obione pendunculata*. The birds of the area are not unusual but include several of those species that come as far as the Channel and tantalisingly no further, plus a range of rare British breeders. In the latter category are avocet and black-tailed godwit, and in the former Kentish plover and icterine warbler. There are gull and tern colonies, and in the drier areas both hoopoe and golden oriole breed. Zwin is particularly attractive during passage periods when most of the western European waders pass through in good numbers. The immediate hinterland which is a separate reserve called Damme holds 2,000–3,000 white-fronts in winter, with several hundred pink-feet and bean geese. It is a breeding place of snipe and godwit. A unique feature, but one of growing popularity abroad, is the aviary collection of over 500 species of birds. These are a considerable attraction and there is a zoo-like 'tea-room and children' atmosphere in this part. In spite of this the bird-watching, as at Slimbridge for instance, is excellent.

SUMMER: greylag goose, shelduck, ringed plover, Kentish plover, black-tailed godwit, oystercatcher, curlew, avocet, black-headed gull, little tern, common tern, hoopoe, golden oriole, icterine warbler.

WINTER: white-fronted goose, bean goose, pink-footed goose.

To get to the Zwin follow the road that skirts the old airfield. During the summer a 'bus service runs between the station of Knokke, the centre of the town, Le Zoute, and the Zwin. Knokke is accessible by 'bus and train from Ostend and Bruges. From the top of the sand dunes there are magnificent views over the mouth of the Scheldt and the Island of Walcheren. Admission fees are 15 BF, and 5 BF for children under 12 years. Knokke and Le Zoute are holiday resorts with plenty of accommodation and an excellent camp site. For the Damme reserve, which lies 7 km from Bruges, contact RNOB, 31 rue Vautier, Bruxelles 4: visits in winter for geese.

# Britain

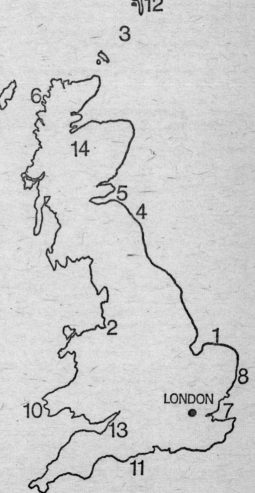

LONDON

BRITISH ORNITHOLOGISTS' UNION,
c/o The Bird Room, British Museum (Natural History), Tring, Herts.

BRITISH ORNITHOLOGISTS' CLUB,
As for the Union.

BRITISH TRUST FOR ORNITHOLOGY,
Beech Grove, Tring, Herts.

NATURE CONSERVANCY,
England: 19 Belgrave Square, London, sw1.
Scotland: 12 Hope Terrace, Edinburgh 9.
Wales: Penrhos Road, Bangor, Caerns.

ROYAL SOCIETY FOR THE PROTECTION OF BIRDS,
The Lodge, Sandy, Beds.

SCOTTISH ORNITHOLOGISTS' CLUB,
21 Regent Terrace, Edinburgh 7.

WILDFOWL TRUST,
Slimbridge, Glos.

READ: *Handbook of British Birds* (1938–41), by W. F. Witherby *et al*: *Birds of the British Isles* (1953–63), by D. A. Bannerman: *Check List* (1970), by BOU: *Where to Watch Birds* (1967), by John Gooders.

## CLEY

The attractive village of Cley lies on the north Norfolk coast and is the best known and most visited bird spot in Britain. To the west lies Blakeney Harbour a haunt of wildfowl and waders enclosed by the peninsula of Blakeney Point, which has good breeding colonies of terns and is a good migration watch point. To the east lie Salthouse Marshes, low-lying grazing intersected by numerous ditches, while Cley itself boasts the reserve of the Norfolk Naturalists' Trust. This is a large area of grazing meadows with extensive reed beds that are the breeding haunts of bittern and bearded tit. The whole is bordered to the north by a huge shingle beach that has seabirds offshore and excellent numbers of shore lark and snow bunting in autumn and winter. Between Cley and Salthouse is the East Bank and Arnold's Marsh, possibly the best worn ornithological path, anywhere. Waders here are always excellent, often outstanding, and occasionally quite incredible. Rarities turn up with such unfailing regularity that ornithologists have put forward theory and counter-theory to explain its unique attractions. But it is not only the waders that are rare, unusual birds like shearwaters on the sea, little gulls on the shore, and spoonbill on the marshes are annual, and the Cley list boasts the rarest of passerines.

Winter brings wildfowl, including brent geese in Blakeney Harbour, and vast numbers of waders. Hen harriers are regular and whatever else is about in the country, be it waxwings or rough-legged buzzards, Cley will have its share.

SUMMER: bittern, garganey, water rail, bearded tit, black-tailed godwit, ruff.

AUTUMN: shearwaters, marsh harrier, spoonbill, wood sandpiper, green sandpiper, curlew sandpiper, little stint, black tern, Arctic skua, little gull, shorelark, bluethroat, great grey shrike, snow bunting.

WINTER: brent goose, wigeon, pintail, knot, bar-tailed godwit.

The A149 passes along this coast through the villages mentioned. The East Bank lies to the east of Cley, there is a small hut on the seaward side of the road. The reserve is open every day except Monday, permits available from Norfolk Naturalist's Trust, 4 The Close, Norwich, NOR 16P. Unsold permits of the day's quota may be obtained from the Warden (ask in the village) at Cley after 10.00 hours on the day concerned. Accommodation at the George Hotel and in several homes in Cley.

## DEE ESTUARY

The Dee is amongst the best places for wildfowl and waders on the west coast of Britain. It lies on the boundary of England and Wales near Liverpool and at low tide offers vast, rich mud banks for feeding waders. The Dee is 20 km long by 10 km wide and is lined by saltings along the eastern bank. Though a flock of 1,000 pintail is still regular here the hundreds of thousands of waders that resort to the islands at Hilbre are the major attraction. Several British bird photographers have found themselves surrounded by waders at high tide on Little Eye and obtained some remarkable pictures. Hilbre Island, Little Hilbre Island, and Little Eye are now a nature reserve. Nearby at West Kirby, the Marine Lake is always worth a look particularly in hard weather, and the Red Rocks promontory on the north-eastern corner of the Dee holds many waders at high tide. Be careful not to put them up, they go straight to Hilbre and that is the end of the bird-watching.

On the other corner of the Dee is Point of Air, an area of mud flats, saltings, dunes, and a small reed bed, that is also used by waders as a roost. This is also a likely place for snow buntings. Numbers of waders at these roosts regularly run into five figure totals for the commoner species.

At the head of the Dee lies 1,000 acres of steel works, with odd freshwater pools and reed beds scattered amongst the buildings, while to the west are brackish lagoons, saltings, and mud flats. Though over 35 species were recorded breeding in the mid-1960s, Shotton Pools have since declined in attraction. Nevertheless there is a good passage of waders, especially freshwater species, and a huge roost of swallows and sand martins.

SUMMER: shelduck, oystercatcher, common tern.

AUTUMN: knot, turnstone, greenshank, sanderling, whimbrel, bar-tailed godwit, black-tailed godwit, hirundines.

WINTER: great northern diver, red-throated diver, wigeon, pintail, scoter, waders, snow bunting.

Hilbre Islands can be reached on foot from West Kirby, leaving there three hours before high water at the latest. It is best to walk to Little Eye then along the rocks northwards to the main island. Permits are necessary for the main island only, contact Hoylake Urban District Council. Point of Air can be reached from the A548 at Talacre Beach.

Shotton Pools can be visited only with the permission of The Works Relations Manager, John Summers and Sons Lt, Hawarden Bridge Steelworks, Nr Chester. The works entrance is just west of the junction of the A548 and A550.

## FAIR ISLE

Fair Isle lies mid-way between Orkney and Shetland and because of its isolation, geographical position, and small size, is world famous as a bird observatory. It is a beautiful island with magnificent bird cliffs and supports a crofting population of over forty people. Eagle Clarke's pioneer studies put Fair Isle on the ornithological map in 1912 and it has retained its pre-eminence ever since. After the last war the island was purchased by George Waterston and the Observatory was opened with Kenneth Williamson as the first warden. In 1954 the National Trust for Scotland took over the island but the Observatory continues as before. Though Fair Isle is mainly a migration study station it does have interesting breeding species like great and Arctic skuas, auks, including the black guillemots that have been the subject of a special study by one of the previous wardens, storm petrel, fulmar, and the Fair Isle subspecies of the wren.

Vagrants, however, are the Observatory's life blood and turn up weekly, if not daily, during the autumn. Up till 1963, 17 species had been added to the British List from their occurrence on this remote island. Anything can turn up here.

SUMMER: storm petrel, fulmar, kittiwake, great skua, Arctic skua, guillemot, razorbill, puffin, black guillemot, wren (Fair Isle subspecies), twite.

PASSAGE: rarities.

The *Good Shepherd* runs between Grutness, Sumburgh, Shetland and Fair Isle twice weekly in summer. It is thus convenient for Sumburgh Airport and the south. Accommodation is available only on a full-board basis. Details from The Warden, Fair Isle Bird Observatory, by Lerwick, Shetland; or between 1st December and 31st March from the Honorary Secretary, Fair Isle BO, 21 Regent Terrace, Edinburgh 7.

## FARNE ISLANDS AND LINDISFARNE

The Farnes consist of some 30 small islands lying off England's north-east coast between Tynemouth and the Scottish border. The majority of the islands belong to the National Trust and are of straightforward public access though the Brownsman is closed during the breeding season. Seabirds are the main attraction including auks, kittiwake and fulmar on the cliffs, puffin and eider inland, and all four British terns on the low lying areas. In particular this is a famous stronghold of Sandwich and the rarer roseate tern though eiders vie for popularity with the closeness of their sitting and immense numbers. Though there is a variety of waders and other species on passage the moulting of greylag geese on the outer islands in late summer is noteworthy.

Immediately west of the Farnes is the Lindisfarne area now mainly a National Nature Reserve covering over 6,000 acres. Most of this area is inter-tidal and rich in birds particularly during passage periods and in winter. To the bird-watcher in the north-east the names of the various areas conjure up pictures of different exciting species. Fenham Flats, Skate Road, Ross Links, Holy Island Lough, Budle Bay, all are outstanding for birds. Wildfowl include a wintering flock of the light-bellied race of the brent goose, odd parties of greylag and pinkfeet and a herd of up to 450 whooper swans. Skate Road is the favourite haunt of sea-duck, divers and three species of grebe. The number of waders in Lindisfarne has not yet been calculated though counts for even some of the areas run into thousands. Even the summer visitor to the Farnes should not miss Lindisfarne.

SUMMER – Farnes: fulmar, eider, oystercatcher, ringed plover, kittiwake, common tern, Arctic tern, Sandwich tern, roseate tern, guillemot, razorbill, puffin.

AUTUMN and WINTER – Lindisfarne: divers, Slavonian grebe, red-necked grebe, brent goose, pink-footed goose, greylag goose, whooper swan, Bewick's swan, eider, scoter, goldeneye, long-tailed duck, grey plover, bar-tailed godwit, little stint, whimbrel, wood sandpiper, spotted redshank, sanderling.

The Farnes are reached by motor boat from Seahouses village and there is a small landing charge. Permits are also required and these must be obtained in advance from the Post Office, Bolton's Garage, or from the Farne Islands Committee, Narrowgate House, Alnwick. The best island is the Inner Farne.

The Lindisfarne Reserve is of free public access though the surrounding farmland is private. The most important access points are:
1. Fenham near Mill Burn.
2. North of Fenham le-Moor at Lowmoor Point.
3. The road east of Beal and the causeway (beware – covered at high tide.) across to Holy Island.
4. North of Elwick to Whitelee Letch.
5. East of Ross a footpath leads across Ross Links to Ross Back Sands and Skate Road.

6.  North-east of Budle.
7.  North-west of Budle at Heather Cottages.
8.  On Holy Island, the road leading north to The Links.
9.  East of Holy Island to Sheldrake Pool.

The A1 passes within 2 km of the area north of Newcastle and direct from London. Accommodation is available in a variety of hotels in Seahouses, and at a hotel and several guest houses at Holy Island.

## FIRTH OF FORTH

The estuary of the River Forth is a vast tidal inlet with some of Britain's most outstanding ornithological sites. As one would expect on the east coast there are many excellent places for waders and migrants in general, but the Forth has one of the largest gannetries and one of the most important colonies of roseate terns in the country. Only the best places along this superb coast have been included and there are many others that deserve the bird-watcher's attention.

1.  **Bass Rock:** 2 km offshore and 5 km north-east of North Berwick at the mouth of the Forth on the southern shore. Its 400 metre square hump holds 6,000 pairs of gannets, and in 1967–69, a black-browed albatross all summer. Check, this bird may well return. A good variety of other seabirds breed. This is the most accessible gannetry in Britain.

    SUMMER: fulmar, gannet, shag, kittiwake, guillemot, razorbill, puffin.

    Boats round the Rock are arranged from North Berwick in summer, and give excellent views of the birds. Access is by permission of the owner. Contact the Scottish Ornithologists' Club, 21 Regent Terrace, Edinburgh 7. The Club organises outings and it is possible to join one of these.

2.  **Aberlady Bay:** east of Edinburgh on the southern shore of the Forth and is the best of the inter-tidal areas. Its 1,400 acres of foreshore and dunes are a local nature reserve and hold terns, waders, and long-eared owl in summer. Autumn passage is particularly good with a large variety of waders and all four grebes on the sea.

    Winter brings many wildfowl including geese and sea-duck.

    SUMMER: dunlin, redshank, common tern, Arctic tern, little tern, long-eared owl.

    PASSAGE: red-necked grebe, black-necked grebe, Slavonian grebe, green sandpiper, wood sandpiper, curlew sandpiper, grey plover, black-tailed godwit, little stint, ruff, skuas, gulls, terns.

    Leave Aberlady village eastwards and stop at the head of the Bay where a timber bridge crosses a stream. In summer access is limited to a small part of the area.

3.  **Inchmickery:** a 3 acre island in the middle of the Forth 6 km from the

centre of Edinburgh. It was heavily built up during the last war but in spite of its ugliness, it holds a breeding colony of over 400 pairs of roseate terns. Other terns also breed.

SUMMER: roseate tern, common tern, Arctic tern, Sandwich tern.

Inchmickery is a reserve of the Royal Society for the Protection of Birds and permits to land can be obtained from their Scottish office, 21 Regent Terrace, Edinburgh 7.

4.  **Largo Bay:** on the northern shore of the Forth adjacent to Elie Ness and Kilconquhar Loch both of which are also good spots for birds. Waders are present at all seasons but wildfowl and seabirds are the major attractions. There are scoter in winter in the Bay and a heavy passage of long-tailed duck, while up to 300 greylags haunt Kilconquhar Loch in winter. Autumn brings large numbers of little gulls, up to 500 having been noted at the Loch, and these birds also visit Largo Bay and Elie Ness. The latter is the best place to watch for divers, skuas, and shearwaters on passage.

AUTUMN: divers, shearwaters, long-tailed duck, waders, little gull, roseate tern, Sandwich tern, black tern.

WINTER: scoter, goldeneye, wigeon, greylag goose.

5.  **The Isle of May:** strategically at the mouth of the Forth 8 km south-east of Anstruther and covers 140 acres. It is ideally situated to receive migrants crossing the North Sea and the commoner night migrants often arrive in considerable falls in autumn. This is also the best season for rarities and though bluethroats and barred warblers are annual, exceptional vagrants do turn up every year. Waders are often numerous and there are always some seabirds including shearwaters to be seen. There are many breeding seabirds. An observatory has long been established on the island.

SUMMER: fulmar, shag, kittiwake, razorbill, guillemot, puffin.

AUTUMN: shearwaters, skuas, warblers, chats, flycatchers, bluethroat, thrushes, Lapland bunting, rarities.

The island is reached by boat from Anstruther. Accommodation is available on hostel lines. Contact Miss N. J. Gordon, 12 Hope Terrace, Edinburgh 9.

With the new Forth Road Bridge Edinburgh is an excellent centre with a vast choice of accommodation and excellent travel facilities.

## HANDA

Handa is everyone's idea of what a bird island should be. Sheer cliffs rising to 400 feet with ledges and crannies packed with breeding seabirds, isolated stacks with crowds of guillemots standing shoulder to shoulder on the top, and no people. Handa is just like that with the added convenience of a regular boat service and a reconditioned bothy to house those who want to stay. There are several thousand pairs of fulmar, shag, kittiwake (the most numerous species with 7,000 pairs), razorbill, and guillemot, and 400 pairs of puffins. There are also great skuas and red-throated divers, and twite breed around the buildings.

To the north and adjacent to the north-western point of the mainland at Cape Wrath lie the fearsome cliffs of Clo Mor, the highest on the British mainland. They hold huge colonies of seabirds, and peregrine and ptarmigan both breed. The endless procession of gannets offshore in summer is a fantastic sight.

SUMMER: fulmar, gannet, shag, golden eagle, peregrine, guillemot, razorbill, puffin, black guillemot, ptarmigan.

Day visits to Handa can be arranged with Mr A. Monro, Tarbert, Foindle, by Lairg, Sutherland. All arrangements for camping or staying at the bothy must be made through the RSPB, 21 Regent Terrace, Edinburgh 7.

For Clo Mor leave the Kyle of Durness to Keodale. Take the ferry across the Kyle and Paul Brown's minibus up to Cape Wrath.


## NORTH KENT MARSHES

These marshes on the southern shore of the Thames estuary are not only the best bird-haunt within 80 km of London but also one of the best in the entire country. From Gravesend to Whitstable stretches a continuous belt of prime bird habitat that is the favourite resort of many bird-watchers. It is not, however, to be covered in a day but forms an excellent area for a winter or autumn holiday. It would take a fortnight to see it all.

The general pattern is a sea-wall along the Thames separating the inter-tidal mud from the fresh grazing marshes. The latter are intersected by drainage ditches and fleets with small areas of reeds. Cutting deep into this pattern is the subsidiary estuary of the Medway and the tidal channel of the Swale. Both have creeks and gutters that further complicate the issue. The following areas have been selected as a cross section of the area.


1. **Cliffe:** the village at the western end of the marshes includes a large series of pits created by the excavation of clay for the cement industry. These are particularly favoured by diving duck and seabirds in hard weather. Waders are always present and most bird-watchers try to arrange a walk along the sea-wall eastwards to Egypt Bay.

WINTER: divers, scaup, merganser, smew, redshank, knot.

Walk through Cliffe and out along a concrete-blocked road to Lower Hope Point past the pits.


2. **Halstow marshes:** similar to the Cliffe area but holding geese in late winter and breeding grey herons in summer. The two bays, St Mary's and Egypt, are high tide resorts of many thousands of waders and the secret is to sit and wait when the tide is rising.

SUMMER: shelduck, grey heron, long-eared owl.
AUTUMN: green sandpiper, little stint, greenshank.
WINTER: white-fronted goose, wigeon, pintail, shelduck, knot.

Leave the A228 westwards to High Halstow at the first signpost after leaving the A2. Continue through the village, bear right and turn left down Decoy Hill Road. Halt at the end, and continue on foot to Egypt Bay. For the Northward Hill Reserve for herons in summer contact the RSPB, The Lodge, Sandy, Beds.

3. **The Medway Estuary:** good for wildfowl and waders and recognised as being of international importance. The best spots are difficult to get at. The Ham Green area is probably the most straightforward, with winter grey plover, bar-tailed godwit, and occasional brent goose, and a good autumn wader passage.

AUTUMN: whimbrel, black-tailed godwit, bar-tailed godwit, spotted red-shank.
WINTER: pintail, goldeneye, brent goose, grey plover, bar-tailed godwit.

Leave the A2 (not M2) northwards at Rainham.

4. **Sheppey:** one vast bird-watching area. The marshes in the south of the island are superb and very difficult of access, and visiting bird-watchers are advised to stick to two basic areas. Shell Ness lies at the eastern end of the island and the stretch of coast between here and Leysdown in winter is crowded with waders. The point is a high tide roost of up to 15,000 knot and many thousands of other waders, and is a good place to observe sea-duck and skuas. The road southwards to Harty Ferry passes Capel Fleet which is a good reedy fresh-marsh area, and leads to the shore for waders and sawbills.

AUTUMN: black-tailed godwit, bar-tailed godwit, grey plover, wood sand-piper, curlew sandpiper, spotted redshank, little stint.
WINTER: white-fronted goose, brent goose, eider, scoter, hen harrier, waders.

Sheppey is reached northwards from the M2 on the A249. Follow the B2008 for Shell Ness and Harty.

The North Kent Marshes are easy to reach by train and 'bus from London. Accommodation can be obtained at several of the village inns within sight of birds.

## MINSMERE

Minsmere is one of the best places to go bird-watching anywhere in Britain, and if the number of species seen is the test of a good day then Minsmere comes out top. It is a reserve of the Royal Society for the Protection of Birds and covers 1,500 acres on the Suffolk coast. The cross section of habitats from the sea westwards is the dune beach (outside the reserve) with some interesting areas of suedia bushes, a sand covered protective seawall, the 'Scrape', reed beds and open pools, flat farmland, deciduous woodland, and open heather heath. The 'Scrape' is the area of coastal pools that has been improved and extended to provide feeding grounds for waders on passage and a series of islands, numbered to facilitate reference, for breeding birds. This direct interference with the process of nature has attracted several hundred pairs of Sandwich and common terns, and enabled the declining little tern to save its fortunes on this coast. Avocets too have returned to breed successfully. Waders here are as good as in any other east coast area and a few rarities turn up every year. Further inland the reed beds have the distinction of being the stronghold of the marsh harrier in Britain and birds can be seen all the year round. Bearded tits also breed and spotted crakes have done so for the last few years. The farmland and woodland hold most of the birds one would expect to find in such areas in southern England and the heath has stone curlew and nightjar. Savi's warblers have returned to breed in some numbers in recent years.

Minsmere is just one, albeit the best, of a series of coastal marshes in Suffolk that make an excellent bird-watching holiday.

SUMMER: shoveler, garganey, spotted crake, marsh harrier, avocet, stone curlew, Sandwich tern, common tern, little tern, nightjar, red-backed shrike, bearded tit, Savi's warbler.

PASSAGE: spoonbill, spotted redshank, little stint, curlew sandpiper, black tern.

Though Minsmere can be seen from two free public hides, entrance to the reserve is strictly by permit. These are available in advance from the Royal Society for the Protection of Birds, The Lodge, Sandy, Beds. Leave the A12 eastwards just north of Yoxford, signposted Westleton. At Westleton take the Dunwich road and turn right after 3 km, signposted Minsmere. Continue along a rough track, paying toll at summer week-ends, park at the end and walk along the coast to the reserve entrance. One can go by train to Darsham, with connections to London, and hire a taxi from a nearby garage.


## OUTER HEBRIDES

The Outer Hebrides lie at the north-western corner of Britain and extend for over 200 km from north to south. They are a land of long sea lochs cutting deep into the coastline and of narrow sounds separating the island groups. These shallow straits are notorious for their peculiar currents and races and only sailors armed with local experts should attempt to navigate them. Geology is of prime importance with the peatlands and infertile eastern coast forming a sharp contrast to the shellsand beaches of the open Atlantic coast and the sweet grass machair. The west coast has farms with cattle and crops while the centre eastwards consists of peat bogs and lochs and is virtually uninhabited.

Though many of the islands are small, uninhabited, ornithologically famous, and hold breeding birds like gannet and Leach's petrel, the best group for the visitor is the central Uists. North and South Uist are both joined to Benbecula by causeways and together form an excellent holiday area for the motorist. North Uist is particularly favoured and a base there is ideal. The shore holds waders throughout the year and the machair and fresh lochs have breeding red-necked phalaropes and post-nuptial flocks of the truly wild greylag geese. Golden eagle, hen harrier, and merlin all breed, together with a variety of waders that includes greenshank. Arctic skuas attack the tern colonies, while the cliffs have a magnificent gathering of auks, fulmars and kittiwakes. Though birds can be seen here, there, and everywhere there are a number of spots that ought to be visited.

1. **Loch Druidibeg:** a large water near Howmore in South Uist. It is a National Nature Reserve covering 4,145 acres and is the stronghold of the native greylags, 40–50 pairs of which breed annually. After the breeding season 300 geese congregate on the machair between Howmore and Eochar. Enquiries for permits and the small hostel should be addressed to The Warden, Stilligarry, Lochboisdale, South Uist.

2. **Balranald:** a reserve of the Royal Society for the Protection of Birds. It has most of the outer Hebrides species including red-necked phalarope, corncrake, waders, gulls, terns, and eight species of duck. It lies on North Uist and visitors are asked to contact the warden at Hougharry.

3. **The Rudha Andvule promontory:** a good spot in South Uist.

4. **Griminish Point in North Uist:** Arctic tern and black guillemot are to be seen and there is a good passage of auks and shearwaters offshore.

SUMMER: black-throated diver, greylag goose, wigeon, shoveler, eider, shelduck, golden eagle, buzzard, hen harrier, merlin, red-necked phalarope, golden plover, greenshank, dunlin, kittiwake, Arctic tern, Arctic skua, guillemot, razorbill, puffin, corncrake, twite.

There is accommodation in many private homes and some guest houses. Write for a brochure and *Where to stay in the Western Isles* to the Western Isles Tourist Association, 21 South Beach Street, Stornoway, OH. There are regular flights to Stornoway and there is an excellent internal air service. There are also regular steamer services from Oban, Mallaig and Kyle of Lochalsh, and a car ferry service from Uig in Skye. There are buses about the islands and boats are not prohibitive to charter.

## PEMBROKESHIRE ISLANDS

Pembrokeshire with its cliffs and islands is one of the most accessible and important of British seabird areas. Though continental bird-watchers can go to the Channel Islands and the Sept Iles Reserve on the Channel coast of France to see gannets, they in no way compare with the 15,500 pairs that can be seen at Grassholm. What is more, the teeming colonies of auks, kittiwakes and fulmars of Skokholm, Skomer, Ramsey, and the many mainland head-lands are on a totally different scale to the Channel sites.

1. **Grassholm:** though holding the gannetry, the smallest, least accessible and, gannets apart, the least attractive of the islands.

2.  **Skomer:** only 2 km from the mainland and the largest, most easily accessible, and best island for birds. Its 200 foot cliffs hold large numbers of common auks, kittiwake, fulmar, and chough, while inland are vast puffinries,
and Manx shearwater and storm petrel colonies. Short-eared owl and buzzard
can be seen in summer though the peregrine no longer breeds.

3.  **Skokholm:** 5 km west of the mainland and the same distance south of
Skomer. Though breeding birds include storm petrel, Manx shearwater,
guillemot, and razorbill the emphasis on the island is on migration. Movements of chats, warblers and flycatchers are frequently very heavy and large
numbers are trapped and ringed. In the latter part of the autumn movement
of finches and thrushes is dramatic. Rarities of all shapes and sizes turn up
with great regularity.

SUMMER: storm petrel, Manx shearwater, gannet, buzzard, puffin, guillemot,
razorbill, chough, short-eared owl.

PASSAGE: seabirds, chats, warblers, flycatchers, finches, thrushes, rarities.

For Grassholm, landing arrangements must be made with the West Wales
Naturalists' Trust, 4 Victoria Place, Haverfordwest, Pembs. Such landings are
extremely infrequent. A nature trail is laid out for visitors to Skomer and the
island is open daily in the summer, boats leaving under normal conditions at
10.30 hours from Martins Haven. There is a landing fee, though members
of the West Wales Naturalists' Trust land free and may stay on the island in
the hostel.

Accommodation is available on Skokholm, on a full-board basis. Access is
on Saturdays and the regular boat service is from Dale. All visitors must
join the West Wales Naturalists' Trust. For transport arrangements and
enquiries, write to The Warden, Dale Fort Field Centre, Haverfordwest,
Pembs.

There are frequent trains from London.


## PORTLAND AND WEYMOUTH

The Isle of Portland juts some 10 km out into the English Channel and is the
site of Portland Bird Observatory and Field Centre. Its geographical position
makes it an excellent place to observe migration in both spring and autumn.
Small dry stone walled fields and thorn hedges are the major haunt of passerines, while the Obelisk at the Bill is an admirable shelter for the excellent sea-
watching where regular species include an autumn up-Channel passage of
Balearic shearwaters. An unusual migrant is the occasional Dartford warbler,
and rarities include melodious and icterine warblers every year. The Observatory is delightfully situated in the converted lighthouse and the accommodation is well above the usual primitive 'observatory' standard. A spring or
autumn holiday is both comfortable and rewarding but book well in advance.

Ferrybridge is where the island meets the mainland, and is a notable haunt
of gulls, terns, and waders. Portland Harbour on the other side of the road is
worth a look particularly in winter when numbers of sea-fowl come in to

shelter. These include all three divers, Slavonian grebe, and eider and merganser.

Radipole Lake lies on the western side of Weymouth and is the backwater of the River Wey. The water level is artificially controlled and the lake was declared a sanctuary in 1948. There are a series of lagoons, much favoured by waders and little gulls (nearly always present in autumn), surrounded by large reed beds. There are many interesting birds to be seen here.

SUMMER: terns, auks.

PASSAGE: Balearic shearwater, Manx shearwater, fulmar, little stint, curlew sandpiper, wood sandpiper, spotted redshank, black tern, little gull, spotted crake, warblers, chats, flycatchers, thrushes, finches, rarities.

For Portland Bird Observatory, leave Weymouth southwards following the signposts to Portland on the A354. Accommodation is available in small dormitories and includes an evening meal in peak periods, from 1 March to 31 October, and at other times by arrangement with the resident warden. Correspondence should be addressed to The Warden, Portland Bird Observatory and Field Centre, Old Lower Light, Portland, Dorset.

Radipole Lake lies beyond a bridge at the north-western corner of the boat basin.


## SHETLAND ISLES

The Shetlands lie 6° south of the Arctic Circle and stretch 120 km from north to south, and about half that from east to west. Only 19 of the hundred or so islands are inhabited. In such a vast and difficult landscape visiting ornithologists have inevitably to be choosy, as spending a full holiday on just a single island can be very rewarding. Nevertheless having come perhaps a 1,000 miles to see northern birds the traveller can be forgiven if he tries to cram everything in. This account, therefore, concentrates on those areas generally considered most worthwhile though omitting Fair Isle which is treated separately because of the different interests of intending visitors.

Shetland is a grim and rugged land with thick peat bogs underlain by hard igneous rock. The vegetation is mainly rough grass supporting sheep and very little else, though Fetlar is called the green isle because of its comparative fertility. This northern island group is one of the most convenient and accessible areas for seabirds in Europe and has the advantage of several other northern species which usually involve visiting far higher latitudes. The seabirds are fantastic. Huge cliffs towering out of the sea are literally splattered with birds. Vast numbers of auks, kittiwakes, and fulmars line the ledges and there are two colonies of gannets both of which are easy to see. Manx shearwater and storm petrel breed out of sight though the former is often seen on the sea on early season evenings. Of the northern species great and Arctic skuas are both numerous, and the great skua (called *bonxie* locally) can be seen more conveniently than anywhere else in the northern hemisphere. Red-throated diver, dunlin and two scarce birds, the whimbrel and the red-necked phalarope, frequent the open land and inland lochs. Amongst wildfowl found in the same areas are red-breasted merganser, wigeon and scoter, and possibly the occasional pair of whooper swans. The visitor who carefully examines every gull in Lerwick Harbour may be rewarded by a summering but non-breeding glaucous or Iceland gull. A pair of snowy owls successfully bred in 1967–1973 but whether this is to be an isolated occurrence or not is too early to say.

SUMMER : red-throated diver, gannet, fulmar, Manx shearwater, storm petrel, eider, scoter, red-breasted merganser, dunlin, snipe, common sandpiper, golden plover, whimbrel, red-necked phalarope, Arctic tern, common tern, Arctic skua, great skua, kittiwake, guillemot, razorbill, puffin, black guillemot, wren, twite, hooded crow.

Almost anywhere in Shetland is good for birds and a good holiday could be had on any of the inhabited islands. The following are high on every visitor's list and visiting one or two of these is probably the ideal way of seeing the islands' birds.


1.  **Unst:** in the extreme north of the group and 20 km by 8 km. The southern half is well cultivated and as green as nearby Fetlar. The cliff scenery is amongst the best in Britain and Hermaness in the north of the island is the culmination of many a bird-watcher's dream. Cliff-nesting seabirds fill the air and offshore lie the stacks around Muckle Flugga with their large gannetry. The cliff tops are honeycombed with the burrows of puffins, while the moors inland are the British stronghold of great and Arctic skuas. The Hermaness Reserve was established in 1955 but there are no restrictions on access. The nearby Loch of Cliff is a favourite freshwater bathing place for many seabirds. Baltasound, the main village, is served by a regular boat from Lerwick, and the ferries between the mainland and Yell, and Yell and Unst, provide an overland route. Accommodation is limited but available in private homes. Contact the Shetland Tourist Association, Information Centre, Alexandria Wharf, Lerwick, Shetland Isles.


2.  **Fetlar:** the smallest of the main islands and though the cliffs are not as impressive as many in Shetland the usual auks, gulls and fulmars manage to breed. Apart from waders Fetlar boasts both skuas, and from 1967 onwards breeding snowy owls. There is a regular boat service from Lerwick and cottage accommodation is available. Apply to the Tourist Association, see Unst.


3.  **The Mainland:** not to be overlooked by bird-watchers arriving hot-foot for the other famous Shetland Isles. It has most of the specialities and with better services and facilities can provide a more varied holiday than any other island and is, of course, the best centre for seeing all the others by day trips. Gannets can be seen fishing in Lerwick Harbour and there are numerous cliffs with seabirds galore. Both species of scoter (only one breeding) regularly

occur in Weisdale Voe and Whiteness Voe is also worth a good look. Ronas Hill National Nature Reserve lies on the north-western side of Mainland and extends along 20 km of coast, including cliffs up to 750 feet with seabirds and skuas. There is a wide choice of accommodation including the Grand Hotel, Hayfield Hotel and Queen's Hotel in Lerwick, the Scalloway Hotel and the Royal Hotel in Scalloway, and a wealth of guest houses. Contact the Tourist Association.

4.  Noss lies 5 km east of Lerwick and though its cliffs drop a mere 600 feet they seem as high as the famous 1,400 foot Conachair of St Kilda. Over 3,000 pairs of gannets breed and the cliffs are covered with auks, kittiwake, and fulmar. On the top are puffin, great and Arctic skuas. There are many tourist trips round Noss by boat from Lerwick which are an ideal way of seeing the sea-bird cliffs. Alternatively, cross from Lerwick to Bressay, walk or take a taxi 4½ km to Noss Sound and call the shepherd to row you across.

5.  Foula lies 24 km west of the Shetland Mainland and is one of Britain's most remote islands. The Kame of Foula is a sea-cliff of 1,220 feet and inferior only to the buttresses of St Kilda in height and in the number of fulmars it holds. Other breeding seabirds are numerous and the island is well worth the trip by *m/v Hirta* out of Scalloway.

BEA fly regular daily services between Sumburgh and Kirkwall in Orkney, and Aberdeen, and Wick on the Scottish mainland. There are connections with other parts of Britain. There are regular twice weekly sailings from Aberdeen to Lerwick via Kirkwall by the North of Scotland and Orkney and Shetland Shipping Co. Ltd.

## SLIMBRIDGE

The New Grounds, Slimbridge, lie on the south bank of the Severn and extend for some 5 km north-east of the Severn Railway Bridge. The 1,000 acres of enclosed pasture and high salt marsh plus the area of sand-flats beyond is managed as a wildfowl refuge by the Wildfowl Trust.

The Trust, formerly the Severn Wildfowl Trust, was established by Peter Scott in 1946 close to the refuge and to the Berkeley New Decoy. A large series of ponds has been excavated and numerous enclosures house the best and largest collection of wildfowl in the world. A unique contribution to conservation has been made at Slimbridge with the building up of a flock of néné or Hawaiian geese that held over half of the world's population of this all but extinct species before a number of birds were sent to Hawaii and released.

The grounds prove attractive to a huge range of birds, especially duck, which fly in from the estuary to feed. The white-fronted geese on the Dumbles usually build up to 1,000 by Christmas and may number 4,000 – 5,000 in the new year. All other species of British geese have occurred here, including lesser white-front in most years. A constantly increasing flock of Bewick's swan winters, spending part of each day in one of the enclosures. Observation hides have been constructed along the sea-wall overlooking the Dumbles to which members are escorted for close views of the geese. The tower gives the ordinary visitor quite excellent views, and there are also hides overlooking the Rushy Pen which is frequented by the wild Bewick's swans.

Waders, too, benefit from the lack of disturbance and on both passages there is an excellent selection of birds.

RESIDENT: waterfowl collection.

WINTER: white-fronted goose, Bewick's swan, duck, peregrine.

PASSAGE: grey plover, whimbrel, black-tailed godwit, bar-tailed godwit, green sandpiper, wood sandpiper, spotted redshank, ruff.

Leave the A38 1 km south of Cambridge and follow signs to the Wildfowl Trust. Admission is daily from 09:30 hours, except Sundays when members only are admitted before 12:00 hours. There are facilities for meals and refreshments.

## SPEYSIDE

The bird-watchers' Speyside lies between the river Spey and the Cairngorms roughly between Kincraig and Grantown. It is a huge, rich, and famous area having one of the largest remnants of the old Caledonian forest in the basins of Rothiemurchus and Abernethy, and with mountain lakes at all heights and the Cairngorms towering high above to 4,084 feet. Until quite recently the area was a virtual nature reserve abutting the actual nature reserve of the Cairngorms to the south. But the arrival of skiing and the development of the area as a holiday playground has changed the situation radically. The forest species like crested tit and black grouse are affected only by picnickers along the fast multiplying roadsides, the osprey has returned to breed and has proved a tourist attraction in its own right, but the rare birds of the area, the dotterel, ptarmigan, and snow bunting of the high tops have been invaded by trippers via the chair-lift at the head of Glen More. To get up and back in a day was a strenuous exercise, now on fine days the general public spend the whole day wandering around the tops. The opportunity is also open to the bird-watcher who it is to be hoped will act responsibly and point out to the layman that his picnic is disturbing the dotterel breeding a few metres away. Incidentally, people are generally fascinated by the sexual role reversal in this species, and therefore more inclined to be moved on a little bit.

The following areas are particularly recommended:
1. The Cairngorms Summit: via the chair lift at the head of Glen More for dotterel, ptarmigan, and possibly golden eagle.
2. Loch An Eilean: for beautiful scenery, nostalgic castle, and crested tit, crossbill, black grouse, and capercaillie in the old pine forest.
3. Loch Garten: for breeding ospreys protected by the Royal Society

for the Protection of Birds. There are good views of the nest from well equipped hides.

4. Loch Morlich: for all the forest species and osprey fishing regularly in the loch – probably the best centre with a camp site and easy access to the Cairngorms.

5. Loch Insh: for winter wildfowl including whooper swan, and hen harrier and, on an early holiday, breeding crossbills.

SUMMER: golden eagle, osprey, greenshank, dotterel, black grouse, capercaillie, ptarmigan, crested tit, siskin, crossbill, snow bunting.

Aviemore on the A9 is a good area to start from with hotels and good transport services, though Loch Morlich is more central. Superb scenery and birds make an excellent holiday.

# Bulgaria

1 Balchik and Baltata Forest
2 Burgas
3 Rila
4 Lake Srebârna

*Danube*

4

1

SOFIA
●

2

3

READ: *The Birds of Bulgaria* (1950), by P. Pateff (in Bulgarian).

## BALCHIK AND BALTATA FOREST

Balchik lies on the northern part of the Black Sea coast to the north of Varna. Founded by the Greeks and famous for its grapes the town is now an important naval base and not, therefore, the ideal place for western bird-watchers to flash around their optical gear. To the south of the town is a range of cliffs that stretch almost without interruption to the Batova River valley which is a prime ornithological area. The cliffs, which are seldom sheer, rise in two stages and the rocky outcrops hold Alpine swift, black-headed bunting, and the extremely rare pied wheatear. This bird is only found in Europe along the Black Sea coast. The cliffs to the north of the Batova River hold the same species and are not subject to the same military objections. Roller, rock thrush, and eagle owl are all to be seen here, and the scrubby headlands are the haunt of olive-tree warblers.

The Batova River enters the sea through a broad valley but in summer amounts to no more than a small stream. To the north of the river lies the Baltata Forest. Covering 2,000 acres and extending to the sea shore this forest is now partly a nature reserve. It is exceedingly wet with a network of channels and bogs and in some places quite open reeded areas, and is predominantly elm with a mixture of ash and robinia. To the south is an open meadow area next to the river, while to the north is agricultural land with vineyards, various crops, and poplars, stretching to the cliffs.

The forest itself holds lesser spotted eagle though there is a better chance of seeing this bird from a vantage point than inside the dense woodland. Black stork and black kite breed, together with Spanish sparrows, and the collared flycatcher here is a local subspecies with an incomplete collar thus eliminating the main diagnostic feature between it and the pied flycatcher! Wild boars are another inhabitant of Baltata. The meadowland to the south holds hoopoe, lesser grey shrike, barred and great reed warblers, and black-headed bunting, and a frequent visitor is the squacco heron. The agricultural land to the north is a haunt of bee-eaters and hoopoes in abundance, and gradually gives way to the cliffs with their own specialities.

SUMMER: black stork, squacco heron, black kite, lesser spotted eagle, eagle owl, Alpine swift, wryneck, roller, hoopoe, bee-eater, lesser grey shrike, rock thrush, pied wheatear, barred warbler, great reed warbler, olive-tree warbler, black-headed bunting, Spanish sparrow.

Although Balchik is nearer and the interesting cliffs are *en route* to Baltata, Varna is probably a better base. It has greater variety of accommodation and the interesting Lake Varna behind. It is, however, further from Baltata which has anyway to be approached from the north. Leave the cliff road to the north of the Batova River on a rough track dropping down toward the forest near the sea.

## BURGAS

Burgas lies on the Black Sea coast and is backed by three large lakes extending inland. Being so near a large town they have been changed and modified to such an extent that only Lake Burgas itself retains any of its natural attributes. Lake Atanosov has been most radically affected and is now a series of settling beds for commercial salt production. This change has not been totally harmful. Salt loving waders like avocet and black-winged stilt which were rare here several years ago are now common. Up to 400 pairs of avocets and 50 pairs of stilts have been counted, and along with terns and Kentish plovers are the typical birds of the area. Lake Burgas still has large reed beds and lying between colourful hills is the most attractive water, though there is an industrial plant complete with smoking chimneys at one end. There are still areas of water meadows and these and the reed beds are full of birds. Recent information shows that the wealth of water-birds that formerly bred here are now only visitors, though they occur regularly and in large numbers even through the summer. The most spectacular of these are the white pelicans which often number several hundred and may yet return to breed. Glossy ibis, spoonbill, and great white heron also fall into this category. Little egrets are always present together with such widespread species as white stork, short-toed lark, and tawny pipit, and there is a good chance of white-tailed eagle.

Migration is phenomenal with literally thousands of waders of many different species. Terns too are excellent and black and white-winged black, whiskered, and gull-billed varieties are all regular. Mediterranean and little gulls are numerous and one can sometimes spot numbers of the rare (here!) black-headed gull. Lake Atanosov is one of the most likely spots outside of the breeding areas for ruddy shelduck.

SUMMER: white stork, great white heron, little egret, spoonbill, glossy ibis, white pelican, ruddy shelduck, white-tailed eagle, avocet, black-winged stilt, Kentish plover, little ringed plover, little tern, common tern, Mediterranean gull, little gull, tawny pipit, short-toed lark, Spanish sparrow.

PASSAGE: little stint, ruff, black tern, white-winged black tern, gull-billed tern, black-headed gull.

Burgas is easy to get to and has a good range of accommodation. The road northwards, route 31, is an excellent vantage point for Lake Atanosov, while that westwards to Ezerovo is a good start to Lake Burgas. Lake Mandra to the south is the least attractive ornithologically though it should not be ignored.

## RILA

Rila lies 105 km south of Sofia in the south-western corner of Bulgaria. It is high in the mountains of the same name with the highest peak in the country Mount Stalin at 9,660 feet nearby. The monastery at Rila is a well known tourist spot with murals covering every inch of space inside, and frescoes and other adornments proliferating outside. Its domes stand out boldly against a background of high snow covered peaks and pine forests. Around the building itself there are many deciduous trees holding a collection of birds that includes grey wagtails and dippers along the streams. Higher up the conifers hold black and other woodpeckers and nutcracker, while the mountains are the haunt of golden eagle and the rare spotted eagle. Rila is also a well known wall creeper area though, as always, these birds are difficult to locate.

North-east of Rila on the other side of the massif is Borovets. The birds here are similar though more thoroughly known, but doubtless anything found on one side could sooner or later be found on the other. Firecrests are common in the Norwegian spruce forest and crested tit, crossbill, and nutcracker all breed. Higher up rock partridge, rock bunting and rock thrush are found, and on the very tops Alpine accentor, shore lark, and Alpine chough. Raptors in this area include short-toed and booted eagles, goshawk, and both common and honey buzzards. The lower valley floors hold hoopoe, roller, and calandra lark, with crag martins overhead.

SUMMER: golden eagle, spotted eagle, short-toed eagle, booted eagle, goshawk, buzzard, honey buzzard, nutcracker, Alpine chough, Alpine accentor, wall creeper, rock partridge, shore lark, water pipit, crag martin, black woodpecker, grey-headed woodpecker, rock thrush, firecrest, crested tit, rock bunting, serin.

Leave Sofia southwards on route 2 to Kočerinovo and turn eastwards on route 164 to Rila and on to the monastery. There is a tourist hotel at the monastery with beds in what were once the monks' cells.

There is a bus from Sofia to Borovets which is near Samokov, and the Balkantourist Hotel is comfortable and recommended.


## LAKE SREBÂRNA

With the demise of the Burgas lakes as areas for breeding birds, and herons in particular, Lake Srebârna has become one of the most valuable and interesting areas in Bulgaria. It lies in the north-eastern part of the country next to the Danube and the Romanian border and adjacent to the spectacular marshes on the river's left bank between Giurgiu and Călărasi and with the excellent Lake Oltina to the east. The lake and surrounding area amounting to 1,500 acres was declared a reserve in 1948. There are extensive reed beds with a growth of scrub but with still a considerable area of open water. To the north and west lie the Popino marshes while along the Danube itself is lush riverain forest with a rich population of song birds including plentiful nightingales as well as barred and icterine warblers, golden oriole, and hoopoe. The marshes have roller, penduline tit and corncrake.

Srebârna itself holds purple heron, little egret, squacco heron, night heron, and little bittern, and there is a colony of Dalmatian pelicans. Marsh harriers wheel over the reed beds and ferruginous duck sit out on the open water, with black and whiskered terns overhead. The reeds themselves hold Savi's warbler, with penduline tit amongst the surrounding scrub.

SUMMER: Dalmatian pelican, purple heron, little egret, squacco heron, night heron, little bittern, ferruginous duck, corncrake, marsh harrier, black tern, whiskered tern, common tern, penduline tit, roller, golden oriole, hoopoe, icterine warbler, barred warbler, Savi's warbler.

Though formerly peasants would take visitors out on the lake in punts the reserve has recently been made a national wildlife sanctuary and permission is needed between March and November. Contact The Committee of Forestry, Department of Nature Protection, Xp. Boteb 55, Sofia. Much of the surrounding area can be explored and all of the interesting birds seen without disturbing the reserve at all. Silistra to the east is the obvious base.

# Czechoslovakia

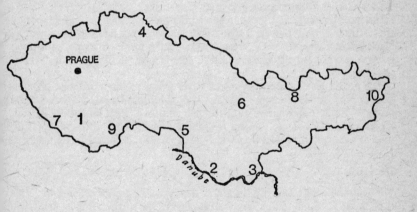

PRAGUE

ČESKOSLOVENSKÁ ORNITHOLOGICKÁ SPOLEČNOST,
Dr W. Černý, Department of Zoology, Viničná 7, Praha 2.

READ: *Prehled Moravskeho Ptactva* (1955) by Z. Kux, *et al* in *Acta Musei Moraviae*, vol 40, pp 156–219: *Faunisticky prehlad slovenskeho Vtacva* 1–111 (1961–1963) by B. Matoušek in *Acta Mus. Slov. Bratislava* vol 7, pp 3–109; vol 8, pp 3–93; vol 9, pp 68–139.

## BLATNÁ

Blatná is a region of ponds and forests in southern Bohemia between Strakonice and Pisek to the north-west of České Budějovice. There are considerable areas of open water surrounded by reed beds, with quite large tracts of damp meadows beyond. The whole is surrounded by coniferous forest. The ponds hold colonies of black-necked grebes, with storks and crakes in appropriate places, and little ringed plover on the open shores. The meadows have black-tailed godwit and crested lark, and the forests hold the usual central European woodpeckers including black and grey-headed. There are also crested tit, golden oriole and firecrest here, and the fields and hedges shelter icterine warbler, serin, and great grey shrike.

SUMMER: black-necked grebe, white stork, gadwall, sparrow hawk, spotted crake, little ringed plover, black-tailed godwit, grey-headed woodpecker, black woodpecker, wryneck, crested lark, golden oriole, firecrest, short-toed treecreeper, crested tit, black redstart, icterine warbler, great grey shrike, serin.

The ponds are on either side of the River Otava to the south-west of Pisek and are of straightforward access. The Hydrobiological Station Blatná provides limited accommodation for five students; write to Dr W. Černý, Department of Zoology, Viničná 7, Praha 2. For ordinary visitors there is no need to write and the Hotel Beránek, Blatná, Okr. Strakonice is recommended.

## DANUBE

The Danube enters Czechoslovakia at Bratislava and after a few kilometres becomes the common boundary with Hungary. The surrounding lowlands are regularly flooded, and there is the typical Danubian complex of marshes, backwaters, and oxbows along both banks. The riverside forests give way to flat sand and gravel land typical of the steppe of the adjacent Hungarian plain. This area between the large and small arms of the Danube between Bratislava and Komárno is the Czech stronghold of the great bustard, total population 750 birds. A reserve covering 22,000 acres was created in 1955 at Zlatná na Ostrově to protect this species.

It is, however, the marshes that hold most attraction for visitors, and the same 'island' between Bratislava and Komárno holds a number of areas that are of importance for breeding and migrant birds. Most are reserves or reser-ves designate. The sand beds of the river itself are important for migrating ducks and geese, thousands of which are regular each autumn. Breeding birds are better amongst the reed beds of the marshes and include 50 pairs of purple heron at Dedinský ostrov and 40 pairs at Parižské močiare where there is also a single pair of great white heron. There is a colony of 65 pairs of cormorant at Istragov and other reedy type birds are marsh and Montagu's harriers, little crake, and a variety of warblers that includes moustached and Savi's. Bearded tits also breed as do bluethroats amongst the surrounding bushes, and black-tailed godwit on the damp meadows.

This is a marshland area in the best tradition and is well worth a thorough exploration even though the better known Hungarian places are only a few kilometres away across the border.

SUMMER: cormorant, great white heron, purple heron, duck, marsh harrier, Montagu's harrier, little crake, great bustard, black-tailed godwit, bearded tit, bluethroat, grasshopper warbler, Savi's warbler, moustached warbler.

The following areas, some of which are reserves, are all close to the Danube and are listed from west to east:

1. Dedinský ostrov: near Gabčíkovo and a major reed bed warbler – purple heron site.
2. Istragov: larger, also near Gabčíkovo with great white heron and cormorants.
3. Zilizský močiar: near Čilizská Radvaň.
4. Člatná na Ostrově: 13 km west of Komárno, with a great bustard reserve.
5. Parížské močiare: near Gbelce, north-east of Komárno, another reed bed area with purple herons.

Komárno is a good centre and the Hotel Europa, ul SNP, is of a high standard.

## KOVÁČOV HILLS

The Kováčov Hills lie near the confluence of the rivers Danube and Hron and are the warmest place in Czechoslovakia. They are covered with deciduous woods that form a base for several species of raptors that hunt over the regularly inundated wetland and marshy lowland forests. These include lesser spotted eagle, honey buzzard, and black kite. There are many woodland birds like Syrian woodpecker, golden oriole and collared flycatcher, while the lowland itself holds stork, night heron, river warbler, and penduline tit. The land to the west near Gbelce is a haunt of great bustard.

SUMMER: white stork, night heron, lesser spotted eagle, honey buzzard, black kite, stone curlew, Scop's owl, bee-eater, roller, hoopoe, Syrian woodpecker, wryneck, golden oriole, penduline tit, rock thrush, river warbler, icterine warbler, marsh warbler, barred warbler, black redstart, collared flycatcher.

Štúrovo is the nearest large town and a good base for exploration of the hills and lowland. The hotel Dunaj, Nábrezie 5, Štúrovo, okr Komárno, is recommended.

## KRKONOŠE NATIONAL PARK

Krkonoše National Park lies on the Polish frontier north-east of Prague and is a large mountainous region. It is 3,500–5,400 feet above sea level and varies from mountain meadowland, through the deciduous and coniferous zones, to dwarf pines and bare open rocks. There are tracks and paths to some of the highest peaks, and the views over these non-Alpine type hills are superb. The dominant birds are those of the coniferous zone with black woodpecker, nutcracker, and black grouse being the most attractive to visitors. Eagle owls breed, as do goshawks, and this is a good area for black storks.

SUMMER: black stork, goshawk, sparrow hawk, black grouse, eagle owl, black woodpecker, nutcracker, dipper, crested tit, ring ousel, fieldfare, redpoll, crossbill, siskin.

Leave Trutnov, which is north of Hradec Králové, into the mountains at Svoboda nad Úpou and Pec pod Sněžkou, where the Hotel Hořec is recommended.

## LEDNICE

At the junction of the rivers Thaya and Morava is a land of marshes and ponds that are of great ornithological interest. The area lies against the Austrian border directly north of Vienna, and is a maze of channels, islands, and backwaters. The whole area including the woodlands is regularly flooded. Though at first sight another of these vast daunting places, the chain of lakes on the Thaya to the south and west of Lednice holds the most interesting birds. They are set in a flat landscape with reeds, and water lilies and other floating vegetation. The colony of black-necked grebes here build their nests out on the open water without any attempt at concealment, and in the region as a whole there are 400 pairs of these birds. Up to 20 pairs of greylag geese breed here, though there are larger colonies at some other areas nearby and there is a colony of 50 pairs of red-crested pochard. Though 10,000 pairs of black-headed gulls breed, the smaller colony here held a single pair of Mediterranean gull in 1967, further evidence of the expansion of this species' range north-westwards. Other breeding birds include 6 pairs of avocet, black-tailed godwit, black and white storks, and the many herons that can be generally seen in the area including purple and night herons, and little and common bitterns. In autumn duck number up to 60,000 with 10,000 geese, and waders of many species pass through in good numbers.

The ponds at Pohořelice hold greylags and red-crested pochard, and the marshes, woodland, and river areas of Panské jezero, Křivé jezero, and Pastvisko hold black-necked grebe, greylag, and gulls, and should be visited. A superb range of breeding passerines includes river, icterine, and barred warblers, lesser grey shrike, and beareded and penduline tits. The nearby Palava Hills are limestone and a noted haunt of rock thrush.

SUMMER: black-necked grebe, bittern, little bittern, night heron, white stork, black stork, greylag goose, red-crested pochard, honey buzzard, sparrowhawk, goshawk, marsh harrier, black kite, black-tailed godwit, roller, hoopoe, black woodpecker, wryneck, golden oriole, bearded tit, penduline tit, black redstart, rock thrush, Savi's warbler, river warbler, grasshopper warbler, marsh warbler, icterine warbler, barred warbler, woodchat shrike, lesser grey shrike, collared flycatcher, serin, ortolan bunting.

Leave Brno southwards on route 2 to Podivin. Turn westwards to Lednice and the ponds which are crossed by two roads and can be easily seen and explored. There is the Uźamku hotel in Lednice na Moravě, okr. Břeclav.

## MALÁ FATRA

Malá Fatra is a minor mountain ridge rising to 5,700 feet to the west of the Tatras. Its subalpine character with deciduous woods, mountain meadows, and vast coniferous forests is an attractive setting in which to see a wide variety of interesting birds. In several places the forests give way to dwarf pine and bare open rocks. This is an excellent and unfrequented area with golden and lesser spotted eagles being the major attractions. There are many interesting woodpeckers including three-toed and white-backed and the usual coniferous species like nutcracker and firecrest. The birds of the more open areas include wall creeper, Alpine accentor, and rock thrush.

SUMMER: golden eagle, lesser spotted eagle, goshawk, sparrowhawk, little ringed plover, hazel hen, black woodpecker, middle-spotted woodpecker, three-toed woodpecker, grey-headed woodpecker, white-backed woodpecker, wryneck, nutcracker, golden oriole, firecrest, dipper, wall creeper, crested tit, ring ousel, fieldfare, rock thrush, icterine warbler, barred warbler, water pipit, red-breasted flycatcher, Alpine accentor, siskin.

The nearest town of any size is Žilina which is a good starting point. The Chata Vrátna, Vrátna dolina, p. Terchová, okr. Žilina provides good accommodation and is an excellent base.

## MODRAVA

Modrava is a mountainous region to the south-west of Prague and geographically part of the Bohemian Forest that forms the German border. The valleys are typical 'Alpine' meadows with some areas of fen, and with extensive forests of beech and other deciduous trees on the hillsides. Higher up these give way to the conifers that dominate the area. Forest birds predominate with woodpeckers of several species including black and three-toed. Both pygmy and Tengmalm's owls breed and other predators include goshawk and sparrowhawk. The coniferous forests are particularly attractive with black grouse and capercaillie, nutcracker, and crested tit amongst others. The scenery is very beautiful and conveniently near the pond areas of Velký and Malý Tisý, and Blatná, as well as Prague.

SUMMER: goshawk, sparrowhawk, black grouse, capercaillie, pygmy owl, Tengalm's owl, three-toed woodpecker, black woodpecker, nutcracker, dipper, crested tit, ring ousel, fieldfare, redpoll, crossbill, siskin.

Leave Sušice southwards into the Modrava region. There is accommodation at the Hotel Šumava, Srní, okr. Prachatice.

## TANAP (Tatra National Park)

The High Tatras are the highest and most beautiful ridge in the wide Carpathian arch, and because of their unique character the whole area was declared a National Park in 1949 covering 500 sq. km. The Park can be divided into two zones, the granite of the High Tatras, and the calcareous Belanské Hills. The highest peak Mt Gerlach reaches 8,743 ft, and 67 per cent of the area is covered with forests, and only 3 per cent is agricultural land and three-quarters of the forests consists of spruce and there is only a tiny area of deciduous trees. The tree line is at 5,000 feet with isolated and stunted trees up to 6,500 feet; at this height the gnarled trees are mainly stone pines. The Park abuts the Polish Tatra National Park to the north which is treated as a separate area.

Though important and famous for its mammals which include lynx, chamois, marmot, and bear, the Tatras are one of the best areas for birds in Czechoslovakia. Golden and lesser spotted eagles breed and there are a number of different owls including eagle and Ural owls, as well as the more widespread Tengmalm's. The woods hold black grouse and capercaillie and several woodpeckers including three-toed. Higher up above the tree line there are Alpine accentor, rock thrush, and wall creeper. The latter is apparently as common here as anywhere in Europe. Black storks are found in some areas.

SUMMER: white stork, black stork, golden eagle, lesser spotted eagle, goshawk, black kite, hobby, pygmy owl, long-eared owl, eagle owl, Ural owl, Tengmalm's owl, black grouse, capercaillie, hazel hen, nutcracker, black woodpecker, three-toed woodpecker, rock thrush, wall creeper, Alpine accentor, red-breasted flycatcher, crossbill.

The centre of the Tatras is Starý Smokovec where there are good hotels and transport facilities. There is also a cable car up into the mountains. To the east Tatranská Lomnica is the Park headquarters and has a cable car to the top of Lomnický Štít which is only a shade lower than Gerlach. There are several hotels amongst the peaks and twelve chalets high up for skiers and summer walkers. Chalets can accommodate up to 120 guests. Contact Czech tourist offices (Cedok) and The Director, TANAP, Tatranská Lomnica, CSSR. The hotel Lomnica, Tatranská Lomnica, okr. Poprad, is a good base.

## VELKÝ AND MALÝ TISÝ

Velký and Malý Tisý (big and little ponds) lie on either side of the western Prague–Vienna road to the north of Třeboň in southern Bohemia. The ponds were created in the thirteenth century for carp rearing and now cover 1,700 acres including a reserve. There are large reed beds sheltering a population of 70 pairs of purple herons, and large numbers of the marsh harriers that are always to be seen. About 50 pairs of night herons breed, and the great white heron does so irregularly. Two species of crake breed and there are 15 pairs of greylags and good colonies of black-necked grebes and black terns amongst the reeds and reed islands. The surrounding wet meadows with willows are rich habitats, and there are many interesting species to be found in the woods and fields outside the reserve. The wealth of passerines here is most impressive with icterine, Savi's and river warblers, together with collared flycatcher and penduline tit. Passage brings regular osprey and little gull, while white-tailed eagles are present in winter. This is one of the richest and easiest to visit places in Czechoslovakia.

SUMMER: black-necked grebe, bittern, little bittern, night heron, great white heron (?), purple heron, white stork, greylag goose, goldeneye, ferruginous duck, little crake, spotted crake, honey buzzard, marsh harrier, hobby, black tern, middle spotted woodpecker, wryneck, golden oriole, crested lark, fieldfare, black redstart, icterine warbler, Savi's warbler, river warbler, penduline tit, great grey shrike, collared flycatcher, serin.

PASSAGE: osprey, little gull.

WINTER: white-tailed eagle.

The ponds lie on either side of the road north of Třeboň and most of them can be seen from public roads and tracks. Exploration is in general unrestricted. The Československá Ornithologická Společnost owns a hut that is used as the headquarters and also provides accommodation for five students. Write to Dr W. Černý, Department of Zoology, Viničná 7, Praha 2. The Hotel Bílý Koníček, nám J. Fučíka 97, Třeboň is recommended.

## VIHORLAT

Vihorlat is a range of volcanic hills in the extreme east of Czechoslovakia that rise to 3,500 feet and are covered with deciduous woods. They are well worth travelling the length of the country for, as they hold several species that are not found elsewhere and are generally rare throughout their range. Raptors are particularly important and in this general area there are golden, lesser spotted, short-toed, imperial, and booted eagles. Red and black kites, goshawk, peregrine, and saker falcon are also found. Visitors should see some of these but numbers are very small. The Ural owl is another outstanding breeding bird, and there is a good range of smaller birds including woodpeckers, roller, rock thrush, rock bunting, and red-breasted flycatcher.

SUMMER: golden eagle, lesser spotted eagle, short-toed eagle, imperial eagle, booted eagle, red kite, black kite, peregrine, saker falcon, goshawk, Ural owl, grey-headed woodpecker, black woodpecker, middle spotted woodpecker, white-backed woodpecker, Syrian woodpecker, wryneck, roller, hoopoe, dipper, crested tit, rock thrush, red-breasted flycatcher, rock bunting.

Michalovce, to the south, is the nearest large town, and accommodation in the midst of the hills is available at Chata pri Morskom oku, p. Remetske Hamre, okr. Michalovce.

# Denmark

1 Blaavandshuk
2 Limfjorden
3 Nissum Fjord to Stadil Fjord
4 Ringköbing Fjord
5 Rold Skov
6 Skagen
7 South Jutland

8 Copenhagen
9 North Sjaelland
10 West Sjaelland
11 Fyn and Langeland
12 Lolland-Falster-Mön
13 Faeroes

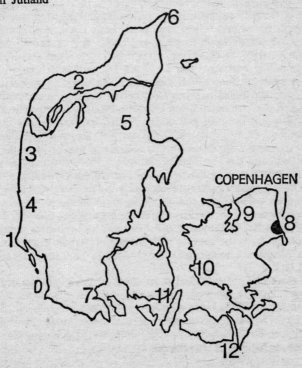

DANSK ORNITHOLOGISK FORENING,
Universitetsbiblioteket, afd 2, Norre Allé 49, Köbenhavn N.

READ: *Danmarks Fugle* (1962–64) by F. Salomonsen and G. Rudebeck
(covers all Scandinavian birds): *Oversigt over Danmarks Fugle* (1963) by
F. Salomonsen: *The Breeding Birds of Denmark* (1946) by P. Jespersen:
*Zoology of the Faroes, Aves* (1935) by F. Salomonsen.

Danish areas have been grouped as follows:
1. Jutland; 2. Sjaelland; 3. Provincial Islands; 4. Faroes.

## JUTLAND

### BLAAVANDSHUK

Blaavandshuk is a sand dune promontory to the north-west of Esbjerg. It has
a lighthouse and a bird observatory with a small area of cover round each, and
the latter owns a Heligoland trap. Migration is often dramatic with a continuous stream of waders, especially knot, redshank, and oystercatcher passing
from the north in autumn. There are usually large numbers of gulls, terns
and skuas, and sea-watching is often good with grebes and divers, and
gannets after westerly winds. Passerine migration is excellent and Blaavandshuk is one of the best places in Denmark for rarities. There are heavy
visible movements of finches, thrushes and pipits. Regular rarities include
bluethroat, Lapland bunting, shore lark, barred warbler, tawny pipit, gull-
billed tern, and black-throated diver. Other birds of the area include Kentish
plover in summer, and black grouse and crested lark throughout the year.

To the south of Blaavandshuk is Skallingen, a wide area of salt-marsh and
dunes. This is exceptionally rewarding for waders and wildfowl with the North
Sea on one side and the Ho Bugt on the other. There is usually a flock of
avocets here in July, often visible from the mouth of the Varde Aa on the east
side of the Bugt. Passage waders are numerous and frequently include broad-
billed sandpiper, while cranes and goshawks are often noted. In winter this
area is noted for snow bunting, shore lark, and grey geese.

Many people arrive in Denmark at Esbjerg and bird-watchers should keep
a sharp look-out from the boat for interesting birds like little gulls and gull-
billed terns. Storks nest on the post office, and the harbour roads are excellent
for crested lark.

Ribe, a small and old cathedral town some 20 km south-east of Esbjerg
has the largest concentration of storks in Denmark, usually about ten pairs.
To the south-west of Ribe is the tidal island of Römö which is joined to the
mainland by a road along a narrow causeway providing excellent views of
waders and duck on a rising tide. Lakolk, on the island, is a good place to see
the immense movements of shorebirds.

AUTUMN: grebes, black-throated diver, knot, redshank, oystercatcher, sanderling, broad-billed sandpiper, Kentish plover, little gull, skuas, gull-billed tern, black grouse, crested lark, shore lark, tawny pipit, bluethroat, Lapland bunting.

WINTER: grey geese, brent goose, black grouse, crested lark, shore lark, snow bunting.

Blaavandshuk is reached by leaving Varde westwards through Oksböl to Oksby. The bird-watchers at the Observatory are usually very friendly towards visitors. For Skallingen take the road southwards from Norballe on Ho Bugt. Accommodation is not available at the Observatory, but visitors can stay at the nearby hotels Blaavandkao and Oksböl.

## LIMFJORDEN

The Limfjorden all but separates the cap of Denmark from the rest of Jutland. It is a huge shallow inlet that at first sight appears unmanageable to the bird-watcher. Fortunately the search can be narrowed to the outstanding area along the northern shore between Tisted and Aalborg. This area is excellent and is well worth a thorough exploration and a holiday at almost any spot. Nevertheless the search can (if necessary) be narrowed even further to the two reserves at Ulvedybet and Vejlerne, and during the breeding season, at least, to the latter alone. It must be repeated, however, that this northern shore of the Limfjorden repays investigation and interesting birds can be found along its entire length.

1. **Vejlerne:** an area of wet grazing meadows with coastal marshes and lagoons created by the failure of a British engineer to construct a satisfactory sea-wall across one of the bays of the Limfjord in the nineteenth century. The resulting fresh marsh is one of the finest in Europe. It has a rich avifauna including vast colonies of gulls and terns: over 25,000 pairs of black-headed gulls have been counted on the narrow belt of marshes that stretches for 6 km down the eastern side. Amongst this horde are several (perhaps 25) pairs of little gulls, and over a hundred pairs of gull-billed terns. The marshes and lagoons hold a magnificent collection of birds at all seasons and include a breeding population of black-necked grebe, black tern, avocet, ruff, black-tailed godwit and dunlin. There are quite extensive reed beds in some places which hold greylag goose, bittern, marsh harrier, and most years a few spoonbills which here reach their furthest north in Europe (see Texel in Holland).

In autumn thousands of duck and waders pass through the area and in late summer it is a moulting ground for greylag geese and numerous duck.

SUMMER: black-necked grebe, spoonbill, bittern, greylag goose, shoveler, marsh harrier, black-tailed godwit, Kentish plover, ringed plover, ruff, dunlin, avocet, black-headed gull, little gull, arctic tern, black tern, gull-billed tern.

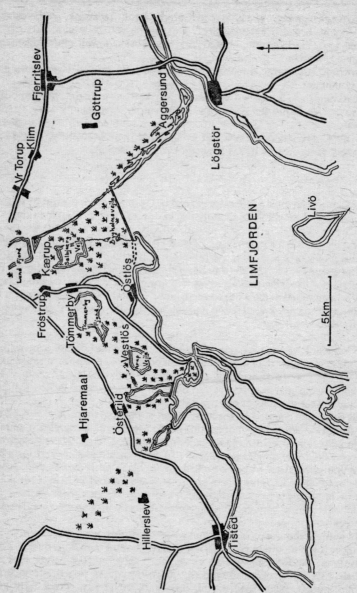

The most interesting area of the Limfjord in northern Jutland.

AUTUMN: greylag goose, teal, wigeon, curlew, black-tailed godwit, bar-tailed godwit.

Vejlerne is a nature reserve with no admission except on the most serious scientific mission. For ordinary bird-watching, however, a great deal can be seen from the surrounding roads particularly from the dam at Bygholm east of Östlös and from the new country road between Tisted and Aalborg. The reserve, in fact, lies between Vestlös and Göttrup south of the A11. Some private marshes nearby can also be overlooked from roads.

2. The other important reserve on the Limfjorden is mainly marshland and shallow water at Ulvedybet which lies east of Vejlerne between Attrup and Vesterby. It is primarily known as a migration haunt of thousands (up to 40,000) of wildfowl, of which the most notable are bean geese.

AUTUMN: teal, wigeon, greylag goose, bean goose.

A walk down the coast from one of the two villages mentioned could be rewarding.

3. Tyborön: a village at the artificial western mouth of the Limfjord. To the south there are a series of lagoons between the road to the village and the sea-wall. Though they vary according to the depth and salinity of the water they can be really excellent – 23 species of wader have been noted in a single day. Breeding birds are also good, with godwits, avocet, ruff, and black tern.

SUMMER: Kentish plover, black-tailed godwit, ruff, avocet, black tern.

AUTUMN: waders.

Leave Lemvig north-westwards to the mouth of the Limfjord.

There are three routes into the area via Oddesund, Aggersund, and Aalborg. There is also a railway that connects with the major cities to the south and which has a line along the northern shore of Limfjord enabling even small villages to be reached by public transport. There is a good hotel at Tisted and a selection of camp sites along the A11.

From Copenhagen the best way to Jutland is by the overnight boat to Aalborg or by direct flight. It is thus possible to get a connection at the capital from any city in Europe. For visitors from Scandinavian countries there are ferries from Kristiansand in Norway to Hirtshals, and from Larvik and Oslo, and Gothenburg to Frederikshavn.

## NISSUM FJORD TO STADIL FJORD

This stretch of the west Jutland coast abuts the Ringköbing Fjord to the south and is in many ways a very similar area. It is treated separately to simplify what would otherwise be a very complex account and because of certain ornithological differences.

Nissum Fjord is a shallow lake with a single outlet to the sea through the coastal dune system. There is an extensive area of pine forest between Bjerghuse and Husby to the south which holds crested tits. The beach, dunes, and lake shore are excellent during migration especially for waders including most of the species one could expect to see in western Europe. In particular, Temminck's stints are more numerous than further west. It is also the main resort of brent geese in Denmark, and an important staging post for pinkfeet. The marshes at Felsted Kog in the south of the fjord form a vast reed bed that is a national game reserve over which a restricted amount of hunting is allowed in the autumn. It is particularly important breeding area for garganey, pintail, shoveler and a variety of waders including black-tailed godwit, ruff, avocet, and wood sandpiper.

To the south of Nissum Fjord lies the pond of Husby Sö which with its surrounding marshes forms an excellent bird area, while further south still is the partly reclaimed (1954) but still excellent Stadil Fjord. This in fact leads into Ringköbing Fjord. Black terns, black-tailed godwit, ruff, dunlin, avocet, and arctic tern are all found in these two areas which are noted for thousands of migrating wildfowl in autumn especially whooper and Bewick's swans, and pinkfeet and greylag geese.

SUMMER: bittern, marsh harrier, Montagu's harrier, pintail, garganey, shoveler, black-tailed godwit, wood sandpiper, ruff, dunlin, avocet, black tern, arctic tern, crested tit, crested lark.

AUTUMN: whooper swan, Bewick's swan, pink-footed goose, greylag goose, brent goose, teal, shoveler, wigeon, marsh harrier, spotted redshank, curlew sandpiper, Temminck's stint, little stint, bar-tailed godwit, black tern, gull-billed tern.

The coastal road along the dunes gives excellent views over the main area of Nissum Fjord and of the pines to the south. There is also access to the water off the minor roads in the north-east between Bövlingbjerg, Nees and Vemb, and the reserve of Felsted Kog can be visited after 1 October. Husby Sö can be seen from the Staby-Husby road, while Stadil to the south is an excellent start to an exploration of the Stadil Fjord and the marshes around Tiim.

The area is easily reached from Esbjerg which is the port of Jutland.

## RINGKÖBING FJORD

Ringköbing is the longest of the west Jutland fjords and also the most famous from an ornithological point of view. All of these lakes are shallow and cut off from the sea by only a narrow belt of dunes along which run various minor roads giving excellent views over the beach and the fjords. Where the dunes are not backed by lagoons there are often large plantations of conifers which hold crested tits with crested larks in the open sandy areas. Ringköbing Fjord itself holds breeding grebes and black terns hawk overhead. The shores of the lake vary from sandy beach to rich salt marsh and water meadow.

The marshes on the island of Klaegbanke have been protected since 1894 and consist mainly of grass and reeds harbouring a rich breeding population of gulls including the occasional little gull, Sandwich and gull-billed terns, marsh harrier and just possibly spoonbill. To the south lies the peninsula of

Tipperne which consists of water-meadows and salt marshes surrounded by a vast area of shallow water with a few islands. The area has been protected since 1894 and a new laboratory for ornithological and ecological research was built in 1954. Breeding birds include a very large colony of avocets, black-tailed godwit and ruff, Sandwich and gull-billed terns, and a host of duck and gulls. Both of these reserves are exceptionally good during autumn passage when almost all the waders and wildfowl that one can see in western Europe occur, often in large numbers. A single day once produced 50,000 wildfowl at Tipperne alone. Amongst these species pink-feet and whooper and Bewick's swans are most important. The similar Vaernengene area is well worth a visit. The lake of Ful Sö to the south is famous for Bewick's swans, up to 8,000 pinkfeet, and regular rough-legged buzzard and hen harrier.

Though the southern end is so rich, the whole of the Ringköbing Fjord is worth exploring and will produce birds. Three areas away from the lake shore deserve mention. The dune and dune stack reserve of Nymindestrommen and Holmslands Klit lies immediately south of Nymindegab and approximates to a southward extension of Ringköbing. Admission is free. The village of Skern on the A11 boasts breeding white storks while the heathland reserve of Borris the east of Skjern holds curlew and black grouse amongst other species.

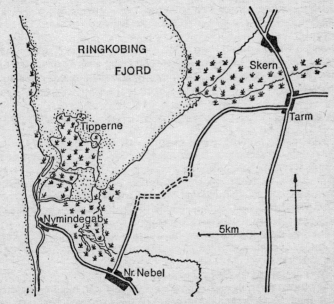

South side of Ringköbing Fjord and the famous reserve of Tipperne. Many of the birds can be seen in the area to the south without entering the reserve.

Unfortunately the area is used for military purposes and watchers must be content with views from the roads.

SUMMER: white stork, marsh harrier, Montague's harrier, Kentish plover, black-tailed godwit, ruff, curlew, avocet, black tern, Sandwich tern, gull-billed tern, black grouse, crested tit, crested lark, collared dove.

AUTUMN: whooper swan, Bewick's swan, pink-footed goose, white-fronted goose, greylag goose, brent goose, teal, shoveler, wigeon, bar-tailed godwit, spotted redshank, Temminck's stint, little stint, curlew sandpiper, wood sandpiper, ruff, avocet.

WINTER: duck, geese, swans, waders.

The road running north and south along the beach, and the roads between Skjern, Ringköbing and Sondervig provide excellent views over the greater part of the Fjord. The beach road north of Nymindegab overlooking the Tipperne peninsula is especially good, and there is free access to the dune reserve south of the latter village.

Klaegbanke is strictly out of bounds for all but the most scientific purpose. Tipperne too is strictly protected but can be visited on Sundays and Wednesday afternoons during June and July by permission of the guard on duty (telephone 0528 1211) at Tipperhuset pr. Nore Nebel, 36. Admission 3 kr. The southern part of these marshes are excellent and are not part of the reserve.

The Borris reserve can be seen from the roads between Skern and Borris, and Ful Sö can be overlooked from the dune Klövbakken along the road to the north.

The area is easily reached from Esbjerg which is the port of Jutland. There is the Grönlund Hotel at Skjern and several camp sites amongst the dunes. There are hotels at Ringköbing that make an excellent base for this and the Nissum area.

## ROLD SKOV

This outstandingly beautiful forest in north-east Jutland is one of the largest woodland areas in Denmark. It is a mixed forest with considerable areas of pure conifers and is a good place for breeding raptors including common and honey buzzards, sparrowhawk and goshawk. Long-eared owls breed, and other birds include nightjar, icterine warbler, and crossbill. It is also the best place for woodcock in Denmark. Rough-legged buzzard and ospreys are noted on passage, and the former frequently in winter as well.

SUMMER: buzzard, honey buzzard, sparrowhawk, goshawk, peregrine, woodcock, long-eared owl, nightjar, wood lark, crested tit, pied flycatcher, icterine warbler, crossbill.

AUTUMN: osprey, rough-legged buzzard.

The E3 between Århus and Ålberg runs through the middle of the forest which is freely open to public access. Try the preserved heath at Rebild Bakker at dusk for woodcock roding and nightjars in courtship display.

## SKAGEN

Skagen is the extreme north tip of Jutland where the Kattegat meets the Skagerak. The huge sand beaches and dunes together with the wild seas make this an exciting area and the stunted pines add to the visual effect. In spring huge flocks of thrushes, finches, and pipits pass up the coast and set off for Sweden and Norway, and there are also large numbers of waders and wildfowl. Though its advantages are less obvious in autumn many small birds are attracted to the lighthouse and the cover provided by the village. There are usually a few raptors to be seen including rough-legged buzzard and occasional kites and eagles. Other rare species that have been seen in recent years include crane, black stork, and red-breasted flycatcher. The movement of corvidae is almost unbelievable.

Sea movements include large numbers of divers, scoter, and Sandwich terns and the best observation place is the Point or along the north beach. For passerines Drachmanns Grav is a likely spot. Tawny pipits breed in the dunes.

In winter kittiwake and the occasional glaucous gull are found in the harbour.

AUTUMN: divers, scoter, rough-legged buzzard, red kite, crane, waders, Arctic skua, Sandwich tern, ring ousel, red-breasted flycatcher.

WINTER: kittiwake, glaucous gull.

SPRING: thrushes, finches, pipits, corvids.

Skagen is reached on route 10.

## SOUTH JUTLAND

Several localities near the German border are exciting in the breeding season for woodland and other birds not found elsewhere in Denmark.

1. The woods at Als hold a few pairs of ravens plus the more usual short-toed treecreeper, golden oriole, and goshawk. Similar species are found on the mainland at Sundeved, particularly at the accessible Gråstens slotspark.

2. Tinglev Mose: the best place in Denmark for grasshopper warbler and one or two other less usual *locustella* have been heard here in recent years. The fen also holds a colony of black terns, with water rail, short-eared owl, and Montagu's harrier. Admission is free, and the best observation point is a track that crosses the fen parallel to and south of the railway from Tinglev to Sönderborg. The marshes to the south at Kragelund and Froslev contain similar species, but are in general rather drier and heathery. Specialities here include great grey shrike and wood sandpiper.

3. Great areas of spruce plantations like those at Froslev and Bommerlund are seldom rich in birds, but these hold great grey shrike, raven, firecrest, goshawk, and crested tit. Access is free on either side of route 8.

**4.  Draved Skov:** to the north-east of the last area and isolated in a large area of heath and bog, is celebrated as a resting place for migrant raptors. It also has a rich variety of small birds, and is freely accessible.

**5.  Ranböl Hede and Frederrikshab Plantage:** well to the north of the other areas, to the south of Silkeborg and west of Vejle, their avifauna is of a similar character. On the heaths there are great grey shrike, wood sandpiper, woodlark, and curlew, while the woods hold black grouse and crested tit.

Black redstarts are more likely to be found in the villages and towns of southern Jutland than anywhere else in Denmark.

SUMMER: goshawk, Montagu's harrier, wood sandpiper, black tern, black grouse, short-toed treecreeper, wood lark, great grey shrike, grasshopper warbler, firecrest, crested tit, golden oriole, raven.

## SJÆLLAND

## COPENHAGEN

The Copenhagen area is more than a convenient place for the busy traveller to get out and see a few birds in a short time. It is an outstanding area for birds in its own right, due mainly to its geographical position in the east of the country. There are a number of public parks several of which have large lakes and which are renowned for the number of wildfowl, gulls and other waterbirds that they attract. In particular Utterslev Mose has a wealth of species in summer including three species of grebe, greylag goose, pochard, common tern, thrush nightingale, and sometimes great reed warbler, in a park completely surrounded by a heavily built up area. Furesoen lake and park in the north-west of the city has a large colony of great crested grebes, a wealth of passerines, and dipper in winter. The best areas are the bays along the north shore of Store Kalv which can be seen from a public footpath. Of the other parks the most notable are Valbyparken (red-throated pipits regular in autumn), and Charlottenlund Skov, the best place for icterine warbler in summer and mealy redpoll by the moat at Danmarks Akvarium in winter.

The major bird areas, however, lie in the southern part of Copenhagen on the island of Amager. Sjaellandsbroen overlooks the largest area of open water in the harbour at the southern end and holds large numbers of sea-birds including smew regularly in winter. The little pond south of the bridge is always worth a look and holds little grebe in summer, a rather scarce bird in Denmark. Kongelunden is a mixed wood with a thick undergrowth in the southern part of Amager and an area of outstanding ornithological interest. Almost all of the passerines that one would expect to find in Denmark are present and one or two more besides. Of outstanding interest to the visitor are barred warbler, icterine warbler, and thrush nightingale. To the west of the forest is an area of salt marshes that regularly hold numbers of waders on passage, though the ringing station on the reclaimed land in the west is on military ground to which there is no entry; it formerly boasted two hundred pairs of avocet. During autumn passage the southward movement of birds of prey through Scandinavia that is particularly well known at Falsterbo can occasionally be seen over the streets of the city. September and October are the best months and honey buzzard, common buzzard, osprey, and sparrowhawk are some-times numerous.

SUMMER: great crested grebe, black-necked grebe, red-necked grebe, little grebe, greylag goose, pochard, common tern, thrush nightingale, great reed warbler, icterine warbler, barred warbler.

AUTUMN: wildfowl, buzzard, honey buzzard, osprey, sparrowhawk, spotted redshank, Temminck's stint, little stint, ruff, warblers, chats, flycatchers.

WINTER: duck, smew, gulls, dipper, kingfisher.

All of the areas mentioned in this section can be visited conveniently by public transport.

1. Utterslev Mose: a public park: tram 5 to Akandevej, 10 and 16 to Bispebjerg Parkalle; 'bus 8 to Akandevej, 43 to Frederiksborgvej.
2. Furesoen: S-train to Holte or Virum; 'bus 160 to Nybro.
3. Charlottenlund Skov: S-train to Charlottenlund.
4. Sjaellandsbroen: part of Copenhagen harbour: 'bus 46 to western side of bridge; tram 3 to Mozarts Plads, then walk 1 km along Borgmester Christiansensgarde.
5. Kongelunden: a wooded area in south Amager: 'bus 31 and 113 direct to centre of forest.

Copenhagen is an international transport centre and has a wealth of accommodation. There are several camp sites including one on the southern shore of Amager.


## NORTH SJÆLLAND

To the north of route E66 on the island of Sjaelland are a number of natural beech woods with a scattering of oak, elm and lime, and with plantations of conifers, and some older swamps. The best known are Gribskov to the north of Hilleröd which is the largest forest in Denmark, and Dyrehave which is a Royal deer park with areas of rough pasture just north of Copenhagen. Icter-ine warblers are the most characteristic birds though they leave in early August, while the nuthatches belong to three distinct sub-species. Those in Jutland are the same as the English form, those in Gribskov and the woods to the north are of the whiter Scandinavian form, and those in Dyrehave belong to the south-east European form. All are numerous and noisy. Thrush nightingales breed but would be impossible to find but for their song, while thickets near open ground are favoured by red-backed shrike. Crossbill breed in the spruces. Though the middle-spotted woodpecker was last recorded in Denmark from Dyrehave in 1961, the black woodpecker has shown signs of colonizing the northern woods from its Swedish strongholds.

A few green sandpipers nest in some of the woods, while white storks breed at Hilleröd (ask anyone in the street), in some of the villages near Gribskov and on the royal palace at Fredensborg. Honey and common buzzards breed in the woods though the best time to see raptors is on passage.

Gilbjerghoved Klint 2 km west of Gilleleje at the northern tip of Sjaelland is a particularly good place for watching visible movements of small birds and raptors in March and April. Up to 100,000 chaffinches and several hundred sparrowhawks can be seen in a day. About 30 km south-west of Gilleleje are the coastal heaths and woods at Melby and Tisvilde which are good for wood lark, nightjar, tawny pipit, and sometimes hobby. The area at Melby is a shooting range, with admission when firing is not taking place.

SUMMER: white stork, buzzard, honey buzzard, green sandpiper, black woodpecker, nightjar, wood lark, red-backed shrike, nuthatch, icterine warbler, thrush nightingale, pied flycatcher, hawfinch, crossbill.

Access to the woods which lie north and south of Hilleröd is normally unrestricted. This is true of almost all the other woods in northern Sjaelland, even though some of them are in private hands. There is an enormous area of beautiful mature forest in which the ornithologist can wander at will.

## WEST SJÆLLAND

In west Sjælland there are several excellent bird places between Nyköbing and Vordingborg.

**1. Hovestrand:** the beach of Sejeröbugt from Höve north towards Lumsaas, north-west of Holbaek. It is broad, sandy, and backed in a good many places by reed beds and pine woods, and is a good place for beach-bird holidays. It is excellent for passage of waders, notably sanderling that are otherwise rare in Sjælland, and little stint. Kentish plover and tawny pipit are both numerous and breed.

SUMMER: Kentish plover, tawny pipit.
AUTUMN: ringed plover, sanderling, little stint.

The beach is of straightforward access from Höve and there are camp sites.

**2. Reersö:** the peninsula that justs into the Great Belt and breaks the coast, line between Kalundborg and Korsör. It is flat, round, and one of the island's favourite wildfowl haunts. Even in late summer there are flocks of shelduck, merganser, pintail, and wigeon, and there are always large flocks of waders. The best places are the mouth of the river on the north side of the neck of the peninsula, and the head of the saltings on the south side.

AUTUMN: wildfowl, osprey, Temminck's stint, little stint, black-tailed godwit, ruff, knot, greenshank, avocet.
WINTER: shelduck, teal, pintail, wigeon, waders.

Reersö is reached by road from the Kalundborg-Slagelse road westwards from Görlev, or the road to the north. The mouth of the Tude Aa, a few kilometres to the south is of similar character but noted for a herd of Bewick's swans on migration.

**3.  Tissö:** a large lake to the east of the Kalundborg-Slagelse road. It is shallow and in many places bordered by thick reeds, and on the east side by beech woods. In the south-east by Saeby Kirke and beside the small road that runs for part of the way along the southern shore a wide fresh mudbank is uncovered in late summer. It is thronged by enormous flocks of waders including up to 500 ruff, with parties of golden plover, wood sandpiper, spotted redshank and greenshank, and by even larger flocks of duck with up to 1,000 greylags. All sorts of things turn up at this season. In winter the lake is noted as one of the principal haunts of Bewick's swan, and holds large flocks of duck and geese, while in summer it is one of the few inland breeding places of little tern.

SUMMER: little tern.

AUTUMN: greylag goose, shoveler, teal, pintail, ruff, golden plover, wood sandpiper, spotted redshank, greenshank.

WINTER: Bewick's swan, greylag goose, duck.

The road down the east side, backed by woods, offers good views, and the little road west of Saeby along the southern shore is excellent in late summer. It is *most important* that the private notices are respected and that observations are restricted to what can be seen from the road. Disturbance could ruin this excellent spot.

**4.  Stigsness:** a point south-west of Skælskör which is outstanding for passage in autumn. The movement of raptors – buzzard, honey buzzard, rough-legged buzzard, osprey, sparrowhawk, harriers, etc. – can on some days equal that at Falsterbo. Crows, piegeons, and passerines are also seen in large numbers.

AUTUMN: raptors, corvids, passerines.

The wood on the point is private, but most of the coast is freely accessible. Halskov Rev, immediately north of the ferry station, is another place to see raptor movements in autumn.

**5.  Karrebæk and Dybsö Fjorde:** immediately south of Næstved and excellent for waders, gulls, and duck at all seasons, they almost invariably hold at least one white-tailed eagle in winter.

AUTUMN: waders, gulls, duck.

WINTER: white-tailed eagle.

Most of the area can be overlooked from the public roads and from Enö, and there is access on foot from Gavnö. Eagles also visit Tystrup-Bavelse Sö (between Næstvedand Sorö) where bean geese are found on the fields on passage.


## PROVINCIAL ISLANDS

## FYN AND LANGELAND

The central islands of Denmark, in most places intensively cultivated and fertile, are nevertheless rewarding for the bird-watcher. There are some

excellent headlands for spring or autumn migration, some fine woods and
coastal areas, and a delightful landscape of orchards, old villages, parkland
and manor houses where birds and sight-seeing mix well together.

The most important localities on Fyn are:

1.  **Knudshoved:** the lagoon just by the embarkation point for the main ferry
over the Great Belt is worth a glance, even in summer, for its colony of
avocets. In spring there is a heavy movement of raptors and songbirds, and
along the coast of the Great Belt a movement of wildfowl, especially eider.
Access is fairly obvious.

2.  **Fyns Hoved and Hindsholm:** the peninsula north of Kerteminde is another
splendid observation point for spring passage. The passerines leave mainly
from the point itself, the raptors and other large birds mainly from further
south, at Bøgebjerg Skov by Stubberun village. Access is free.

3.  **The North coast:** the flats at Glydensten (near Bogense) and Egebjerggård
are best, with breeding colonies of wildfowl and waders, such as greylag
geese, shelduck, ruff and avocet. There are large flocks of knot, dunlin, grey
plover, ringed plover and bar-tailed godwit on passage. Access is limited, but
much can be seen from public paths.

4.  **The lakes round Brahetrolleborg:** this area lies off the A8 in south Fyn
about 10 km north-east of Fåborg. There are colonies of greylags at Arres-
kovsø and Brændegårdssø, and a population of breeding buzzards and honey-
buzzards in the surrounding woods, with a chance of ravens. Icterine warbler,
thrush nightingale and other typical Danish woodland birds occur in these
woods as elsewhere on Fyn. On passage there are large flocks of greylag and
other wildfowl, with occasional but regular visits from both golden and white-
tailed eagles. The latter has also summered here.

5.  **Small islands south of Fyn:** in the triangle between Fyn, Aerö and Langeland is a host of small islands, many uninhabited. Most hold colonies of gulls
and terns, and a good many have colonies of avocets, ruffs and a handful of
breeding turnstones. On passage there are many other waders in smaller
numbers, and great flocks of eider and some brent. On Langeland the outstanding locality is at Keldsnor.

This is the southern tip of the island. In the period from the end of July to
the beginning of November there is a continuous passage of almost every
category of Danish migrant. The movement of waders is mainly concentrated
between 20 July and 10 September, and on the lagoon and surrounding flats
it is possible on a good day to see more than twenty species, including red-
necked phalarope and broad-billed sandpiper. Night migrants are seen in
large numbers in the woods and hedges, especially warblers, chats, red-backed
shrikes and flycatchers. From the first week in September the raptors begin
to move, the honey buzzards of the early period being replaced by common

buzzard later on, both often passing in large numbers. Many other raptors occur with them. There is also a large daily movement of small passerines in the mornings, and a big movement of duck, mainly eider, along the coasts and out over the Baltic. This locality, for variety and drama in the daily migratory movements, can thus almost bear comparison with the great Swedish stations of Falsterbo and Ottenby. Though the total volume of birds moving is usually smaller, it has the distinct advantage that the number of bird-watchers watching them is smaller as well, for the place is virtually unknown outside Denmark.

Passage is most easily observed from the top of Dovns Klint. A road reaches it from a turning on the main road between Magleby and Bagenkop, and access is virtually unrestricted.

SUMMER: greylag goose, shelduck, buzzard, honey buzzard, ruff, turnstone, avocet, gulls, terns, icterine warbler, thrush nightingale.

AUTUMN: greylag goose, brent goose, eider, golden eagle, white-tailed eagle, honey buzzard, buzzard, knot, grey plover, bar-tailed godwit, red-necked phalarope, broad-billed sandpiper, warblers, chats, flycatchers.

## LOLLAND-FALSTER-MÖN

These three islands form the southern part of Denmark and have sufficient interesting bird-watching places to make a very good holiday.

1. **Gedser:** the most southerly point of Denmark lies at the end of the peninsula at the tip of Falster. It is a good place to watch autumn hawk migration, and buzzard, honey buzzard, sparrowhawk, peregrine and the occasional osprey can usually be seen. It is also a likely place for passing cranes. Passerines can be very numerous around the lighthouse area. It is an excellent spot off the beaten track for autumn migrants.

AUTUMN: crane, buzzard, honey buzzard, osprey, peregrine, sparrowhawk, warblers, chats, flycatchers.

Leave Nyköbing southwards on route A2 (E64) to Gedser where there is a hotel. A minor road leads to Frisenfelt and the lighthouse.

It is worth stopping 20 km north of Gedser on the A2 where the road overlooks the reserve of Boto Nor. This is a resting place for flocks of geese, duck, and waders in spring and autumn. In particular bean geese and occasional cranes are noteworthy.

2. **Naskov Indrefjord:** one of the country's outstanding reserves covering 500 acres, and the site of the only breeding colony of red-crested pochard, up to 30 pairs of which have bred annually since 1940. There is a large lagoon with reed beds and marshes that are also the haunt of garganey. Marsh harriers quarter the reeds which hold great reed warbler, with colonies of black-necked grebe, black tern, and mute swan. The area is excellent for passage and winter wildfowl and waders. There is an ornithological station here.

SUMMER: black-necked grebe, red-crested pochard, garganey, mute swan, marsh harrier, black tern, great reed warbler.

PASSAGE; WINTER: duck, geese.

Though a reserve, the area is freely accessible by the footpaths on the north side.

3. **Maribo Söerne:** south of Maribo on Lolland and a good place for water-birds, occasionally holding the odd osprey and white-tailed eagle. The surrounding woodland has an excellent cross-section of Danish woodland birds including thrush nightingale, golden oriole and honey buzzard.

SUMMER: honey buzzard, golden oriole, thrush nightingale, icterine warbler.

AUTUMN: waterfowl, osprey, white-tailed eagle.

There are roads and view points throughout the area.

4. **Brunddrager and Hyllekrog:** at the southern point of Lolland, and one of Denmark's best places for observing passage in autumn. In the last week of August and the first of September the most numerous raptors are honey buzzard, later replaced by common buzzard. Both species may sometimes be counted in thousands on a single day. Other raptors, osprey, sparrowhawk, harriers, and falcons, are also numerous, and this is one of the very few places that kites are seen regularly. There are also good movements of passerines, and large flocks of terns and waders gather on the peninsular of Hyllekrog itself.

5. **Ulfshale:** an area of marshes and woodland at the northern tip of Mön, mainly known for the colony of avocets that breed on the nearby Nyord Island marshes and that are frequently seen in the area. Other breeders here include ruff, dunlin, shoveler and garganey. The chalk cliffs to the east at Möns Klint are good for peregrine, and for raptor and thrush migration in spring.

SUMMER: shoveler, garganey, goosander, ruff, dunlin, avocet.

Leave Stege northwards on minor roads. Birds can be seen all the way but admittance to the reserve area is not usually allowed.

# FAROES

Though geographically nearer Iceland, Norway and Britain politically and culturally, the Faroe Islands are part of Denmark though in fact the people speak a language (Faroese) of their own. There are 18 inhabited islands covering a total of 540 square miles with a population of 35,000, lying approximately half-way between Shetland and Iceland. The economy is based on deep-sea fishing for foreign markets though sea-birds are taken for food on most islands, eggs (guillemot), young (fulmar, manx shearwater, and gannet), and adults (guillemot, puffin, and fulmar). Adult birds are skilfully and daringly taken by hunters hanging from the cliffs using the famous flegg nets.

Visitors to Faroe must expect bad weather during even the best time for a visit, which is June to mid-August. There can be drizzle for weeks on end with continuous cloud down to sea level. The seabird colonies are amongst Europe's finest ornithological sights. There is a gannetry of 1,000 pairs on Mykines, vast colonies of guillemot, razorbill, puffin, kittiwake and fulmar on almost all the islands but particularly on Streymoy, Mykines, Eysturoy, Kallsoy, Vidoy, Fugloy, Sandoy, and Skúvoy. There are great and arctic skuas on Streymoy, Svínoy, Sandoy, and Skúvoy, also Leach's petrel on Mykines, and Manx shearwater and storm petrel on Mykines and Skúvoy. Eider, whimbrel, golden plover, Faroe snipe and Faroe wren breed all over the place, while one or two lakes hold red-necked phalarope, red-throated diver, Slavonian grebe, and several wildfowl species. In the north-eastern group of islands there is always a chance of purple sandpiper and snow bunting high up on the fjells.

SUMMER: red-throated diver, Slavonian grebe, gannet, Manx shearwater, fulmar, Leach's petrel, storm petrel, greylag goose, wigeon, pintail, scaup, scoter, merganser, eider, purple sandpiper, whimbrel, golden plover, oyster-catcher, Faroe snipe, red-necked phalarope, great skua, Arctic skua, kitti-wake, greater black-backed gull, Arctic tern, guillemot, black guillemot, razorbill, puffin, redwing, Faroe wren.

The Faroe Islands

The following is a list of the most likely islands that an ornithologist would want to visit:

1.  **Streymoy:** the main island with Torshavn the Faroe capital. The town's plantation holds breeding redwing and the cliffs mainly in the north-west holds wrens, auks, and other seabirds. The valley near Saksum in the north of the island has a great skua colony. There are hotels in Torshavn which is reached by boat and air from Copenhagen or Iceland. It should be possible to arrange a boat excursion around the Sandoy cliffs. Accommodation in houses on this and other Faroe islands can be arranged through The Faroese Tourist Board, Foroya Ferdamannafelag, Torshavn, Faroe Islands, who will answer any queries on transport, accommodation, etc.

2.  **Mykines:** the most westerly island with Faroes' only gannetry. There are colonies of cliff-breeding seabirds, storm and Leach's petrel, Manx shearwater, and Arctic skuas. There are boats from Vagar and one can thus be on Mykines quite quickly from Glasgow, and from Torshavn.

3.  **Eysturoy:** northeast of Streymoy. It has seabird cliffs at its northern tip and the lake of Toftavatn near the southern tip. The latter holds red-throated diver, Slavanion grebe, and red-necked phalarope. Possible accommodation can be arranged in homes.

4.  **Kallsoy, Vidoy, and Fugloy:** part of the north-eastern group of islands with very large seabird colonies on their northern ends.

5.  **Svinoy:** has a great skua colony; and on both this and the previous islands there is a chance of purple sandpiper and snow bunting on the high tops. Access to the group is by boat from Torshavn to Klaksvik, the second town of the islands.

6.  **Sandoy:** south of Streymoy and one of the best islands for birds. The lakes, especially those around Sand (Sandsvatn and Grothusvatn), hold red-throated diver and most of the wildfowl and waders, including red-necked phalarope. Seabirds breed on the cliffs and Arctic and great skuas on the hills. There are regular boats from Torshavn to Skopun whence 'bus to Sand. Accommodation is possibly available in homes.

7.  **Skúvoy:** a smallish island to the south of Sandoy, but has some magnificent sea-bird cliffs. Manx Shearwater and storm petrel breed on the grassy slopes and great and Arctic skuas in the hills with waders including purple sandpiper. Boats go from Sandoy and Torshavn and there is possible accommodation in houses.

READ: *The Atlantic Islands*, K. Williamson: *A Mosaic of Islands*, K. Williamson and J. Morton Boyd.

# Finland

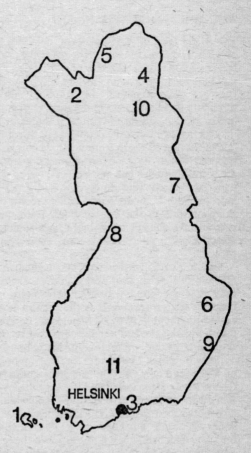

5

4

2

10

7

8

6

9

11

HELSINKI

3

1

SOCIETAS PRO FAUNA ET FLORA FENNICA,
Snellmaninkatu 9–11, Helsinki.

SUOMEN LINTUTIETEELLINEN YHDISTYS RY (FINNISH ORNITHOLOGICAL SOCIETY),
Pohjois – Rautatiekatu 13 B, Helsinki.

SUOMEN IUONNON SUOJELUYHDISTYS RY (FINNISH LEAGUE FOR NATURE CONSERVA-
TION), Lapinlahdenkatu 29B, Helsinki.

READ: *Finnish Birds, their distribution and numbers* (1958) by E. Merikallio.


## ÅLAND ISLES (AHVENANMAA)

The Åland Isles, all 6,544 of them, lie about halfway between Finland and Sweden. They are rising from the sea at the astonishing geological rate of 150 feet per 5,000 years and a mosaic of islands and indented coastlines is emerging. Bare rock is a common feature of the islands especially in the east though there are grassy meadows with woods including some quite extensive stands of mature deciduous trees in the west. Over a third of Åland's 22,000 people live in Mariehamn on the southern shores of the main island and to make matters more complex the people speak Swedish.

The smallest islets are almost entirely bare of tree vegetation and scrub-like juniper grows in the cracks on an otherwise smooth surface. The larger islands are sometimes bare but more often covered with a growth of deciduous or coniferous (predominantly spruce and pine) woodland. The mainland is indented with a characteristic Baltic growth of reeds and rushes along the shoreline, due to the lack of tides. Even quite small islets are inhabited permanently, though many more have summer villas, and even the tiniest skerry might produce a hay crop. The surrounding waters are intensively fished.

The birds of Åland represent, like the human inhabitants, a strange mixture of Swedish-Finnish, east-west elements. There are breeding thrush nightingales that are found virtually nowhere else in Finland, and several more typically eastern species. It is the Finnish headquarters of the white-tailed eagle with about 8–10 pairs. Signildskär and the other western isles hold the thrush nightingale, and it is this area that boasts most of the 80 odd pairs of Caspian terns that are found on Åland, though these birds have bred within a short distance of Mariehamn. In the extreme east barred warblers are found on Kokar and only one other area (the Turku archipelago) in the country. Of the auks only the razorbill and black guillemot breed in Finland and both are found here on the outer islands, the Kobbaklintar archipelago being particularly noted for razorbills. Duck include velvet scoter, eider, goosander, and scaup which are not common in Finland. Similarly shelduck and dunlin, both breeding here, are not numerous in the rest of the country. Of the more spectacular species there might be twenty pairs of eagle owls, and breeding osprey, goshawk, and greylag goose.

SUMMER: white tailed eagle, osprey, peregrine, goshawk, eider, goosander, velvet scoter, scaup, mute swan, greylag goose, shelduck, turnstone, dunlin, Caspian tern, Arctic skua, common gull, razorbill, black guillemot, eagle owl, black grouse, nutcracker, thrush nightingale, barred warbler, siskin, willow tit.

Clearly even a long holiday does not suffice to visit every one of the islands in this group and unlike the Lofoten Islands off Norway, there is not a single island or group that has everything that all the others have. Visitors to Åland will want to see the western and eastern species as well as the notable birds like white-tailed eagle. For this bird Föglö is recommended, though the islands of Kumlinge and Vordö, and the northern and western parishes of Geta, Hammarland, and Eckerö are also known haunts. Other islands have already been mentioned and visitors can take their choice. There is a good selection of accommodation even on the smaller islands including pensions and hundreds of summer cottages. For details and reservations write to Åland Travel Association, Norra Esplanadgatan 1, Mariehamn, Åland.

Travel is straightforward and fast.

From Finland: there is an air service from Turku to Mariehamn (50 minutes) with connections to Helsinki. A modern car ferry (Silja Line) caters for the same route (6 hours).

From Sweden: there is an air service from Stockholm to Mariehamn (45 minutes). The same modern car ferry route continues Mariehamn–Norrtalje (4 hours but there are six other routes plus a hydrofoil service Stockholm–Mariehamn (2½ hours in summer).

Internal transport is by a complex service of boats here, there and everywhere. There are, however, only three cars for hire; contact the Travel Association.


## ENONTEKIO

Enontekio, previously called Hetta, is one of the nicest Lapp villages. It lies near the Norwegian and Swedish borders away from the main route 21, and is either specifically visited or not by tourists passing towards the North Cape. It is situated by a lake shore just south of the limit of coniferous forests along route 21 100 km south of Kilpisjärvi. The area is typical taiga with open hillsides, lakes, bogs, and marshes and holds an excellent selection of Lapland species including crane, smew, whooper swan, a variety of waders, Siberian jay, and great grey owl. The latter is everywhere a scarce bird but a number of sources show it to be seen regularly in this area. Being so near the northern limit of the taiga a small increase in height takes one into the tundra zone, and the National Park of Pallas-Ounastunturi across the lake from Enontekio rises to 2,630 feet. This 50 km long park is a wilderness with the comfort of frequent wilderness huts (autiotupa) enabling the whole range to be walked from Enontekio to Pallastunturi. It is also the most regular haunt of snowy owls in Finland and holds long-tailed skua and possibly bar-tailed godwit and other waders. The whole area is the most likely in the country for gyr falcon.

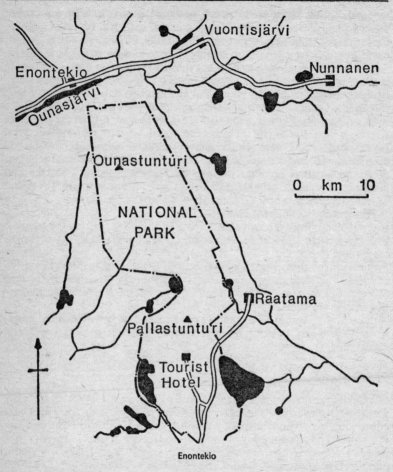

Enontekio

The vistas from the tops over the forests and lakes into Sweden and to the lonely beaches of the eastern lakes are magnificent by any standards. Add the birds in this exceptionally rich area and you have a paradise – provided you can stand the mosquitoes.

SUMMER: smew, whooper swan, crane, gyr falcon, greenshank, spotted redshank, red-necked phalarope, long-tailed skua, snowy owl, great grey owl, hawk owl, Siberian jay, Arctic warbler, Lapland bunting, snow bunting.

There is a 'bus service on route 21 to Enontekio from Rovaniemi which is reached by train-sleeper or air from Helsinki. The road continues eastwards to Vuontisjärvi and Nunnanen both of which are good for birds and remote.

The Hetta Tourist Hotel at Enontekio was opened in 1963 and is the ideal centre for exploration of the taiga zone and the lake shores. There is also a hostel and a camping site. Across the lake, Ounasjärvi, lies the beginning of the 60 km Pallas-Hetta Trail to Pallastunturi Tourist Hotel via a series of huts. There is no village at Pallastunturi just the hotel, a camp site and an interesting natural history museum, but there are regular bus services to Rovaniemi and back along route 21 to Enontekio so that those desperate for snowy owls can make a 3–4 day round trip of it. On the other hand a day trip from Enontekio should suffice for most of the tundra species.

## HELSINKI

Helsinki is good for birds and the surrounding area could make an enjoyable bird-watching holiday. It is unlikely, however, that anyone would do this with all the wonders to the north, and so we offer a very few sites for anyone with a day or a few hours to spare in the capital.

1.  **Vanhankaupunginselka Bay:** the large bay in the centre of the city. It can be seen from almost anywhere. Around Sannalahti is a reed bed with marsh warblers and the only reliable great reed warblers in Finland. This is also a possible spot for bittern. The bay occasionally has the odd little gull.

2.  **Grönträsk:** a small shallow lake in the north-western suburbs, surrounded by houses and a fringe of reeds. There are scattered birch trees but no apparent 'garden' ownership and one can walk between the houses round the lake. Both red-necked and Slavonian grebes breed and Caspian terns visit to feed.

3.  **Otaniemi:** a suburb to the west of Helsinki at the far side of Laajalahti Bay. This is a good place for Caspian tern and little gull, as well as a few land birds like hazel hen, ortolan bunting and icterine warbler. Leave Helsinki westwards on Itämerenkatu and turn right at the far side of the bay.

4.  Though not really Helsinki and not included in the check-list below, Aspskar Bird Reserve is an island off Lovisa and the breeding haunt of 70 pairs of Caspian tern, and a few pairs of guillemots – the only established Finnish locality.

SUMMER: red-necked grebe, Slavonian grebe, bittern(?), pochard, water rail, Caspian tern, marsh warbler, great reed warbler.

## LAKE INARI

This is the largest lake in Lapland and the third largest in Finland. It lies 260 km north of the Arctic Circle, and is 70 km long and 30 km wide. In some places the shoreline merges into fringe marshes while at other spots the pine forests that cover most of the surrounding area come right down to the rocky shore. There are numerous islands and inlets holding an important population of breeding duck including red-breasted merganser, goldeneye and smew. Though it lies within the pine belt, typical tundra type species such as Lapland bunting, snow bunting, and long-tailed skuas can be found in the area. There is a possibility of a gyr falcon here and cranes can be found at Akujärvi near Ivalo.

The surrounding woods and hills hold most of the interesting Lapland species including Arctic warbler, pine grosbeak, little and rustic buntings, Siberian jay, and Siberian tit. Needless to say such a vast lake in such a vast and remote area is largely inaccessible but a reasonable exploration is possible from a single centre, and the many wilderness huts (autiotupa) make long journeys quite feasible. As with every other Lapp area the mountain walking precautions of clothing, map, compass, and especially experience, apply. This is also probably the worst part of Finland for mosquitoes.

SUMMER: crane, smew, red-breasted merganser, goldeneye, dotterel, long-tailed skua, owls, Siberian tit, Siberian jay, Arctic warbler, pine grosbeak, shore lark, rustic bunting, Lapland bunting, little bunting, snow bunting.

The following areas are known to be good but roads are very rough:

1.   Leave Ivalo eastwards on the road to Akujärvi and after 4 km turn left onto a small road to Veskoniemi. The lake can be viewed from the end of the road and watch for crane-type marshes *en route*.

2.   Leave Ivalo as in 1. and continue to Akujärvi. Keep left here on the road to Virtaniemi. Areas of the lake can be seen from this village and at Nellimö.

3.   Leave Ivalo northwards towards Inari on route 4 and view the lake at several points along the road.

4.   Leave Ivalo southwards on route 4 and turn left after 30 km signposted Kaunispää; continue to the summit where there is a restaurant and camp site. This is an extremely easy spot to visit for the higher altitude tundra species like dotterel and shore lark. Buses from Rovaniemi and Ivalo stop here.

The forest is fairly uniform and most travellers prefer to explore the area around the more attractive Inari, though in fact Ivalo is a better all round centre. There are boat trips on the lake from Inari (information from the Tourist Hotel) which provide good opportunities to see wildfowl. The Inari Tourist Hotel overlooks the rapids of the Juutuanjoki and there are other hotels in Inari and Ivalo. Ivalo can be reached by plane from Rovaniemi (55 minutes) and Helsinki, and there are good bus services along route 4. Autiotupa, mountain huts, are found in all directions and make hiking exploration simple.

Some maps show a road running eastward along the northern shore of the lake from Kaamanen. This is a snow-route and only usable in winter when the ground and lake are frozen.


## KARIGASNIEMI

Karigasniemi is one of the most northern villages in Finland. It lies at almost 69° 30′ north near the Norwegian border on route 4,100 km beyond Inari.

There are only a few wooden Lapp huts here but being on a main road it is an excellent base for exploring the surrounding countryside. This consists of open tundra in the main though there are some dwarf birches in the valleys. Some 6–7 km south is an excellent marshy area called Luomos and though probably no different to many other similar spots in all directions it is known to hold a superb collection of breeding waders. These include spotted redshank, wood sandpiper, broad-billed sandpiper, Temminck's stint, and just possibly bar-tailed godwit. This, however, is not all there is to Karigasniemi. To the north is the nearly 2,000 feet Ailigas which holds really Arctic birds. Lapland bunting, shore lark, long-tailed skua, and possibly gyr falcon might be found. The whole area has golden plover, whimbrel, and rough-legged buzzard. The woodland areas, notably along the Tenojoki River are the stronghold of the waxwing, and Arctic warblers occur in suitable places. Most of the species mentioned also breed in the Kevo Natural Park which covers 85,000 acres between the Karigasniemi and Utsjoki roads. But this is difficult to get to and not really necessary anyway.

SUMMER: whooper swan, long-tailed duck, gyr falcon, rough-legged buzzard, spotted redshank, wood sandpiper, broad-billed sandpiper, ruff, whimbrel, Temminck's stint, bar-tailed godwit(?), dotterel, red-necked phalarope, long-tailed skua, ptarmigan, waxwing, Siberian tit, shore lark, red-throated pipit, bluethroat, Arctic warbler, snow bunting, Lapland bunting.

There are 2 hotels in Karigasniemi, a youth hostel and a camp site. The village lies on a bus service from Ivalo and Rovaniemi, but it is a long journey. A good trip is from Outakoski to Utsjoki by the post boat along the Tenojoki River. This takes 9 hours and the return is 2 hours longer. In winter the same trip can be done by snow bus on the frozen river – but birds are then decidedly scarce.

## KOLVANAN UURO

This small but deeply wooded valley lies just north of Joensuu in east central Finland. The woodlands are mixed and well developed and the stream that has formed the 'canyon' opens out at one point to form a small lake sufficient to harbour a pair of black-throated divers. It is, however, the woods that are the main attraction and the area is noted as being one of the likely spots for finding the greenish warbler. Walking conditions are fair and there is little chance of getting lost in the narrow valley.

SUMMER: black-throated diver, hazel hen, capercaillie, thrush nightingale, greenish warbler, siskin.

Take route 18 north from Joensuu. Shortly after passing the village of Uuro look for a minor road on the right signposted Kolvanan Uuro. Follow signs through a series of minor roads and eventually stop at the end of the road looking down into the valley. A footpath leads to the valley floor and the lake. Explore here and northwards along the valley for 2 km. The nearest accommodation is at Joensuu, a large town 20 km away.

## OULANKA NATIONAL PARK

The Oulanka National Park lies just south of the Arctic Circle near the Soviet border, covers 27,000 acres, and was created in 1956. It is a region of savage grandeur along the River Oulankajoki, with waterfalls, rapids, ravines, meadows, and fields of flowers. The flowers are particularly interesting as fjell species are here found in the forest zone. The woodlands are predominantly birch and not as dense as those in other parts of the country. There are also numerous small lakes and marshes, though the conditions for walking are not as rough as in many other parts of Finland. It would suit those who prefer to use established footpaths rather than venture into the virgin forest with consequent rough going and the danger of getting lost.

Ristikallio is a beautiful gorge of the Oulankajoki and part of the National Park. It is chiefly attractive as a haunt of Arctic woodland species and in particular is noted as a haunt of the elusive red-flanked bluetail. A visit in the small hours of the morning is recommended, between 01:00 hours and 06:00 hours, in mid-summer as this is not only the best time for birds but also the time of minimum insect activity. Common birds of the woodlands are brambling, redpoll and Siberian, and crested tits, while the marshes hold wood sandpiper, and an interesting variety of duck. Owls include Tengmalm's and eagle, while smew and whooper swan are regular, if rare, breeding species. Golden eagles are frequently seen and probably breed.

As in most parts of Finland there are large areas of country still ornithologically little known. Interesting birds must not be thought of as confined to a particular area where they have been seen but rather as occurring in similar nearby, but unknown, spots as well. Thus lesser white-fronted geese breed near Salla to the north of Oulanka, and broad-billed sandpiper, little bunting and red-flanked bluetail breed near Kuusamo to the south. Certainly if holidaying here, try the peak of Rukatunturi 1,400 feet and the vast lakeland east of Kuusamo.

SUMMER: black-throated diver, crane, wigeon, pintail, smew, whooper swan, golden eagle, wood sandpiper, eagle owl, Tengmalm's owl, Siberian tit, crested tit, Siberian jay, red-flanked bluetail, crossbill, brambling.

Leave Kuusamo northwards on route 5. After 30 km, and passing Rukatunturi prominent on the right, turn right on to a minor road to Käylä. Fork right to Kiutaköngas which is the centre of the park and has a camp site. There is a path westwards from here along the Oulankajoki which leads to the Salla road in 12 km. A round trip should not be beyond the imagination of four people with a car. There are several hotels and a youth hostel in Kuusamo.

## OULU

Oulu is the largest and most important town in northern Finland and a far cry from the former fur, fish and tar trading station of the last century. Its

industrial plant and busy port make it a dynamic centre and a surprising place
for a bird-watching holiday. In fact a large variety of interesting birds can be
seen very close to the town which lies almost at the head of the Gulf of Bothnia.
The best known bird is the terek sandpiper for which this is the only non-
Soviet European breeding spot. The birds are extremely scarce even here and
their whereabouts should not be disclosed. Access is all but impossible
anyway, though there is a chance of seeing the birds at one of their feeding
grounds. Yellow-breasted buntings breed near Oulu and at few other places
in Europe, and other interesting species include crane, hawk owl, the elusive
great grey owl, and scarlet grosbeak.

The meadows and marshes at Liminka, 23 km to the south of Oulu, are
worth exploring as there are a variety of wader species including breeding
ruff, red-necked phalarope, and a northerly population of marsh harriers.
Hailuoto is a large offshore island with fishermen, farmers, and large sandy
beaches. It is about the right size for a holiday and is well worthwhile from
a bird point of view. It is rich in breeding waders including Temminck's stint
and duck of six species. Spotted crake reach their furthest north in the world,
and there is a colony of little gulls. Further north of Li are the Krunni Isles.
These too, hold Temminck's stint and a wealth of duck but are more difficult
to get to, though you get Caspian tern for your trouble.

SUMMER: crane, garganey, pintail, marsh harrier, turnstone, Temminck's
stint, ruff, little ringed plover, terek sandpiper, hawk owl, great grey owl,
ortolan bunting, yellow-breasted bunting, scarlet grosbeak, siskin.

The following areas are recommended:

1.  **Oulunsalo:** follow route 4 southwards and turn right after 6 km signposted
to the airport (*lentoasemat*). Stop after ½ km and explore the damp bushy area
to the right of the road and down to the shore. Likely species here include
yellow-breasted bunting, ortolan, scarlet grosbeak and various waders and
wildfowl. Access is generally unrestricted except to cottage gardens. Continue
through Oulunsalo to Varjakka which is an area of mature pine woods with
drier ground than the inland forests and a number of reed-fringed inlets
holding garganey, pintail and waders.

2.  Take route 4 northwards but turn left on to the Hietasaarentie road before
leaving the town (see street plan). Continue past the camping site until the
road finishes at the oil port. This is an unsalubrious spot that will bring a
breath of home to rubbish dump bird-watchers and may provide terek sandpiper feeding at about 4 a.m. Other birds include Temminck's stint, turnstone,
and pintail. Access is unrestricted along the shore, though the going becomes
progressively more difficult north-eastwards.

3.  Leave Oulu on route 20 but turn right on to route 77 on the outskirts.
After 10–15 km take any minor road to the left and explore marshes and
forest. The area is typical of central Finland with dense birch and pine forests

with a fair amount of secondary growth alternating with flat open marshy areas with occasional trees. Cranes might be seen well away from the roads, though a compass or local guide are essential. Other species are owls, ruff, and crossbill. Access is unrestricted but walking conditions are rough.

4.   There are regular boats to Hailuoto 20 km to the west where there are two small hotels the Kahvimaja and Merivilla, and a camp site at Marjaniemi 16 km from the landing stage.

5.   To reach the Krunni Isles a boat would have to be chartered at Li; staying would be an expedition.

Oulu provides a range of accommodation. Hotels; Anina, Pakkahnoneen Katu 16; Kauppahotelli, Asemakatu 7; Ovlas, Rautatienkatu 8; Tervahovi, Hallituskatu 13–17. There is also a youth hostel and camping site.

Travel from Helsinki by air (1¾ hours) or by route 4 (626 km).

## PARIKKALA

Probably the most interesting of Finnish birds are those species that reach their furthest west and breed nowhere else outside of the USSR. Terek sandpiper and yellow-breasted bunting are scarce but relatively simple to identify once found. But Blyth's reed warbler is a real connoisseur's bird. There might be 30–40 pairs outside Russia; all are in eastern Finland and some are found here. Parikkala lies in the Finnish lake district where there is literally as much water as land, right against the Russian border. It stands on a large lake fringed with reeds and with some marshy edges. The surrounding countryside is largely agricultural though there are quite extensive areas of pinewoods.

Blyth's reed warbler is to be looked for in the willow saplings along the lake edge and not among the reeds themselves. Indeed any 'reed warbler' found in reeds in southern Finland is likely to be the reed warbler! Apart from this rarity which is difficult to find and identify except by its song, the lake and its surrounds hold an interesting variety of species including spotted crake and other rails, thrush nightingale, golden oriole and ortolan.

SUMMER: great crested grebe, duck, rails, spotted crake, marsh harrier, little gull, golden oriole, thrush nightingale, Blyth's reed warbler, ortolan bunting.

The following areas should be explored:

1.   The lake shore in and around the village.

2.   Leave the village southwards and shortly after joining the main route 6 look for a marshy lake on the left.

3.   The woodlands behind the village. Though access is generally unrestricted do not trespass in the village timber yards. Avoid approaching too close to the Russian border – there are warning signs.

Parikkala lies just west of route 6 and visitors coming from either direction should watch for signs to the village. There is a camp site but little or no hotel accommodation though there is a tourist hotel at Punkaharju 30 km to the north. There are frequent buses and trains on the Helsinki–Joensuu route.

## SOMPIO NATURAL PARK

This area lies north of the 68° parallel and rises to a maximum height at Nattaset of 1,650 feet. It has no road and can be reached only on foot from the south and west from route 4 where the sole village is Vuotso 3 km outside the Park boundary. There are large areas of pine and birch woods that give way to open tundra on the fjells, with peat bogs and marshes. One excellent area of marsh is at Mutenia outside the Park to the south. Just west of Mutenia village there is a bridge over a stream draining the marshes which lie to the north-west. They consist of a peatbog with tussocks of sphagnum, scrubby bushes, and a considerable amount of shallow water. Care should be exercised in walking over the marshes which can be dangerous. The surrounds are mixed pine and birch woods which are decidedly good (i.e. bad) for insects though the open marsh is less so. This area is a haunt of broad-billed sandpiper, spotted redshank, and wood sandpiper, with waxwing and Siberian tit and willow grouse in the woods.

Higher up, in the Park itself, which covers 45,000 acres there are bluethroat and rough-legged buzzard, and on the tops shore lark, Lapland bunting, and dotterel.

SUMMER: rough-legged buzzard, golden plover, broad-billed sandpiper, ruff, spotted redshank, greenshank, jack snipe, wood sandpiper, dotterel, ptarmigan, willow grouse, capercaille, Siberian tit, waxwing, shore lark, bluethroat, brambling, Lapland bunting.

Vuotso tourist hotel is less luxurious than most of the others but is clean and adequate. It is also the only accommodation. It lies on route 4, 73 km south of Ivalo. For the Mutenia marshes turn eastwards at Vuotso toward Lokka. Stop at the bridge just before Mutenia village. There are 'buses from Rovaniemi and Ivalo to Vuotso, and from Vuotso to Mutenia. If motoring northwards, do not miss Kaunispää, see Lake Inari number 4.

## VESIJAKO NATURAL PARK

Vesijako Natural Park lies north-west of Lahti in south central Finland and was declared a reserve in 1956 covering 300 acres. It is an old forest area with several lakes typical of the surrounding countryside and this part of Finland. In many ways its birds are typical too, with chaffinch, siskin, spotted and pied flycatchers, goldcrest and all the other usual Scandinavian woodland birds. Vesijako, however, boasts a few species in a comparatively small area that are not typical and therefore very interesting. The osprey is one and though this species is by no means rare it is nice to have a sure spot. Pygmy and Ural owls are found and so is the red-breasted flycatcher. Good bird-watching in attractive surroundings is to be found here.

SUMMER: osprey, pygmy owl, Ural owl, spotted flycatcher, pied flycatcher, red-breasted flycatcher, goldcrest, siskin.

Leave Lahti northwards on route 58 and turn left after 60 km at Arrakoski. Bear left and the Park is on the left in 3 km. The Evo Research Station near here should be able to help. Their area contains Ural and hawk owls, three-toed woodpecker, and black-throated diver.

# France

1 Lac du Bourget
2 Baie de Bourgneuf
3 La Brenne
4 Camargue
5 Dombes
6 Port de Gavarnie
7 Gorges du Tarn
8 Lac de Grand Lieu
9 Les Landes

10 Languedoc
11 Golfe du Morbihan
12 Île de l'Olonne
13 St Flour
14 Sept-Îles
15 Sologne
16 Somme Estuary
17 Vanoise National Park
18 Baie de Veys

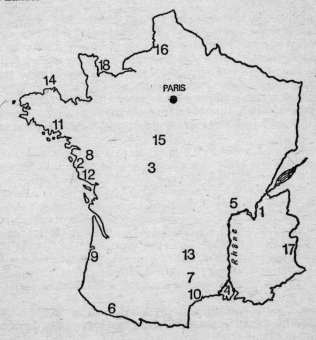

SOCIÉTÉ ORNITHOLOGIQUE DE FRANCE,
55 rue de Buffon, Paris 5e.

SOCIÉTÉ D'ÉTUDES ORNITHOLOGIQUES,
80 rue du Ranelagh, Paris 16e.

LIGUE POUR LA PROTECTION DES OISEAUX,
129 Boulevard St. Germain, Paris 6e.

SERVICE DE CONSERVATION DE LA NATURE,
57 rue Cuvier, Paris 5e.

READ: *Inventaire des Oiseaux de France* (1953–1963) by N. Maynard in *Alauda* Vol 21, pp 1–63; with supplements in *Alauda* Vol 24, pp 53–61; vol 25, pp 116–121; vol 27, pp 211–229; vol 28, pp 287–302; vol 30, pp 46–64; vol 31, pp 36–51. *Opportunities for co-operation with French Ornithologists* (1960), by G. Mountfort in *British Birds* vol 53, pp 193–199.


## BAIE D'AIGUILLON

This huge inter-tidal inlet lies to the north of the important west coast naval port of La Rochelle, and is generally recognised as the most important area in France for waders. Like many other similar places along this coast, the bay was under threat of a barrage, but the most recent information is that this is now unlikely. There are nevertheless many drainage schemes gradually encroaching into this major wetland. There is, for instance, an 8 km sea wall being built along the northern shore to prevent flooding of the Lay Valley. Between the bay and Niort lie the magnificent and famous Pointevin Marshes, but it is the bay and the two sandspits to the north that are the main centres of interest.

In summer the marshes hold breeding teal and garganey while the black-tailed godwit is here at the very southern tip of its range. Black-winged stilts breed as do between 50 and 100 pairs of black tern. Marsh and Montagu's harriers can be seen overhead. Autumn brings perhaps 200,000 waders of most species that one could expect to see passing down the Atlantic coast. But over half of this number stay to winter, including 30,000 each of knot and dunlin, 15,000 black-tailed godwit and 500 bar-tails, 5,000 grey plover, and no less than 3,000 avocets – the most important flock that winter in the country. There are also several hundred spotted redshank. Wildfowl too are numerous with 30,000 shelduck, thousands of the commoner surface feeding duck, and 4 species of geese. Of these only the brent and white-fronted ever reach three figures.

The major interest in spring is the March flock of 50,000 black-tailed godwit, and the several thousand ruff that haunt the marshes. Most of these

species can be seen on the bay but many resort to the Reserve Nationale de la
Point d'Arcay at high tide. This 5 km long sand bar is extensively planted with
pines, but in the south the sandy shore and marshes are thronged with birds.

SUMMER: marsh harrier, Montagu's harrier, teal, garganey, black-tailed
godwit, redshank, black-winged stilt, black tern, short-eared owl.

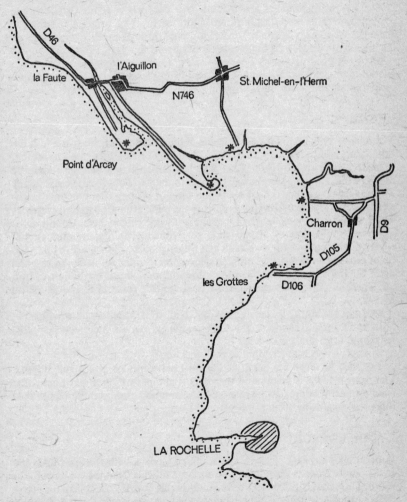

Baie d'Aiguillon – main vantage points marked with asterisks. Most waders gather in the northern
part of the bay at high tide.

AUTUMN: black-tailed godwit, bar-tailed godwit, whimbrel, ruff, little stint, golden plover, spotted redshank, green sandpiper, wood sandpiper.

WINTER: shelduck, teal, pintail, wigeon, brent goose, white-fronted goose, greylag goose, bean goose, golden plover, grey plover, black-tailed godwit, bar-tailed godwit, spotted redshank, knot, dunlin, avocet.

SPRING: black-tailed godwit, ruff.

The Pointevin Marshes are crossed by a network of roads that facilitate exploration. Those on the northern shore of the bay running southwards from the N746 near St Michel-en-l'Herm pass through excellent wader areas. This road also leads to La Faute a seaside town from where a road runs southwards to la Point d'Arcay. The bay itself can be seen from several places in the south and east notably at la Pelle, les Grottes, and west of Bourg Chapon. Accommodation is not difficult to find along this coast.


## BAIE DE VEYS

The Baie de Veys lies on the eastern side of the Cherbourg Peninsula and is the tidal estuary of the River Vire. It is slowly silting up and there are provisional plans to convert it to a fresh water lake by constructing a barrage across the mouth while allowing the passage of ships to the parts of Carentan and Isigny by specially constructed canals. At the time of writing, the outcome is unsettled. A barrage would certainly destroy the main attraction to bird-watchers which is the enormous flocks of passage and wintering waders. Counts show a winter population of 50,000 each of oystercatcher, curlew and dunlin, together with many knot, redshank and ringed plover. There are also up to 100 brent geese and the nearby Carentan depression is noted for geese, swans, and duck on the winter floods. In spring and autumn almost anything can turn up. There is a small reserve covering the high tide roost at Sainte Marie du Monts.

SUMMER: shelduck, garganey shoveler, teal, oystercatcher, terns, snipe.

AUTUMN: green sandpiper, wood sandpiper, curlew sandpiper, spotted redshank, little stint, godwits.

WINTER: oystercatcher, dunlin, curlew, knot.

The Baie de Veys lies north of the N10 between Cherbourg and Bayeux. The nearest town is Isigny and there are a number of lanes and tracks that enable the whole area to be explored. Accommodation is quite plentiful in this area even away from the coast.


## LAC DU BOURGET

Bourget lake lies east of Lyon and south of Geneva with the Spa of Aix-les-Bains on the eastern shore. The nearest large town is Chambéry 11 km to the south. Though it is 1,000 feet above sea-level this is an excellent lake for marsh birds particularly at the southern end in the large reed beds between Bourget, Viviers-du-Lac, and Voglans. The marshes of Lavours at the northern end between the lake and the Rhône are also excellent, and there are reeds along several of the rivers that flow into the lake. The surrounding land is agricultural though with several Mediterranean elements. The hills and cliffs rise to 2,750 feet, and the juxtaposition of marshy land and high cliffs makes Bourget an attractive area with a good range of birds. The small size makes it an excellent area for a holiday.

The lake holds great crested grebe with little bittern and great reed warbler common in the reed beds. Savi's warbler breeds on the Lavours marshes and Cetti's warbler is present throughout the year. While breeding marsh warblers are found around the marsh edges the penduline tit found in the same place has not yet been proved to nest. Black kites are common, and the surroundings hold honey buzzard and short-toed eagle, both of which are frequently seen. The cliffs have Alpine swift and crag martin, and in the winter wall creeper. In particularly hard weather the latter descend to the lake edge. Bonelli's is the commonest warbler but melodious are found here and there. Cirl and ortolan buntings breed as do rock buntings at the edge of the cliffs.

SUMMER: great crested grebe, little bittern, black kite, honey buzzard, short-toed eagle, curlew, penduline tit, Alpine swift, crag martin, Cetti's warbler, Savi's warbler, great reed warbler, marsh warbler, melodious warbler, Bonelli's warbler, cirl bunting, ortolan bunting, rock bunting.

WINTER: wall creeper.

From Lyon take the N6 eastwards to Chambéry. N201 and 491 run along the lake, and N92 runs along the Lavours marshes and the D83 from Lavours crosses them. N491 *bis* gives access to the top of the cliffs. There is a large choice of hotels at Aix-les-Bains, and three camping sites, including one excellent one.

## BAIE DE BOURGNEUF

The Baie de Bourgneuf is a shallow inter-tidal area to the south-west of Nantes. It is bound to the south and west by the Île de Noirmoutier aud to the east by the marshes and salines of the Île de Bouin which is part of the mainland. These gradually give way to the Machecoul marshes and then the Lac de Grand Lieu. The marshes and salines are a notable haunt of the black-winged stilt, and Cetti's warbler and white-spotted bluethroat are not uncommon. But above all it is the shallow bay itself that is the major attraction to birds and bird-watchers. It is an important area for wintering wildfowl with 1,500 brent geese and several thousand wigeon, teal and other duck. Vast numbers of waders are also found including grey plover and knot. During passage periods the area often holds a superb variety of wader species and the Île de Noirmoutier is then noted as an excellent area. There are salines and woods as well as the open shore here, and L'Herbaudière is an excellent place for a sea-watch. A boat trip into the gulf north of Noirmoutier is recommended in autumn for petrels and shearwaters, though in the right circumstances these species can be seen from the shore. The passage of birds of prey including short-toed eagles is said to be good. Breeding birds on Noirmoutier include short-toed lark.

SUMMER: black-winged stilt, short-toed lark, Cetti's warbler, bluethroat.

PASSAGE: petrels, shearwaters, raptors, curlew sandpiper, little stint, grey plover.

WINTER: brent goose, wigeon, teal, grey plover, ringed plover, knot.

The Île de Noirmoutier can be reached by bridge and there are marinas, many hotels and two good camp sites. The Bouin area is worth exploring thoroughly and the marshes and scattered salines are crossed by roads in all directions. Rather surprisingly this area has not been thoroughly explored and more information would be welcomed.

## LA BRENNE

This outstanding wetland area lies near the centre of France between Château-roux and Le Blanc to the north of the River Creuse. It is a plateau holding something like 500 lakes and ponds of varying sizes and covering an area 25 km by 20 km. Though in the major area the larger lakes are grouped quite close together, there are so many outlying waters that it would be a pity to miss La Brenne as it can occupy a considerable holiday.

The ponds are shallow with a varying growth of fringe vegetation mainly of reeds which in some cases, at the Étang du Couvent for instance, have completely covered the water and created a single reed bed. Many have islands of reeds and some islands of firm land with trees. A number are dry, at least seasonally, and some are or have been drained. The southern half of the Étang Montiacre for instance is now good agricultural land. Though frequently compared with the Sologne to the north La Brenne differs considerably from that area. The pond surroundings are basically open agricultural land rather than the forest and heath that is so typical of the more northern area. This certainly means that the variety of birds is not as great but the countryside is less monotonous and the Chasse Gardé notices are much less frequent. Most of the lakes can be seen from roads and farmers, unlike gamekeepers, are prepared to let you walk across their land if asked. The area is rather more important for breeding birds like purple heron and for the three harriers and other raptors. Bittern and little bittern breed commonly amongst the reeds and a wide variety of duck are found. Crakes, including Baillon's are quite common and a good variety of waders is found. Breeding terns include both black and whiskered and numbers of these in autumn can be very impressive. The surrounding land holds most of the species commonly found in central lowland France but is particularly important for little bustard and stone curlew.

Autumn passage brings a wide variety of wildfowl, raptors, terns, and other species to the area.

SUMMER: great crested grebe, black-necked grebe, little grebe, grey heron, purple heron, little bittern, bittern, shoveler, teal, marsh harrier, Montagu's harrier, hen harrier, Baillon's crake, water rail, snipe, curlew, little bustard, stone curlew, black tern, whiskered tern, Savi's warbler, great reed warbler, reed warbler, sedge warbler.

AUTUMN: raptors, terns.

All of the ponds are worth looking at and can be examined from roads and tracks with the aid of a good local map. The following can definitely be seen from the public highway: the Étangs de Notz; Moury, with reeds and good for duck; Couvent, a vast reed bed; Miclos, often one of the best with reeds and terns and an interesting rough marsh to the north west; Beauregard, reeds; Gabriére, one of the largest waters with duck and reeds; Gabrieu, water lilies, reeds, grebes and terns; Lerignon, water lilies and reeds; Mardassan, a reed bed; Purais, reed edges; Hardouine, reed edges; La Mer Rouge, a vast water with reeds, terns, duck, etc; Montiacre, reed beds and open water; Blizon, attractive with reeds and islands; Le Sault, reed edges. The Étang de Bignotoi differs from the other lakes by being surrounded by rough land with gorse and recent plantation of conifers and a large wood to the north-east. Northwards the land is much bleaker and gives a distinct impression of being good for birds. Harriers are numerous and black and whiskered terns are found. The Étang de Bernadoux to the north is part of this area.

There is a railway to Le Blanc, which is a good centre for exploration and has a camp site. It would, however, be better to stay at one of the villages like Meziéres en Rosnay, though accommodation would be very limited.

## CAMARGUE

The Île de la Camargue proper lies between the two arms of the river Rhône where it reaches the Mediterranean south of Arles. Almost all accounts of the area, however, include the whole of the delta area of the river and most visitors wish to see the Petite Camargue to the west of the Petit Rhône; the strange Crau, which owes more to the River Durance than the Rhône, east of the Grand Rhône; and the Roman town of Les Baux. The Camargue was once more cultivated than it is today but the embankment of the channels, begun in the eighteenth century, halted the annual floods that were responsible for washing the salt from the land. Thus the characteristic saline lagoons are a comparatively modern creation.

The picture of the Camargue as a land of cowboys, horses, and fighting bulls liberally laced with interesting gipsy festivals at Stes Maries de la Mer is attracting increasing numbers of tourists. The *cabanes* formerly occupied by the *guardiens* are fast being converted to holiday cottages and there are more and more people exploring the area. Luckily, protection of the most important areas is covered by the Reserve Naturelle, while the important salt pan area in the south is industrially developed and unattractive to tourists. Perhaps the biggest threat to the region is from the practice of rice growing which is expanding southwards year by year.

If a line is drawn from the coast northwards the following succession of habitats can be noted:

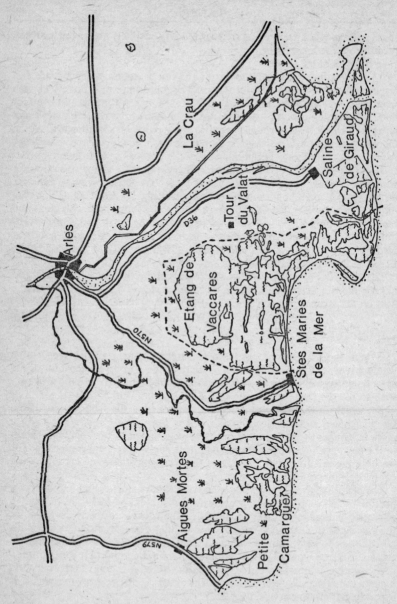

**The Camargue:** the line of dashes shows the reserve boundary, but the whole area is of outstanding ornithological interest.

Waxwings are sporadic in their occurrences over most of Europe and can be guaranteed only in the extreme north of Scandinavia

Glimpses, like this, of the magnificent black woodpecker are all that most bird-watchers get of this widespread but not common bird

The pygmy owl is essentially a northern bird and,
like most owls, very difficult to get to grips with

*above* Migrating dunlin – the staple bird of all visitors to European shores

Two Scandinavian birds, greenshank (left) and spotted redshank, pass through Europe in large numbers on their way southwards

Wood sandpipers gather in large numbers on some southern European marshes prior to a direct crossing of the Mediterranean and Sahara

Ruffs displaying at their lek. These birds seem to be slowly increasing with a spread into new areas including Britain

1. Sandy shore varying in width from a few yards to several hundred and harbouring Kentish plover.

2. Coastal dunes likewise varying in width but over a mile wide in the Petite Camargue where there are also woods of stone pines. Only the tawny pipit and short-toed lark breed amongst the dunes though the woods of the Petite Camargue hold heronries of little egrets, and night and squacco herons.

3. Saline lagoons occupy most of the better known area of the Camargue and almost all of the Reserve. They vary from the highly saline and commercially exploited salt pans in the south to the mainly brackish pools in the north. Nearest the sea the salines hold the famous flamingoes, many avocets, and a wealth of autumn waders and terns. In winter they are deserted. The population of the larger lagoons is concentrated on the islands and consists mainly of colonies of gulls and terns including gull-billed tern, a few slender-billed gulls, as well as red-crested pochard and black-winged stilt. There is a huge passage of autumn waders here too. The ground surrounding the lagoons is flooded during the winter but dries out in spring and is partly covered with glasswort. It is occupied by short-toed lark and Kentish plover, and in the less saline areas by spectacled warbler, crested lark, tawny pipit, and pratincole. Wherever dried and more densely vegetated areas occur, great grey shrikes and bee-eaters are typical. Here and there in this area disused drainage ditches have become overgrown with tamarisks and in some places with elms and poplars. They form one of the richest bird zones in the whole of the Camargue. Breeding species include black kite, hoopoe, penduline tit, fan-tailed warbler, Scop's owl, Sardinian warbler, and lesser grey shrike. In the densest woods Cetti's and melodious warblers and golden orioles are found.

4. Marshes are generally shallow with a wealth of emergent vegetation and breeding red-crested pochard, black-winged stilt and whiskered tern. In some areas reedbeds are extensive with purple heron, little bittern, spotted, Baillon's and little crakes, marsh and Montagu's harriers, great reed, Savi's and moustached warblers.

There are three specialized areas not covered in this transection:

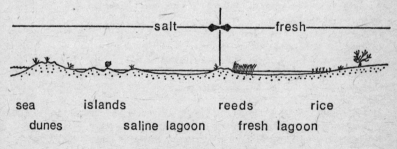

Section through the Camargue

1.   **La Crau:** a plain consisting of stones up to the size of a man's fist, with bare earth and a growth of aromatic herbs. Sheep roam the flat landscape which is interrupted only by their folds and occasional telegraph poles. Interesting birds include lesser kestrel, little bustard, pin-tailed sandgrouse, calandra lark, short-toed lark, crested lark and black-eared wheatear. The Entressen rubbish dump should be visited, it has most of the rubbish of Marseille to be picked over.

2.   **The riverain forest:** along both arms of the Rhône consisting of poplar, elms, willow, and some oaks. Birds include black kite, Scop's owl, golden oriole, Cetti's and melodious warblers, and the colonies of little egrets and night and squacco herons.

3.   **Les Baux-de-Provence:** an old roman town thronged by tourists and requiring an entry fee to the ruins to get the best out of the bird-watching. Views southwards are fantastic over the Camargue to the sea, and birds include Alpine swift, blue rock-thrush, subalpine warbler, and possibly Egyptian vulture. *En route*, the attractive groves of Barbegal are worth looking over for roller, hoopoe, and melodious warbler.

SUMMER: purple heron, little egret, squacco heron, night heron, little bittern, flamingo, red-crested pochard, marsh harrier, black kite, lesser kestrel, crakes, Kentish plover, avocet, black-winged stilt, slender-billed gull, whiskered tern, gull-billed tern, pin-tailed sandgrouse, Scop's owl, bee-eater, roller, hoopoe, calandra lark, short-toed lark, crested lark, golden oriole, penduline tit, black-eared wheatear, Cetti's warbler, Savi's warbler, moustached warbler, great reed warbler, melodious warbler, Sardinian warbler, subalpine warbler, spectacled warbler, fan-tailed warbler, tawny pipit, great grey shrike, lesser grey shrike, woodchat shrike.

AUTUMN: passage waders, notably sandpipers including regular marsh sandpiper.

WINTER: teal, wigeon, gadwall, shoveler, pintail, red-crested pochard.

Visitors should ensure an exploration of all of the major habitats mentioned above keeping to roads and rights of way. The following should be included:

1.   THE RESERVES ZOOLOGIQUES ET BOTANIQUES DE CAMARGUE: permits available from Monsieur G. Tallon, 2 Rue Honore Nicholas, Arles, B. du R. by personal application.

It is, however, quite possible to see most of the specialities without disturbing the Reserve at all.

2.   THE ÉTANG DE VACCARÈS on roads D36B and D37 looking towards the Étang for reed and water species and inland for herons and waders. Good stopping points are at Notre-Dame d'Amour, La Capellière and in the Tour du Valat area.

3.   SALIN DE GIRAUD where a road runs southwards past riverain forest and amongst the commercial salt pans to the shore.

4.   LES STES MARIES on D85A and eastwards towards Pertuis de Rousty.

5.   PETITE CAMARGUE westwards from the D85, reached from the N570

out of Les Stes Maries and the car ferry across the Petit Rhône. Also eastwards from le Grau du Roi and the excellent N579 out of Aigues Mortes.
6. From La Crau at Retour des Aires on N568 walk eastwards, and at
Entressen inspect the village rubbish tip. *En route*, the D35 along the Grand
Rhône is good for woodland species and gulls, terns, and herons over the
river.

Most people stay in Arles and motor into the Camargue daily to avoid the
mosquitoes; it is, however, a long trip. There are hotels at Albaron and Les
Stes Maries that are more central and one can camp in several places. It is
possible for serious students to stay on the Reserve at la Capellière and Salin
de Badou, arrangements to be made with the Conservator Monsieur Tallon
as above.

There are international air services to Marseilles and 'bus routes to Arles.

## DOMBES

Glancing at a series of distribution maps of French birds one's attention is
drawn to the extension northwards of the range of several species up the
Rhône valley. In most cases this northwards protrusion is due to the presence
of southern species in the ponds of the Dombes. These lie north-east of Lyon
between the rivers Soane and Ain and cover a vast area between Lyon and
Bourg, and Châtillon and Meximieux. Most of the larger and more important
waters lie around Villars on either side of the N83 which bisects the district.
The ponds are shallow with emergent vegetation mainly of reeds which form
quite sizeable beds in some places, and there is considerable commercial
exploitation for fish. The surrounding land is agricultural though there are
quite large areas of woodland along the eastern boundary north and east of
Chalemont. In the extreme south lies the large marsh area of Echets while on
the east side of the N83 immediately south of Villars is the area that was made
a nature reserve in 1963.

The most important and interesting birds of the Dombes are undoubtedly
the herons the following numbers of pairs of which bred in 1965; grey heron
(50 pairs), purple heron (150 pairs), little egret (100 pairs), night heron (150
pairs), squacco heron, here reaching its furthest north-west, as well as untold
numbers of bittern and little bittern. Duck are well represented in the marshes
and on the pond fringes and include red-crested pochard. Crakes, a variety of
waders including black-winged stilt, black and whiskered terns, two harriers
and black kite, and a whole wealth of warblers outstanding amongst which
is the tiny fan-tailed warbler here reaching its most northern outpost in the
world, can all be found.

Being so far south there is also a rich avifauna unconnected with the ponds
and found generally throughout the area.

SUMMER: great crested grebe, black-necked grebe, little grebe, grey heron,
purple heron, little egret, night heron, squacco heron, little bittern, bittern,
marsh harrier, Montagu's harrier, black kite, goshawk, garganey, gadwall,

shoveler, red-crested pochard, spotted crake, curlew, black-tailed godwit, black-winged stilt, black tern, whiskered tern, woodchat shrike, fan-tailed warbler, great reed warbler.

AUTUMN: heron, duck, waders.

The network of roads on either side of the N83 ensures that a great many of the ponds can be seen from public roads and particularly the Étang du Grand Glarcins and the Étang du Grand Birieux which are the two largest waters. The reserve south of Villars can be seen from the N83 and views of purple heron, little egret and squacco heron can be obtained without bothering the *mairie* (town hall) in Villars at all. The marsh at Echets lies north and east of the village which is due east of Neuville and on the N83, which provides an excellent vantage point.

Lyon is an international centre with its own airport, and buses and rail run to Villars which is the best centre and which has a choice of hotels and a very good camp site.


## PORT DE GAVARNIE

Gavarnie lies in the French Pyrénées and immediately to the north of the Ordesa National Park across the border in Spain. Most visiting bird-watchers include the whole of the valley from Lourdes southwards when they talk about Gavarnie and it is certainly necessary to include the lower area. Booted eagles, for instance, are only found low down, and Egyptian vultures seldom get above 2,500 feet. The valley is pine clad on its lower slopes but becomes progressively more open and rocky the higher one goes. The scenery has been described, by people who ought to know, as some of the best in the world.

At the top, around Gavarnie itself and beyond, water pipits are perhaps the commonest species, but interesting birds like black-eared wheatear, snow finch and Alpine accentor are quite widespread. Alpine and common choughs occur in mixed flocks of over 100 and the elusive wall creeper is known to breed. A little lower, below 5,000 feet, citril finch, ortolan and rock buntings, and crag martin are found, while rock thrushes are found at most altitudes. Lower still black, white-backed, and middle-spotted woodpeckers appear in the woods with red-backed shrikes in the meadows up to 4,000 feet.

Gavarnie has been the subject of investigation by several students of migration. In autumn passerines can be watched pouring over the col, though one must be there early and actually at the crossing point to see them. There is also an exciting movement of butterflies into Spain. It is, however, for birds of prey that most visitors come. These on the whole are similar to the birds of the Spanish side with griffon and Egyptian vultures and the rare and magnificent lammergeier. Golden and Bonelli's eagles are found high up with booted eagle in the valley forests. Red and black kites can be seen and there are goshawks, peregrines and hobbys.

SUMMER: griffon vulture, Egyptian vulture, lammergeier, golden eagle,

Bonelli's eagle, booted eagle, red kite, black kite, goshawk, peregrine, hobby, Alpine chough, chough, wallcreeper, black woodpecker, white-backed woodpecker, middle spotted woodpecker, Alpine accentor, crag martin, rock thrush, black-eared wheatear, dipper, black redstart, red-backed shrike, citril finch, rock bunting, snow finch.

There are good transport facilities from Lourdes to Gavarnie where there is the Hotel Voyageurs. There is a camp site lower down at Gèdre, and many more near Lourdes. Beyond Gavarnie camping wild is general.

## GORGES DU TARN

The Gorges du Tarn are frequently quoted in the brochures as Europe's answer to the Grand Canyon, which is unfair to this area of France because it obviously is not, and tourists are disappointed as a result. With the rise of the Massif plateau the rivers cut deep valleys that can in places properly be called gorges, the Tarn being the most famous and spectacular of them. It stretches downstream from the picturesque village of Ispagnac on the N107 south of Mende to Millau on the N9, a distance of 50 km as the crow flies and certainly two or three times longer by the twisting river. The Gorges du Tarn is undoubtedly beautiful. Its sides rise hundreds of feet vertically through limestone cliffs in places, while in other parts terracing has created an agricultural community. In some places the valley is wide enough for fields and small towns are often placed on knolls surrounded by crops. It is an ancient area with medieval churches and a wealth of folklore and caves high up on the hillsides. Above all, it is now a tourist area.

The Gorges du Tarn cut deeply through the Caussés, those bare limestone plateaux that are covered with a desert flora of aromatic herbs on a rough base of stony earth at about the 3,000 ft mark. Even mild days can be bleak up here and only the shepherd and goatherd disturb the keen bird-watcher.

There are basically three major habitats to be explored, the valley floor with the river, the wood along its banks, and the fields and terraces of the gentler lower slopes. Then there are the cliffs and crags, and the gorge edge, and lastly the open Caussés, the Caussé de Sauveterre and the Caussé Mejean. The Tarn itself is bare but the tangled undergrowth and woods along its banks hold a few warblers while the fields hold finches and cirl buntings. Overhead fly Alpine swifts and crag martins while the steep sides and crags have black redstarts, choughs, and ravens. Birds of prey are sometimes numerous on the rising air along the gorge edge and include red kite and short-toed eagle. The Caussés require careful examination to get good views of the larks, pipits, buntings, and wheatears that live there.

To the east of the gorge proper but adjacent and immediately north of the Tarn lies the Cevennes National Park centred on Mont Lozère and Mont Aigoual. This area is one of the last strongholds in France of the golden eagle and other raptors.

SUMMER: red kite, short-toed eagle, golden eagle, Alpine swift, swift, crag martin, raven, chough, larks, pipits, grey wagtail, wheatear, warblers, cirl bunting, ortolan bunting.

There is a railway to Millau at the western end that runs along the gorge for several kilometres and enables those without transport to get going. There are roads along the entire length to Ispagnac, though to get the best out of the area it is best to travel by boat. Peyrelcan and Ste Enimie are probably the best centres, the latter having roads in four directions leading to a number of minor roads over the Caussés. It is also full of tourist spots and has a choice of accommodation and camp sites.

The Cevennes National Park is best approached via Florac, then along the N598 to Pont de Montvert and northward on the mountain road to the Col de Finiels. The village of that name would make an excellent base for this area.


## LAC DE GRAND LIEU

This lake lies south of the Loire near Nantes. It covers 22,240 acres (measured in winter when the water level is highest) of shallow water with large areas covered by water lilies and floating debris especially in the west. Around the edges is a truly huge reed bed of unknown dimensions with a jungle of sallows and dwarf willows which are the breeding site of one of the largest mixed heronries in western Europe. The night heron is dominant but little egret and grey heron also breed. The reed beds hold purple heron, bittern, and little bittern and an unmanageable collection of small brown warblers including Cetti's. In the south-west the marshes gradually merge with the Machecoul marshes and change into open grazing lands with a collection of ferocious looking bulls. These marshes in turn continue to the shallow Baie de Bourgneuf. The meadows here hold the furthest south black-tailed godwits, while to the west are the furthest north black-winged stilts. The grazing marshes are flat and open, the skyline interrupted only by a few trees around the farmhouses and lines of tamarisks along the ditches. These are the haunt of bluethroats.

In winter the Lac de Grand Lieu is the principal Atlantic coast resort of diving duck, and there are usually Bewick's and whooper swans, and a few greylags present. During passage periods there are hordes of waders and large numbers of garganey, and a regular number of spoonbills.

SUMMER: bittern, little bittern, purple heron, little egret, night heron, garganey, shoveler, hen harrier, black-tailed godwit black-headed gull, black tern, short-eared owl, bluethroat.

WINTER: tufted duck, pochard, Bewick's swan.

PASSAGE: spoonbill, waders, terns.

Being so good for birds because of its impenetrable zone of reeds and willow thickets the lake is also decidedly difficult to get at. The bulls on the surrounding farmland do not help. It is private property and is a carefully managed shoot which means no winter disturbance. The village of Passay which is as near open water as you can get, has boats and someone might be persuaded to take you out. Many bird-watchers have seen a great deal from the surrounding roads and villages. Use the Institut Geographique National's 1:100,000 colour-map section 'Nantes'. For the Machecoul marshes St Lumine and St Philbert de Grand Lieu are the best centres.

## LES LANDES

The Landes coast of France lies between the mouth of the Gironde and the Pyrénées and the distance from Pointe de Grave in the north to Bayonne near the Spanish border is 230 km. Even a long holiday would not suffice to explore such a vast area ornithologically but fortunately the birds of the area differ little in spite of a change of two degrees of latitude. It is thus possible to choose any reasonably sized section as a sample of the whole area, though any scientifically-minded ornithologist with plenty of time on his hands could as an interesting study decide exactly what difference, if any, two degrees of latitude makes to comparable bird populations.

The area is dominated by the sand that has been built up by the sea into a huge dune system running roughly north and south. The dunes stretch inland for several kilometres and culminate in the dune at Pyla which is the highest in Europe and a well known tourist attraction. Amongst the dunes are many damp slacks and a series of large lagoons. These from north to south are the Étangs d'Hourtin (called de Carcans in its southern half), de Lacanau, the Bassin d'Arcachon, and the Étangs de Sanguinet and de Biscarosse. Of these only the largest at Arcachon is joined to the sea. Almost the whole of the Landes is covered with conifers.

The area taken as a sample is that between the Bassin d'Arcachon and Mimizan. The Étang de Biscarosse and the Petit Étang de Biscarosse are apparently suitable for water birds with huge surrounding reed beds. Unfortunately this whole area is one of the most intensively shot over in France and breeding marsh birds especially of any size are remarkably few. Even the passage of sizeable birds appears light probably because of the pressure of shooting, and raptors in particular are either shot or pass through quickly. Black kite and marsh harrier are quite likely to be seen but otherwise the birds of the lakes are the more secretive species like Cetti's, great reed, and grasshopper warblers. In winter there are large numbers of duck and up to 1,000 brent geese at Arcachon.

The dunes with a vegetation of marram and scrub hold little but crested lark and Dartford warbler while the sea is notable only for an autumn passage of gannet and scoter. In this area most of the trees are maritime pines with occasional Corsican pines, bordered along the roadsides with oak, eucalyptus, and other deciduous species, and with a considerable growth of bracken and gorse. The dominant warbler is Bonelli's, more commonly found at a considerable altitude in France. Other species include short-toed treecreeper, firecrest, serin and a small range of predators including sparrowhawk, buzzard and hobby.

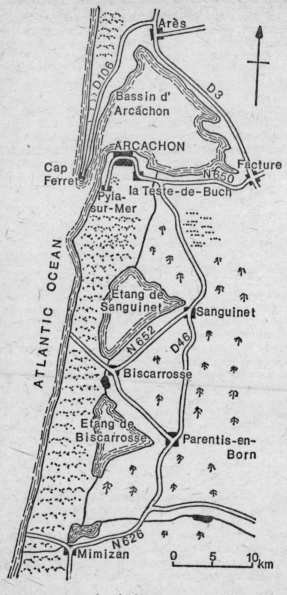

Les Landes

The final habitat is the area of original heath notably between La Teste on the Bassin d'Arcachon and Sanquinet. These are mainly heather and bracken, with invading birch scrub. Birds here include hoopoe, woodchat shrike, red-backed shrike, nightjar and crested lark.

SUMMER: black kite, marsh harrier, buzzard, sparrowhawk, hobby, hoopoe, woodchat shrike, red-backed shrike, nightjar, crested lark, short-toed tree-creeper, crested tit, stonechat, redstart, Cetti's warbler, great reed warbler, grasshopper warbler, Dartford warbler, Bonelli's warbler, firecrest, serin, cirl bunting.

AUTUMN: gannet, scoter, osprey, black tern.

Access to the whole area is straightforward and mainly open. Bird-watchers should try to find the least disturbed areas. Les Landes is easy to get to via Bordeaux and regular public transport services exist. There is a wealth of holiday accommodation ranging from first class hotels in Arcachon to nudist camp sites along the coast. Most of the towns have a *plage*.

# LANGUEDOC

The whole of the Languedoc coastline between the Camargue and the foothills of the Pyrénées is broken by lagoons. These have been created by the build-up of sand along the coast forming a series of bars and by small feeder rivers. Wherever a larger river enters the sea lagoons have not been created though there is still a low lying marshy coastline. Though large areas are covered by water there are not the vast marshes that are found in the Rhône delta and this makes birds of several species rather fewer. The major habitat is the open water itself varying from salty to virtually fresh. There are considerable areas of salines in several places, and various fresh marshes and reed beds. But in general the strong salt element is the dominant factor and emergent vegetation is rather sparse. The lagoons from north to south are:

1. **The Étang de Maugio:** lying to the west of le Grau du Roi and the Canal de la Radelle which is usually regarded as the boundary of the Camargue. There is a large area of marsh to the north-east and many birds of the Camargue can be found.

2. **The Étang de Pérols:** a bare lake south of Montpellier.

3. **The Étang de l'Arnel and the Étang de Vic:** joined together the latter having a little marsh and saline area to the north.

4. **The Étang d'Ingril:** a large area of salines and marshes to the east of Frontignan holding most of the typical Languedoc species. It has a good road and track network and together with nearby Séte offers an excellent choice of hotel accommodation and camp sites.

5. **The Bassin de Thau:** the largest lagoon covering 65 sq km with the N108

and a major railway line along the sandbar is the most familiar of the lagoons to the ordinary traveller. The vast beach can be very crowded in summer and incredibly hot. The interesting areas here lie behind the beach rather than on the far shore and consist of marshes and a small area of salines.

There is then something of a gap though almost every stream along the coast has or had its own marsh system. In particular

**6. The Étang de Vendres:** at the mouth of the Aude and totally overgrown is a good place for reedy birds. But any of the dune lagoons along this stretch should be worth exploring.

**7. The Étang de l'Ayrolle and the Étangs de Bages et de Sigean:** the next large waters and also one of the best areas. There are several marshy areas especially at the north end of Ayrolle, extensive salines notably at St Martin, and several smaller lagoons on the north side. There is à camp site at Port la Nouvelle.

**8. The Étang de Lapalme:** a smaller water with good areas of salines and marsh.

**9. The Étang de Leucate:** a huge rather bare water connected to the sea in several places. There is a good marshland area on the west side north of Salses.

**10. The Étang de Canet et de St Nazaire:** the southernmost lagoon and has a smaller lagoon and marsh in the south.

SUMMER: little egret, marsh harrier, black kite, Kentish plover, avocet, black-winged stilt, common tern, tawny pipit, woodchat shrike, great grey shrike, hoopoe, bee-eater, short-toed lark.

PASSAGE: flamingo, herons, waders, gulls, terns.

WINTER: wigeon, tufted duck, pochard.

Though well worth a visit in summer, especially as one is never quite sure what occurs where, in autumn this coast receives all of the Rhône valley herons and an excellent variety of passage waders. It is thus a first class area for those who cannot stomach the idea of chasing hundreds of other bird-watchers round the Camargue in summer, or who are unable to get south until late July or August. There are many places with hotels and pensions and a superb choice of camp sites near the sea and an excellent beach.

## GOLFE DU MORBIHAN

The Golfe du Morbihan lies on the Atlantic coast south of Vannes and the N165. It is a vast shallow inlet about 20 km wide but whose mouth is only about 1 km. Its many creeks cut deep into the land and there are a vast number of islands, the largest of which are inhabited. At low water the whole basin empties out and becomes a gigantic wader feeding ground. Fortunately bird-watchers do not have to explore the whole area as most of the interesting species can be seen in two places on the eastern side. This is also the best side for the many ponds and salt marshes that line its shores but which are separated from the Golfe itself. The Noyalo-Séné inlet has been isolated from the inter-tidal zone by a causeway and a fresh water lake has been created. This is a particularly attractive spot with fresh marshes and salt marshes juxtaposed, and is becoming a major breeding ground for gulls and terns. In the south of the Golfe the Bay of Sarzeau is extremely rich in zostera, the weed found particularly attractive by many wildfowl species. It is this area more than any other that has made Moribihan the most important French Atlantic coast wildfowl area. Between 4,000 and 6,000 brent winter, the principal European wintering ground outside Britain. Wigeon, however, outnumber all other wildfowl combined and sometimes amount to 40,000. Pintail reach 10,000 and eider and merganser are among the other regular duck. Waders on passage and in winter are very numerous and the variety is sometimes outstanding with 'fresh' and 'salt' waders both present in large numbers.

Compared with its status as a wintering and passage ground the breeding population is poor. Terns, shelducks, gulls, and a few waders breed on the island reserve of Meabon for instance, but autumn and winter are the times here.

SUMMER: shelduck, black-headed gull, common tern, roseate tern, Sandwich tern.

AUTUMN: wigeon, teal, black-tailed godwit, bar-tailed godwit, whimbrel, curlew sandpiper, greenshank.

WINTER: brent goose, wigeon, pintail, teal, tufted duck, pochard, eider, red-breasted merganser, waders.

The best vantage point for this area is the shortest route between Vanne and Sarzeau along the eastern shore of the Golfe. This passes close to all of the best spots.

## ILE DE L'OLONNE

The Île de l'Olonne lies immediately north of Les Sables d'Olonne on the Atlantic coast of France between La Rochelle and the mouth of the Loire. It is not really an island at all though at one time a tidal creek separated the sandy offshore bank from the mainland. Today the tidal creek is merely a large area of marsh land crossed at several points by roads leading to the vast dune beach which is thronged by holiday-makers throughout the summer. It is still tidal at each end and though the commercial salines have been abandoned they still form brackish lagoons. Further inland and away from the influence of the sea there are areas of reeds, lagoons with muddy margins much frequented by waders, and a number of fish ponds. In many places the old walls of the former creeks still exist and make excellent paths and view

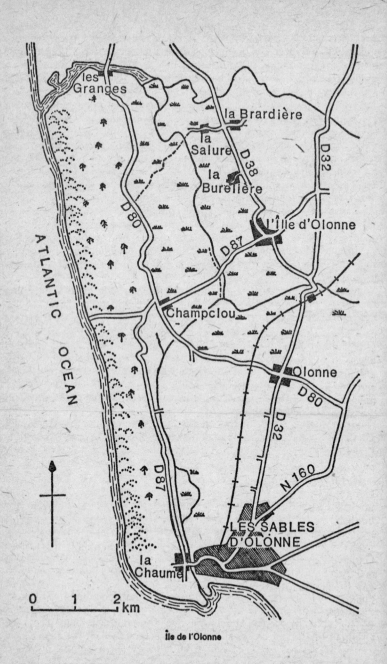

Île de l'Olonne

points. The Ile is 13 km long and has been extensively planted with pines which together with the dune beach and marshes make an attractive landscape. The outstanding breeding bird is the avocet which breeds on the disused salines. This is the only colony on the French Atlantic coast. Black-winged stilts breed too but they are also found at the Baie du Bourgneuf to the north. Garganey and ruff also breed, together with many other interesting birds. During passage periods this area is outstanding. Little egret, spoonbill, and a superb collection of waders pass through, and marsh harriers are almost continuously present. Many species of raptors haunt the marshes and duck find it an excellent feeding ground.

SUMMER: garganey, avocet, black-winged stilt, ruff, cirl bunting.

PASSAGE: little egret, spoonbill, marsh harrier, black kite, honey buzzard, spotted redshank, curlew sandpiper, bar-tailed godwit, little stint.

Cross to the Île at la Chaume from Les Sables d'Olonne. Various roads cross back to the mainland; the whole area can be explored on foot along tracks and paths except for the Chanteloup reserve. There is a camp site at Les Sables d'Olonne and an excellent one at Brétignolles-sur-Mer to the north. There is a good choice of hotels.

## ST FLOUR

St Flour is a picturesque town perched on a hillside and bypassed by the N9. It is one of the most flourishing holiday centres in the Massif Central with a wealth of attractions in a very beautiful setting. The town, however, is also a good centre from which the visiting bird-watcher can explore the surrounding countryside which consists of rolling cornfields with belts of conifers and quite steep hills covered with twentieth-century pine plantations. To the north the Col de la Fageole rises to 3,500 feet in rolling agricultural country and is an excellent place for birds of prey. These sometimes soar above the hill itself but are generally distributed in the area. Species include red kite, Montagu's harrier, booted eagle, and many buzzards. The small pine wood and adjacent fields at the top hold cirl bunting.

Further north the road runs through the superb Gorges de l'Allagon to Lempdes. This is another good raptor area and buzzards are almost constantly in view. Lempdes itself lies at the mouth of the gorge and the river is here bordered by an excellent riverain forest full of small birds. Red-backed shrike, wryneck, cirl bunting and many other small passerines are common.

In the hilly pine clad district to the south of St Flour lies the Viaduc de Garabit. This is a favourite bathing place for many people in the artificial lake, and the wooded hillsides hold crested tit, black redstart, short-toed treecreeper, and firecrest. The general area has woodchat shrikes and is excellent for a holiday.

SUMMER: booted eagle, red kite, buzzard, Montagu's harrier, woodchat shrike, red-backed shrike, wryneck, crested tit, firecrest, black redstart, cirl bunting.

The whole area lies along the N9 and is attractive in a non-dramatic mountain way. There are hotels and camp sites at St Flour and Lempdes. The camp at the latter is adjacent to the riverain forest.

## SEPT-ÎLES

The Sept-Îles lie off the north coast of Brittany and are the most important site in France for breeding seabirds. Lannion, at the end of the N167 is the nearest town, and Perros-Guirec the nearest sea-side resort, and usual setting off point. These islands are not only the best place in France, but they are also important as the southernmost breeding site of two typical North Atlantic seabirds, the puffin and the gannet. The latter has increased on Rouzic from 2 to 1,400 pairs in the short period since its establishment. Other species include razorbill and guillemot, cormorant, and kittiwake. Storm petrels breed but are, of course, seldom seen, and peregrine and raven haunt the cliffs. The latest addition to the Rouzic breeding list is the fulmar which finally arrived in 1960.

SUMMER: storm petrel, fulmar, gannet, peregrine, kittiwake, puffin, guillemot, razorbill, peregrine.

The Sept-Îles were declared a reserve in 1912. Lying only a few kilometres off the coast they are visited by thousands of tourists each year in 'trips round the rocks' organized by the boatmen at Perros-Guirec. In fact landing is forbidden on Rouzic, Malban, and Cerf islands, and though allowed on the others (two incidentally are mere rocks) the animals and birds must not be interfered with. Excellent views including the whole of the gannetry can be obtained from these tourist trips which approach very near. There are birds all round the boat. Permission to land might be granted for high scientific endeavour; in this case contact the Ligue Francaise pour la Protection des Oiseaux, 129 Boulevard St Germain, Paris 7e.

## SOLOGNE

The damp marsh area of the Sologne lies between the arms of the rivers Loire and Cher less than 150 km south of Paris. Though ponds are scattered throughout this huge triangle eastwards beyond Orléans, the central part of the Sologne is concentrated into a comparatively small area between Ferté-St-Aubin and westwards along the Cosson to the N156, southwards to Chemery, then east to Romorantine and Salbris, and north on the N20 to Ferté. Even within this rectangle the area between the villages of Neung, St Viatre, and Marcilly holds many of the more attractive bird haunts.

The Sologne is a plateau of damp heath interrupted by a multitude of ponds. The vegetation is predominantly mature deciduous woodland with quite often extensive forests notably the Parc du Chambord which is a hunting reserve. Such woodlands often hide nearby lakes from view and the Chasse Gardé notices and heavily keepered hunting preclude examination. Most of the ponds are shallow and marshy with extensive fringe vegetation of reeds forming large reed beds in some places. Many are heavily overgrown and some almost dry mud. There are drainage schemes and the Étang de Marcilly for instance is now dry. Many of the waters have heavy growths of water lilies and look very beautiful in late summer.

In the north of the area woodland gives way to heathland with heather and birch scrub and holds a different avifauna to the woodland ponds. There are also extensive stands of pines as well as new plantations in this area. Though hunting is the major interest of the area it remains an excellent area for bird-watching providing one does not trespass to do so. The ponds hold purple and night herons and common and little bitterns as well as a wide variety of duck. Marsh, hen, and Montagu's harriers breed as do many waders on the surrounding marshes including black-winged stilts and black-tailed godwit, and colonies of 3,000 black-headed gulls. Black and whiskered terns hawk over the larger lakes while the reeds around the edges hold an interesting collection of warblers.

Migration is particularly good in autumn with waders, geese, raptors and cranes being regular.

SUMMER: great crested grebe, black-necked grebe, little grebe, grey heron, purple heron, night heron, little bittern, bittern, shoveler, pochard, marsh harrier, hen harrier, Montagu's harrier, black kite, Baillon's crake, little ringed plover, curlew, black-tailed godwit, common sandpiper, black-winged stilt, black tern, whiskered tern, black-headed gull, short-eared owl, Savi's warbler, great reed warbler.

AUTUMN: crane, geese, raptors, waders.

Most of the ponds and marshes are worth inspection and one could spend a lengthy stay productively searching the whole area. Many ponds can be seen from the roads with the aid of a good map though in a number of cases views are most unsatisfactory and anyone staying in the area for any length of time would be well advised to try to contact the local gamekeepers. The Étang de Biévre for instance can be partially viewed from the road at the north-east corner, while a walk of 25 metres down a gravelled drive would give excellent views of almost the whole lake, and it is a productive lake too. Other lakes in the central area that can be seen from the road include the Étang de Marguilliers, mainly mud and marsh with reed beds; Favells, open water; Pontbertas; Menne; Beaumont, an excellent little lake that requires farmers' permission for closer approach; Malzone; and Panama. This list is not exhaustive.

The hunting reserve at Chambord lies south of the village in the north-west of the Sologne near the Loire. Many of the most interesting species can be seen by walking along the public roads and tracks. There is also good forest bird-watching along the Marcilly-Millancay road in the north of the Forêt de Bruadan. The road north of Chaumont is excellent for heath land and pine forest birds.

Any of the N20 towns like Ferté-St-Aubin, Lamotte-Beuvron, Nouan, and

Salbris would make an ideal base for exploration, though the villages amongst the ponds like St Viatre would be better for those without transport. There is an attractive hotel at Chaumont. Nearest camp sites are at Ferté-St-Aubin and Romorantin. Orléans to the north has excellent transport services.

## SOMME ESTUARY

It is easy when looking at a map of France to overlook the small estuaries on the north coast and go for the vast bays and marshes of the west. Yet the estuary of the Somme is of the same sort of size as Langstone Harbour in Sussex and is virtually ignored. At low tide the basin empties out leaving sand and mud banks that attract large numbers of wildfowl and waders. The banks are particularly rich in marine life and attract hordes of French holiday-makers. During the summer months low tide sees the estuary covered with people of all ages all armed with buckets, and shellfish are the staple diet of the many campers who spend their holiday here. Out beyond the shell-fishers a few lone gun men patrol the water line. At dusk the waders flight in by the thousand. Throughout the year the Somme is over-hunted and as a result breeding birds are almost non-existent. Even during autumn passage, early mornings when the tide is right is the rule. In winter, hunting continues but there are then no trippers to contend with.

This is an important area for migrants and black- and red-throated divers are plentiful on the sea with scoter and sawbills. Brent geese pass through (quickly) as do whooper swans, shelduck and many other duck. There are usually a few predators about, ospreys are for instance annual, and the passage of waders can be very heavy. Black and bar-tailed godwits, and whimbrel often form very large flocks, while other species like wood and green sand-pipers haunt the small marshes behind the beach to the north. This sandy northern shore is also one of the few French haunts of snow bunting and shore lark in winter. Duck and waders do winter but hunting is really out of hand here.

PASSAGE: black-throated diver, red-throated diver, whooper swan, brent goose, shelduck, teal, garganey, wigeon, scoter, red-breasted merganser, peregrine, osprey, bar-tailed godwit, black-tailed godwit, whimbrel.

WINTER: waders, duck, shore lark, snow bunting.

The northern shore with dunes to the west of Le Crotoy, where there is a camp site, is of open access.

## VANOISE NATIONAL PARK

The Vanoise lies against the Italian border in the Savoie Alps to the north of a line joining Grenoble and Turin, and corresponds to the famous Italian Gran Paradiso National Park. It covers 150,000 acres, but with a pre-park of a further 280,000 acres, and rises from about the 3,000 foot mark to over 12,500 feet at Mont Casse. The lower valleys are typical of Alpine France with fields and agriculture; from 2,500 feet there are forests mainly of pine; the Alpine stage, between 5,000 feet and 6,500 feet, consists of more scattered and hardier conifers, while above this, trees disappear and rock and open ground predominate. At 9,000 feet almost all plants disappear.

The Vanoise is an excellent place for a holiday especially for those that like their birds in beautiful surroundings. It is not, however, to be ignored by the experts. Eagle and pygmy owls both breed, as do three-toed woodpeckers, the latter two being right on the edge of their range here. The rare wall creeper is described as widespread and, therefore, a certain attraction to a considerable number of bird-watchers. Otherwise the Park boasts most of the typical Alpine birds. The open tops have Alpine accentor, snow finch, both choughs, the Alpines being particularly abundant, and ptarmigan. Lower in the forests are hazel hen, Tengmalm's owl, black woodpecker, nutcracker, crested tit, and citril finch. Golden eagles soar overhead and there are numbers of Alpine swifts and crag martins.

SUMMER: golden eagle, ptarmigan, black grouse, hazel hen, rock partridge, Tengmalm's owl, eagle owl, Alpine swift, black woodpecker, three-toed woodpecker, crag martin, nutcracker, chough, Alpine chough, crested tit, wall creeper, Alpine accentor, citril finch, crossbill, snow finch.

The Park is reached by two major roads, the N90 and N6. These are joined by the N202, which is the only road inside the Park proper. For a full exploration and glorious walking holiday, stay at one of the mountain refuges, Refuge du Palet near Tignes, Refuges Felix-Faure and Péclet-Polset near Pralognou, the chalet hotel Entre-deux-Eaux in the Doron valley near Termignon and Chavière chalet. Transport is from Chambery and Grenoble.

# German Democratic Republic

Visitors to East Germany are not free to wander as they like about the countryside. It is generally necessary for those who do not wish to join an organized tour to submit details of their intended stops and destinations in advance for approval. It would seem that flashing binoculars and telescopes, not to mention cameras and telephoto lenses, would be a decidedly risky business in such a set up, and reluctantly the German Democratic Republic has been omitted from this book. Reluctantly, because there are many outstanding bird areas including the huge wildfowl wintering grounds of the Mecklenburg coast, and the lakes in north-western Mecklenburg that hold breeding greylags, red-crested pochard, and many other birds. The Muritz lakes have breeding white-tailed eagle, and the ponds at Niederspree hold crane, greylag, goldeneye, black tern, and black stork, while the same species plus white-tailed eagle, bittern, and roller breed in the pond area to the north of Gorlitz.

Further information especially from bird-watchers who have tried to visit East Germany would be very welcome.

# Germany (Federal Republic)

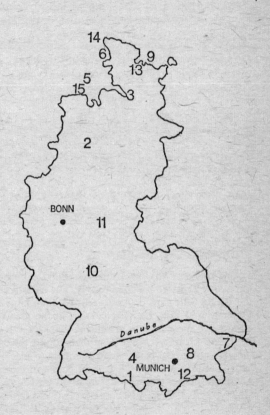

GERMAN SOCIETY FOR THE PROTECTION OF BIRDS:
Deutscher Bund für Vogelschutz,
6 Frankfurt M-Fechenheim, Steinauer Strasse 33.

Each State has own ornithological station and centre:
VOGELWARTE RADOLFZELL,
Schloss Möggingen, über Radolfzell, Bodensee.

VOGELSCHÜTZWARTE FÜR HESSEN, RHEINLAND-PFALZ UND SAARLAND,
6 Frankfurt M-Fechenheim, Steinauer Strasse 44.

STAATLICHE VOGELSCHÜTZWARTE FÜR BADEN-WÜRTTEMBERG,
714 Ludwigsburg, Favoritepark, Forsthaus.

VOGELWARTE HELGOLAND,
2940 Wilhelmshaven – Rüstersiel.

STAATLICHE VOGELSCHÜTZWARTE DES LANDES NORDRHEIN – WESTFALEN,
43 Essen – Bredeney, Ägidiusstrasse 94.

ORNITHOLOGISCHE ARBEITSGEMEINSCHAFT EMS-WESER-NIEDERELBE,
2 Hamburg – Sasel, Ilsenweg 11.

READ: *Die Vogel Deutschlands* (1964), G. Niethammer, H. Kramer, H. E. Wolters; *Handbuch des Deutschen Vogelkunde* (1936–1942) G. Niethammer.

## BODENSEE-UNTERSEE

Lake Constance, as the British insist on calling it, lies on the frontiers of Germany, Switzerland and Austria. The eastern end, particularly the area of the Rhine delta, lies in Austria and we are here concerned with the smaller Untersee and the extensive marshes in the area of Constance. Of these the largest and most famous are the Wollmatinger Ried. They have an excellent collection of breeding marsh birds amongst the reeds and lagoons including 200 pairs of great crested grebe, 50 pairs of black-necked grebe, 100 pairs of black-headed gull, and 50 pairs of common tern. Duck are quite numerous and there is an interesting colony of 50 pairs of red-crested pochard, many of which breed on the tiny 2½ acre reserve of the Deutscher Bund für Vogelschütz.

The Untersee is also shallow and marshy with large reed beds and submerged vegetation. The fringe marshes hold gulls and terns with occasional marsh harriers, but are mainly known as the most important inland area for migrating and wintering waterbirds in Germany. Maxima include 10,000 mallard, 480 shoveler, 3,000 teal, 650 pintail, 1,000 gadwall, 19,000 pochard, 6,000 tufted, and no less than 8,000 red-crested pochard. The observatory at Radolfzell, which was formerly on the Baltic coast at Rossitten, studies the migration of birds through the area, particularly on the Mettnau peninsula, which is a reserve.

The Einkircher marshes on the Bodensee are a water-bird reserve of the DBV.

SUMMER: great crested grebe, black-necked grebe, garganey, red-crested pochard, bittern, little bittern, spotted crake, little crake, black-headed gull, common tern, great reed warbler.

PASSAGE: duck, waders.

WINTER: mallard, shoveler, pintail, teal, gadwall, pochard, tufted duck, red-crested pochard.

Access is straightforward with the aid of a good map but contact the Staatliche Vogelschützwarte für Baden-Württemberg, 714 Ludwigsburg, Favoritepark, Forsthaus. Serious students of migration should contact the Vogelwarte Radolfzell, 7761 Schloss Möggingen, über Radolfzell, Bodensee.

## DUMMER

Dummer is a shallow lake some 5 km square to the north-east of Osnabrück. It is one of the best inland bird sites in Germany and a considerable area is protected as a nature reserve. There is considerable growth of emergent vegetation amounting to large reed beds in some parts, which gives away to natural peat fen, open meadows, and some interesting woods. Though mainly known for its typical marshland breeding birds including little bittern, bittern, marsh harrier and a wealth of duck amongst the reeds, Dummer is also noted as a migration and wintering haunt of duck. No less than 30 different species have been seen at one time or another. The surrounding meadows hold black-tailed godwit and ruff, and black tern hawk over the water and breed on the floating vegetation debris.

SUMMER: grey heron, bittern, little bittern, teal, garganey, gadwall, pintail, shoveler, pochard, marsh harrier, curlew, black-tailed godwit, ruff, black tern.

AUTUMN; WINTER: duck.

Leave route 51 at Hude which is 45 km northeast of Osnabrück. Though large areas are in fact nature reserve most of the lake can be worked from public roads. In spite of it being comparatively small, exploration of the local woods adds the typical wealth of German woodpeckers and woodland species, and forms a useful holiday centre. There are camp sites at Hude and Lembruch.

## ELBE ESTUARY

The whole of the south-eastern corner of the North Sea, from Sylt to the central Friesian island of Borkum, which lies in German territory is good for birds. Parts of the area at Uthörn, Husum, and Wangerooge have been treated separately and this really leaves only the three estuaries of the Ems, Weser, and Oder plus the tidal Jade Bay to be accounted for. All are good for birds particularly for wildfowl and waders and especially during the winter. Though references to winter birds can be found in this guide there are intentionally very few specifically winter areas. Nevertheless at least one major area for wildfowl along this coast must be included and the Elbe is in many ways the better and best known. What is more, it has considerable attractions at other times of the year. In autumn it receives huge numbers of geese and these stay for a couple of months before moving on to Holland and Britain. Greylags are numerous in the upper estuary and barnacle geese at the mouth at Dieksanderkoog. Duck, especially pintail and wigeon, are numerous and there are sizeable flocks of sea-duck off Cuxhaven. Knechtsand at the mouth is the major moulting ground of European shelduck. Waders pass through in vast numbers on migration with grey plover, turnstone, bar-tailed godwit, and knot dominant. Waders also breed and there are avocets near the mouth on the northern shore and black-tailed godwits on the marshes higher up.

Three large areas are particularly noted for birds. At the mouth is the rich reclaimed farmland and land in process of reclamation to the west of Maine. These go by names such as Kronprinzenkoog, Kaiser-Wilhelm Koog, etc. and are excellent at dusk and dawn and at high tide. Follow roads as far west as possible then continue on foot to the saltings via Dieksanderkoog. Across on the southern shore is Balje marsh which has geese and breeding godwits. Finally, and a long way upstream towards Hamburg, is the Pagensand-Bishort area off Hohenhorst and particularly the Wedel marshes. These are noted as an excellent place during migration particularly for a wide variety of waders including dotterel and broad-billed sandpiper, little gull, and red-throated pipit. Any one of these areas would be worth a visit at any time of the year.

SUMMER: avocet, black-tailed godwit, ruff.

SPRING: geese, dotterel.

AUTUMN: greylag goose, white-fronted goose, barnacle goose, pintail, wigeon, eider, shelduck, broad-billed sandpiper, wood sandpiper, whimbrel, Temminck's stint, little gull.

WINTER: duck, waders.

Hamburg is immediately adjacent to the excellent marshes at Wedel which are the best bird-watching within striking distance of the city. The Alster lakes in the city centre often hold interesting duck in winter, and the Sachsen Wald east of the city is a good spot for black woodpecker, honey buzzard and red-breasted flycatcher. Dieksanderkoog is easy enough to find with the aid of a good map.


## FEDERSEE

Federsee is the largest nature reserve in Baden-Württemberg and the largest and most important area of marshland in south-west Germany. It lies between Stuttgart and Lake Constance west of Biberach near the village of Buchau. Though only 330 acres of open water remain there is a total of 3,500 acres protected as the reserve. A large part of this consists of huge reed beds, but there is an open flat marsh that is particularly rich botanically. All of the main ecological stages from open water to pine forest can be seen and have the appropriate birds. Federsee was declared a reserve in 1939 and an ornithological station was set up in 1958.

Amongst the marsh birds there are all of the indigenous rails, marsh harrier, bittern, and a colony of 450 pairs of black-headed gulls. There is also a small colony of common terns and a medium-sized heronry nearby. Both kites, mute swan, white stork, a selection of ducks, and perhaps night heron and Savi's warbler also breed. Certainly over a hundred species of birds breed annually.

SUMMER: black-necked grebe, garganey, gadwall, mute swan, bittern, little bittern, heron, white stork, night heron(?), marsh harrier, hobby, black kite, red kite, spotted crake, little crake, water rail, curlew, black-headed gull, common tern, long-eared owl, black grouse, willow tit, blue-headed wagtail, grasshopper warbler, Savi's warbler.

The Federsee is reached by an 1100 metre long path of wooden boards, so one should take gumboots. On the lake shore the Radolfzell Bird Observatory has built a bird-tower with a hide. Visiting is allowed and guides are available all the year round. But apply to Dr Gerhard Haas, 7952 Bucha/Federsee, Inselstrasse 4, beforehand. Leave the E11 autobahn at Um and take route 311. Turn eastwards to Buchau just before Riedlingen. There are good hotels at Biberach 15 km to the east.

# HELIGOLAND

Heligoland lies 60 km north of the German mainland in the south-eastern corner of the North Sea, and since 1720 has consisted of two islands. Oberland, which is the largest, was originally surrounded by 200 feet sandstone cliffs but wartime modifications added land at the foot of the eastern cliffs and a harbour at the southern end. The cliffs left on the north and west coasts hold Germany's only breeding guillemots and kittiwakes. To the north-east lies Dune Island which is one of the major attractions to the huge tourist industry which currently attracts almost half a million visitors annually. Perhaps duty free cigarettes and spirits also have something to do with the island's popularity. It is thus a sharp contrast to the isolation and sense of frontiersmanship that pervade Europe's second most famous bird observatory at Fair Isle.

The pioneering work of Gatke led to the establishment of the bird observatory in its present form in 1910. It is situated in the centre of the Oberland plateau and the garden contains almost the only vegetation in any direction for 40 miles. Elder, hawthorn, and bramble predominate but the area is only 150 yards by 30 yards with a small pond in the middle and a number of Heligoland traps. These traps were first used on this island, though there is hardly an observatory anywhere without one now. Being right in the middle of the south-west migration route and in perfect isolation, Heligoland receives huge numbers of migrants most of which concentrate in the observatory garden. Ringing numbers are much higher than any similar station treated in this book. The chats, warblers, and flycatchers are often involved in heavy falls and regular numbers of barred warblers, red-breasted flycatchers, bluethroats and ortolan buntings occur in autumn, and the most extreme vagrants turn up with surprising regularity. Apart from passerines all sorts of migrants are noted including an interesting collection of waders on the shore especially on Dune Island, and a variable number of raptors.

Dune Island is easy to get to by boat and holds many of the migrants that prefer a more open landscape such as Lapland buntings, though binoculared ornithologists should refrain from chasing rarities through the beach reserved for nude bathing.

SUMMER: kittiwake, guillemot.

AUTUMN: geese, buzzard, sparrowhawk, purple sandpiper, curlew sandpiper, little stint, skuas, wryneck, warblers, chats, flycatchers, barred warbler, red-breasted flycatcher, bluethroat, ortolan bunting, Lapland bunting, rarities.

The observatory welcomes help from experienced bird watchers and particularly from qualified ringers. Anyone wishing to help should write to Dr G. Vauk, Voegelwarte Heligoland, Germany, but note that the observatory does not provide accommodation other than for its resident staff. All visitors, therefore, must stay at one of the many new hotels or at the modern youth hostel. Camping is allowed only on Dune Island which is inconvenient for daily visits to the observatory. Casual bird-watchers may call at the observatory, but are not normally allowed into the garden. However, an excellent holiday can be had from the periphery, as it were.

During the summer modern ships ferry the thousands of trippers across from Wangerooge in the East Frisian Islands, Wilhelmshaven, Bremerhaven, Cuxhaven, Hamburg, Brunsbuttelkoog, Büsum and Hörnum on the Island of Sylt. Hamburg is the most convenient port for the south and west but visitors from Scandinavia find the Hörnum service most convenient.

# HUSUM

1. **Spätinge:** Husum lies on the west coast of Schleswig-Holstein and is a convenient centre for the surrounding area of reclaimed marshland, lagoons, and saltings. Parallel walls show the various stages of the reclamation that has been a preoccupation in this area for centuries. Many of the new meadows are used by cattle and their drinking ponds are the favourite haunt of black terns. Larger fleets fringed with reeds and in some cases with extensive reed beds hold marsh harriers and colonies of black-headed gulls. The fields themselves hold breeding ruff and black-tailed godwit. There are a number of small colonies of avocet, and white storks breed in the village. The creation of a new reservoir by cutting back a dyke 9 km south of Husum near Simonsberg has enhanced an already excellent area and this together with the Spätinge area is now a nature reserve of the DBV.

SUMMER: white stork, garganey, marsh harrier, Kentish plover, ruff, black-tailed godwit, avocet, black tern, black-headed gull, blue-headed wagtail.

The Spätinge of Adolfskoogs lies south of Husum near Simonsberg. There is a hut in Koog giving good views over the area. Further information from the Deutscher Bund für Vogelschutz.

2. **Hamburger Hallig** is a low lying grass covered island north of Husum and west of Bredstedt which is connected to the mainland by a dam. Due to constant land reclamation, the island is increasing in size, though it is not safe from flooding and large numbers of terns lose their eggs each year. For decades this has been a favourite wintering ground of barnacle geese.

SUMMER: ruff, black-tailed godwit, terns.

WINTER: barnacle goose.

Though a reserve of the DBV there are no restrictions on access.

3. **Westhever** is another area of grassland with a sandy beach further west than Simonsberg. It is a reserve of the DBV and is frequented by many sun-bathers as well as bird-watchers. Most of the breeding birds of the North Sea coast are established here with the advantage that guided trips can be made during the breeding season.

SUMMER: ruff, avocet, black tern.

The warden's hut is near the lighthouse.

## INN LAKES

The River Inn runs along the Austro-German border for the lower part of its course before joining the Danube at Passau. The recent construction of dams has changed an area of meadows holding nothing but a few teal into one of the most important wetland areas in this part of central Europe. At present there is only one nature reserve, the Bay of Hagenau in Austria south of the dam at Schärding, but more of the marshes and reed beds will probably soon be protected. The area is particularly important as a staging post in the spread of south-eastern species notably the river warbler. Other breeders include purple and night herons, little bittern, common tern, and penduline tit, and red-crested pochard have attempted to breed, and black-winged stilt have bred once. There is a strong passage of waders including up to 6,000 ruff at Inn-Stausee near Simbach in March, these being the birds that pass through Italy after a trans-Saharan flight. In autumn hordes of wildfowl include 15,000 tufted, 9,000 pochard, and 1,000 goldeneye, and many remain through the winter.

SUMMER: purple heron, night heron, little bittern, gadwall, tufted duck, pochard, red-crested pochard, black-winged stilt, black-headed gull, common tern, penduline tit, river warbler, bluethroat.

AUTUMN: tufted duck, pochard, goldeneye, waders.

WINTER: duck.

SPRING: waders, ruff.

The best approach is from the German bank and virtually the whole stretch between Simbach and Passau is worth investigating. The lake above the dam at Schärding should not be missed nor should the Inn-Stausee east of Simbach. There are hotels and camp-sites nearby.

## ISMANINGER TEICHGEBIET

This is a privately owned and carefully protected, artificially dammed lake, with an area of fish ponds, and a sewage farm, all situated in a former swamp to the north-east of Munich. It is an exceptionally rich group of habitats and one of the most important wetlands in Germany. The lake has an ample fringe of emergent vegetation that provides excellent breeding sites for large numbers of waterbirds. Up to 150 pairs of black-necked grebes breed, together with excellent numbers of the commoner ducks. There is also a small population of breeding red-crested pochard, and a large black-headed gullery (500 pairs).

Many herons pass through on migration and there is always a large population of moulting and wintering duck. The following maxima speak for themselves: teal 2,500, garganey 400, gadwall 530, shoveler 630, red-crested pochard 300, tufted 5,000, pochard 11,200, ferruginous duck 60, smew 100, goosander 415. There is also a good passage of waders.

SUMMER: great crested grebe, black-necked grebe, gadwall, shoveler, tufted duck, pochard, red-crested pochard, black-headed gull, penduline tit.

AUTUMN; WINTER: red-crested pochard, ferruginous duck, smew, waders.

This area is not accessible to the public. Ornithologists, and to qualify for this title it would be advisable to carry proof of membership of one of the national ornithological organizations eg BOU, BTO, may apply for a key to Professor W. Wüst, 8 München 19, Hohenlohestrasse 61.

Follow the road from Munich to Ismaning.

## KIEL BAY

Almost the entire coastline of Kiel Bay is excellent for birds and it forms one of those large areas where it is particularly difficult to pick out one place as better than another. It stretches from Kiel in the west along the south-western Baltic to Heiligenhafen and then continues along the western shore of Fehmarn. A number of places are particularly good though the birds of one area are generally found in adjacent areas as well.

1. Bottsand is a sandy half-island east of the Kiel Fjord and has been a nature reserve since 1961. The principal habitats are dunes backed by dykes and large areas of saltmarsh, and the avifauna is accordingly rich with a colony of avocets, and one of the largest colonies of little terns on the western coast of the Baltic. Caspian terns are regular in autumn. Bottsand is managed by the local DBV group led by Mr Erwin Schneider, 23 Kiel-Wik, Flensburger Strasse 18. To get to the reserve take the road to Probstei in the direction of Barsbeker, and pass the Barsbeker lake to the coast.

2. **Kleine Binnensee** lies further to the south-east near the village of Hohwacht. It is a shallow water surrounded by marshes and separated from the sea by only a beach in typical Baltic fashion. The marshes hold many waders and the beach has little tern and ringed plover. The lake itself is excellent for duck especially during migration periods, and is a reserve of the DBV. The two nearby lakes of Grosse Binnensee and the Sehlendorfer See are also worth a look.

Kleine Binnensee is managed by the Eutin group of the DBV which has accommodation on the edge of the reserve for the warden.

3. **Heiligenhafen** is a holiday resort on Fehmarn Sund and is noted as an excellent area for migrants.

4. **Fehmarn** is a low sandy island of considerable size, the western half of which has some quite extensive areas of marshland that support a rich avifauna. Breeding red-crested pochard and greylag geese are outstanding but there are many other attractive breeding birds and a wealth of migrants particularly terns, waders, and duck. Fehmarn is connected to the mainland by bridge.

SUMMER : red-crested pochard, greylag goose, avocet, oystercatcher, little tern.

AUTUMN : duck, Caspian tern.

# KÜHKOPF

Kühkopf is an island in the Rhine between Mainz and Mannheim. In this part of its course the river formerly meandered over a broad valley floor but most of its more lavish eccentricities are now backwaters or oxbow lakes. Nevertheless there are many islands enclosed between the Rhine and its backwaters in the stretch between Karlsruhe and Mainz, the largest of which is the Kühkopf immediately west of Darmstadt. A wide variety of habitats has attracted 115 breeding species, 82 migrants, and 5 vagrants. There are large areas of farmland with many fields as well as borders planted with fruit trees, and meadows with established hedges. Extensive areas of pollarded willows are found and the old still water arms of the Rhine are covered with a wealth of emergent and aquatic vegetation. There are beautiful old woods as well as new plantations, and the sandy and muddy banks of the river are exposed according to the varying water level. The latter attract many waders, particularly *Tringa* species.

Amongst the 115 breeding species, the marsh birds are found along the old arms of the Rhine. They include little bittern, four species of crake, and several dabbling duck. The woodland holds a variety of raptors, owls, and woodpeckers including most of the species one would expect to find in this part of Germany, with red and black kites, goshawk, and irregularly the honey buzzard. There are five species of owl and six of woodpecker. There are four species of shrike, and a few nice attractions like white-spotted bluethroat and serin. Black woodpeckers are usually easy to see.

The good passage of waders often includes a few oddities and there are regular autumn records of harriers, herons, and cranes.

SUMMER: garganey, shoveler, little bittern, goshawk, red kite, black kite, buzzard, honey buzzard, hobby, spotted crake, little crake, Baillon's crake, corncrake, quail, long-eared owl, short-eared owl, grey-headed woodpecker, middle-spotted woodpecker, black woodpecker, great grey shrike, lesser grey shrike, woodchat shrike, red-backed shrike, hoopoe, golden oriole, blue-throat, icterine warbler, firecrest, serin.

AUTUMN: waders.

There are trains from Frankfurt, Darmstadt, Wiesbaden, Mainz and Mannheim to Goddelau-Erfelden and to Stockstadt. From Goddelau it is a 20 minute walk or 'bus to Erfelden where a ferry crosses to the Kühkopf. A bridge crosses to the island at the south end. The island is now partly a reserve and visitors should contact Vogelschutzwarte für Hessen, Rheinland-Pfalz und Saarland, 6 Frankfurt am Main-Fechenheim, Steinauer Strasse 33.

## MARBURG

Marburg is an ancient university town on the River Lahn to the north of Frankfurt and the E4, and is dominated by a castle on a steep hill. The Castle park (Schlosspark) has several attractive birds including serin, black redstart, marsh and willow tits, and short-toed treecreeper. The surrounding pine-clad hills boast a number of species, and the large cemetery (Friedhof) which extends through the slopes on the western boundary of the town is as good a place as any to see them. They include all of those species found at the castle plus woodpeckers, crested tit, and goldcrest. The river Lahn itself has black-bellied dipper and little grebe. The coniferous woodland to the south and east of Cappel abounds with the commoner birds and has breeding buzzard, while the Allna valley, 6 km south-west of Marburg, has breeding hawfinch, serin, marsh warbler, red-backed shrike, buzzard, and black kite.

This is a typical area of central Germany and an excellent holiday spot.

SUMMER: buzzard, black kite, woodpeckers, red-backed shrike, black redstart, short-toed treecreeper, black-bellied dipper, marsh tit, willow tit, crested tit, goldcrest, marsh warbler, serin, hawfinch.

The cemetery is entered from the Ockershauser Allee between Marburg and the village of Ockerhauser which is now a suburb. There are walks along the paths between the graves. The other areas are of straightforward access.

## OBERAMMERGAU

Though known to the outside world as the scene of the ten-yearly passion play Oberammergau is an ideal centre for exploring the bird life of the Bavarian Alps. The village lies in the valley of the River Ammer adjacent to the first real mountains south of Munich. The whole valley north-westwards to Saulgauts and south-east to Ettal lies between two and three thousand feet and the steep sides of the valley are covered with an extensive growth of conifers. Up to four and a half thousand feet firs predominate but then gradually give way to pines which progressively thin out to the tree limit at six thousand feet. The valley floor is mainly meadows of varying degrees of dampness and apart from a beech wood at Staffelsee there are few deciduous trees and bushes. Birds found in this habitat include red-backed shrike, pied flycatcher, golden oriole (in the birches near the Wahrbuhel), black redstart, wryneck, serin and tawny pipit, the latter on the dry cattle pastures. The valley-side fir woods hold crested tit, nutcracker, fieldfare, crossbill, siskin and a variety of woodpeckers including grey-headed (commonest), green and great-spotted. There are also lesser spotted, middle spotted, three-toed and white-backed woodpeckers, and though not yet observed there are doubtless black woodpeckers in the area enabling all the western European woodpeckers to be seen in a single mountain valley.

Above the tree line crag martin, Alpine accentor, and the highly aerial Alpine chough can be found, while golden eagle, honey buzzard, and goshawk are frequently seen overhead. A total of 112 species was seen in the area in a 15-day holiday recently.

SUMMER: golden eagle, goshawk, honey buzzard, buzzard, long-eared owl, great spotted woodpecker, middle-spotted woodpecker, lesser spotted woodpecker, white-backed woodpecker, three-toed woodpecker, green woodpecker, grey-headed woodpecker, wryneck, capercaillie, Alpine chough, golden oriole, nutcracker, fieldfare, Alpine accentor, crag martin, red-backed shrike, tawny pipit, water pipit, short-toed treecreeper, firecrest, crested tit, pied flycatcher, serin, siskin, citril finch, crossbill.

This is the sort of area that gets explored during a refreshing mountain holiday, nevertheless some areas should be visited.

1. Staffelsee: the large lake north of Murnau is generally bare except for the odd great crested grebe, but the beech wood on the south side is excellent for woodpeckers.

2. Sonnenberg (5,562 feet) for high altitude species and crag martins on the way up.

3. Noth Kar-Spitze (nearly 7,000 feet) for high altitude species, and citril finch amongst dwarf pines near the top.

4. Aurschling Kopf (5,180 feet) for high altitude species.

Transport is reasonably easy by bus from Munich, and there are several local hotels, inns, and pensions, as well as camp sites at Oberammergau and Unterammergau.


## LAKES IN SCHLESWIG-HOLSTEIN

The lakes on the eastern side of south Jutland form the western end of the vast series of glacial lakes that stretch right across Germany, Poland and Russia. They are the equivalent of the Muritz Lakes in East Germany, and the Masurian Lakes in Poland. The classic bird of the lakes is the white-tailed eagle and this bird still occurs in Schleswig-Holstein. The area is well worth visiting and fits in very well with an exploration of the nearby coast treated separately as Kiel Bay.

The most important lakes are Westensee south-west of Kiel which has grebes and thrush nightingale, and Lebrade which is immediately north of Plön where breeding birds include black-necked grebe, greylag and gadwall. Plön itself is excellent for duck and grebes and is another thrush nightingale spot. Warder See which lies south of the others between Lübeck and Neumüntser is a good spot for migrants.

SUMMER: black-necked grebe, greylag goose, gadwall, white-tailed eagle, thrush nightingale.

All of the lakes can be seen from roads and examined via public paths, tracks, etc.

## UTHÖRN

The island of Uthörn lies in Königshafen north of List and Sylt. It is a sandy island with shallow seas that are an attractive feeding place for thousands of migrant waders. These include most of the commoner species, and an interesting large flock of whimbrel summer here. Formerly Uthörn was a virtual paradise for breeding seabirds and waders, and Caspian terns had their most southerly breeding ground here. Though reduced there are still large colonies of terns and gulls as well as eider and red-breasted merganser. They have been carefully protected for many years. The surrounding mud banks are a winter haunt of brent geese, particularly between Ellenbogen and Uthörn.

SUMMER: eider, red-breasted merganser, whimbrel, ringed plover, common tern, little tern, gulls.

AUTUMN: knot, greenshank, godwits, green sandpiper, spotted redshank.

WINTER: brent goose, waders.

The DBV use two huts on the island from which they organise guided tours for the large number of interested visitors who holiday on Sylt, from where it is easily reached.

## WANGEROOGE

This North Sea island is the easternmost of the Friesian Isles and one of the most popular beach resorts in Germany. Like the other islands it is the product of sea and tides and consists of a vast sandy beach in the north and the gently shelving sand and mud banks of the Waddensee in the south. Between the two, in the centre of the elongated saucer lies an area of marshy meadows that are the favourite haunt of many waders. Outstanding amongst a good collection of breeding birds are the large colonies of terns of four species, and the numerous black-headed gulls. Short-eared owl, shelduck, and Kentish plover all breed as do an interesting variety of smaller birds. On passage there are frequently many thousands of waders.

SUMMER: shelduck, oystercatcher, Kentish plover, black-headed gull,

common tern, Arctic tern, Sandwich tern, little tern, short-eared owl.
PASSAGE: waders.

Wangerooge can be reached from Bremerhaven and Wilhelmshaven but most conveniently from Harlersiel just across the Waddensee. There are four reserves which can be visited by permission of the warden at Wangerooge. There are camping facilities.

# Greece

1 Gulf of Arta
2 Asprovalta
3 Axios Delta
4 Corinth
5 Delphi
6 Evros Delta
7 Lake Ioannina

8 Lake Koronia
9 Mesolongion Lagoons
10 Metéora
11 Nestos Delta
12 Central Peloponnesos
13 Porto Lágo
14 Pyrgos

Though not included in this edition the major islands of Crete and Corfu have proved of great interest to visiting ornithologists. A lengthy report on the birds of Crete is currently in preparation.

READ: *A specific Check-list of the Birds of Greece* (1957) by A. Lambert in *Ibis* 99, pp 43–68: *Die Vogelwelt Macedoniens* (1950) by W. Makatasch: *Catalogus Faunae Graeciae II: Ave* by W. Bauer, M. E. Hodge, *et al* (German with English summary).

## GULF OF ARTA

This 100,000 acre inlet lies on the west coast between the Albanian border and the Gulf of Corinth. Though one of the four most important wetlands in Greece it is surprisingly little visited by bird-watchers, who are perhaps daunted by its vast size. Fortunately, apart from a small place on the southern shore, only the northern area need be considered. In the extreme south-eastern corner just north of Amfilokhía lies a small area of mudflats at the end of one of the arms of the Gulf. This is a good spot for passage waders and a bird's-eye view of the area can be obtained from the hill on the E19 to the north. In the northern area part of the Gulf, to the south of Arta, are two river mouths, marshes, and large reed-fringed lagoons with areas of meadows beyond. For the lagoon birds Saloara and the road leading to it is excellent, and birds include crakes and waders. Pygmy cormorants and pelicans are regular here. East of this area around Aliki and the mouth of the Arachthos are salt pans that are exceedingly good for waders. But the whole area needs more attention.

SUMMER; AUTUMN: white pelican, purple heron, squacco heron, pygmy cormorant, duck, little crake, Baillon's crake, spotted crake, waders.

Three routes from Arta are major starting places:
1. Aliki road and salt pan area.
2. Saloara road and meadows and lagoons.
3. Preveza road alongside the River Luoros at its mouth.

## ASPROVALTA

Asprovalta is a convenient coastal area between Thessaloniki and Kavala with the main E5 running along behind the beach. The shingle gives way to areas of grass with a considerable growth of bushes and trees that is lush by Greek standards. A wide variety of species has been seen here and it is obviously a particularly good place for seabirds in early autumn. Slender-billed Audouin's, and Mediterranean gulls are all seen, with numbers of Cory's and Balearic shearwaters. Breeding birds include rufous warbler, black-headed bunting, pratincole and Kentish plover. This is also one of the most reliable spots for masked shrike in the country. Though more of a place for a day or two than a holiday, the attractions might be extended to include the Strymon mouth to the east. This varies a great deal according to the water level but has been good.

SUMMER: Kentish plover, pratincole, Mediterranean gull, woodchat shrike, masked shrike, hoopoe, grey-headed woodpecker, rufous warbler, black-headed bunting.

AUTUMN: Cory's shearwater, Balearic shearwater, Mediterranean gull, slender-billed gull, Audouin's gull.

The E5 runs through the area and there are camp sites either side of the village, as well as excellent wild camping between the road and the sea.

## AXIOS DELTA

Across the bay from the city of Thessaloniki lies a vast delta area created by four rivers. The eastern Gallikós is separate from the others and is ornithologically unimportant. The three others the Axios, Aliakmon, and Loudhias have built up an elaborate system of lagoons and channels with extensive areas of salt marshes and a gently shelving seashore that is generally known as the Axios Delta. The rivers, particularly the Axios, have been straightened and a considerable area of former marshland has been reclaimed, though flooding is still regular in some areas in winter. The two larger rivers the Axios and Aliakmon are better than the third and should be visited first by those with only limited time for exploration. Breeding birds include an excellent variety of waders such as Kentish plover, black-winged stilt, and pratincole, and superb terneries that include gull-billed tern. Smaller birds include penduline tit, black-eared wheatear and Cetti's warbler.

To the south but separate is the area of salines around Lake Alyki which is excellent for passage and breeding waders, and for the generally distributed species found in this part of the country.

SUMMER: garganey, shelduck, spotted crake, pratincole, little ringed plover, Kentish plover, black-winged stilt, little tern, Sandwich tern, gull-billed tern, short-toed lark, black-eared wheatear, tawny pipit, penduline tit, Cetti's warbler.

Lake Alyki and the salt pans lie immediately south of Alyki village which is 4 km east of Kitros on route E92. The delta is crossed by a network of roads and tracks that are best explored with a good map. Naturally the river banks and coast itself are excellent routes for birds. There are two camp sites and many hotels in Thessaloniki.

## CORINTH

Corinth is only 84 km west of Athens and its birds are typical of the arid Mediterranean macchia landscape that dominates the Peloponnesos. There are intermittent small farms and orchards and the area around the Canal, Old Corinth, and Acro (High) – Corinth offers a good range of the typical birds. These include the exotic bee-eater, roller and hoopoe, the red-rumped swallow, black-headed wagtail (*M.f.feldegg*), a superb collection of warblers including olivaceous and olive-tree, both rock thrushes, Cretzschmar's bunting, and rock sparrow. The lagoon across the main road from the ruins is a stopping place for migrant water-birds but offers little cover. Terek sandpiper and other rarities have been noted.

SUMMER: lesser kestrel, Scops owl, Alpine swift, bee-eater, roller, hoopoe, red-rumped swallow, black-headed wagtail, Cetti's warbler, olive-tree warbler, olivaceous warbler, orphean warbler, Rüppell's warbler, Sardinian warbler, subalpine warbler, Bonelli's warbler, fan-tailed warbler, black-eared wheatear, rufous warbler, rock thrush, blue rock thrush, sombre tit, rock nuthatch, Cretzschmar's bunting, black-headed bunting, Spanish sparrow, rock sparrow.

Corinth is easy to reach from Athens and has good accommodation.

# DELPHI

Delphi is, of course, on every tourist's list of places that it is unthinkable to miss in Greece. It has an open air theatre, Temple of Apollo, stadium and all the other wonders of ancient Greek civilization. The ruins are beautiful with cream-coloured columns and pavements against a slightly darker cream soil and the odd clumps of bushes and small trees. High above the city Parnassos rises to 8,068 feet, and away toward Amphissa stretches the largest olive grove in Greece.

Delphi is not to be missed ornithologically either. The ornitho-philistine can sit in the theatre listening to Sophocles with one ear and rock-nuthatches with the other. The surrounding ruins, in spite of the thousands of visitors, hold an incredible number of the warblers of the *sylvia* family. Whitethroat, lesser whitethroat, Sardinian, subalpine, and orphean warblers can all be found, and the collection is completed by the highly localised Rüppell's warbler. Rock thrushes and rock sparrows are also typical birds of the ruins. Amongst the higher ruins on the lower slopes of Parnassos where there are more trees and shrubs, sombre tits can be seen and higher still where the trees and shrubs are sparser but where there are still a few monuments, buntings take over. Ortolan, cirl, rock, and Cretzschmar's buntings are all found, and overhead Alpine swift, red-rumped swallow, and the abundant crag martin hawk for insects.

High above it all stands Parnassos with its magnificent cliffs and buttresses. Peregrine and buzzard are comparatively common and all four vultures can sometimes be seen. Griffons are usually present and there are frequently Egyptian and black. The lammergeier is decidedly scarce but turns up occasionally. The best time to watch for raptors is late morning but there has been a decline in numbers in the last few years. The lower slopes of the mountain particularly the coniferous woods above 3,000 feet are excellent with firecrest, and black woodpecker, and the surrounding countryside, notably the 1,000-year-old woods towards Amphissa is full of birds including olivaceous warbler.

SUMMER: griffon vulture, black vulture, Egyptian vulture, golden eagle, Alpine chough, rock thrush, rock nuthatch, black woodpecker, Alpine swift, red-rumped swallow, crag martin, sombre tit, black redstart, Sardinian warbler, Rüppell's warbler, subalpine warbler, orphean warbler, olivaceous warbler, Cretzschmar's bunting, ortolan bunting, rock bunting, rock sparrow.

Delphi is on the northern shore of the Gulf of Corinth and there is excellent bathing (and Mediterranean gull and shearwaters) at Itea. Exploring the ruins is straightforward and it is a simple matter to wander off up Parnassos to find more birds. For the higher birds and a more thorough exploration of some of the intermediate areas the road running northwards out of Arakhova crosses the lower slopes of the mountain and a walk westwards is advised. Try the local rubbish tip for vultures on the ground.

## EVROS DELTA

The River Evros has the unenviable distinction of being the boundary between Greece and Turkey and though shooting here is unusual the mutual distrust could be pushed to extremes by the sight of hordes of foreigners staring with binoculars and telescopes. It is a good area for spies. Bird-watchers have been turned away from the marshes and Gala lake on the Turkish side but the Greek side seems easier. It is certainly worth trying as the delta is the most important wetland in the country. Though large parts have and are being reclaimed the resulting meadowland is still attractive to birds. Nevertheless the area near the sea with its lagoons and reedy areas is the most important. Breeding birds include glossy ibis and spur-winged plover as well as a vast number of other less rare and less spectacular species like black-winged stilt, various herons, bee-eater, roller, various terns (possibly only summering), and the two specialities, Isabelline wheatear and masked shrike. There are two good and accessible spots, the lagoons in the west near the coast and the river area itself, but a full exploration is needed.

The Avas Gorge lies to the north of Alexandroupolis and is a totally different area from the delta. It is, however, near the town and thus is a likely place for anyone working the marshes to spend a day. Its sheer 200 foot cliffs drop to the scrubby gorge floor where the river and road run. There is a good chance of raptors including golden eagle, Egyptian and griffon vultures, booted eagle, and lanner. Other birds include eagle owl, woodpeckers, sombre tit, blue rock thrush, black-eared wheatear, and crag martin. To the south 5 km before the gorge, is a rock with a ruined castle on the western side of the road. This is known as a likely place for black stork and masked shrike. Between this rock and Alexandroupolis the road runs beside the railway, and this is one of the most reliable places in Greece for seeing Isabelline wheatear. Staying in Alexandroupolis in August is excellent for the Audouin's gulls that pass along this coast.

The Evros in winter holds an excellent collection of raptors and wildfowl, especially greylags and whitefronts but with regular numbers of lesser white-fronts and red-breasted geese.

SUMMER–Evros: Dalmatian pelican, black stork, little egret, glossy ibis, white-tailed eagle, imperial eagle, spur-winged plover, black-winged stilt, pratincole, Caspian tern, gull-billed tern, hoopoe, bee-eater, roller, masked shrike, Isabelline wheatear.

SUMMER–Avas: black stork, golden eagle, Egyptian vulture, booted eagle, lanner falcon, eagle owl, grey-headed woodpecker, middle spotted wood-pecker, Syrian woodpecker, crag martin, red-rumped swallow, masked shrike, lesser grey shrike, blue rock thrush, black-eared wheatear, Isabelline wheatear, sombre tit, subalpine warbler.

Leave the E5 south of Ferai southwards on a track where the road bends through a right angle to head north-westwards towards Alexandroupolis. Some short distance down the track is a T junction, where one must turn right for the lagoons, left for the river. The tracks run along the tops of embankments and are just motorable. Alexandroupolis is the nearest accommodation and there is a camp site.

For Avas Gorge leave Alexandroupolis northwards on the eastern side of

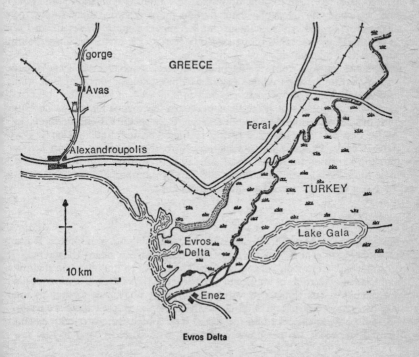

**Evros Delta**

the town on a minor road signposted to Aisymi and follow it beyond Avas village to the gorge.

## LAKE IOANNINA

Lake Ioannina lies in north-western Greece to the east of the town of that name. It is quite a sizeable water with bare sides except in the south around the major feeder river where there are muddy and reedy areas. The town itself has a colony of several hundred pairs of lesser kestrels, a profusion of white storks, and Egyptian vultures frequent the rubbish dump. Though the usual Greek species are found, the lake is at its best during autumn passage when huge numbers of waders, terns, and herons pass through. These include gull-billed and Caspian terns, purple and squacco herons, and glossy ibis. There is also a good passage of eagles here.

SUMMER: white stork, Egyptian vulture, lesser kestrel, hoopoe, roller.

AUTUMN: glossy ibis, purple heron, squacco heron, little bittern, raptors, black-winged stilt, gull-billed tern, Caspian tern, black tern.

Mount Astraka lies near Konitsa to the north of Ioannina but is best reached from the latter. It rises to nearly 6,000 feet and is a superb and little known area for many mountain species and raptors. The tops hold snow finches, while the limestone cliffs harbour wall creeper, three species of vulture, up to 400 Alpine choughs, and Alpine accentor. Lower down the area round the Vikos River long-legged buzzard, rock partridge, dipper, and sombre tit can be noted.

SUMMER: griffon vulture, Egyptian vulture, lammergeier, long-legged buzzard, rock partridge, Alpine accentor, Alpine chough, rock nuthatch, wall creeper, sombre tit, snow finch.

For the south side of Lake Ioannina leave the town southwards on E19 and turn eastwards along a rough lakeside track at the far end of the lake. At the end of 1 km walk 200 metres to the lake shore and reed beds. For Astraka leave Ioannina northwards on the road to Konitsa. 16 km before that town turn eastwards to Aristi and continue to Papingon. From here a mule track leads northwards to the cliff face of Astraka.

Accommodation can be had only in Ioannina.

## LAKE KORONIA

Lake Koronia is one of the best known bird-watching areas in Greece. It lies 15 km east of Thessaloniki, 200 metres north of the main Thessaloniki–Kavala road, from which it can be seen. The lake is 10 km by 5 km, shallow and fringed with reeds at either end – particularly the eastern end where reeds are extensive. The water level varies considerably and being so shallow the lake can grow or shrink quite dramatically. If the water is low there is a fringe of mud between the lake and the reeds. If it is high the water may extend beyond the reeds to the grassy surrounds. The adjacent land is flat, dry agricultural land with a few trees and scrubby bushes. In general a glance at the water level is a good indication of what birds are likely to be seen. Low water is good for waders but poor for herons and pygmy cormorant, and the reverse is true for high water. Breeding birds include little egret and probably some of the others that are regularly noted like night and purple herons. Pygmy cormorant, Dalmatian pelican, and glossy ibis are three of the major attractions. Though they do not breed they are frequently present particularly in late summer. Other species likely to be seen in summer are long-legged buzzard, avocet, stilt, Kentish plover, pratincole, and a good variety of smaller birds including Cetti's, Savi's and rufous warblers. Koronia is outstanding during passage periods when waders of many species form quite large flocks and black, whiskered, and Caspian terns pass through. There is nearly always an osprey present in autumn.

SUMMER: little egret, night heron, purple heron, pygmy cormorant, Dalmatian pelican, glossy ibis, long-legged buzzard, Kentish plover, avocet, black-winged stilt, pratincole, calandra lark, short-toed lark, crested lark, hoopoe bearded tit, Cetti's warbler, Savi's warbler, subalpine warbler, rufous warbler, Spanish sparrow.

AUTUMN: black stork, glossy ibis, osprey, green sandpiper, little ringed plover, greenshank, Temminck's stint, little stint, black tern, whiskered tern, Caspian tern.

The lake is immediately obvious from the main E5 road, from which the open southern shore is readily investigated. To reach the reedy eastern end, leave the E5 northwards in the village of Langadikia on to a rough road. Cross the stream that runs out of the lake by a ford (cars can cross it with care) and walk along the banks to the lake. The stream itself is good for 'reedy' warblers. If the water level is low, one can walk on the mud between the reeds and the water at both ends. There is a sandspit at the north-western corner that is a favourite haunt of waders, which can be reached by walking round the western end from the E5. This walk is particularly rewarding when the water is low.

'Buses between Thessaloniki and Kavala pass the lake. Though camping 'wild' in the immediate neighbourhood is possible, there are hotels and camp sites at Thessaloniki. This is a rewarding area that is easy to work.

NB Neighbouring Lake Volvii is deep, steep-sided, and no good for birds.

## MESOLONGION LAGOONS

These lagoons and marshes lie on the northern shore of the mouth of the Gulf of Corinth on the Greek west coast, and are an excellent area particularly for waders and terns. The outstanding spots lie on either side of the causeway running south from Mesolongion which is raised and provides an excellent viewpoint for the river on the right and a vast area of salt pans to the left. These cover several square kilometres and are excellent for Kentish plover, avocet, and black-winged stilt in summer and a good variety of other waders on passage including broad-billed and terek sandpipers. Across the salines lies the River Eúenos with an area of marshland delta beyond but little is known of the birds here. To the north the causeway at Aitolikon is a good vantage point for Lake Aitolikon which is worth a careful look. West from here lies the mouth of the River Acheloos – probably the best part of the area. There are colonies of terns including gull-billed, as well as pratincoles and the commoner waders, but the delta is difficult to penetrate and not well known.

SUMMER: Dalmatian pelican, garganey, avocet, black-winged stilt, Kentish plover, pratincole, little tern, common tern, gull-billed tern, short-toed lark.

AUTUMN: gulls, terns, broad-billed sandpiper, terek sandpiper.

Mesolongion village lies just south of the E19. Turn into the village and then south along the causeway with birds on either side to the sea where there is a restaurant. For Lake Aitolikon turn west in the village and view towards the north; continue along this road to Oeniadae which is a good place to start an exploration of the Acheloos Delta and has interesting ruins. There is a ferry across the Gulf of Corinth to Kruneria which is east of the Eúenos mouth and marshes.

## METÉORA

Metéora lies just north of the E87 between Ioannina and Larisa and is on every tourist's list of 'musts'. Pillars of brown sandstone rock rise to 1,820 feet above sea level and were believed to be meteors hurled by an angry god. Their inaccessibility provided a safe refuge for hermits in the fourteenth century and many refugees subsequently expanded into monasteries. Only five monasteries remain today but all save Aghios Stephanos are too poor to offer the traditional liqueur or coffee. Historically, the most important monastery, the Great Meteoron, was founded on a particularly inaccessible pinnacle the first ascent of which was, according to tradition, made by way of a rope fastened to an eagle's leg whose nest lay at the top. Eagles and other raptors remain the major attraction for the bird-watchers, and Meteora is famed as a likely place for all four species of vulture, four different eagles, and breeding lanner falcons. Other birds include rock and cliff haunting species like red-rumped swallow, crag martin, and Alpine swift.

SUMMER: black vulture, griffon vulture, Egyptian vulture, lammergeier, golden eagle, short-toed eagle, booted eagle, Bonelli's eagle, lanner falcon, Alpine swift, crag martin, red-rumped swallow, sombre tit.

Leave the E87 northwards at Kalabáka to Metéora which is frequented by tourists.

## NESTOS DELTA

The River Nestos reaches the sea almost opposite the island of Thasos to the south of the E5 between Kavalla and Xanthi. Below Krisoúpolis it winds its way through a flat marshy landscape, and then near its mouth divides into two channels that reach the sea only a short distance apart. Just north of Krisoúpolis a small stream leaves a lake and winds its way westwards to reach the sea in the Gulf of Kavalla. Between and around these two channels is the Nestos Delta. Near the coast are a series of brackish lagoons surrounded by bare sandy ground, and on the western shore is a large sandy inlet backed by extensive marshland. Inland there are meadows with reedy channels forming an ideal feeding ground for herons. Little egret and squacco heron are generally to be seen and breeding birds include the diminutive fan-tailed warbler and rare spur-winged plover. The latter has spread from Asiatic Turkey and first bred in Greece in 1960. It can now be found at several places along this coast and could be looked for at any suitable area in the Balkans. The Nestos is a good place for Dalmatian pelican and ruddy shelduck. Thasos is mountainous and has breeding white-tailed eagle, black-eared wheatear, bee-eater, abundant hoopoe, and olivaceous warbler. Anyone working the Nestos with a few days in hand should have a good time on the island.

SUMMER: Dalmatian pelican, ruddy shelduck, little egret, squacco heron, glossy ibis, ferruginous duck, marsh harrier, spur-winged plover, pratincole, roller, tawny pipit, fan-tailed warbler, short-toed lark.

AUTUMN: red-footed falcon, waders, terns, Audouin's gull, bee-eater.

The main area is along the road from Krisoúpolis to Keramoti which is the colourful port for Thasos and an excellent headquarters. Just north of Keramoti are some lagoons on the eastern side of the road. Another road runs northwards just outside Keramoti to Pegai and this is rewarding where it crosses the minor river. Walk along the banks. The other approach to the delta is to stop on the E5 east of Kavalla where the delta begins and the road leaves the sea. Pylons cross the road at this point. A sea wall runs southward for 2 km and gives excellent views over the marshy areas to the east. This part holds many harriers, glossy ibis, and fan-tailed warbler at different times of the year. There are 'buses from Kavalla and accommodation there would fit in very well with a quick autumn visit, which should include the town rubbish dump. This is by the coast and the main road to the east of Kavalla, and is the unsalubrious haunt of Audouin's gull. There are boats from Kavalla to Thasos and one could return on the ferry to Keramoti where there is a camp site.

## CENTRAL PELOPONNESOS

The best approach to the mountains and forests of the Peloponnesos is a tour between Olympia, just 22 km in from Pyrgos on the west coast, and Vytina in Arcadia, which is just about in the centre. Around Olympia, worth a visit for its spectacular ruins and good museum, are Scop's owl, bee-eater, short-toed and calandra larks, tawny pipit, Bonelli's warbler, and golden oriole, while to the north the oakwoods at Kapellis, once the best deciduous stand in the Peloponnesos if not the whole of Greece, have breeding middle-spotted and white-backed woodpeckers, and 'half-collared flycatcher'. Higher still around Vytina in or above any of the coniferous forests there are Bonelli's, golden, and short-toed eagles, nightjar, rock bunting, and many other of the commoner birds of further north.

From November to April Lake Takka, just south of Tripolis, has open water and large numbers of duck including ferruginous. Lake Stymphalía, is reached by turning south at Kiáton near Corinth. Black-necked grebe, little bittern, night and squacco herons, glossy ibis, harriers, lesser kestrel and waders are all more or less regularly present. Blue rock thrush and sombre tit are resident, the latter at the northern end of the lake. There is a good hotel at Kastania on the paved road over the pass to the west into the next valley of the Pheneós. For the ambitious, continuing from there along the dirt road over the next pass towards Zaroúchla gives the best access to the land above the timberline at Mt Chelmós just to the west. Here there are shore lark, dipper – in the outlet of the Styx – Alpine accentor, and ortolan bunting.

SUMMER: Bonelli's eagle, golden eagle, short-toed eagle, Scop's owl, blue rock thrush, white-backed woodpecker, sombre tit, bee-eater, short-toed lark, calandra lark, shore lark, tawny pipit, collared flycatcher, Bonelli's warbler, Alpine accentor, ortolan bunting, golden oriole.

SPRING: black-necked grebe, little bittern, night heron, squacco heron, glossy ibis, hen harrier, marsh harrier, lesser kestrel, little ringed plover, great reed warbler.

Corinth is the obvious starting place for a trip to the Peloponnesos and a tour from there through the centre of the island to the west coast at Pyrgos, returning via Argos should produce many of the 124 species that breed on the 'island'.

## PORTO LÁGO

Porto Lágo is a village lying on a sand spit between a large lake and the sea. The lake is connected to the sea by two sluices and is not really very good for birds, and fortunately the village is not an exciting tourist spot. Nevertheless Porto Lágo is one of the most famous names in recent Greek ornithology. The bird areas are salt pans, the shore and some fresh water lagoons, together with the surrounding flat grassy land which is almost bare. The four principle areas are the salt pans 2 km west of the village immediately north of the E5 and clearly visible from it; a further area of salt pans due south of the first group but situated by the coast; the coast itself especially adjacent to the salt pans and particularly where the generally shallow muddy shore runs out in spits; and the lagoons south of the road immediately east of Porto Lágo village.

Breeding birds include Kentish plover, stone curlew, Caspian tern, and a variety of smaller birds including fan-tailed warbler. There is always a chance of spur-winged plover. During passage periods the area is quite outstanding and an unrivalled place for waders. Marsh sandpipers are common, broad-billed sandpipers frequent, and terek sandpipers sometimes occur. Temminck's stints and curlew sandpipers are everywhere. Slender-billed and

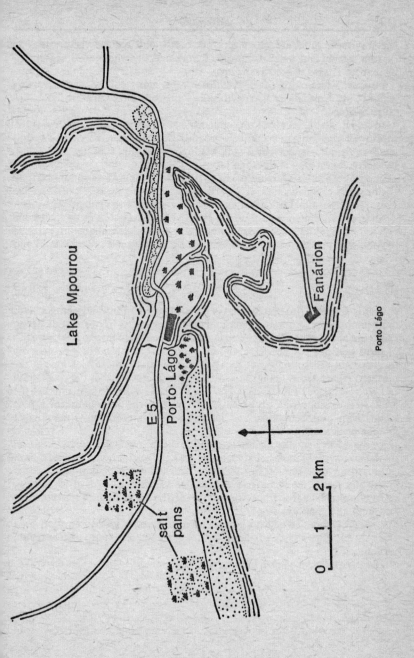

Lake Mpourou

E 5

Porto Lágo

salt pans

Fanárion

Porto Lágo

2 km

0    1    2

Mediterranean gulls are often very numerous, and regular visitors include raptors, Dalmatian pelican, squacco heron, and the white-tailed eagles that fly in from Thasos to feed at the lake.

SUMMER: white-tailed eagle, Kentish plover, stone curlew, avocet, black-winged stilt, Caspian tern, crested lark, short-toed lark, calandra lark, fan-tailed warbler.

AUTUMN: Dalmatian pelican, squacco heron, spoonbill, Bonelli's eagle, short-toed eagle, marsh sandpiper, broad-billed sandpiper, Temminck's stint, terek sandpiper, slender-billed gull, Mediterranean gull, Caspian tern, roller, bee-eater, lesser grey shrike, fan-tailed warbler.

The whole area is of free access and each of the four areas should be fully explored. In particular it is well worth walking the entire length of shoreline from the western end of the salines to the sluice near the village. There is a small area of conifers to the south of the village near the quay that some visitors have found interesting. Camping is unrestricted almost everywhere (try the west end of the village) though the nearest hotels are at Xanthi and Komotini.


## PYRGOS

Pyrgos is centrally situated in what is probably the best bird-watching area in the Peloponnesos. A series of coastal lagoons separated from the sea by long sand bars and surrounded by extensive swamps and pine forests hold a wealth of birds that has not yet been fully investigated. Lake Mouria is reached by turning right just before Pyros to Ágios Ioannis and is most profitable at the northern end. Lake Agoulinítsa can be scanned directly from the road south of Pyrgos. The spa of Kaíapha offers little, but just before the sign a turn to the right, towards the sea, leads at least 8 km northwards through excellent pine woods with brush, swamps, and Lake Agoulinítsa eventually on the right and the open shore on the left.

To the north a smaller lagoon is joined to the sea through a narrow channel to the south of Manolas. Its shoreline and the surrounding marshes have produced an excellent variety of species including Dalmatian pelican and glossy ibis. Leave the main road at Lechaina to the south side of the lagoon, or alternatively take a track westwards off the main road 7 km north of Lechaina at the 50 km stone.

SUMMER: Dalmatian pelican, glossy ibis, purple heron, little egret, short-toed eagle, black kite, roller, calandra lark, Cetti's warbler, fan-tailed warbler, penduline tit.

There is a camp site north of Pyrgos at Kourouta.

# Holland

1 Biesbosch
2 De Hoge Veluwe and
  Het Veluwezoom
3 Naardermeer
4 Nieuwkoop and
  Botshol Lakes
5 Oostelijk Flevoland
6 Rhine Delta
7 Texel
8 Vlieland
9 Westzaan Reserve and
  Alkmaardermeer
10 Zwanenwater
11 Zwartemeer

AMSTERDAM

ROTTERDAM

NEDERLANDSE VERENIGING TOT BERSCHERMING VAN VOGELS,
De Ruyterkade 100, Amsterdam.

VERENIGING TOT BEHOUD VAN NATUURMONUMENTEN IN NEDERLAND,
Herengracht 540, Amsterdam.

READ: *Avifauna van Nederland* (1962) by K. H. Voous *et al.* in *Ardea* 50, pp
1–103.


## BIESBOSCH

This area of low lying pastureland lies south-east of Rotterdam between the
Nieuwe Merwede and the Bergsche Maas as they join to form the Hollandsch
Diep. The maze of dykes, walls, and tidal creeks becomes an intricate pattern
of islands and saltings in the south, and is one of the best bird-watching areas
in the country. In particular it is a ringing centre and is much frequented by
Dutch aficionados and the rarity brigade. Breeding birds include avocet and
night heron but in spring and autumn the area is outstanding for passage
waders with Kentish plover, spotted redshank, etc. It is a major staging post
for wildfowl including huge numbers of greylag and especially white-fronted
geese, many of which stay for the winter. With the completion of the delta
works this area will gradually become fresh with most interesting results.
See the section on the Rhine Delta.
    SUMMER: avocet, night heron, terns, waders.
    AUTUMN: avocet, Kentish plover, spotted redshank, wood sandpiper, green
sandpiper, curlew sandpiper, white-fronted goose, greylag goose, wigeon,
pintail, rarities.
    WINTER: wildfowl, waders, harriers.
    Cross the bridge over the Nieuwe Merwede near Goringchem and turn
westwards along the southern bank of that river. There are many small roads
southwards linking the islands and the 'main' road continues almost to the
confluence of the two rivers. *En route* from the north in summer there is a
stork's nest just east of Molenaarsgraaf in the Alblasser Ward.


## DE HOGE VELUWE AND HET VELUWEZOOM

Though bird-watchers often refer loosely to the sandy forest area between
Arnhem and the Ijsselmeer as the Veluwezoom it is as well to be clear as to
what the name really refers. In fact there are three quite distinct areas that are
worth distinguishing in this general area which consists of a varying wooded
landscape with some very impressive old pine forests. If all three have the same
birds it does not mean that a trip to one is a substitute for visits to the others.
They are quite excellent places with very good birds.

1.  **De Hoge Veluwe:** a 'private' national park administered by a foundation
aided by the Dutch government and covering 14,500 acres to the north-west

of Arnhem. The park can be entered at the following places, Otterlo, Hoenderloo, Schaarsbergen, Oud-Reemst, and at the main entrance along the Otterlo–Hoenderloo road. There are large areas of heath with pines, birches, and a variety of deciduous trees. Mammals include moufflon, wild boar, and red and roe deer. The birds are typical of the area with goshawk, black woodpecker, and great grey shrike the most obvious attractions.

**2. Het Veluwezoom:** a similar area to the north-east of Arnhem covering 9,750 acres administered by the Vereniging tot Behoud van Natuurmonumenten, Herengracht 540, Amsterdam. Though there are roads through the area many of the tracks are kept in a rough state to discourage cars. The habitats and birds are similar to the Hoge Veluwe.

**3. Putten and the Hulshorst woods:** in the north near Harderwijk are similar if inferior examples of the same habitats. A quick visit enables most of the typical birds to be seen. This is ideal for the polder-watcher.

SUMMER: goshawk, sparrowhawk, buzzard, Montagu's harrier, hobby, black grouse, woodcock, curlew, long-eared owl, black woodpecker, wryneck, great grey shrike, golden oriole, crested tit, tawny pipit, short-toed treecreeper, redstart, wood warbler.

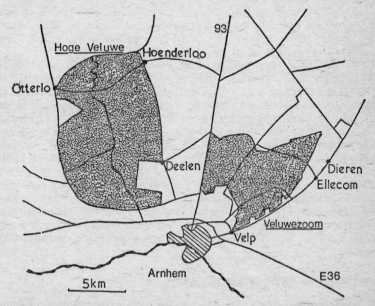

Hoge Veluwe and Veluwezoom, showing the relative position of these two important forest areas near Arnhem.

## NAARDERMEER

The lake of Naarden lies 10 miles south-east of Amsterdam and is the oldest and most famous nature reserve in the Netherlands. It covers 1,842 acres on both sides of the Amsterdam–Amersfoort railway and is probably the most visited reserve in the country. Most of the other lakes in the area are the result of human peat digging activities but Naardermeer is a natural lake that has twice been reclaimed and was finally preserved by its purchase by Natuur-monumenten in 1906. The lake is surrounded by alder and willow fen and large reed beds while at the eastern end there is a working decoy that is used for ringing studies. The area holds one of the richest bird populations in a country that has itself an enviable ornithological reputation. There are two colonies of spoonbills here and, with the exception of the dune colonies on Texel and at Zwanenwater, no others nearer than the Neusiedlersee in eastern Austria. Similarly the colonies of purple herons here and in a few other Dutch localities are hundreds of miles away from the nearest breeding colonies in the Dombes in France. The reserve also holds the largest colony of cormor-ants in the country and a wealth of marsh birds including marsh harrier, bittern, little bittern, red-crested pochard, black tern, great reed and Savi's warblers, and bearded tit.

SUMMER: spoonbill, purple heron, grey heron, bittern, little bittern, cormor-ant, garganey, pochard, red-crested pochard, marsh harrier, hobby, black tern, golden oriole, bearded tit, grasshopper warbler, sedge warbler, reed warbler, Savi's warbler, great reed warbler, icterine warbler.

Visit is by permit only available from Vereniging tot Behoud van Natuur-monumenten in Nederland, Herengradt 540, Amsterdam-C (phone 020–246212), on weekdays during office hours 09:00 to 12:30 and 14:00 to 17:00 hours. Applications should preferably be made two weeks in advance and offer alternative dates as access is by rowing boat on a three or six hour trip. Visitors must pay the boatman's wages—not excessive. There are only a limited number of trips on Sundays. The trip to the spoonbill and heron colonies passes along canals and across smaller lakes and is good for birds all the way.

By car, take the Amersfoort road from Amsterdam and turn right sign-posted Muiderberg just before a viaduct some 3 km after crossing the river Vecht. Instead of joining the viaduct turn right again and continue parallel with the main road. After 1 km turn right again to the fisherman's house, Visserij. By bus alight at 'halte viaduct Googweg' and follow car instructions on foot.

## NIEUWKOOP AND BOTSHOL LAKES

These shallow lakes lie 17 km apart to the south of Amsterdam, while the same distance to the west lies a further group consisting of Westeinderplassen,

Braasemermeer, and Kagerplassen. Nieuwkoop is the larger and is reed-fringed with considerable areas of open water. It lies to the south of the village and the best part of the lake is the extreme south-western corner. This is one of the most reliable spots to see little bitterns. There are a large number of other breeding birds including common bittern, purple heron (a large colony is found at the reserve of Slikkendam), marsh harrier, several terns and duck, and a variety of warblers including Savi's and great reed.

Botshol is the smallest of a group of lakes and lies immediately east of the village of Waver. It has similar birds to Nieuwkoop, with the added attraction of red-crested pochard, but is rather more reedy and overgrown.

SUMMER: little bittern, bittern, purple heron, garganey, red-crested pochard, marsh harrier, black tern, common tern, grasshopper warbler, Savi's warbler, marsh warbler, great reed warbler, icterine warbler.

Nieuwkoop village lies on the west side of the lake. Boats are available to the south-western part. Botshol lies west of the E9 road south of Amsterdam and is best approached via the village of Waver.

## OOSTELIJK FLEVOLAND

The enclosing of the former Zuiderzee in 1932 and the creation of a huge shallow inland lake the Ijsselmeer has changed the ornithology of a vast area of the Netherlands. Huge reclamation projects are enclosing the various polders all of which are at present at different stages of development. The Noordoostpolder has been completely reclaimed and now consists of rich agricultural land intersected by dykes. Birds are the ordinary meadowland species, though dotterel breed in the neighbourhood of Emmeloord. To the south and separated from it by the Ketelmeer lies Oost-Flevoland. Most of this polder which was separated in 1957 is now agricultural land with dykes, but drainage is not complete and there are huge reed beds and lagoons along the south western dyke. These are gradually becoming smaller though some will be left as wildfowl refuges. Further south lies Zuid-Flevoland which was finally embanked in 1968-9. The process then involved pumping out the water and when muddy, sowing reeds from the air. A vast reedbed was thus created and the birds of this area in the early 1970s were approximately the same as those on the previous polder in the late 1950s. A further polder, the Markerwaard, is in the process of creation and European bird-watchers can look forward to at least a further 15 years of outstanding marshes in this area.

Oost-Flevoland presents three basic habitats: the drained low-lying fields, the lakes that separate it from the mainland, and the marshes. The latter are mainly reed beds with extraordinary numbers of reedy species. Over 500 marsh harriers were shot here in a single season some years ago because they had reached pest proportions, but they are still numerous. Other species include bearded tit, water rail, spotted crake, and many warblers including Savi's. The lagoons hold avocet, commic tern, and visiting spoonbill, while the fields are frequented by black-tailed godwit and ruff. The whole area is excellent for a vast number and variety of breeding duck amongst which red-crested pochard and wigeon are outstanding. The area around Dronten is unique as the below sea-level breeding haunt of dotterel, and the forestry plantation on the Kampen road holds golden oriole and icterine warbler. Lastly the Veluwemeer and Ketelmeer provide frequent close views from good vantage points along the dykes of red-crested pochard, pintail, and visiting

Oostelijk Flevoland

white storks and black terns. Passage can bring regular little gull and occasional gull-billed and Caspian terns, as well as hoards of wildfowl, including thousands of Bewick's swan, greylag, white-fronted and pink-footed geese, and tens of thousands of pintail, wigeon, shoveler, tufted duck, pochard, goldeneye, and scaup.

SUMMER: red-crested pochard, wigeon, shoveler, garganey, pintail, gadwall, greylag goose, marsh harrier, white stork, spoonbill, spotted crake, water rail, dotterel, black-tailed godwit, ruff, avocet, common sandpiper, black tern, commic tern, long-eared owl, blue-headed wagtail, bearded tit, golden oriole, Savi's warbler, icterine warbler.

AUTUMN: waders, little gull, gull-billed tern, Caspian tern, Bewick's swan, greylag goose, pink-footed goose, white-fronted goose, wigeon, pintail, shoveler, tufted duck, pochard, goldeneye.

WINTER: wildfowl.

There are three bridges on to Oost-Flevoland at Kampen, Elburg and Harderwijk. Though most bird-watchers prefer to stay at the latter because of its closeness to the western marshes, Kampen makes an attractive base for the Zwartemeer area as well. The western marshes can be seen from the Harderwijk-Lelystad road along the top of the dyke, and Veluwemeer from the similar road along the northern shore. Dronten lies in the north of the polder. Harderwijk is 50 miles east of Amsterdam by road, and can at present be reached by ferry which could be an ornithologically rewarding journey.

## RHINE DELTA

At the mouth of the Rhine lies a huge expanse of mudbanks, creeks, saltings, islands, fresh marshes and lagoons, and reclaimed pasturage. Immediately to the south and separated from it by only a narrow neck of land lies the similar estuary of the Wester Schelde. The coastline itself is sandy and huge dune systems have been built up leaving several gaps through which the Rhine disgorges.

Behind the dunes and protected from the North Sea tides, large delta islands have been built up and then reclaimed as water-meadows. The arms of the river itself are shallow and uncovered at low water. Like the dunes along the rest of the dutch coast the Delta dunes hold several bird-rich lakes. Those on the island of Voorne, particularly Breede Water and Quackjeswater, are outstanding for breeding waders, duck, grey heron, and notably spoonbill, and are also excellent for passage waders. The shore itself holds Kentish plover. Away from the dunes there are a series of lagoons along the inner edge of the islands with those on the island of Schouwen being excellent for passage waders and breeding avocet. The two other habitats are however the most important and are best during passage and winter periods. The mudflats hold hordes of waders, duck, and thousands of brent and other geese. The grazing lands in autumn and winter represent one of the largest zones of concentration for wildfowl in Europe. All three swans reach four figures, and greylag, white-fronted and bean geese often five figures. Duck, including pintail, wigeon, and shoveler are even more numerous.

Unfortunately (or fortunately) this whole area is going to· be radically changed with the completion of the Delta works currently in progress costing £300 million and due to be finished in 1980. Barrages are to enclose the Haringvliet and Grevelingen completely, and the mouth of the Ooster Schelde will be closed forming a huge inland lake. This will slowly pass through the saline and brackish stages and eventually become fresh. The Veersegat Dam and Grevelingen Dam are already finished. These changes will completely alter the nature of the area and its birds. Perhaps the grey geese will stay finding safe roosts on the offshore banks or the continuing open Wester Schelde. Waders, brent geese, shelduck and other inter-tidal species must decline. But the gains from a fresh marsh of this size should be most exciting and might well prove even more attractive in the future than the draining of the Ijselmeer.

SUMMER: shelduck, spoonbill, grey heron, avocet, little ringed plover, Kentish plover, common tern, Arctic tern, Sandwich tern, little tern.

AUTUMN; WINTER: Bewick's swan, whooper swan, greylag goose, white-fronted goose, bean goose, brent goose, shoveler, pintail, wigeon, harriers, spotted redshank, wood sandpiper, curlew sandpiper, Kentish plover.

Over such a vast area selection or exploration is a necessity. Though the latter is far more rewarding, if selection must be made the following spots are well worth visiting:

1. The barrages at the eastern end of Grevelingen and at either end of Haringvliet.
2. The dunes and lakes of Voorne, particularly Breede Water and Quackjeswater for which the village of Rockanje is a good centre.
3. The lagoons and pools on the southern side of Schouwen.

NB Wildfowl, geese, and waders can be found everywhere.


## TEXEL

Texel is the southernmost of the Friesian islands and lies 80 km north of Amsterdam. It is 15 km by 11 km and with no less than 19 distinct bird reserves is one of the most outstanding bird areas in the sub-continent, and ideal for a full holiday of exploration. Texel was formed by sea, sand, and wind and takes the form of a shallow saucer. In the west and open to the full force of the North Sea a huge marram covered dune system has been built up forming an excellent bathing beach. On the landward side and overlapping onto the adjacent land large mixed forests were planted at the beginning of this century while the dunes themselves contain marshy slacks and lagoons that hold Texel's most interesting birds. The reserves at De Krim and Slufter, De Muy, Westerduinen, De Bollekamer and De Geul hold a wealth of marsh birds including the most northerly regular colony of spoonbills in Europe as well as avocet, black-tailed godwit, and marsh and Montagu's harriers. Inland from the dunes and pines lie extensive grazing marshes intersected by numerous dykes that form a perfect habitat for the extraordinarily numerous black-tailed godwit, redshank and sheep. The centre of the saucer is the Waalenburg area which is very marshy pasture holding black-tailed godwit and especially ruff. Grazing meadows continue to a dyke and sea-wall that protects the coast from the sea. Beyond lie the extensive mudflats of the Waddenzee.

SUMMER: black-necked grebe, bittern, spoonbill, garganey, pintail, shoveler, eider, marsh harrier, Montagu's harrier, water rail, little ringed plover, Kentish plover, black-tailed godwit, ruff, avocet, common gull, commic tern, Sandwich tern, long-eared owl, short-eared owl, blue-headed wagtail, red-backed shrike, stonechat, grasshopper warbler, great reed warbler, marsh warbler, icterine warbler, short-toed treecreeper, siskin, golden oriole.

The following reserves are concentrated in the west of the island amongst the dunes and are owned by the Staatsbosbeheer (State Forest Service). Permits are available from the State Forester's Office, Boswachterij, K52, De Koog ('phone 02228–227). The office is open weekdays 08:30–12:30 hours and Sundays 08:30–09:30. There are two excursions per day and a maximum of 15 persons are allowed per excursion. Book well in advance, and see the map for location.

1.  **Muy:** a small lake set amongst the dunes and probably the most famous of Texel's reserves. There are large reed beds with willow and elder along the shore and on the islands that hold the breeding colonies of spoonbill and grey heron. Marsh and Montagu's harriers quarter the reeds that hold a wealth of warblers, while the water holds an excellent collection of breeding duck. Escorted tours only can be made from March to September.

2.  **Slufter and Krim:** a solitary tidal creek breaking the dune system of the west coast and leading to the salty beach plain of the Slufter known as the desert of Texel. Storms may completely cover the area with salt water. The Krim is the dunes to the north of the area with an access road. The dunes hold a large colony of eiders, while avocet, black-tailed godwits, Kentish plover, and terns breed on the Slufter. This is an excellent site for migrant waders. Escorted tours are only from March to mid-July.

3.  **Westerduinen:** on the coast and important for its colony of breeding herring gulls (about 700 pairs) and common gulls (about 20 pairs), as well as for jackdaw, stock dove, and shelduck all nesting in rabbit holes. Other birds include grasshopper warbler and red-backed shrike. Conducted tours only can be made from mid-April to mid-August.

4.  **Bollenkamer:** a chain of artificial waters lying amongst the dunes and supplying water to the town of Den Hoorn. It consists of the lakes of Noordulak, Grotevlak, Pompevlak, and Wattevlak which hold duck including garganey and many warblers, and the surrounding land which harbours

black-tailed godwit and short-eared owl. The dunes can be entered along many tracks.

5. **Geul:** a reed fringed lake with adjacent lagoons and dunes. It holds a small colony of spoonbills and a rich breeding population of birds including avocet, short-eared owl, black-tailed godwit, marsh and Montagu's harriers, long-eared owl, and herring gull. Conducted tours only can be made from mid-March to mid-September.

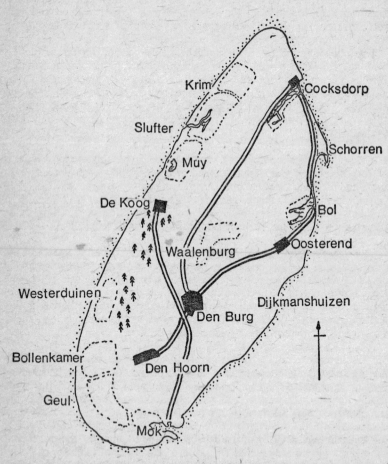

Texel, showing the major reserves. To the east lies the Waddenzee, one of Europe's most outstanding bird areas.

The group of reserves in the east amongst the water meadows and mudflats belong to Natuurmonumenten (Dutch Society for Conservation of Nature Reserves). Permits for individual visitors are available from the warden Mr C. G. Boot, Polderweg 2, De Waal ('phone 02220–2590) between 19:00–20:00 hours. Permits for groups must be arranged with Vereniging tot Behoud van Natuurmonumenten in Nederland, Herengracht 540, Amsterdam-C ('phone 020–246212). As places are limited visits should be arranged well in advance.

6. **Schorren:** a promontory of mudflats and saltmarsh lying outside the island's protective dykes. Breeding birds include colonies of black-head gulls and common terns with avocet, eider, and Kentish plover. The mudflats and especially the Wadden shallows are excellent for migrant waders which are driven on to the promontory and thus close to the observer at high tide. No access permit is required.

7. **Bol:** creeks and an area of low lying meadows. Breeding birds are not special but visitors include spoonbill and avocet, and a wealth of migrant waders including spotted redshank, wood sandpiper, duck, swans, and especially brent geese at high tide. There is limited access but good views from road and dyke.

8. **Dijkmanshuizen:** a carefully controlled wetland with lagoons, reed-beds, and meadows. Amongst a wide variety of breeding birds are avocet, common tern, black-tailed godwit, ruff, and various warblers. It is also a good area for migrating duck and waders. There are some conducted tours but there is a track through the reserve, and the road along the dyke between Oudeschild and Oostereud gives good views of avocet, etc.

9. **Waalenburg:** one of the richest bird-watching areas on Texel. The low lying meadows are flooded in winter and then attract a huge population of wildfowl. Lagoons are left in summer when the breeding birds include black-tailed godwit, ruff, shelduck and shoveler. The reserve is closed but excellent viewing can be had from public roads between De Koog and De Waal.

Amongst a further huge list of places to visit for birds are:

10. **Mokbaai:** an area of mudflats in the south of the island near the ferry harbour particularly good for passage waders.

11. **Petten:** a small lake reserve easily seen from the adjacent road, holding colonies of avocet, common tern, common and black-headed gulls, and a few blue-headed wagtails. It lies just west of Mokbaai.

12. **Cocksdorp:** on the north-east coast. To the north of the town is an area of mudflats with a promontory of salt marsh that is excellent for waders.

Further north near the lighthouse is the best area for watching migration and many rarities have turned up here.

13.   **Dennen:** the largest area of woodland between De Koog and Den Hoorn holding most of the woodland species found on Texel including sparrowhawk, woodcock, long-eared owl, nightingale, icterine warbler, short-toed treecreeper and golden oriole. There are no restrictions on access.

Texel is reached by a frequent and fast car ferry from Den Helder which is reached from Amsterdam by hourly train services.

## VLIELAND

The island of Vlieland lies north of Texel, is smaller, has only one small town, and is generally neglected by foreign bird-watchers. Its structure is basically the same as the better known island with a dune coastline facing the North Sea with a somewhat narrower agricultural and marshland area to the south. Vlieland is thus dominated by sand though there are considerable areas overgrown with heather and planted with conifers. Some of the plantations in the north-east of the island are quite extensive. In the western part of the island there are some neglected polders, several of which are flooded or partially flooded. Though numbers vary, colonies of up to 100 pairs of avocets are found here, and there are several other breeding waders. The reed beds hold the odd pair of marsh harriers, and there are several excellent colonies of eiders, and large colonies of herring gulls.

The extensive mud-banks, notably the Posthuiswaard flats, attract thousands of waders on migration and in winter. These include grey plover, spotted redshank, godwits, and avocet.

SUMMER: eider, shoveler, shelduck, marsh harrier, Montagu's harrier, avocet, curlew, terns, herring gull.

AUTUMN: wigeon, pintail, shoveler, shelduck, harriers, grey plover, spotted redshank, golden plover, black-tailed godwit, avocet.

The main town of Oost Vlieland is in regular ferry contact with Harlingen which can be easily reached from Amsterdam by the exciting road across the dam enclosing the Ijsselmeer.

## WESTZAAN RESERVE AND ALKMAARDERMEER

These wetland areas lie north-west of Amsterdam and make excellent day trips from the city, as do Naardermeer to the south-east, and Botshol and Nieuwkoop to the south. Westzaan lies north of Zaandam and is a wet marshy nature reserve holding black-tailed godwit and other flood meadow species. Alkmaardermeer is a large lake with islands, reeds, and swamps which together with the nearby waterland area of dykes and meadows holds an interesting collection of breeding waders including ruff and black-tailed godwit. Spoonbill are frequent non-breeding visitors to this area.

The area to the south around Jisp and Wormer also has ruff and black-tailed godwit, and a reed bed that holds bittern and both great reed and Savi's warblers. Black tern breed and there is a large colony of common terns.

SUMMER: spoonbill, duck, ruff, black-tailed godwit, redshank, black tern, sedge warbler, reed warbler.

1. After passing northwards through Zaandam turn left to Westzaan. The reserve is north of the road.
2. For Alkmaardermeer turn right to Akersloot between Zaandam and Alkmaar, or take the road round the eastern side of the lake.
3. Jisp and Wormer lie eastwards off the main road at Wormerveer to the north of Zaandam.

## ZWANENWATER

This lake is one of the largest of the Dutch dune lakes that are such a feature of the country's ornithology. It is rich and shallow with a strong growth of reeds and other emergent vegetation. Lying north of Amsterdam it is often overlooked by bird-watchers in their mad race to Den Helder and Texel but it is quite comparable with any other bird area in the Netherlands. Breeding birds include spoonbill and avocet, with Kentish plover along the beach and goldcrests in the pines. It is an outstanding area in autumn when a wide variety of passage waders is present.

Spoonbills are also frequent visitors to the small reserve of Hondsbossche a few kilometres down the coast near Petten. This is an excellent little place and well worth a visit for the dozen or so pairs of avocet, plus other breeding waders including Kentish plover.

SUMMER: spoonbill, garganey, avocet, hobby, goldcrest, woodcock, Kentish plover, common tern, long-eared owl, crested lark, sedge warbler, reed warbler.

Zwanenwater is a reserve lying immediately south of Callantsoog which lies on the coast west of the Alkmaar–Den Helder road. Permits, which are cheap, are available on the spot.

## ZWARTEMEER

Zwartemeer is really an area of the Ijsselmeer extending eastwards between the Noordoostpolder and the mainland north of Zwolle, and providing an outlet for the rivers Zwarte Water and Meppelerdiep. To the north lies the Schinkelland a series of rich shallow lakes and patches of seasonal and permanent swamp. Most have a considerable growth of emergent vegetation and there are some large areas of reeds. Breeding birds include purple heron, red-crested pochard, garganey, shoveler, marsh and Montagu's harriers, black tern, and the usual warblers and rails. Autumn and winter are excellent for duck.

SUMMER: purple heron, white stork, cormorant, red-crested pochard, garganey, shoveler, water rail, Montagu's harrier, black tern, sedge warbler, reed warbler, great reed warbler, Savi's warbler, bearded tit.

Zwartemeer is worth a close inspection and the vast reed beds along the edges are excellent for warblers. The lakes of Vollenhover, Beulakerwijde and Belterwijde are easy to work from the roads that cross them and the Boven-wijde and area to the north are reasonably accessible by road. There are white storks on a traditional platform in the village of Grafhorst just north-east of Kampen.

# Hungary

1 Bakony Hills
2 Balatonelle
3 Budapest
4 Csákvar
5 Hortobagy

6 Kisbalaton
7 Ócsa Forest
8 Sasér Reserve
9 Sodium Lakes of the
      Danube-Tisza Plain
10 Lake Velence

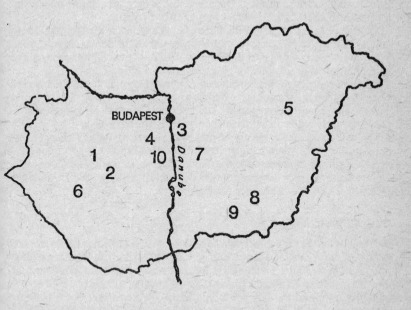

HUNGARIAN INSTITUTE OF ORNITHOLOGY,
Garas u.14, Budapest 11.

NATURE CONSERVANCY OFFICE,
Egyetem tér 5, Budapest V.

READ: *Aves-Madarak* (1958) by A. Keve *et al*: *Nomenclator Avium Hungariae* (1960) by A. Keve.

## BAKONY HILLS

The Bakony Hills run parallel with the northern shore of Lake Balaton and continue to the north as the Vértes Hills. They are of gentle gradient rising to between 1,200 and 1,800 ft, and are in the main wooded. One of the most interesting areas is in the south around Sümeg where the beech woods to the north of the town hold some interesting woodland birds. These include Syrian and middle spotted woodpeckers and serin, while in the town itself there are rock thrushes around the ruined tower on the hill. To the south-west near Bazsi is another ruin at Tatika. The beech woods here are a nature reserve and a haunt of black woodpecker and red-breasted flycatcher.

Though not strictly part of the hill avifauna anyone in the area should not fail to examine the fish ponds on the western side of the Sümeg-Tapolca road. These are typical of this part of Hungary and hold great white heron, purple heron and other species, many of which breed.

SUMMER: white stork, great white heron, purple heron, little bittern, buzzard, black tern, black woodpecker, middle spotted woodpecker, Syrian woodpecker, grey-headed woodpecker, gooden oriole, crested lark, rock thrush, black redstart, red-breasted flycatcher, icterine warbler, serin.

The woodland areas are easy to find and one merely needs to keep an eye open on the right when coming from Sümeg to Tapolca for the ponds. A permit might be necessary for the Tatika reserve; contact The Council for Nature Conservation, Egyetem tér 5, Budapest V. Many visitors work this area while staying in Keszthely for Kisbalaton.

## BALATONELLE

Balatonelle lies on the southern shore of Lake Balaton which is the largest lake in western and central Europe and covers 640 sq km. It is also the most important resort area of Hungary and not really worth the bird-watcher's attention. Instead he should concentrate his efforts on the wonderful reserve at Kisbalaton, and the fish ponds and marshy lagoons that occur here and there around the shore. Of these the most important are the fish ponds 6 km south of Balatonelle. They are reed and sedge fringed with some quite extensive reed beds that hold bearded tit and great reed warbler. Herons are not numerous: the most likely species is the little bittern, but both Baillon's and

little crakes are present and all three marsh terns can be found. Ferruginous
duck are often present in large numbers.

SUMMER: black-necked grebe, little bittern, ferruginous duck, Baillon's
crake, little crake, whiskered tern, black tern, white-winged black tern,
common tern, ruff, bearded tit, great reed warbler, Savi's warbler, red-
backed shrike.

Balatonelle lies roughly half way along the southern shore of Lake Balaton
on route 1. Turn southwards on route 67 to the ponds. There are many hotels
and camp sites to choose from around Balaton.

## BUDAPEST

Varosliget is a park in central Budapest. It is much the same as any other city
centre park in any other country in Europe. Though there are the usual
fountains and statues it is perhaps rather more wooded than some. For the
time-pressed tourist the park is an ideal and convenient spot to pick up many
typically Hungarian species in a brief excursion. The birds of the area include
Syrian woodpecker, icterine warbler, golden oriole, hoopoe, collared flycatcher (numerous) and serin. Not bad for a walk in the local park!

The second area near Budapest for those who have no time for birds in
Hungary or who have a spare day, is the Buda Hills to the north-west of the
city. These steep carstic but well wooded hills give excellent views over Budapest and are an excellent bird-watching area. Chances of seeing the breeding
eagle owl must be slim but the collection of great, spotted, middle-spotted,
Syrian, green and black woodpeckers is worth looking for, and both collared
and red-breasted flycatchers can be found. A warning in this respect must be
given, as migrant pied flycatchers are easy to confuse with collared and are
frequently present well into the breeding season.

SUMMER: **Varosliget Park:** Syrian woodpecker, wryneck, golden oriole, hoopoe, crested lark, collared flycatcher, wood warbler, icterine warbler, serin.
**Buda Hills:** eagle owl, great-spotted woodpecker, middle-spotted
woodpecker, Syrian woodpecker, green woodpecker, black woodpecker,
wryneck, golden oriole, hoopoe, rock thrush, red-breasted flycatcher, collared
flycatcher, hawfinch, ortolan bunting.

Varosliget Park is of straightforward access from the city centre and is
marked on all tourist maps. The Buda Hills lie immediately outside the city
limits and are easily reached by public transport. A walk to the top and general
exploration is advised.

## CSÁKVAR

Csákvar is 25 km north of Székesfehérvár to the west of Budapest. It lies in
the flat grassland landscape that one thinks of as typical of the Hungarian
plain, and is noted as one of the few remaining strongholds of steppe type
birds. Outstanding amongst these is the great bustard, but these birds are

under great pressure and are not easy to find. Rather more common are stone curlew, and the whole plain is alive with skylarks and tawny pipits. The golden barrenness of the steppe is interrupted here and there by odd oaks, by marshy areas containing perhaps the odd Baillon's crake, and by the disused bauxite quarries of Csákvar. These provide a broken rocky landscape and introduce species like the rock thrush into an otherwise unsuitable area. They also provide bee-eaters with breeding cliffs, and are a frequent haunt of imperial eagles.

Away to the north are the Vértes Hills with their thick covering of oaks, and magnificent views over the adjacent plain. These too are noted as a haunt of imperial eagle, several pairs of which breed. There are also most of the other woodland birds of this part of the country including a good range of woodpeckers and the interesting flycatchers. The other major attraction of the hills is the saker falcon which breeds and can often be seen from a high viewpoint.

SUMMER: imperial eagle, Baillon's crake, stone curlew, great bustard, rock thrush, bee-eater, roller, hoopoe, lesser grey shrike, middle spotted woodpecker, tawny pipit.

Leave Budapest westwards on the E5 and turn southwards to Csákvar. There are roads in several directions across the plain that provide a good chance of great bustard. There are several routes across and into the Vértes Hills to the north but exploration on foot is best. Do not omit the disused bauxite quarries. These are State property and can be entered by permit obtained from The Director of State Properties, Budapest V, Kossuth Lajos ter 11.

## HORTOBAGY

This area of the Hungarian plain is one of the most famous ornithological spots in an exceptionally bird-rich country. Were it not for post-war travel restrictions there is no doubt that the European bird-watcher would be listing the Puszta Hortobagy along with his list of Camargue, Coto, and Lapland as the sub-continent's outstanding bird haunts. Basically the area is steppe, but there are areas of marsh, pasture, woodland and ponds. An excellent steppe area lies immediately east of Hortobagy along the road to Debrecen. The plains are here interrupted by marshy areas that attract many interesting species including greylags, garganey and pratincole, as well as by the more typical birds of the steppe such as great bustard, short-toed lark, and tawny pipit. This area is also excellent for raptors including short-toed eagle and red-footed falcon.

To the north-west of Hortobagy are a series of the fish ponds that are so characteristic of Hungary. These are shallow lakes bordered by rushes and reeds and with a varying growth of willow. They are used to breed fish for food in an inland country that is otherwise unable to obtain this form of protein. The ponds are state property and a great deal of toleration is shown to the birds of the area which are of exceptional interest. Amongst the duck, ferruginous are the most interesting but the breeding herons include spoonbill, little bittern, little egret, squacco, purple and night herons. Black storks are seen and white-winged black terns hawk over the pools and penduline tits breed along the ditches. There are many other fish ponds around this area that are worth exploring and which hold other species including great white heron. In winter there are many geese here, though not the 100,000 of pre-war days.

SUMMER: greylag goose, garganey, gadwall, ferruginous duck, spoonbill, little bittern, little egret, squacco heron, night heron, purple heron, black stork, saker falcon, buzzard, hobby, short-toed eagle, red-footed falcon, marsh harrier, black-tailed godwit, great bustard, pratincole, white-winged black tern, golden oriole, hoopoe, penduline tit, tawny pipit, short-toed lark.

The steppe is state farm and though many of the marshes and most of the birds can be seen from roads and tracks, permits can be obtained from The Director of State Properties, Kossuth Lajos ter 11, Budapest, V. The same office issues permits to visit the fish ponds and in this case for good bird-watching such permits are highly recommended. Many can, however, be seen from roads and tracks quite adequately.

Debrecen is the nearest accommodation centre though the peasant restaurant in Hortobagy has delighted many visiting bird-watchers with its five-course dinner.

## KISBALATON

Though Lake Balaton is so huge only the south western area at Kisbalaton (Little Balaton) is of any real ornithological importance. But this area around the 8,600 acre reserve, covering in all perhaps 13,000 acres, is outstanding even by Hungarian standards and is one of Europe's most important wetlands. At one time there was considerable area of open water but encroaching vegetation has turned almost the whole area save only a small pool into a single vast reed-bed. Red sedge grows here and nowhere else in Europe. There are some areas of willows that stand high above the reeds and are the site of a large colony of cormorants. Many trees have been killed by these birds and now form vantage points for the herons of the area. The reserve is bisected by the River Zala which then continues into Lake Balaton between dykes. Kisbalaton holds three important species, other than the cormorant, that are not found at the other outstanding marsh area at Lake Velence, the squacco and night herons, and the little egret. Both great white heron and spoonbill breed more numerously than at Velence though the former is still very much on the danger list. Most of the other specialities are also reedy species including three species of crake to be listened for on summer evenings, a variety of warblers including Savi's, moustached, and marsh, the odd pair of greylag geese, marsh harrier, and perhaps the occasional glossy ibis.

The surrounding land is mainly agricultural with the usual sprinkling of interesting birds, though perhaps the penduline tit which is found on the marsh edge and along the overgrown ditches is most worth searching for. Golden oriole, lesser grey shrike, icterine and barred warblers complete the scene.

SUMMER: white stork, purple heron, great white heron, little egret, squacco heron, night heron, spoonbill, glossy ibis, pintail, garganey, shoveler, gadwall, ferruginous duck, greylag goose, marsh harrier, little crake, spotted crake, Baillon's crake, long-eared owl, nightjar, golden oriole, lesser grey shrike, penduline tit, Savi's warbler, moustached warbler, icterine warbler, barred warbler.

Kisbalaton is a nature reserve and access is strictly by permit only. These are obtainable from The Council for Nature Conservation, Egyetem tér 5, Budapest V, and guided tours go up the River Zala from the lake. It is possible, however, to walk eastwards along the banks from the bridge that crosses the river just north of Kisbalaton village. Most herons are seen in the occasional clearings amongst the reeds.

## ÓCSA FOREST

This interesting area lies 25 km south of Budapest to the east of the Danube. On one side of the road lies an area of water-meadows with lagoons and patches of reeds bisected by a track running along the top of a dyke and bordered by poplars. This holds golden orioles, roller, lesser grey shrike and more characteristically marsh and Montagu's harriers, and black-tailed godwit. Red-footed falcons are sometimes seen. The Forest proper lies on the other side of the road and being likewise low-lying is very wet. It is a seemingly impenetrable jungle of ash and alder with some stands of oak and is a nature reserve most famous for wild boar, tree frogs, spider's webs, mosquitos, and river warblers. The latter here find ideal conditions and are comparatively common. The commonest woodpecker is the Syrian and both lesser and red-backed shrikes are numerous around the edges. Amongst a vast collection of interesting birds lesser spotted eagle, saker falcon and goshawk are the most interesting, if elusive, to the visitor.

SUMMER: lesser spotted eagle, goshawk, black kite, marsh harrier, saker falcon, Montagu's harrier, hobby, red-footed falcon, Baillon's crake, black-tailed godwit, roller, golden oriole, Syrian woodpecker, lesser-grey shrike, red-backed shrike, river warbler.

Ócsa is a reserve and can be entered by permit obtained from The Council for Nature Conservation, Egyetem tér 5, Budapest V. The area can, however, be fully worked from the road and tracks and the best chance of raptors is undoubtedly to wait for them to soar over the area. There is a military camp in the area and foreign bird-watchers should use discretion.

## SASÉR RESERVE

The reserve at Sasér is an 150-acre island in the River Tizsa to the west of

Hódmezövásárhely which is north-east of Szeged. It is the centre of the
marshy area to the north and south along the river and has poplar and salix
woods that are one of the best heronries in the south of Hungary. Night
herons are dominant with up to 150 pairs but they are followed by little egret
(60–70 pairs), squacco heron (30 pairs), and grey heron (30 pairs). Cattle
egrets have summered here every year in the last few years, and pygmy
cormorants do so exceptionally. Duck breed and so in many years do white-
tailed eagles. The area is regularly flooded and the marsh meadows are an
important area for migrant waders and waterfowl. Naturally the surrounding
land holds most of Hungary's regular birds including corncrake, quail, and
barred warbler.

SUMMER: pygmy cormorant(?), little egret, night heron, squacco heron,
grey heron, cattle egret, white-tailed eagle, corncrake, quail, lesser grey
shrike, roller, barred warbler.

Sasér is best visited from Szeged when working the sodium lakes area.
It can be entered with a permit from The Council for Nature Conservation,
Egyetem tér 5, Budapest V.

## SODIUM LAKES OF THE DANUBE – TISZA PLAIN

Between the Danube and Tisza to the south of Budapest lie a series of unique
alkaline sodawater lakes. In particular the area between Szeged and Kecskemét has a great concentration, though there is another large group to the west
of Kecskemét, which is Hungary's fruit farming centre. The water level is
entirely dependent on rainfall and many ponds are almost dried up in summer.
Maps tend to show either very few or a great many waters and though not
exactly correct the latter are to be preferred from an ornithological point of
view. The most famous of these lakes is Lake Fehértó which though part of
the Szeged-Fehértó reserve has been extensively modified by the construction
of fish ponds and by huge settling beds for the extraction of soda. At one time
this was one of the principal wintering haunts of white-fronted geese and
with them red-breasted geese, but these flocks have now diminished and the
red-breasted goose in Hungary is reduced to only a few wintering individuals.
Nevertheless the lake remains one of the best spots for breeding marsh birds
including the exceptionally numerous little bittern, and penduline tit. The
large colony of black-headed gulls contains a few pairs of Mediterranean gulls,
a species that is extending its range to the north-west at present. To the north
near Kecskemét, the Szivós lakes are an excellent example, and hold breeding
avocet, black-winged stilt, Kentish plover, and a gull colony. Many of the
lakes apart from Fehértó have been turned into commercial fisheries with
little but a few rushes around the edges. Others remain alternately wet and
dry with large reed beds, and hold bittern, little bittern, purple heron, ferruginous duck and a good variety of other species including white-winged black
tern. Lesser grey shrike, roller, and hoopoe breed in the surrounding areas
which include pasture, cereals, and sunflower seeds. During migration

thousands of waders pass through the area including whimbrel and Temminck's and little stints.

SUMMER: black-necked grebe, bittern, little bittern, purple heron, white stork, ferruginous duck, greylag goose, marsh harrier, avocet, black-tailed godwit, Kentish plover, black-headed gull, Mediterranean gull, white-winged black tern, spotted crake, crested lark, penduline tit, lesser grey shrike, roller, hoopoe.

AUTUMN: whimbrel, Temminck's stint, little stint, ruff.

The area to the east of the Kecskemét–Szeged road is the best and many of the lakes can be seen from roads and tracks. They vary so immensely from season to season that a list of names is virtually useless – a good map is the key. The Szivós lakes are recommended. The reserve at Szeged-Fehértó can be entered by permit available from The Council for Nature Conservation, Egyetem tér 5, Budapest V. There is a reserve hut and a bird observation tower. Szeged is the obvious place to stay though Kecskemét is noted for its beautiful buildings.


## LAKE VELENCE

Lake Velence covers ten and a half square miles and is thus quite small when compared with nearby Balaton. It lies 50 km south-west of Budapest but as one of the country's primary bird haunts merits a section on its own rather than just a day trip from the capital. It is a shallow lake surrounded by reeds which in some places form extensive beds. The open water with duck and hawking black terns can be seen from nearby hills while marsh and Montagu's harriers hunt over the reed beds. These are densest at the western end of the lake where the famous great white herons and spoonbills breed. Both of these species can easily be seen almost anywhere around the lake and their breeding sites should not be disturbed. The reeds also hold purple heron, little bittern, little crake, and a wealth of warblers including great reed, Savi's, moustached, and marsh. Though no longer breeding, the glossy ibis is sometimes seen.

Between the main Budapest–Szekesfehervar road and the lake lie the Dinnyes marshes centred on the quaint village of that name. These marshes are an important feeding ground for the birds of the lake but are also an important breeding ground in their own right including ruff, black-tailed godwit and white-spotted bluethroat. The odd trees hold lesser grey shrike, golden oriole, and roller, while the usual harriers and duck are easy to see. A small pond near the village well is a little gem. Black terns are almost always present and the reedy fringe has great reed and moustached warblers.

The surrounding farmland and countryside boasts an excellent selection of birds including barred warbler, bee-eater, and quail, and almost every village has a pair of white storks.

SUMMER: white stork, purple heron, great white heron, spoonbill, little bittern, glossy ibis, ferruginous duck, pintail, garganey, greylag goose, marsh harrier, Montagu's harrier, buzzard, little crake, water rail, ruff, black-tailed godwit, black tern, common tern, quail, roller, bee-eater, hoopoe, golden oriole, bearded tit, lesser grey shrike, bluethroat, great reed warbler, Savi's warbler, moustached warbler, marsh warbler, barred warbler.

Access around the edges of the lake is generally free and unrestricted and the nearby hills enable most of the water to be seen. The Dinnyes marshes can be explored from a rough track that runs in a loop from the main road on the southern side of the lake. The pond is right in the village itself. The lake, at least the western end with breeding herons, is a nature reserve. Permits for guided tours are available from The Council for Nature Conservation, Egyetem tér 5, Budapest V.

There is a small inn with six rooms at Gardony, and first class camping sites at Agard and Velence.

# Iceland

1 Grimsey
2 Huna Floi
3 Myvatn
4 North-western Peninsula

5 Reykjavik
6 Snaefellsnes Peninsula
7 Thingvallavatn
8 Westmann Islands

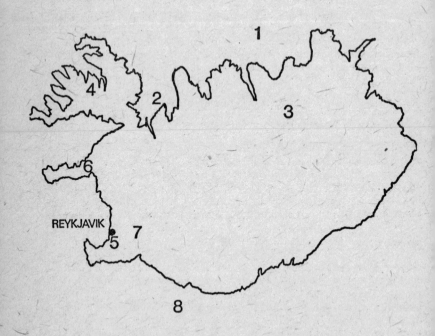

READ: *Die Vögel Islands* (1938–1949), by G. Timmerman (in German).

## GRIMSEY

The island of Grimsey is the most northerly point of Iceland, liable to vol-canic disturbance, and lies fairly and squarely on the Arctic Circle off the north coast. It is less than 4 km long and half as wide and is the permanent home of a hardy breed of shepherds, fishermen, and bird-catchers. This is particularly significant for otherwise Grimsey would be another of those bird-paradise islands that beckon so many and are attained by so few. The island boasts thirty-six nesting species including the last of Iceland's little auks. Numbers were recently down to four pairs and the species may well be extinct by now. This is probably due to amelioration of the climate rather than perse-cution, for the Icelanders have enforced strict measures to protect this bird at its last stand in the country. Though it will be Iceland's loss little auks are so incredibly numerous at Jan Mayen and other Arctic strongholds that the loss is only an inconvenience to bird-watchers. Visitors cannot expect to see little auks in Iceland.

There are, however, vast colonies of other auks on Grimsey including Brunnich's guillemot and puffins, over 8,000 of which were formerly taken annually without any ill effect. Kittiwake and fulmar breed on the cliffs, the latter which includes the rare blue phase is the oldest known colony in the world (1640). Inland red-necked phalaropes frequent the pools and snow buntings are said to be abundant. Gannets bred but apparently do so no longer, the nearest colonies being the Skrudur Islands and the Raudinupur headland.

SUMMER: fulmar, razorbill, guillemot, Brunnich's guillemot, puffin, little auk, kittiwake, red-necked phalarope, snow bunting, raven.

Access to Grimsey is reasonably regular by boat from Akureyri, which is in daily contact with Reykjavik by plane, 'bus, and boat. Accommodation might be possible to arrange in private houses but local enquiries in Akureyri should be made before any trip. Camping is, of course, comparatively straightforward.

## HUNA FLOI

Huna Floi is typical of the valleys of the north coast of Iceland and has been chosen because of its central position on the Hunafloi on the road between the two areas most frequented by visiting bird-watchers. This is not to say that it lacks attractions of its own though its birds can on the whole be found at any of the other major fjords along this coast. At the head of the fjord is an ex-tensive green area of low lying marshland and saline lagoons intersected by various river channels with fresh ponds and bogs. Mountains rise steeply in the east to 2,500 feet. Out towards the fjord mouth, and of easy access by road, are cliffs with razorbill, puffin, guillemot, and fulmar. The guillemots are mainly Brunnich's and the fulmars include one in a hundred of the blue phase. In the marshes eiders are common though they are most frequently seen on the fjord and lagoons together with the non-breeding specialities of the area, Iceland gull (which does not breed in Iceland) and king eider. Other non-breeders that are frequently seen here in early summer are pinkfeet and barnacle geese *en route* to their breeding grounds. The greylag goose however breeds in the marshes as do whooper swans. The usual north Iceland birds are found on the sides of the hills and great northern divers breed on some of the remoter waters.

SUMMER: great northern diver, eider, king eider, scoter, greylag goose, pink-footed goose, barnacle goose, whooper swan, purple sandpiper, whimbrel, golden plover, Iceland gull, glaucous gull, guillemot, Brunnich's guillemot, razorbill, puffin, kittiwake, fulmar.

Huna Floi can be reached by bus from Reykjavik and Akureyri daily, and by regular boats from the same places. Blonduos is the ideal centre on the fjord with roads running in all directions. The roads to Svinavatn is particularly worth a bird-watcher's attention though the road southwards to Reykjavik is also excellent. There are two hotels in Blonduos, the Kvennaskolinn and the Hotel Blonduos, both of which are quite reasonable. This is an excellent area and an ideal stop between Snaefellsnes and Myvatn.


## MYVATN

It is, of course, unthinkable that any one should go to Iceland for birds without visiting Myvatn, but it comes as a surprise that no one visiting Iceland for any reason whatsoever should miss a trip to this northern lake. There is no area of comparable size in the country that is so interesting from a vulcanological point of view. Five km east lies the Namafjall area with its solfataras, or bubbling muddy sulphur pools, an incredibly colourful sight. The whole area is split into narrow strips by faults and fissures and littered with volcanoes of a multitude of types and shapes, from the explosion crater Ludent visible from the hill at the entrance of Dimmuborgir, to ring-wall crater Hverfjall – best seen halfway between Myvatn and Dimmuborgir.

Myvatn is set in a landscape of lava flows and is incredibly indented so that long-distance views are almost unattainable within its basic 8 km × 10 km framework. It is the third largest lake in Iceland and is nowhere much deeper than 12 feet. It has been called the bird-watchers' Mecca because there is no larger concentration of breeding ducks in Europe. Reliable estimates put the number of duck at the end of the breeding season at something like 150,000. Three species of duck are American birds and can be found nowhere else in Europe. The harlequin and Barrow's goldeneye have long been famous but a recent addition in the past few years has been the American wigeon breeding in Europe for the first time. Another bird found nowhere else in Europe is the great northern diver which prefers the more remote upland lakes but which is frequently noted amongst the throng on Myvatn. Fifteen species of duck breed of which scaup is the commonest, and in 1959, 15,000 eggs were taken from a single island.

Sandvatn to the north-west has birch scrub that are the only trees for miles. Duck are numerous here too, including the American species, and there is more likelihood of seeing the magnificent gyr falcon here than at Myvatn. Apart from duck there are perhaps 200 pairs of Slavonian grebes, and thousands of Arctic terns and red-necked phalaropes in the area as a whole.

Graenavatn are the marshes at the southern end of the lake and are handy to explore from Skutustadhir. Greylag, merlin, and the usual waders, are found here, and pinkfeet are frequent passage migrants. Dimmuborgir is a likely area for gyr falcon as well as a vantage point for crater gazing. Incidentally though 'my' is Icelandic for 'fly' there are no mosquitoes in Iceland.

SUMMER: great northern diver, red-throated diver, Slavonian grebe, whooper swan, greylag goose, mallard, teal, gadwall, wigeon, American wigeon, pintail, shoveler, pochard, tufted duck, scaup, scoter, harlequin, long-tailed duck, Barrow's goldeneye, goosander, gyr falcon, Arctic tern, red-necked phalarope.

Myvatn is not the place for a day trip and any visitor will do his own exploration of the area. The following will be on his list:

1. The Laxa River seen west of Myvatn when approaching or leaving the area is a most reliable place for the harlequin that are found only on swiftly flowing streams of this nature. It is also a good place for Barrow's goldeneye.
2. The Marshes at the north-western corner.
3. Sandvatn to the north-west.
4. The Lava Fields, Craters, and Sulphur Pools to the east.

Accommodation is available at two hotels in Reykjahlidh the Reynihlio and Reykjahlio which is slightly cheaper. There is a summer hostel and youth hostel at Skutustadhir where the post office has a few beds.

There are buses every day from Akureyri from mid-June to the end of August. Akureyri is in daily contact with Reykjavik by bus, plane (2–3 flights a day), and boat. The latter is an excellent way of seeing the exciting and relatively little known north-west peninsula.

# NORTH-WESTERN PENINSULA

The remote north-western corner of Iceland is almost cut off by the extensions of the Breidafjord and Hunafloi. It is a harsh, mountainous and rugged landscape that because of its inhospitality and inaccessibility has remained the stronghold of the two famous Icelandic birds of prey, the gyr falcon and the white-tailed eagle. Its deeply indented fjord coastline rises steeply from the sea to a plateau at about 2,500 feet and gives rise to a vast range of cliffs that are occupied by huge colonies of seabirds. Notable are the auks with puffin, razorbill and guillemot being joined by Brunnich's guillemot and a

few non-breeding little auks. Another regular non-breeding summer visitor is
the king eider, but one should remember that the North Cape of the peninsula
is only a few kilometres from the Arctic Circle. The cliffs also hold large
numbers of fulmars about one in a hundred of which is of the blue phase.
Other seabirds include shearwaters, but these are most often seen from ships
while travelling to and from the area.

Most of the rivers that run into the fjords have created little deltas at their
mouths. These are excellent for birds and many hold eider, Arctic tern, red-
necked phalarope, and other waders. The higher slopes hold purple sandpipers
but they are very difficult birds to find.

SUMMER: great northern diver, red-throated diver, Slavonian grebe, whooper
swan, king eider, eider, long-tailed duck, Barrow's goldeneye, white-tailed
eagle, gyr falcon, merlin, harlequin, whimbrel, golden plover, red-necked
phalarope, purple sandpiper, Arctic skua, Arctic tern, glaucous gull, guillemot,
Brunnich's guillemot, razorbill, puffin, little auk, ptarmigan, snow bunting.

The peninsula is remote and harsh and needs mountain experience and
ability to 'rough it' to get the best out of it. Really it is almost expedition
country but it is possible to get to Isafjordhur by bus, plane, and ship. As so
much of the area is difficult of access a mixture of boat in and bus out would
enable an excellent section of the country to be seen. Indeed using buses,
stops could be made at a whole succession of villages along the southern
shore of the largest sea inlet. For those who could not stand either journey
there are planes every weekday from Reykjavik. No matter how one arrives a
boat trip up the fjords and out to the north-western coast is an essential for
seeing seabirds. For accommodation the National Tourist Board in Iceland is
very helpful.

# REYKJAVIK

All journeys to and from Iceland inevitably start and end in Reykjavik and
most travellers have a day at the start and/or end of a trip to spend sightseeing
in the town. Ornithologists in such situations are notorious philistines and will
probably want to go bird-watching. Reykjavik not only has several convenient
places for birds but also has a speciality if not of its own then at least confined
to this corner of the country. The grey phalarope is the fifth American species
found in Iceland and nowhere else in Europe but it is not a numerous bird and
visitors have been disappointed at not finding them at one of the four places
that they breed. The nearest to Reykjavik are at Midhnes and Gerdhar but
they can also be found being tossed around on the waves at Stokkseyri. There
is, however, no need to travel so far from the town for bird-watching. There
is an eider colony at Alftanes, and an auk colony including a few Brunnich's
guillemots at Hafnarbjorg. The park lake, Lake Tjornin, in the centre of
Reykjavik has an island with a large colony of Arctic terns, red-necked
phalarope, and a wide variety of duck. The Seltjarnarnes peninsula near
the golf course is an unfrequented haunt of many breeding birds including a

colony of Arctic terns that give the golfers hell. There are rocks and weed along the shore and two interesting lagoons that hold summering non-breeders like turnstone, purple sandpiper, glaucous gull and red-necked phalarope.

SUMMER: red-breasted merganser, red-necked phalarope, grey phalarope, redshank, turnstone, purple sandpiper, ringed plover, glaucous gull, kittiwake, Arctic tern, guillemot, Brunnich's guillemot, razorbill.

Gerdhar and Midhnes lie on the peninsula 30 km west of Reykjavik at the south-western corner of Iceland and can be reached by bus. Most of the other places are shown on a decent map of the town surrounds. There are many hotels of varying price and comfort, and cars can be hired by the day. There is a summer youth hostel.

There are two other trips from Reykjavik that should be mentioned one of which fills a spare day rather well. These are to Kulusuk near Angmagsalik on the eastern coast of Greenland by air for a day, and to the west coast at Narssarssuag for a four-day trip. Details from National Tourist Offices.

## SNAEFELLSNES PENINSULA

This area lies on the west coast to the north of Reykjavik and amongst those that know, Snaefellsnes is as famous as Myvatn, though for totally different reasons. Snaefellsjokull itself rises nearly 5,000 feet straight from the sea and is a now defunct volcano that dominates the scenery of the area, and incidentally the scene of Jules Vernes' *Journey to the Centre of the Earth*. Most of the south side of the peninsula consists of rather boring lava flows though there are areas of sandstone that make good seabird cliffs. This area is noted as the most accessible area for Brunnich's guillemots this side of the Atlantic, and as a breeding haunt of other auks, gulls, and fulmar. There is also a good chance of a gyr falcon. The best cliff is at Malarrif on the south-western tip of Snaefellsnes.

The north coast is scenically more interesting with sandy lagoons rocky shores, and a multitude of offshore islands many of which are good for birds without holding any species that cannot be seen easier elsewhere. It is the coast of two species basically, the glaucous gull and the white-tailed eagle. The gull is quite numerous along this coast with fifteen breeding colonies, but the white-tailed eagle is down to ten pairs in the whole of Iceland, all in the Breidafjordur area and the north-west peninsula. The decline of this magnificent bird is taken very seriously by the Icelanders who attempt to keep disturbance to a minimum. There is a hefty fine for photographing either gyr falcon or the sea eagle at the nest, and even a shot of an eyrie could technically be an offence!

Inland the usual Icelandic species include whooper swan, greylag, whimbrel, golden plover, ptarmigan, and snow bunting, with divers on appropriate lakes.

SUMMER: divers, fulmar, whooper swan, greylag goose, white-tailed eagle, gyr falcon, glaucous gull, Brunnich's guillemot, guillemot, razorbill, puffin, black guillemot, Arctic skua, Arctic tern, ptarmigan, golden plover, whimbrel, snow bunting.

There are roads round the perimeter of the peninsula and across the middle enabling the whole area to be thoroughly explored. On the south coast where the cliffs are the major attraction especially in the south-west, the following are likely places: Bulhahaaun, Stapi, Londrangar, Rif and Olafsvik. On the north coast the road is as good a place as any for seeing the specialities. Boats to the bird islands leave from Stykkisholmur.

There are hotels at Budhir, Hotel Budhir, and at Stykkisholmur, and there are buses three times a week on alternate days from Reykjavik.

## THINGVALLAVATN

Thingvallavatn is the largest lake in Iceland and lies 40 km east of Reykjavik in an attractive landscape of mountains and lava flows covered by rich vegetation. Lying on the road to Geysir, where the Great Geysir gave its name to all other geysirs in the world, and being the scene of the foundation of the Icelandic open air parliament in 930 a.d., Thingvallavatn is on every tour list out of Reykjavik. It is a marshy area reminiscent of parts of the European mainland and one is not, therefore, surprised to find breeding black-tailed godwits, though Iceland is this species' furthest north in the world. The great northern diver breeds here and the rivers running into the lake on the eastern side are fast flowing and hold harlequin duck. Perhaps Thingvallavatn is not as good as Myvatn but there are two of the species found nowhere else in Europe; even Barrow's goldeneye turn up sometimes to make a third. The other birds of the area include several species of duck, golden plover, whimbrel, Arctic tern, ptarmigan, and snow bunting. It is also acknowledged to be one of the best areas in Iceland for gyr falcon.

SUMMER: great northern diver, whooper swan, goosander, harlequin duck, tufted duck, scaup, Barrow's goldeneye, greylag goose, gyr falcon, merlin, black-tailed godwit, whimbrel, golden plover, Arctic tern, ptarmigan, snow bunting.

The lake can be easily explored from the road though there are no restrictions on access to any part of the area.

The Hotel Valholl in Thingvellir is not expensive and there are buses every day from Reykjavik. One can, as almost everywhere in Iceland, camp 'wild'.

## WESTMANN ISLANDS

The Westmann Islands lie off the south coast of Iceland and are one of the most important seabird haunts in Europe. The group consists of twenty mainly volcanic lumps though only the 5 km long Heimaey is of any size and holds any people. The island of Surtsey lies to the south-west of Westmann and has been burning since its emergence from the sea in 1963. Planes to

Reykjavik from Britain and other European countries fly over this new island as do those from the capital to Westmann.

The islands are the only Icelandic breeding locality for Manx shearwater, Leach's petrel, and storm petrel, though the nocturnal habits of all three are not exactly conducive to easy bird-watching. Nevertheless, shearwaters can be seen in the early summer on the sea prior to coming ashore in the evenings. More obvious are the gannetries on four of the outlying islands and these birds are frequently seen about the group. Five species of auk breed including a few Brunnich's guillemots (the dominant guillemot further north in Iceland) and enormous numbers of puffins that have been exploited by the islanders to the tune of 50,000 birds per annum without apparent harmful effect. The bird cliffs are truly one of the outstanding sights in European ornithology.

Many other birds breed including the usual Icelandic waders and great skua and glaucous gull.

SUMMER: gannet, cormorant, shag, Manx shearwater, Leach's petrel, storm-petrel, fulmar, guillemot, Brunnich's guillemot, black guillemot, razorbill, puffin, glaucous gull, kittiwake, great skua.

Heimaey can be reached by plane from Reykjavik every day, and by boat on alternate days. There are also boats regularly from Stokkseyri.

There is a hotel and many homes take people in, but beware of visits coinciding with the local festival when every bed will be taken. The island of Ellidaey has a comfortably furnished hut for overnighting fishermen that can be used. Travel within the group is simple to arrange on Heimaey though chartering is the rule.

# Ireland

IRISH SOCIETY FOR THE PROTECTION OF BIRDS,
21 Merrion Square, Dublin 2 (Eire)

ROYAL SOCIETY FOR THE PROTECTION OF BIRDS,
58 High Street, Newtownards (Northern Ireland)

READ: *Ireland's Birds* (1967) by R. F. Ruttledge.

## AKEAGH LOUGH

Akeagh Lough is the only stretch of permanent fresh water in northern Kerry, but this by itself does not mean very much. What it does mean is that it is also one of the nearest stretches of fresh water to North America. Akeagh Lough lies behind the sand dune beach at the head of Ballyheighe Bay to the south of Kerry Head. It is a shallow water of 6–7 acres normally, but sometimes almost dries up in summer. It is set in a flat landscape and a slight change in water level affects its size considerably. Its marshy surrounds are grassy and typical of those favoured by ruff, while there are also considerable areas of reeds. It is noted as the Irish stronghold of gadwall, and other duck occur according to the water level. It is, however, its position 'across the sea' from America that has brought Akeagh ornithological fame as the eastern 'home' of Nearctic waders. Pectoral sandpipers are annual visitors and others have included killdeer, lesser golden plover, dowitcher, least sandpiper, Baird's sandpiper, white-rumped sandpiper, and western sandpiper. American duck sometimes turn up as well and of course, many interesting Palearctic birds occur too.

AUTUMN: ruff, little stint, greenshank, rarities.

Akeagh Lough, which is private property, lies south of Ballyheighe village and can be best looked over from route 105 which passes it on the landward side.

## CAPE CLEAR ISLAND

Cape Clear lies at the very south of Ireland with only Fastnet rock beyond. The bird observatory was established in 1959 by a band of enthusiastic amateurs and has continued to function on a purely amateur basis ever since. Though it was established to study migration, emphasis in the late 1950s was on passerines, and particularly on night migrants, drift, and all that. It was, of course, an excellent place for an observatory at the south-western tip of Ireland and many rarities have turned up to prove the pioneers right. Cape Clear does not attract vast numbers of migrants and doubtless interest would have lapsed had it not been for the discovery that there were large movements of seabirds to be seen offshore. So started the craze for sea-watching that has since spread infectiously through British ornithology and is now being followed elsewhere in Europe. Every autumn sees observers perched on the southern points of Cape Clear such as Pointanbullig, Blananarragaun, and Pointabullaun for hours at a time watching and counting the migrations (if that is what they are!) of a wide variety of seabirds. The outstanding birds are sooty, great and Cory's shearwaters. Until Cape really got going all three, and particularly the last two, were considered rare off British coasts, yet in mid-September 1965 no less than 5,000 great shearwaters were identified in a single day. This was exceptional but the average observer with a two-week autumn holiday should see something of these birds. Other regulars include storm petrel, Manx shearwater in vast numbers, fulmar, gannet, great skua, and all the common gulls, terns, auks, and sea-duck. Rarities have included black-browed albatross, little shearwater and some petrels that might well be Wilson's petrel.

Passerines do not get ignored but might get overlooked. There is little ringing but a number of birds like icterine and melodious warblers, and red-breasted flycatcher turn up every autumn. The breeding birds are not exciting but do include chough and black guillemot.

SPRING: seabirds.

AUTUMN: great shearwater, Cory's shearwater, sooty shearwater, Manx shearwater, fulmar, storm petrel, gannet, scoter, great skua, kittiwake, terns, puffin, guillemot, razorbill.

Cape Clear is reached from Baltimore by mailboat. Baltimore is reached by bus or car service from Cork, which is in turn reached from Dublin, Fishguard, etc. Accommodation may be available on the island, but would-be visitors should make arrangements well in advance. Camping is usually staightforward and food is available. Contact the BTO if serious migration studies are planned.

## DUBLIN BAY

The celebrated River Liffey reaches the sea via central Dublin and Dublin Bay beyond. The shallow waters here are one of Ireland's principal bird haunts, and being adjacent to the city are ideal for the casual visitor. There are five areas that are particularly important:

1. **Howth Peninsula:** the cliffs here are impressive scenically, hold fulmar, guillemot, razorbill, black guillemot, and rock dove, and are easy to get at and see the birds.

2. **Bull Island:** just off the northern suburbs of Dublin it is a low sandy island 3 km long and about 1 km offshore. It is connected to the mainland by two causeways from the middle and southern end and has two golf courses and a vast sandy beach that attracts many week-end bathers. Between the island and the mainland is a huge inter-tidal mud bank that holds a wintering flock of 400 pale-breasted brent geese. This area is also excellent for a wide variety of wintering duck and waders including greenshank. The northern part of the

island is one of the few places in Ireland that regularly has snow buntings and there is also the occasional Lapland bunting. Passage brings many waders including spotted redshank and bar-tailed godwit.

3. **Dun Laoghaire Harbour:** the harbour to the south of Dublin is a favourite winter haunt of sea-duck, divers especially red-throated and great northern, and purple sandpipers at East Pier.

4. **Ireland's Eye:** a small offshore island with the same breeding seabirds as the Howth cliffs, plus a small colony of puffins.

5. **Lambay:** a larger island further out to sea. It has the same breeding seabirds but in the larger numbers that are a part of the experience of seeing these birds.

SUMMER: fulmar, razorbill, guillemot, black guillemot, rock dove.

PASSAGE: spotted redshank, snow bunting, short-eared owl.

WINTER: great northern diver, brent goose, pintail, wigeon, shoveler, goldeneye, merganser, long-tailed duck, bar-tailed godwit, knot, greenshank, kittiwake, short-eared owl.

Route 86 out of Dublin leads to Howth, and Bull Island and Dun Laoghaire can be found with almost any map. Boats to Ireland's Eye can be obtained at Howth Harbour. Lambay Island is owned by Lord Revelstoke and permission to land must be obtained through The Steward, Lambay Island, Rush, Co. Dublin. Rush is the usual point of departure. There is plenty of accommodation of great variety in Dublin.

## LOUGH ERNE

This area lies in County Fermanagh in north-western Ireland and consists of two large lakes Lower and Upper Lough Erne. Both have a wealth of islands, though at the southern end of the Upper Lough it is difficult to decide whether there are more islands or more water. The surrounding land and most of the islands are wooded and form an important breeding ground for many species of birds. In particular they are the only regular breeding haunt of common scoter in Ireland with about 50 pairs in 1954. In an effort to preserve and increase this number the Royal Society for the Protection of Birds has established reserves at Horse Island and Duck Island in Lower Lough Erne. Both tufted duck and merganser also breed. Other breeding birds on the islands are black-headed and common gulls, and in some years Sandwich terns, with garden warblers around the Lough Shores. Up to 50 whooper swans winter with occasional geese, and several species of duck.

SUMMER: tufted duck, red-breasted merganser, scoter, black-headed gull, common gull, Sandwich tern, garden warbler.

WINTER: whooper swan, duck.

There are a maze of roads by which to explore this area, and Enniskillen is an excellent base between the two Loughs.

## KERRY ISLANDS

The westernmost points of the British Isles are a collection of small largely uninhabited islands off the coast of County Kerry. They lie in three groups as continuations of the peninsulas separated by Dingle Bay and the Kenmare river. Nobody can tell you how many birds there are here but all species of breeding British seabirds, with the exception only of Leach's petrel, are found. Even Leach's petrel might breed though conclusive proof is at present lacking. The islands have romantic-sounding names and part of their attraction lies in the manner of reaching them by fishing boat from the charming western Ireland fishing villages. The islands are:

Northern group
  1. Inishtooskert: storm petrel, Manx shearwater.
  2. Inishtearaght: large colonies of storm petrel, Manx shearwater, puffin.
  3. Inishabro: storm petrel, Manx shearwater, fulmar.
  4. Inishvickillane: large colonies of storm petrel, Manx shearwater, with fulmar, puffin, razorbill.
Middle group
  5. Puffin Island: 20,000 Manx shearwater, fulmar, puffin.
  6. Little Skellig: 20,000 gannet (second only to St Kilda in British Isles).
  7. Great Skellig: storm petrel, Manx shearwater.
Southern group
  8. Bull Rock (actually in Cork): 500 gannet, kittiwake, razorbill.
Figures represent breeding pairs.

It is possible to charter boats from the adjacent fishing villages, price by negotiation. Remember that petrels and shearwaters are only about at night, and that unless you intend to camp and stay for several days it is as well to choose one of the islands where birds, like auks and gannets, can be seen during the day. Landing is difficult and really unnecessary, but can be a marvellous holiday for ringers, etc, who organise thoroughly. Camping on the Blaskets is prohibited except on Great Blasket.

## LOUGH NEAGH

Lough Neagh is 25 km long by 17 km wide and covers nearly 100,000 acres. It lies inland from Belfast and is the blank rectangle on maps showing the breeding distribution of many birds in Britain. It is vast, unmanageable, and incredibly rich. The north, as a sort of appendix, is Lough Beg covering a mere 1,700 acres but an important area nevertheless. The loughs are shallow reed-fringed especially at Lurgan on the southern shore, and the haunt of vast numbers of wildfowl. Indeed, there are no satisfactory estimates of the number of birds wintering here though 30,000 tufted duck have been counted, with 28,000 pochard, 4,000 goldeneye, 1,000 scaup, 350 whooper and 50 Bewick's swans. There are perhaps 500 pairs of tufted breeding together with vast numbers of great crested grebe. American duck and waders turn up regularly in winter and passage periods.

Lough Beg lies on the river Bann to the north of Lough Neagh. It is a shallow lake with a winter flood area to the west, several parts of which are permanent water. The largest of these is known locally as Oystercatcher Pool and is a favoured haunt of rare birds particularly American waders. Dowitcher, yellowlegs, and buff-breasted sandpiper have all been seen. Here too there are large flocks of duck in winter including wigeon and pintail as well as the diving duck. The southern shore has been extensively excavated for sand and some of the pits are flooded. They are extensively overgrown and are a good place for passerines and hold breeding colonies of black-headed gulls and common terns.

SUMMER: great crested grebe, tufted duck, black-headed gull, common tern.

WINTER: great crested grebe, tufted duck, pochard, goldeneye, scaup, red-breasted merganser, whooper swan, Bewick's swan.

AUTUMN: waders, rarities.

There are roads all round Lough Neagh which can be thoroughly explored. The water can be very rough in winter and it is as well to remember that duck too prefer a sheltered shore. Lough Beg, which is private property, is best approached from the west off route 182.

## STRANGFORD LOUGH

Strangford Lough is a sea lough south-east of Belfast that empties out at low tide exposing a huge expanse of mud. The western shore has many low islands and these form an ample resting ground for the large numbers of waders that use Strangford in winter and on passage. The sea outside the lough is also worth a look with regular sea-duck and divers. Amongst the wintering waders knot and bar-tailed godwit are the most interesting though a few greenshank are regularly present.

Wildfowl are, however, the major attraction and the lough holds up to 3,500 brent geese, and 12,000 wigeon. The Downpatrick marshes to the south hold a decreasing flock of 300 greylags, and increasing whitefronts (250). Scaup, goldeneye, merganser, and scoter all winter, sometimes in large numbers, and there are always great northern and red-throated divers to be seen. The usual wader species occur on passage and as in most other large Irish waters, American birds turn up with some regularity. In summer the lough is a haunt of breeding terns, black-headed gull, and duck including merganser.

SUMMER: red-breasted merganser, shelduck, black-headed gull, Arctic tern, Sandwich tern.

WINTER: great northern diver, red-throated diver, brent goose, white-fronted goose, greylag goose, wigeon, tufted duck, scaup, goldeneye, red-breasted merganser, scoter, knot, bar-tailed godwit, greenshank.

PASSAGE: spotted redshank, curlew sandpiper.

The usual way of working this area is to go south down the coast and north along the lough. It is a long walk but more manageable by car southwards on the A2 and northwards on the A20. It makes a nice round trip from Belfast.

## WEXFORD SLOBS

The North and South Slobs of Wexford Harbour are the most celebrated bird haunt in all Ireland. Basically they are an area of saltmarsh and reclaimed pasture land particularly liable to flooding and the winter haunt of 6,000 Greenland whitefronts and 4,000 brent. They lie at the south-eastern corner of Ireland. The North Slob consists of meadows intersected by salt creeks and likely to flood, a dune and marram area, and the muddy harbour itself. In spite of reclamation the latter is still a vast mud bank at low tide. To the south the Slob is dominated by a marshy channel fringed with reeds running down the middle and the huge dune coastline which extends northwards to Rosslare Point. This is a scrubby area that is particularly noted for migrants and is generally considered to be the best area for passage waders.

Though there are more whitefronts on the North Slob this area is private and inaccesible and visitors should work the South Slob (also private but accessible in parts) which nevertheless has several thousand of these birds. It is also the most likely area for rarities which in this part of the world means American waders. These are of almost annual occurrence. Apart from the two dominant geese there are always the odd barnacles, greylags, and pinkfeet each winter, and recently there has been a snow goose every year. Both wild swans occur, the whooper regularly, and there is a wide variety of duck including a peak of 3,000 scaup. Wintering waders include a flock of up to 3,000 black-tailed godwit, though a great variety of these birds is present during passage periods.

The Slobs are not a dead place in summer. Three species of tern breed on a small island at the harbour entrance, along with several duck, and tree sparrow. This is one of the few places in Ireland that the latter is found. They frequent ruins exclusively in sight of the sea.

SUMMER: teal, terns, sedge warbler, tree sparrow.

AUTUMN: whimbrel, curlew sandpiper, ruff, black-tailed godwit, spotted redshank, American waders.

WINTER: Slavonian grebe, brent goose, white-fronted goose, pink-footed goose, greylag goose, wigeon, pintail, shoveler, scaup, goldeneye, red-breasted merganser, whooper swan, black-tailed godwit.

The South Slob is reached from route 8 south of Wexford. Turn left to Rosslare past Killinick and continue to Burrow which is a good starting point and one of the best spots. There is accommodation in Wexford which overlooks the harbour with views of brent geese and waders.

## SOUTH WEXFORD

On the south coast of County Wexford and not far from the Wexford Slobs is a series of excellent bird habitats that cater for all the needs of bird-watchers at all seasons. At the extreme south-east is Carnsore Point which has low cliffs and is an excellent vantage point for sea-watching for Manx shearwater and auks. To the west is Lady's Island Lake which is a very shallow inlet with muddy corners much favoured by waders. Ruff, little stint, and curlew sandpiper are frequent on autumn passage and it is also a likely place for black tern and little gull. This is the only place in Ireland for turtle dove and is a regular place for spring oddities like hoopoe. Tacumshin Lake lies further west and is a shallow inlet with hordes of waders. Grey plover, bar-tailed godwit, and greenshank winter and there are many more on passage. Up to 200 brent appear here in the later part of the winter. In summer it holds Sandwich and little terns.

Further west still lie the Gull and Bannow Bays. Both have extensive mudflats which are the haunt of wigeon, shelduck, and many waders. A flock of brent frequent Bannow Bay and spotted redshank use the Cull. Offshore lies Great Saltee a low cliff-fringed island packed with auks, kittiwakes, fulmars, and a small colony of gannets. Manx shearwaters also breed. Saltee is a good place for migration and while the island was inhabited was the site of a bird observatory. It boasted the usual migrations of passerines, falls of night migrants, rarities, and sea-bird movements. Those who want to look at sea birds are better off elsewhere.

All of these areas are reached from Wexford. There is a track to Carnsore Point, but most of the other places involve a certain amount of walking. Saltee can be seen from boats out of Kilmore Quay, and camping trips can be arranged.

# Italy

1 Abruzzi National Park
2 Capri
3 Valli di Comacchio
4 Gargano Peninsula
5 Gran Paradiso National Park
6 Greggio
7 Orbetello
8 Oristano
9 San Giuliano Lake
10 Venetian Lagoons

ROME

ASSOCIAZIONE ORNITOLOGICA ITALIANA,
via Belfiore 11, Milan.

LEGA NAZIONALE CONTRA DISTRUZIONE DI UCELLI,
Lungarno Guiccardini 9, Firenze.

READ: *Elenco degli uccelli italiani* (1945) by E. Moltoni.

## ABRUZZI NATIONAL PARK

The Abruzzi is an area of rugged mountain peaks and lush green valleys 100
km east of Rome. It embraces some of the highest peaks in the Appenines
rising to almost 7,000 feet. The area is a surprising contrast to the bare, dry,
scrubby land that is so typical of much of the Mediterranean area. In the
valleys there are 'Alpine' pastures with bushes and small deciduous trees, and
quite a large area is covered by deciduous forests. In summer the Park offers
pleasant relief to the often oppressive heat of the lowlands. The mountains
frequently have bare precipitous peaks, and there are some fine gorges. In
the flatter places at high altitude above the tree line there are areas of barren
ground with sparse dry grass.

The bird population of the woodlands tend to be reminiscent of similar
areas in England. Nuthatch, marsh tit, blackbird, chaffinch and buzzard are
typical species, and it is only the odd middle-spotted woodpecker that reminds
one that this is Italy. The more open parts have the very common red-backed
shrike. Higher up, the steep rocky areas have blue rock thrush and black
redstart with Alpine chough, lesser kestrel and crag martin overhead. The
fine gorge north of Scanno is an excellent and easily accessible spot for these
birds. The bare open hillsides at this height have several of the same species
but with the addition of tawny and water pipits. Higher still there are Alpine
accentor and possibly snow finch. The Park is noted for bear and chamois.

SUMMER: buzzard, lesser kestrel, Alpine chough, chough, middle-spotted
woodpecker, crag martin, tawny pipit, water pipit, blue rock thrush, black
redstart, red-backed shrike, marsh tit, Alpine accentor, snow finch.

The park is of unrestricted access and a number of roads and motorable
tracks facilitate exploration. Pescasseroli on route 83 has 3 hotels and 3
pensions and is an ideal base. Amongst the places definitely worth a visit are
the *Chamoiserie* near Villetta Barrea which has woods and meadows and a
road leading to a mountain ampitheatre allegedly good for chamois; the gorge
north of Scanno; and the high openlands particularly along the Anversa
d'Abruzzi–Pescina road. Camping is allowed throughout the Park area.

## CAPRI

Apart from being one of the outstanding tourist attractions on the Italian
coast Capri is also the site of a splendid and enterprising Swedish bird

observatory. It was started in the spring of 1956 at headquarters provided by the San Michele Foundation (see *The Story of San Michele* by Axel Munthe) and has operated a ringing station every spring and some autumns since. Capri is a small rocky island 6 km by 2 km, rising to a maximum of 1,800 feet, immediately south of Naples. It is covered by macchia, olive groves, vineyards, and some pine woods and is notoriously poor in breeding species. Migrants, however, are often exceedingly numerous and in the tenth century the local bishop was known as the Bishop of Quails because he existed almost exclusively on dues collected from the catching of these birds. The observatory functions in a 12 acre oasis established as a sanctuary by Axel Munthe in the 1920s, and catches large numbers of birds for ringing. Amongst the most interesting regular species are nightjar, hoopoe, the very numerous golden oriole, black-eared wheatear, redstart, nightingale, vast numbers of icterine warblers (melodious are very rare) and garden warblers, wood warbler, flycatchers including a sprinkling of collared, woodchat, serin, and Italian sparrow. Honey buzzard and black kite pass through in spring and there are a sprinkling of records of Egyptian vulture, and the odd eagle.

SPRING: black kite, honey buzzard, Egyptian vulture, hoopoe, golden oriole, black-eared wheatear, icterine warbler, collared flycatcher, serin, Italian sparrow.

AUTUMN: migrants.

The observatory has accommodation for only four workers and this is fully occupied by the staff in April and May. There are both cheap and expensive hotels in Anacapri which is near the observatory. There is no 'good' place for migrants and when the circumstances are right the island is literally flooded with birds. During busy mornings the observatory do not appreciate visits by bird-watchers but then birds can be found easily without help. At other times the staff can be quite helpful – though remember they have a job to do. Capri is ¾ hour by boat from Sorrento and 1½ hours from Naples with its international airport. Bona fide research workers wishing to work on Capri should contact Carl Edelstam, Naturhistoriska Riksmuseet, Vertebratavdelningen, 104 05 Stockholm 50, Sweden.


## VALLI DI COMACCHIO

At the head of the Adriatic on the northern and western shores of the Golfo di Venézia lies a huge delta area and series of lagoons similar to those that extend westwards along the coast of Languedoc from the delta of the Rhône. The most famous of these is the Laguna Venéta with Venice perched on one of its marshy inner islands. In many ways the southernmost of these lagoons, the Valli di Comacchio, is also the best for birds. It is a vast water separated from the sea, and with a significant inflow of fresh water the salinity varies from very high to merely brackish. In the seaward area salinity is as high as 46 per cent. The surrounding land is in many places marshy and often broken by smaller lagoons. The area is exceptionally rich ornithologically and in winter probably holds upwards of 50,000 birds. The flock of up to 30,000 pochard is particularly important but other species are well represented. Passage brings many waders, while this is an important breeding site for black-winged stilt, avocet, pratincole, and several species of gulls and terns.

SUMMER: black-winged stilt, avocet, pratincole, gulls, terns,

PASSAGE: waders, terns.

WINTER: pochard, tufted duck, wigeon.

The Valli can be well seen along the northern shore from the road between Ostellato and Porto Garibaldi, and southwards from this road along the coast road, and on the road across the lagoon from Spina to Alfonsine. There are many camp sites and hotels along the coast and this is an excellent area for an early summer exploration holiday.

## GARGANO PENINSULA

The Gargano peninsula is the spur of the boot of Italy on the Adriatic coast. It rises to over 3,000 feet and is separated from the rest of the country by the low lying valley of the Candelaro. The whole area is very attractive scenically. There are four important areas for birds here.

1. **Margherita di Savoia Salinas** lie in the flat coastal plain between Margherita di Savoia and the village of Zapponeta to the south of Gargano. They extend for 15 km along the coast and from 1–2 km inland, and are very important economically. The lagoons nearest Margherita di Savoia are small and not attractive to birds but the others are larger and shallower with mud banks when partially dried making them very attractive to waders. Autumn passage here is excellent with large flocks of greenshank, curlew sandpiper, little stint and ruff and a scattering of many other species. Black terns are also common, and fan-tailed warblers breed amongst the scrubby bushes by the coast road. The surrounding countryside is flat and devoted to intensive cultivation of melons and tomatoes.

AUTUMN: redshank, greenshank, curlew sandpiper, little stint, ruff, knot, spotted redshank, little ringed plover, little tern, black tern, fan-tailed warbler.

The salt-pans are private but good views of those nearest the coast may be obtained from the main coast road, route 159. They can also be seen from a small rough road leading inland on the north-western outskirts of Margherita di Savoia signposted Trinitapoli. This gives views over the pans on either side of the road, and from it there are tracks along the inland edge of the salt-pans. On the south-eastern outskirts of Zapponeta there is another rough road similarly signposted. Tracks lead off to the left to the salt-pans which do not actually border the road. Accommodation at Margherita di Savoia is not luxurious though the largest hotel should be good, and the area is not everyone's idea of a holiday spot – it is strictly for the birds!

2. **Candelaro**, or the lower part of that river, is a low lying marshy area that is frequently flooded, with some areas of reeds and salt marsh. Though there is reclamation in hand it will probably not affect this area and its status as the most important site in Italy for geese. Up to 4,700 whitefronts winter with a few bean geese and large numbers of the commoner duck including wigeon and pintail. Recent agricultural activities have driven the geese away, it is hoped only temporarily. The area would clearly be worth a look in summer too.

WINTER: white-fronted goose, bean goose, wigeon, teal, pintail.

Routes 89 and 159 cross the area but great care should be taken not to trespass and offend the understanding landowner, or to disturb the geese into range of the local shooters.


3. **Gargano Mountains** rise to 3,500 feet and are geologically distinct from the Apennines consisting of limestone more akin to the mountains of the Dalmatian coast. The lower slopes are fairly bare but become increasingly wooded at higher altitudes, and in the centre of the area lies the Forest of Umbra. This is a protected State Forest of fine mature beechwoods very similar to Burnham Beeches and holding the same sort of birds. Nuthatches are very common and chaffinch, blue tit and great tit make the northern visitor feel at home. The lower slopes have buzzard, black kite, Scop's owl, and the three shrikes are comparatively common. Black-eared wheatears are found on the rockier parts.

SUMMER: buzzard, black kite, Scop's owl, little owl, lesser grey shrike, woodchat shrike, red-backed shrike, nuthatch, blue tit, great tit, black-eared wheatear, chaffinch.

The hills are mainly rough grazing or not farmed at all and access is generally free.


4. **Lake Lesina** lies immediately west of the Gargano Hills and is separated by a very narrow and inaccessible neck of land from the sea. The lake is 15 km long by 3 km wide and is extremely shallow and fringed by varying amounts of reeds, the largest reed beds being at the eastern end. There are several mud banks in the open water part and thus the lake is good for waders as well as duck and marsh birds. Bittern and little bittern are found amongst the reeds and little egret in the more open parts. Marsh harriers probably breed at the eastern end with great reed warbler and possibly bearded tit. Penduline tit occur in the willows bordering the lake and fan-tailed warbler amongst the surrounding cultivation.

Lake Varano to the east is much less marshy though it does hold some duck and terns; it is also very difficult to approach as the road along the isthmus is always some distance from the water's edge.

Passage of waders here is good with Lesina again the best. Wood sandpiper and greenshank are common and there is a scattering of other species including quite decent numbers of black-winged stilts.

SUMMER: bittern, little bittern, little egret, marsh harrier, penduline tit, bearded tit(?), fan-tailed warbler, great reed warbler.

AUTUMN: black-winged stilt, wood sandpiper, greenshank, spotted redshank, black tern.

Because of its reed marsh edges the lake is difficult to approach. The village of Lesina itself is a good spot though there is a chance of exploring the reed beds at the eastern end by tempting one of the local fishermen. They are most likely to be found by the pumping station which is accessible by motorable tracks westwards off the Torre Mileto–Sannicandro road. The lake is extensively shot over at week-ends and the optimum time for a visit is therefore a Friday. There is a wide choice of accommodation on the Gargano Peninsula but not unfortunately at Torre Mileto. Rodi Garganico is a pleasant place with hotels further down the coast. This is the ideal base for the whole area.

## GRAN PARADISO NATIONAL PARK

The Gran Paradiso lies in the north-western corner of Italy against the French border and covers 140,000 acres of the high Alps. The protected area extends into France as the Vanoise National Park. Protection of the Gran Paradiso dates back to 1836 but the National Park in its present form originated in 1947. The peak of Gran Paradiso itself rises a magnificent 13,380 feet and drops a full 8,000 feet before reaching the tree line and pine forests. The scenery is typically Alpine with the fierce snow laden peaks of bare rock rising over the pines and meadows below, and with water everywhere in spring.

Though mainly famous for its 4,000 ibex the park is undoubtedly one of the best areas for watching birds in Italy. In general the birds are much the same as for the Vanoise National Park which has been dealt with fully under France. Golden eagle, ptarmigan, black grouse, Tengmalm's owl, eagle owl, Alpine swift, woodpeckers, and the birds of the high tops are all found including wallcreeper and snow finch.

SUMMER: golden eagle, ptarmigan, black grouse, hazel hen, rock partridge, eagle owl, Tengmalm's owl, Alpine swift, crag martin, three-toed woodpecker, black woodpecker, nutcracker, Alpine chough, crested tit, wall creeper, Alpine accentor, citril finch, snow finch.

Leave Turin northwards on route 460 through Cuorgne to Locana. At this point the Park lies northwards and westwards. Continue to Noasca which lies at the foot of Gran Paradiso and then up the valley to the Col du Nivolet, after this the road becomes more a project than a reality though it might now be finished. This is the most convenient habitat transect but a holiday walking the mountains in this beautiful scenery is ideal. There are 4 Alpine refuges, 2 chalet-restaurants, and 11 overnight bivouacs for walkers, as well as many hotels in the adjacent villages.

## GREGGIO

The Oasi di protezione di Greggio lies on the western bank of the River Sesia between Milan and Turin. It consists of oak and hornbeam woods in the north, with an area of scrub in the south. There are also plantations of poplars along the river bank. It is of considerable importance in this industrial region of Italy as a sanctuary for birds and is particularly noted for its large heronry. Little egret and night heron breed, and other marsh edge birds like Savi's warbler and penduline tit are found. The surrounding countryside holds crested lark, hoopoe, and melodious warbler.

SUMMER: little egret, night heron, crested lark, hoopoe, penduline tit, melodious warbler, Savi's warbler.

Leave the Milan–Turin autostrada at the Greggio signpost. The reserve lies north of the road from Greggio station on the west bank of the river.

## ORBETELLO

Mount Argentario, complete with its sixteenth-century Spanish forts, lies picturesquely offshore to the north of Rome. The three sandy promontories that connect it to the mainland enclose the large salt water lagoons of Orbetello. These are thronged by holiday-makers from the adjacent holiday villages, but are known as one of the best places for waders during both spring and autumn passage periods. The northern end of the lagoon is a reserve and its shallow waters and marshes hold some twenty pairs of black-winged stilts. A pair or two of Kentish plovers survive on the beaches. During passage periods large numbers of little stints, wood sandpipers and spotted redshanks can be found. Herons and egrets are invariably present, little egrets regularly over-winter, and marsh harriers are present throughout the year.

To the south, the lagoon of Burano is too deep for waders, but it too is a reserve, mainly for duck in winter. The surrounding land holds the usual 'scrub' warblers, plus reported Marmora's warblers.

SUMMER: purple heron, little egret, black-winged stilt, Kentish plover, blue rock-thrush.

AUTUMN: ruff, spotted redshank, wood sandpiper, little stint, Montagu's harrier.

WINTER: little egret, marsh harrier, hen harrier, pintail, wigeon, tufted duck.

SPRING: ruff, garganey.

The Orbetello reserve is reached from the N1, halfway between Quatro Strade and Albinia, westward via a farm. Notices mark the route. The beach is also a fine vantage point. The reserve at Burano can be visited by contacting the guardian at nearby Nunziatella.

## ORISTANO, SARDINIA

Sardinia is too large an island to explore fully in a short holiday and so the best place for birds is described to whet the appetite of prospective visitors. Recent years have seen the island opened up to tourists and there are now plenty of hotels and modern accommodation.

Oristano is a small town on the west coast near the River Tirso which reaches the sea at the shallow Bay of Oristano. There are several lakes and lagoons in this low lying neighbourhood and many are both marshy and overgrown. To the south of the town there are extensive salt pans and the whole area is attractive to breeding marsh birds and passage migrants. Duck are numerous in winter and there is a strong spring passage of garganey. Migrant warblers and raptors are often numerous and waders though seldom numerous are often interesting species. Breeding birds are quite outstanding including purple gallinule, white-headed duck, little egret, and bee-eaters, and flamingos are often present. Cetti's and Sardinian warblers are everywhere and both pallid and Alpine swifts hawk overhead. Sardinia also offers Marmora's warbler to those who search the hills, and Eleanora's falcon and Audouin's gull to those who know what they are looking for or where to look.

SUMMER: flamingo, little egret, white-headed duck, purple gallinule, osprey, Eleanora's falcon, Audouin's gull, bee-eater, Cetti's warbler, Sardinian warbler.

PASSAGE: duck, waders, terns, passerines.

WINTER: duck.

Sardinia can be reached by air from many European cities and by car ferry from several places in Italy. Oristano has a choice of accommodation but the village of Marina di Torre Grande is the place to stay in this area.


## SAN GIULIANO LAKE

Lago di San Giuliano lies in southern Italy in Basilicata 15 km south-west of Matera, a part of the country that is generally unknown and not visited by tourists. The water level is subject to considerable variations being at its highest in early spring and lowest in autumn, though the surrounding land is so bare that there are good muddy margins for waders at all seasons. Being an artificial lake the only area of reeds is at the north-western end. The surrounding countryside is very dry and the hills with a sparse covering of grass rise up on either side of the broad river valley. There are a few groups of trees and some conifer plantations particularly along the southern shore. The lake is private and a fence with danger notices protects it from trespass. It can, however, be seen adequately at many points.

What little is known of San Giuliano is encouraging. There are numbers of great crested and little grebes and garganey, and black, white-winged black, and whiskered terns have all been seen on migration. At such times there is a good collection of waders including wood sandpiper, greenshank, curlew sandpiper, black-tailed godwit, and Kentish plover. Little egret and grey heron are seen and marsh harriers quarter the shore. The surrounding area holds breeding lesser grey shrike and the quite common woodchat and red-backed. Fan-tailed warblers appear common and short-toed lark and black-eared wheatear inhabit the more arid regions.

SUMMER: great crested grebe, garganey, kite, roller, lesser grey shrike, woodchat shrike, red-backed shrike, green woodpecker, short-toed lark, black-eared wheatear, fan-tailed warbler.

AUTUMN: grey heron, little egret, wood sandpiper, greenshank, curlew sandpiper, black-tailed godwit, Kentish plover, black tern, white-winged black tern, whiskered tern.

The main road between Potenza and Matera passes the dam and there are buses. Matera has accommodation. The main viewpoints are along the rough but motorable road on the southern side of the lake; there is a better surfaced road along the northern shore but it is not as close as in the south and the light is adverse except in the early mornings.


## VENETIAN LAGOONS

The most famous lagoons in the world lie at the head of the Adriatic with Venice set squarely in their midst. They are shallow with a maze of islands on the landward side and have been created by the build-up of sand bars along the coast on one of which the Lido di Venézia stands. The lagoons are intersected by long and sometimes deep canals and support an active fishing industry. About a fifth of the whole is reserved for shooting the numerous duck and waders that occur on passage and in winter. Though the 100,000 duck here in the winter of 1962–3 might be exceptional there are always huge numbers of wigeon, pintail, and diving duck present, the latter including up to 25,000 tufted duck. In spring up to 4,300 garganey have been counted. Clearly the area is one of the most important wetlands in Europe. With careful management and control it could become a more important breeding area as well, in spite of commercial exploitation. Passage waders are numerous and rich and as well as the more usual species Temminck's stint, broad-billed sandpiper, and marsh sandpiper have occurred.

AUTUMN: golden plover, spotted redshank, marsh sandpiper, greenshank, little stint, Temminck's stint, broad-billed sandpiper.

WINTER: wigeon, pintail, teal, pochard, tufted duck, waders.

SPRING: garganey, waders.

In an area of 140,000 acres exploration is never easy, but as most visitors will be based on Venice boat trips are obviously best. Out of season these are cheaper. There are roads round the lagoons giving good views over the fringe of the area.

# Malta

READ: *The Birds of Malta* by E. L. Roberts.

## MALTA

Malta lies 100 km south of Sicily and 250 km east-south-east of Cape Bon in Tunisia in mid-Mediterranean. The group consists of four islands, Malta 200 sq km, Gozo 65 sq km, and the two much smaller islands of Comino and Filfla all within 5 km of each other. The islands are composed of limestone that forms 800 foot cliffs between Jebel Chantar and Dingli in the south-west, and a series of high barren ridges in the north-west. Agriculture is confined to the valleys with irrigation, and the wadieu (water courses) that are tree lined. The Maltese are great hunters and thousands of birds are slaughtered annually on migration. In particular quail and turtle doves are much sought after. Nevertheless there are a number of breeding birds and about 125 species are noted each year.

The best areas for bird-watching are the terraced valleys in north-western Malta where cultivation provides plenty of cover for birds and watchers. Likely places are the Boschetto Gardens near Rabat, the San Anton Gardens at Balzan, and particularly the wadieu. The south-western cliffs hold herring gull, rock dove, and blue rock thrush, while the cliffs of Ta'chench in Gozo, and Filfla have breeding Cory's shearwater and the occasional peregrine. Balearic shearwaters are often seen offshore and possibly breed on Gozo and Comino. The salt pans and creek of St Paul's Bay are a good place for migrant waders and wildfowl, as are the fishponds at Marsaxlokk and the pool at Ghadira north of Mellicha. Purple heron, little egret, and night heron are frequent here in good numbers, while other migrants include a selection of raptors like honey buzzard, marsh and hen harriers, hobby, and lesser kestrel in the north-western uplands.

Breeding birds include the resident spectacled and Sardinian warblers, short-toed lark, and the Malta sparrow which is a race of the Spanish sparrow.

SUMMER: Balearic shearwater, Cory's shearwater, peregrine, herring gull, quail, blue rock thrush, short-toed lark, rock dove, spectacled warbler, Sardinian warbler, Malta sparrow.

PASSAGE: purple heron, night heron, little egret, honey buzzard, marsh harrier, hen harrier, hobby, lesser kestrel, quail, turtle dove, black-eared wheatear, woodchat shrike, icterine warbler.

There are frequent air services to Malta especially from Britain, and a wealth of accommodation at Valetta. Most people speak English.

# Norway

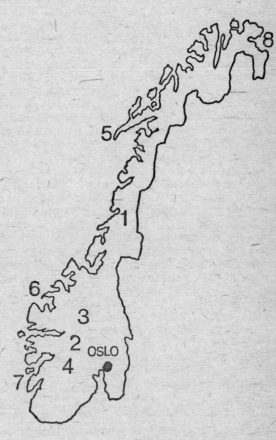

1 Börgefjell
2 Djupvatn
3 Dovrefjell
4 Hardanger Vidda
5 Lofoten Isles
6 Runde
7 Utsira
8 Varanger Fjord

ZOOLOGISK MUSEUM,
Sars gt.l., Oslo 5.

READ: *Håndbok over Norges Fugler* (1947–50) by H. L. Lovenskiold.

## BÖRGEFJELL

Börgefjell lies on the borders of the provinces of Nordland and Nord-Tröndelag roughly half way between Trondheim and the Lofoten Isles. The major mountain rises to over 5,500 feet and while the rivers on one side descend quickly to the Atlantic those to the east run right across Sweden before entering the Baltic in the Gulf of Bothnia. The valleys have birches that hold the usual Scandinavian redwing, fieldfare and brambling, and siskins are common about the houses. Goosander and goldeneye are found on the major rivers, with pied flycatcher and willow warblers amongst the pines. There are many lakes at different altitudes with varying surrounds, and marshes are commonplace. These hold breeding waders including Temminck's stint and red-necked phalarope, and in some places long-tailed duck. Higher still this area really begins to shine with two species of geese to add to the more widespread ptarmigan and snow bunting. Long-tailed skuas also haunt the tops and so occasionally do snowy owls.

Though outside the area, the vast Rösvatn to the north is worth exploring. It holds black-throated diver and scoter, and many of the waders and passerines are found around its shores. This is a good spot for rough-legged buzzard. The whole area is excellent walking country and though roads are particularly few in the southern part there are sufficient for car-bound watchers to see many of the characteristic birds without too much effort. But lesser white-fronts and bean geese deserve hard work.

Börgefjell is a National Park covering 250,000 acres.

SUMMER: lesser white-fronted goose, bean goose, long-tailed duck, scoter, goosander, goldeneye, rough-legged buzzard, Temminck's stint, red-necked phalarope, long-tailed skua, willow grouse, ptarmigan, snowy owl, bluethroat, fieldfare, redwing, brambling, siskin, snow bunting.

Leave southern Norway or Trondheim up the major northern road route 50 to Fellingfors. This makes an excellent base but going eastwards on route 640 leads to Rösvatn and the excellent centre of Hattfjelldal where there is a camp site. From here there are roads in three directions including a close approach to the highest tops at Ivarrud.

## DJUPVATN

Djupvatn lies roughly halfway between Bergen and Oslo to the north of route 20 and the country's main railway at Geilo. It is one of the favourite recreational areas with skiing in winter and hiking from hut to hut during the summer. The huts enable areas completely off the beaten track to be explored and are thus excellent bases for bird-watching. Djupvatn is a convenient name for the area around the northern end of that lake, the plateau land to the south-west, and the Strandafjord-Raggsteindal area beyond. For those who want typical Scandinavian birds in beautiful surroundings this is the area. Raggsteindal is a lakeside hotel-hut with birches rising from the lakeside marshes alive with redpolls and bramblings. Cross the lake, boats being arranged by the hotel, and climb up the slope following the marked footpath towards Iungsdal. The plateau at the top gradually slopes northwards with odd lakes and marshes that hold waders, and with ptarmigan and dotterel on the drier spots. Continue across quaking bogs – more frightening than they are dangerous – and up across Stolsbergi for ring ousel, peregrine, just possibly gyr falcon, and on down to Iungsdal. There is an excellent marsh with dwarf willow on hillsides sheltering fieldfare.

SUMMER: peregrine, waders, dotterel, ptarmigan, ring ousel, redstart, redpoll, siskin, brambling.

This is a good area for exploring from the two huts at Raggsteindal and Iungsdal. Approaching from the south, there is a road to the former and to Djup where there is another hut near Iungsdal. Do not be tempted to try the route between Iungsdal and Bjoberg – you will regret it. Train and bus to Geilo (walk) or Hol (bus) for a start. Join Den Norske Turistforening which owns or runs the huts.

# DOVREFJELL

The Fokstua area of the Dovrefjell has been famous for its birds since the early part of the nineteenth century, and though the wettest part of the marsh was destroyed in 1916–17 with the construction of the Dovre Railway the region remains one of the great bird areas in Europe. The reserve itself covers a tiny 7½ sq km alongside route E6 but the surrounding area of fjell, marsh, and lake is worth exploring in its own right. Indeed some species like rough-legged buzzard, dotterel, and ptarmigan do not breed in the reserve at all.

Though the numbers of species breeding on the Fokstua marsh declined during the last century there has been an increase in the last fifty years. Since 1958 both ruff and great snipe have been present again, the latter between the railway station and Lake Harrtjern, while hen harriers have bred since the 1930s. Three new species to the area are whimbrel, Lapwing and common gull while in 1962–3 a pair of lesser white-fronted geese bred. The most recent colonist is the Temminck's stint which probably bred in 1966. In the surrounding birch forests typical Scandinavian species include fieldfare, bluethroat, brambling, siskin, and redpoll with dippers along the streams. Higher up many tundra type species like snow bunting and shore lark breed, while on the exposed tops it is possible to find the purple sandpiper. The most exciting birds of all are the cranes, several pairs of which breed in the reserve.

This wonderful area of marsh, woods, lakes and open fjells is concentrated, beautiful, and absolutely ideal for a short holiday.

SUMMER: red-throated diver, crane, hen harrier, peregrine, rough-legged buzzard, whimbrel, golden plover, dotterel, Temminck's stint, ruff, purple sandpiper, red-necked phalarope, great snipe, great grey shrike, dipper, ring ousel, fieldfare, bluethroat, shore lark, brambling, siskin, redpoll, snow bunting, Lapland bunting.

The land surrounding the reserve is of straightforward open access and many of the more interesting birds can be found amongst the wooded hillsides and above the tree line to north and south of the valley. The reserve itself is sacrosanct between 25 April and 8 July except along a marked trail between 7 a.m. and 11 p.m. though specialist workers may get special permission. However, the marked trail wanders through the most exciting part of the reserve and all visitors are given a booklet with a map showing what they can expect to see *en route*. The E6 which runs along the south-eastern boundary is an excellent vantage point for that part of the reserve that cannot be seen from the trail. Cards of permission are available from the guard on the far side

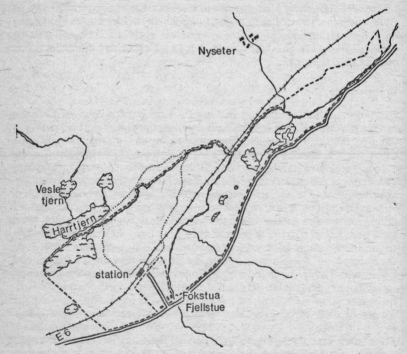

Dovrefjell: the dashes show the reserve boundary and the only part that is restricted in this magnificent area. The dotted line is the route taken by permit holders. A great deal can be seen without entering the reserve at all.

of the railway near Fokstua station but he might restrict the number of visitors at any particular time. There is the Fokstua Fjellstue hotel at Fokstua and a choice of hotels, youth hostels and camp sites at nearby Dombås. International access is via Oslo or Trondheim and thence by road (E6) or rail.

## HARDANGER VIDDA

The Hardanger Vidda is the southernmost and best known of the Norwegian fjells and is a winter and summer playground for the people of Oslo and Bergen. There are many organised holidays including pony trekking and bird-watching, and in winter Norwegian style cross-country skiing is very popular. Because of its geographical position the Hardanger is the furthest point south for a number of interesting Artic and sub-Arctic birds though it reaches only a modest 5,000 feet in height. In fact the best areas are the lowlands in the north rather than the higher more mountainous south. Pine woods and birch copses line the valleys and surround the low lying lakes, but higher the trees die out and dwarf willow scrub and open marshes alternate with bare moss covered areas. Though dependent on the number of lemmings and voles there is often a good population of raptors including golden eagle and merlin. Other breeding species include the numerous dotterel, together with great snipe, whimbrel, wood and purple sandpipers, and Temminck's stint. There is a good collection of duck, and owls include Tengalm's and pygmy. One of the most characteristic passerines is the bluethroat though brambling, fieldfare, and redpoll are all comparatively common.

SUMMER: golden eagle, osprey, merlin, scaup, goldeneye, velvet scoter, greenshank, great snipe, whimbrel, wood sandpiper, purple sandpiper, Temminck's stint, dotterel, Tengalm's owl, pygmy owl, three-toed woodpecker, black woodpecker, fieldfare, bluethroat, brambling, redpoll.

The best centres are in the north from the Bergen–Oslo road at Dyranut where there is a mountain hostel. Striking south from here are several well marked paths to other huts spaced at walkable distances, and the Norwegians make quite a thing of these 'trips' as they call them. Huts supply accommodation varying from private rooms to small dormitories and most supply meals and packed lunches. Recommended places for birds are the Bjoreidal valley immediately south of Dyranut, Randhelleren on Lake Langesjöen, and Sandhang on Lake Normannslågen and Hadlasker to the west-north-west. All are huts and offer accommodation. For information on organised bird-watching holidays write to TTK, 1 Slottsgaten, Bergen.

## LOFOTEN ISLES

The very idea of the Lofoten Isles is enough to make most people shiver and when a jagged row of peaks is seen rising from the sea many are convinced that their feelings have been confirmed. Yet in spite of lying totally north of the Arctic circle the Lofotens are really green and lush. There are sheltered

bays and sandy beaches and many fishing villages contrasting with the harsh
rugged mountains inland. For the bird-watcher the low rounded hills of
Röst, entirely covered with grass, are the most likely destination. Röst
consists of a large number of islands at the very south of the Lofotens.
Röstlandet is a beautiful fishing village with gaily painted houses standing
half over the deep blue water of the sheltered harbour. The Röst group and
nearby Vaeröy are the seabird centres of the Lofotens. There might be five
and a half million birds here. Dominant are the auks, puffin, guillemot and
razorbill with black guillemot in suitable places. There are many thousands
of kittiwakes, the storm petrel is said to breed, and the fulmar does so.
Eiders are plentiful and the down is collected by the islanders on a commercial
basis. Arctic skuas breed, pursuing the plentiful terns and waders on the
moorland hillsides. The two best islands Vädöy and Storfjell are uninhabited
and the largest island Röstlandet holds a population of 800.

SUMMER: storm petrel, fulmar, eider, white-tailed eagle, red-necked phalarope, curlew, kittiwake, Arctic skua, guillemot, razorbill, puffin, black guillemot.

Röst can be reached by local steamer from Vest-Lofoten or direct from
Bodö. The latter is the best route as it connects with Oslo by air (2 hours)
then by boat to Röst (6 hours). Train from Oslo to Bodö is cheaper but longer
(26 hours). The only accommodation on Röst is the guesthouse of Röst
Fiskarheim which can take twelve people. There are, however, several
rorbuer, wood-built winter fishing huts with good facilities, that can be hired.
Contact the Lofoten Travel Association, Svolvær. Otherwise camping is usual.


## RUNDE

The island of Runde lies in the northern part of the fjord coast off Ålesund. It
is mountainous and the cliffs that form the west coast drop 1,000 feet to the
sea and hold two million (who counted them?) seabirds. Unlike many such
islands off the British coasts Runde is inhabited by 3,000 people which is an
extremely useful and attractive factor in its favour. The largest bird rock is
Rundebranden near the village of Goksöyr. Kittiwake and puffin are the most
numerous species, but there are also thousands of razorbills and guillemots.
The fulmar colonized Runde in the 1920s and has since increased to about 300
pairs, while a more recent colonist the gannet was first proved to breed in 1957
and had increased to 75 pairs by 1966. Gannets occupy the steepest section of
Rundebranden and the fulmars are found on the northern part of the island.
Other birds include shag, oystercatcher, curlew, eider, and shelduck, and this
is the right part of the coast for white-tailed eagle and eagle owl both of which
are found on or around Runde.

SUMMER: fulmar, gannet, shag, eider, shelduck, peregrine, white-tailed
eagle, curlew, oystercatcher, kittiwake, puffin, guillemot, razorbill, eagle owl.

There are two villages, Runde and Goksöyr, joined by a narrow road on the
east coast. There is no hotel accommodation but local fishermen and farmers

do put people up. They also take visitors out in boats to see the bird cliffs. There are regulations about disturbing the birds and departing from a clearly defined route. Special permission to take photographs away from the route can be obtained from Vestlandske Naturvernforening, Botanisk Museum, Universitet, Bergen. Runde is reached in 2 hours by local steamer from Ålesund, which is in contact with Bergen by air (1 hour) or by sea (17 hours). From Oslo it is train to Åndalsnes (8 hours) and 'bus (3 hours).

## UTSIRA

Utsira is a small island off the south-west coast of Norway near Haugesund and to the north-west of Stavanger. It is roughly 3 km across in any direction, rises to over 200 feet, and is in an isolated position 15 km from the nearest land. It offers little in the way of cover for birds the vegetation consisting largely of grass and heather but with some fields and cultivation in the central valley and around the houses. There are three small woods of conifers and it is these plus the cultivated areas that are the main interest to bird-watchers. Initial investigations in 1934 and 1936 showed that Utsira was an excellent spot for studying migration and managed to add three new forms to the Norwegian list in a single season. Subsequent work has shown that vagrants are regular but that mass migration is better studied on the mainland at places like Lista.

Several seabirds breed including shag, and razorbill and guillemot on Spannholmene 3 km south-west, but it is the autumn migration that is the main reason for visiting the island. Rarities of annual appearance include yellow-browed warbler, red-breasted flycatcher, probably Richard's pipit, as well as the more usual passerine migrants. Waders are never very numerous but seabirds can be quite interesting.

AUTUMN: Richard's pipit, red-breasted flycatcher, pied flycatcher, Greenland wheatear, yellow-browed warbler, northern chiffchaff, scarlet grosbeak, short-toed lark.

There is no doubt that systematic mist-netting on Utsira would produce valuable records of rarities for the Norwegian coast. The island is reached by boat from Haugesund 3 or 4 days a week and though there is no hotel or hostel there is a possibility of cottage accommodation or camping. Enthusiasts should contact the Zoology Department at Stavanger Museum.

## VARANGERFJORD

Varanger lies on the 70° of latitude and is the most north-easterly coastline of the European mainland. The fjord opens out eastwards, is truly part of the Arctic Ocean, and receives far less benefit from the warming gulf stream than areas even a little further south and west. It is consequently more barren and cold. The birds are also typically high Arctic; the white-billed diver for example is much more likely to be met than the great northern. And it is the only place in Europe where one can go to and reasonably expect to see both Steller's

and king eider. There are also the only European Brünnich's guillemots
outside Iceland.

The habitat becomes progressively more barren as one proceeds eastwards
from Varangerbotn, the village at the head of the fjord, and one is conscious
of the falling temperature. Bird-watchers find that shirt sleeves at Utsjoki
200 km south-west by road give way to thick sweater by Varangerbotn, two
thick sweaters and gloves at Ekkeröy, and duffle coat, scarf, the lot at Vardö
– full January salt marsh gear. At Varangerbotn there are still dwarf birches
growing near the fjord edge but these become progressively more stunted and
virtually disappear by Vadsö, leaving low scrub only in sheltered places, and
bare tundra elsewhere. There is an area of mud at Varangerbotn which attracts
numbers of waders and is a particularly good spot for summer plumaged knot
and bar-tailed godwit. The coast is relatively flat as far as Vardö with gently
shelving shingle well covered with seaweed. North of Vardö the scenery
becomes spectacular with bare precipitous cliffs and screes interspersed with
sandy bays. There are a number of places to visit:

1. **Varangerbotn:** a muddy area for waders, goosander – which is very much
a sea duck in this part of the world – and a chance of Arctic warbler.

2. **Nesseby:** has a picturesque wooden church on a promontory that is
excellent for waders, with a little pool next to the church which is a red-necked
phalarope feeding ground. Black-throated diver occur on the sea together with
king eider which appear anywhere from here onwards.

3. **Vadsö:** the main town of the area with shops, hotel, etc, and a daily bus
service from Utsjoki. The rubbish tip lies on a small island south of the town
reached via a wooden bridge (navigable by car). It is a likely spot for odd
gulls like glaucous and Iceland, and just occasionally has ivory gull and
Ross's gull. Temminck's stint breeds and little stint sometimes, about the only
place they do breed in this book.

4. **Kiby-Ekkeröy:** a good place for sea-watching which is best done at night
when the sun is in the north and the light is often good. Seabird movement
seems to occur all night unlike passerine activity which is lowest from about
18:00–01:00 hours. The main species to be seen at sea are Arctic and long-
tailed skuas with a possibility of pomarine as well, white-billed diver, eider,
king eider, long-tailed duck, glaucous gull, Brunnich's guillemot, and velvet
scoter. There are flat shingle areas here suitable for camping by the coast and
near Kiby there is an Arctic tern colony beside the road.

5. **Ekkeröy Island:** one of the best places on the whole coast. There is a low
sandy shore on the north side and precipitous cliffs on the south. The latter
holds 5,000 pairs of kittiwake. There are literally masses of Temminck's
stints, red-throated pipits, Lapland buntings and shore larks, with red-necked

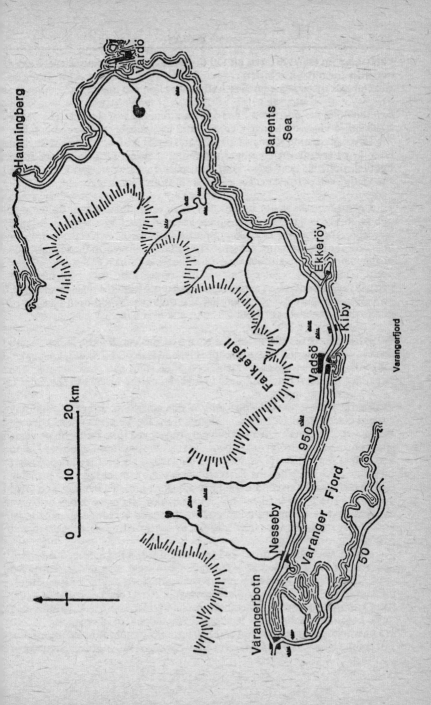

phalaropes on the little pools on top of the island. Bean goose, Steller's eider and little stint are often seen on passage along this part of the coast. One can drive across the sandy causeway to the village on the island.

6. **Falkefjell or 'falcon-hill':** lies inland from the above area. The lower scrub holds bluethroat, mealy redpoll and just possibly Arctic redpoll, and the very common red-throated pipit. Pools hold red-necked phalarope, and large lakes long-tailed duck and red-throated diver. Further up are snow bunting, dotterel, long-tailed skua, and purple sandpiper, and a chance of snowy owl and gyr falcon. Temminck's stints are everywhere.

7. **Vardö:** remarkable for its difficulty of access and unpleasant dirtiness. It is a relatively large town lying on an island reached by regular and fairly frequent ferry from the mainland opposite. Cars can only be taken across at high tide, the loading ramp being too steep at other times. On the seaward side of the main island is an islet with a lighthouse on which five species of auk breed. There is no regular boat but one of the local fishermen might be persuaded to ferry visitors across. Looking across from the main island often provides an opportunity of seeing birds on the sea. Vardö itself consists of unattractive grey houses, a foul harbour, and a stinking fish-glue factory.

8. **Hamningberg:** at the end of the road past the Vardö ferry. It has superb scenery with snow still at sea level in July, and is good for skuas, king eider, long-tailed duck and possible gyr falcon, little stint, and glaucous gull. The habitations marked between Vardö and Hamningberg have been abandoned.

9. **Pasvik Valley:** the odd man out in this collection. It is the politically curious extension of Norway southwards from the Varanger Fjord between Finland and the Soviet Union. It can only be reached from the north on route 955 from Kirkenes to Nyrud, where the road crosses into the Soviet Union and comes out again at Virtaniemi in Finland. This part is closed. Dwarf birch and birch scrub line the valley with bare tundra on the hill tops. Breeding species include Arctic redpoll, bean goose, yellow-breasted bunting, and great grey owl. The lakes hold red-necked phalarope while the more extensive marshes have breeding bar-tailed godwit. Kirkenes is quite a sizeable town and can be reached by bus from Utsjoki, by coastal steamer from Bergen and Trondheim, or by plane.

SUMMER: white-billed diver, red-throated diver, bean goose, long-tailed duck, velvet scoter, eider, king eider, Steller's eider, gyr falcon, bar-tailed godwit, Temminck's stint, little stint, purple sandpiper, red-necked phalarope, dotterel, kittiwake, Arctic tern, glaucous gull, Arctic skua, long-tailed skua, great grey owl, snowy owl, bluethroat, Arctic warbler, shore lark, red-throated pipit, Lapland bunting, snow bunting, Arctic redpoll, mealy redpoll.

The whole area is reached by route 950 turning off route 50 at Varangerbotn. But continue on route 50 for the Pasvik Valley. The 950 is gravel but good in general as far as Vardö ferry. Thereafter it is driveable but needs care. Access is unrestricted everywhere though there is a possibility of being questioned about optical gear near the Soviet border. The optimum time for a visit is late June to early July when bird-watching can take place twenty-four hours a day. 'Evening' is the least productive period and an excellent time to sleep. It is generally very cold and winter clothes are needed but there is no mosquito problem and the weather is generally fine. There are hotels at Vadsö, and Kirkenes, and guest houses at Varangerbotn, Kirkenes (2), and at Skogfoss in the Pasvik Valley.

This is a superb and unique area in Europe, but one that is being progressively disturbed. Many bird-watchers are now finding the adjacent fjords more wild and therefore less predictable bird-wise.

# Poland

1 Barycz Valley
2 Puszcza Białowieska
3 Biebrzanski Marshes
4 Bieszczady Zachodnie
5 Jezioro Druzno
6 Gdańsk
7 Goplo Lake

8 Masurian Lakes
9 Pieniny Mountains
10 Słowiński National Park
11 Tatrzanski National Park
12 Warsaw
13 Wolin Island

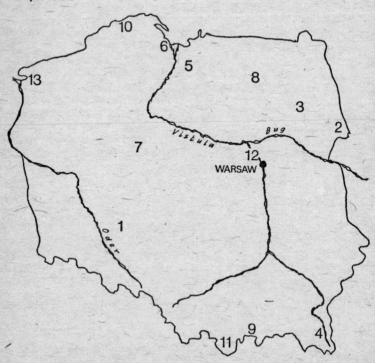

ZAKLAD OCHRONY PRZYRODY POLSKA AKADEMIA NAUK
(Polish Conservation Research Centre),
Krakow 2, Arianska 1.

READ: *Ptaki ziem Polskich* (1958) by J. Sokolowski.

## BARYCZ VALLEY

The River Barycz, a tributary of the Oder, wanders across its flat valley 50 km north of Wroclaw. Since the fourteenth century the area has been noted for the production of carp and the ponds created in former river beds by the Cistercian monks have been largely preserved by subsequent generations. At present there are 16,000 acres producing 1,300 tons of carp annually. The valley has been known as an area of outstanding interest to ornithologists since the 1890s, and in recent years 215 species have been observed, no less than 161 of which have been proved to breed.

The ponds can be roughly divided into two types. In the Zmigród and the southern part of the Milicz valleys they are surrounded by swampy meadows and deciduous woods and hold large number of passerines and raptors. Around Milicz itself the land is less damp and there are more geese and grebes though rather fewer raptors. The larger groups of ponds from west to east are Radziqdz, Ruda Sulowska, Milicz, Krośnice, Potasznia, and most of them are drained each autumn to catch the carp, though some ponds in each group hold fry and are kept filled. Though individual ponds extend over 1,000 acres there are many tiny ones and the average depth is only a few feet. The surrounding vegetation is in such circumstances luxurious with reeds, sedges, osiers, alders and woodland. There are often islands of reeds and in some cases up to half of the total area may consist of reed beds. There are several areas where the artificial raising of the water level has resulted in the flooding of adjoining woodland.

The main habitats are as follows:

1. **Ponds:** sedges holding colonies of black-headed gulls with a mixture of black-necked and red-necked grebes; edges with reeds hold great reed warbler and Savi's warbler (a newcomer to the area); islands of reeds with marsh harrier, bittern, mute swan (only place in Southern Poland), greylag (300 pairs), the three diving duck pochard, tufted and ferruginous, water rail, and Poland's only breeding purple herons; alders and flooded woods have a wealth of wildfowl and an interesting variety of woodpeckers plus penduline tit.

2. **Meadows:** the damper the meadows the more interesting the birds. Typical birds include garganey, black-tailed godwit, grasshopper warbler, and blue-headed wagtail.

3. **Woods:** vary from the dry pines of the sandy areas to the alder swamp

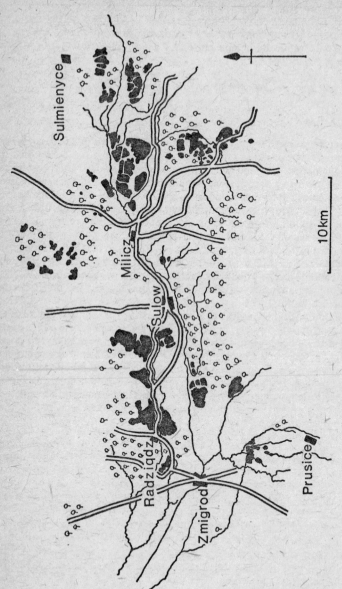

The Ponds of the Barycz valley.

jungles round the ponds. There are extensive beech woods on the Trébnica Hills south of Milicz and these come down to the Barycz Valley near Zimgród, though there are mixed deciduous woods throughout the area. Birds include a wide variety of raptors, including a few pairs of white-tailed eagles, black stork, roller, a selection of woodpeckers, hooded crow, river and icterine warblers, and red-breasted flycatcher.

4. **Fields and Pastures:** hold a few interesting birds not found elsewhere including tawny pipit, great grey shrike, and ortolan.

In the autumn there are regularly good numbers of white-tailed eagles and mute swans, and a passage of duck and waders.

SUMMER: red-necked grebe, black-necked grebe, purple heron, little bittern, bittern, white stork, black stork, pintail, ferruginous duck, greylag goose, lesser spotted eagle, goshawk, red kite, black kite, white-tailed eagle, honey buzzard, marsh harrier, osprey, peregrine, crane, spotted crake, little crake, black-tailed godwit, green sandpiper, ruff, black tern, roller, hoopoe, green woodpecker, grey-headed woodpecker, great spotted woodpecker, white-backed woodpecker, middle spotted woodpecker, lesser spotted woodpecker, black woodpecker, golden oriole, penduline tit, redwing, bluethroat, river warbler, Savi's warbler, great reed warbler, icterine warbler, barred warbler, red-breasted flycatcher, tawny pipit, great grey shrike, woodchat shrike, serin, ortolan bunting.

Milicz, which is the ideal centre, is easy to reach by train, 'bus and car from Wroclaw. Most of the ponds can be seen from roads and paths and many are of straightforward access. There are a number of reserves including the excellent Stawy Milickie. Scientific information available from Stacji Badawczej Universytetu Wroclawskiego in Rudzie Sulowskiej; and permits from Wojewódzki Konserwator Przyrody, Wroclaw, Plac Powstańców Warszawy, Prezydium Wojewódzkiej Rady Narodowej, Wydzial Leśnictwa i Rolnictwa.

## PUSZCZA BIAŁOWIESKA

The Białowieska Forest lies in the extreme east of Poland and continues across the Soviet border. It is the best known natural history site in the country and is the home of the only wild herd of European bison, and a good spot for elk. Białowieska is the largest remnant of the original central European forests, and 12,500 acres are now a National Park. Beeches are entirely absent and the dominant tree is hornbeam with alders, oaks, birches, lime, maple, elm and considerable areas of pines. The Forest proper involves a much larger area perhaps 130,000 acres but not all of this is woodland. There are open areas and considerable tracts of marshes that attract many of the 200 species of birds that have been seen here, and most notably breeding cranes. Perhaps the most interesting feature of the avifauna of the Forest is the northern and eastern influences. Great grey owls for instance are probable breeders. Both lesser spotted and spotted eagles breed, and the short-toed eagle probably does. One can add eagle owl to the great grey, while the pygmy owl is said to be common. Amongst the smaller birds collared flycatchers are very common and red-breasted flycatcher, roller and firecrest all breed.

The European bison had been protected here for several centuries and though hard pressed during the Napoleonic War, it survived and increased prior to World War I. The sight of such food was too much for hungry soldiers and the last wild bison was shot in 1921. Three Swedish animals were sent to Białowieska in 1929 and despite the setback of World War II they have thrived and multiplied to the present free roaming herd of just under a hundred animals.

SUMMER: white stork, black stork, crane, lesser spotted eagle, spotted eagle, short-toed eagle, red kite, black kite, ruff, great grey owl(?), short-eared owl, eagle owl, pygmy owl, white-backed woodpecker, three-toed woodpecker, black grouse, capercaillie, roller, hoopoe, redwing, collared flycatcher, red-breasted flycatcher, firecrest, thrush nightingale, barred warbler, crossbill, ortolan bunting.

There are trains from Warsaw to Białowieska which lies against the Soviet border south-east of Białystok. There are plenty of roads and tracks, though entry to the reserve must be obtained through the Dyrekcja (Director) Białowieskiego Parku Narodowego, Białowiesza, pow Hajnówka, woj. Białystok. All information can be obtained from Zakladzie Badania Ssakow Polskiej Akademii Nauk, and Stacji Badania Lasów Pierwotnych Instytutu Badán Lesnych, both in Bialowiezy.

## BIEBRZANSKI MARSHES

These fantastic marshes are the Polish equivalent of the famous Pripet Marshes on the other side of the Soviet boundary and to the south. They lie along the River Biebrza between Augustów and Lomza to the north-east of Warsaw near Białystok. The river twists and turns and has created thousands of oxbow lakes and backwaters adjacent to its present course. There are islands formed as the river divides and rejoins and many small lakes, the whole being surrounded by a vast area of marshland extending to some 200,000 acres. The area is in several places well wooded with some quite considerable forests including pines, though wet meadows, marshes and peat bogs predominate. There are tracks and roads but they are infrequent and the area is sparsely inhabited. Needless to say there are many question marks about what species are found in such a vast unmanageable area and even the status of the obvious stars like spotted and lesser spotted eagles, white-tailed eagle, and osprey is unsure, though all are probable breeders.

The variety of habitats is shown by the wealth of breeding birds which include typical marshland species like ruff, curlew, and bittern together with a variety of woodpeckers and more specialized species like black grouse and hazel hen. Crane, black stork, penduline tit, and red-breasted flycatcher are all found. Eagle owls breed, and the area lies at the extreme edge of the winter and irruptive range of a number of typical high Arctic owls that occur here with some regularity. These include Ural, great grey, hawk, and Tengalm's owls.

SUMMER: black stork, bittern, crane, mute swan, goldeneye, spotted eagle, lesser spotted eagle, white-tailed eagle, osprey, red kite, hobby, ruff, curlew, eagle owl, black grouse, hazel hen, black woodpecker, white-backed woodpecker, penduline tit, red-breasted flycatcher.

Apart from its size this area is difficult to penetrate, though things are easier in winter on skis. Białystok which can be reached by train and 'bus is the best starting place. From here public transport can be used to the edge of the marshes. Exploration other than on the few tracks is something of an expedition and camping equipment and food must be carried. There is a reserve of over 5,000 acres at Czerwone Bagno which is in the heart of the least spoilt area, and the lakes at Drenstwo and Tajno are obvious attractions. If the prospect seems daunting and unclear it must be remembered that this is one of Europe's outstanding wetlands and an opportunity to break new ground. Permits for Czerwone Bagno, and for the other reserve of Grzedy, can be obtained from Wojewódzki Konserwator Przyrody, Białystok, ul. Mickiewicza 5. Prezydium Wojewodzkiej Rady Narodowej, Wydzial Leśnictwa i Rolnictwa.

## BIESZCZADY ZACHODNIE

The Bieszczady mountains lie 80 km south-east of Rzeszów in the corner of Poland sandwiched between the Ukraine and Czechoslovakia. They rise to only 3,400 feet at Tarnica but hold many of the Alpine species found in the Carpathians. The hills are separated by wide valleys running from north-west to south-east and can be divided into a number of vertical stages. Up to 3,000 feet there are forests of various trees but above this level are open meadows with a characteristic Alpine flora. Due to the ravages of the last war the landscape is poor and a large number of people have left the area. It is now partly controlled by the Polish military.

Apart from the usual wealth of mammals over 150 species of birds have been recorded for the area which has received a fair amount of study. The commonest birds are nutcracker, redwing, ring ousel, and hazel hen but there are the two exciting flycatchers, woodpeckers including black, Ural, eagle, and pygmy owls, and probably four species of eagle. This is a remote area and well off the beaten tourist track for those who like their birds wild.

SUMMER: golden eagle, lesser spotted eagle, spotted eagle(?), short-toed eagle(?), red kite, osprey, eagle owl, Ural owl, pygmy owl, black woodpecker, three-toed woodpecker, white-backed woodpecker, hazel hen, nutcracker, Alpine accentor, ring ousel, redwing, red-breasted flycatcher, collared flycatcher, crossbill.

Trains run to Ustrzyki Dolne which is the best base. 'Buses run into the mountains from here to Ustrzyk Gornych which is the ideal centre for a holiday. Permits to roam around the area can be obtained from the local military authorities wop at Lutowiskach and Wetlinie. Permits for reserves in the area from Wojewodzki Konserwator Przyrody, Rzeszów, ul. Grunwaldzka.

There are two other areas nearby that repay the attention of the motorized watcher:

1. The old river bed of the River San at Hurko near Przemysl which holds many marsh species including little bittern, penduline tit and Savi's warbler, all of which have recently spread into the area. Other interesting birds include roller, black-tailed godwit and black tern.
2. Along the River San from Przemysl to just north of Jaroslaw there were ten breeding colonies of bee-eater in 1965, the only ones in Poland.

## JEZIORO DRUZNO

Druzno Lake lies immediately south of Elblag to the south-east of Gdańsk in the Baltic depression, and covers 5,800 acres. It is shallow with extensive areas of reeds and scrub and surrounded by marshy areas totalling 3,500 acres particularly in the south and east. The average depth is about 2 feet though there is perhaps 20 feet of soft mud. Semi-floating islands of reed and vast reed beds are the most characteristic feature of this vast impenetrable swamp. The lake is outstanding for breeding and passage birds and is now a reserve.

The wealth of birds in such a comparatively small area is outstanding and compares very well with any similar area anywhere in Europe. There are two species of harrier, night heron, bittern and little bittern, crane, two species of crake, many duck and a superb range of passerines including river and Savi's warblers, scarlet grosbeak, and penduline tit. The bearded tit apparently no longer breeds here but would be worth searching for. Colonies of little gulls (14 pairs) and black terns (10 pairs) breed, and lesser spotted eagles if not breeding are at least regularly present. The area is excellent during passage periods and is the wintering ground for many wildfowl.

SUMMER: red-necked grebe, black-necked grebe, night heron, bittern, little bittern, pochard, tufted duck, ferruginous duck, hen harrier, marsh harrier, lesser spotted eagle, crane, little crake, spotted crake, little gull, black tern, bluethroat, icterine warbler, marsh warbler, barred warbler, river warbler, Savi's warbler, scarlet grosbeak.

In effect Druzno is the centre of a vast reclaimed depression. It is largely overgrown and only gradually passes into 'solid' land that is itself very marshy. The reclamation has involved building a series of high walls and a great part of the lake can be overlooked from them. Elblag to the north is the ideal base and there is a tourist information centre. The Elblag canal runs through Druzno amongst the reeds and is an excellent way of seeing the birds by boat. This canal is unique in that ramps and inclines are used to haul boats across the narrow strips of land that separate the lakes. Elblag can be reached by train and 'bus from Gdańsk. Permits from Wojewodzki Konserwator Przyrody, Gdańsk, ul. 3 Maja 9.

A white stork comes in to its bulky nest in a rush.
These birds are widespread over most of temperate Europe except France

A party of bean geese arrives at pasture in Germany. The low lying southern shore of the North Sea is the most important area in Europe for wintering wildfowl

A pratincole at its nest in the Camargue. These tern-like waders are common summer visitors to the Mediterranean region

The flock of flamingos in the Camargue is one of the most famous bird-sights in Europe.
Sometimes these birds also breed at a secret place in southern Spain

Confined to the north and east as a breeding bird, cranes can be seen at many places
as they pass through on migration

Goosanders, like the other sawbills, are northern birds as far as most European bird-watchers are concerned

A great skua pursues a pale phase arctic skua at the island of Foula

# GDAŃSK

There are a number of outstanding areas within striking distance of what was formerly Danzig. Most are on the Zatoka Gdańsk shore and the first is virtually in the city's suburbs.

1. **Vistula Mouth:** the Vistula originates high up in the mountains of Sudeten Czechoslovakia and passes through Krakow and Warsaw before reaching the Baltic; 30 kilometres from its mouth it divides into two channels. The eastern one the Negat joining the Zalew Wislany the former Frisches Haff, and the western branch dividing into three outlets near Gdańsk. Though all four exits are good for birds, and the eastern one into the all but land locked haff passes through a vast area of reclaimed marshes, it is the middle of the three western mouths that concerns us here. As the river flows westwards parallel to the coast it turns northwards on the outskirts of Gdańsk and passes through the dune coastline to reach the Baltic. Part of this channel has been improved by building stone banks and this operation has enclosed the large dune lakes that form the nature reserve at Ptasi Raj to the north-west of Gorki Wschodnie. The two shallow lakes have large areas of reeds and scrub and are ideally situated next to the sea and the muddy river banks. The wealth of breeding birds, which includes wood sandpiper and ruff and a wide range of reed birds such as bearded tit, and river and Savi's warblers, is augmented by a colossal passage along the coast. Amongst the regular species are spotted redshank, curlew sandpiper, Arctic skua, Caspian tern and up to 800 little gulls. The adjacent woodland holds the usual species for this part of Europe.

SUMMER: wood sandpiper, little ringed plover, ruff, little gull, bearded tit, barred warbler, icterine warbler, river warbler, Savi's warbler.

AUTUMN: hen harrier, white-tailed eagle, spotted redshank, curlew sandpiper, sanderling, bar-tailed godwit, Arctic skua, little gull, Caspian tern, Sandwich tern, bluethroat, great grey shrike.

The road eastwards along the northern bank of the Vistula in Gdańsk leads to a ferry across the outlet and to the Ptasi Raj reserve.

2. **Mierzeja Wislana:** this is the strip of land that almost separates the former Frisches Haff from the Baltic and is more or less a continuation of the famous strip of dunes that encloses the notable Kurskij Zaliz (Kurisches Haff). The famous bird observatory at Rybačij (Rositten) lies on the northern peninsula but being now part of the Soviet Union is of difficult access. The Mierzeja Wislana, which lies half in Poland, holds no observatories but the village of Krynica Morska is the ideal spot for watching one of the most dramatic bird migrations. A month of watching from mid-September recently produced nineteen species of duck, fourteen species of raptors, sixteen of waders, and up to 2,000 chaffinches per minute! Almost a hundred species were observed including oddities like little crake, bittern, penduline tit, and bearded tit.

AUTUMN: black-throated diver, black stork, scaup, ferruginous duck, velvet scoter, eider, smew, white-fronted goose, lesser white-fronted goose, bean goose, whooper swan, golden eagle, rough-legged buzzard, white-tailed eagle, honey buzzard, marsh harrier, hen harrier, Montagu's harrier, little crake, Arctic skua, little gull, nutcracker, penduline tit, bearded tit, serin, crossbill.

There is a road eastward from Gdańsk to Krynica Morska amongst the dunes. Petrol can be bought in the village.

3. **Rewa:** to the north of Gdańsk in the Gulf of Puck is the sand promontory at Rewa. This is bordered to the north by the marshes of the river Reda and a fringe of peat bogs. It is an excellent area for migrating shorebirds twenty-two species of which were recently noted in a fortnight, and all sorts of terns occur. A hill between the Rewa road and the Reda river rises to 150 feet and is well forested, adding breeding passerines to the variety of birds that can be seen in the neighbourhood.

AUTUMN: scaup, scoter, whimbrel, bar-tailed godwit, black-tailed godwit, wood sandpiper, green sandpiper, Temminck's stint, little stint, curlew sandpiper, broad-billed sandpiper, Arctic skua, little gull, black tern, Caspian tern.

Leave Gdańsk northwards on route 52 and turn right to Rewa just after Gdynia.

4. **Kartuzy:** Kartuzy lies 30 km west of Gdańsk and is typical of this part of Poland. Most of the land is agricultural but a considerable area is covered by forest and there are some quite large lakes. To the south-west of Kartuzy are a series of post-glacial lakes, the largest of which are Raduńskie, Kiodno, and Ostrzyckie. They are not rich in fringe vegetation and do not hold large numbers of birds, nevertheless the variety is impressive. Little bittern, the two storks, garganey and probably goldeneye breed and three species of grey geese are frequent winter and passage visitors. Birds of prey of eight species, including white-tailed eagle, breed in the neighbourhood, and cranes may do so. There is the usual array of warblers and other small birds.

SUMMER: red-necked grebe, little bittern, white stork, black stork, golden-eye(?), goshawk, black kite, white-tailed eagle, hen harrier, osprey(?), crane(?), little ringed plover, golden oriole, thrush nightingale, river warbler, great reed warbler, marsh warbler, barred warbler, red-breasted flycatcher, serin, ortolan bunting.

Kartuzy can be reached by train and bus and there is a good network of roads through the lake area.

## GOPLO LAKE

The lake is situated in the plains of central Poland 40 km south of Torun. It covers 33 sq km and its long indented shoreline supports a thick growth of emergent vegetation in several places giving way to considerable tracts of marshes. There are some areas of woodland but most of the surrounding land is agricultural. Though it boasts no eagles, no less than four species of harrier have been seen here, three of which breed, and the pallid harrier is an occasional visitor. Montagu's harrier is something of a local speciality as is the red kite. Greylags number about a hundred breeding pairs, and seven species of duck breed. From two to five pairs of cranes breed each year in three widely separated spots and there are colonies of black and common terns. Fifteen species of warbler breed and the lake's most recent acquisitions are penduline and bearded tits, and Savi's warbler. A total of 182 species has been recorded here but no less than 131 of these were breeding.

SUMMER: red-necked grebe, black-necked grebe, little bittern, bittern, white stork, ferruginous duck, greylag goose, cormorant, black kite, red kite, Montagu's harrier, marsh harrier, hen harrier, goshawk, black tern, common tern, roller, nightingale, thrush nightingale, penduline tit, bearded tit, great grey shrike, Savi's warbler, great reed warbler, icterine warbler, barred warbler, serin, ortolan bunting.

Goplo can be seen from many vantage points around its shores and is best approached from the west via Poznan, from where there are trains to Inowroclaw. Knuszwica at the northern end would be a good base for the marshes on the eastern side.


## MASURIAN LAKES

The Masurian Lake District lies in the north-eastern corner of Poland between the Soviet border and the River Vistula and thus extends over 350 km from east to west. The whole complex is glacial in origin and the landforms are resultingly varied. Though many of the lakes are shallow with a wealth of emergent vegetation some are decidedly deep with a consequent lack of plants. Known as 'Kraina Tysiąca Jezior', the land of the thousand lakes – though in fact there are well over four thousand – the area is a beautiful holiday playground that regularly attracts thousands of visitors. There are regular boat services from one part of the lakes to another, several of which pass right through interesting ornithological areas. The lakes are set in forests of deciduous and coniferous trees and they are of significant value to birds of prey. There are many ornithological reserves which can be visited, and which hold excellent collections of birds.

1.  **Lake Sniardwy:** in the east of the region and the largest lake in Poland covering 25,000 acres. Waves frequently reach 4 feet in height and the shoreline in some places has been cut into cliffs. There, however, extensive reed beds and small islands that shelter birds.

2.  **Lake Lukniary:** near Mikolajki adjacent to Lake Sniardwy with a large reserve that is the home of a thousand pairs of mute swan the largest concentration of this species in the world – Britain's Abbotsbury is artificially restricted to eight hundred pairs.

**3. Jezioro Siedmiu Wysp:** also has mute swans and a wealth of other interesting species like crane, black stork, greylag and bean geese, and is also a reserve.

**4. Lake Mamry:** the second largest lake only marginally smaller than Sniardwy and lies north of Gizycko. It has several islands one of which is named after the colony of cormorants that breed on it, and has areas of reeds and sedge. Amongst an interesting collection of birds both species of nightingale and river warbler are outstanding.

**5. Lake Kruklin:** south-east of Mamry and tiny in comparison, a mere 500 acres. It has ten thousand pairs of black-headed gulls and is quite a good place for autumn waders. Odd species like Caspian tern are sometimes seen here.

**6. Oswin Lake:** north of Mamry near the Soviet border and quite small. There is a bird reserve.

**7. Pogubie Wielkie Lake:** a small lake with an island bird reserve south of Sniardwy.

**8. Karas Lake:** away from the main area south-west of Ostroda. The whole area is included in a bird reserve of almost 2,500 acres. To the west is a marshy reedy area almost as big as the lake itself.

SUMMER: black-necked grebe, red-necked grebe, cormorant, grey heron, bittern, white stork, black stork, mute swan, greylag goose, ferruginous duck, goldeneye, goosander, lesser spotted eagle, goshawk, marsh harrier, black kite, white-tailed eagle, osprey, peregrine, black-tailed godwit, ruff, quail, crane, spotted crake, thrush nightingale, aquatic warbler, ortolan bunting.

The best centres are in the Sniardwy–Mamry complex and the villages of Mrągowo, Ruciane, Gizyeko, and Węgorzewo are recommended locally. Boats can be hired at all four and long trips made through the chains of lakes. Trains run to three of the villages and Olsztyn is the best starting point. Ruciane, Mrągowo and Gizycko have camping sites and the latter boasts the Mazurski Hotel, Plac Grumwaldzki 17.

As a tourist and holiday centre the Masurian Lakes are well served with facilities and with or without a car form an excellent bird-watching region. Permits from Wojewódzki Konserwator Przyrody, Olztyn, ul. Kopernika 48.

## PIENINY MOUNTAINS

The Pieniny mountains are near neighbours of the more famous Tatras, are much inferior in height, and yet have a delightful charm of their own. They are more wooded and park like with extensive pine woods but are not without a ruggedness that is most obvious in the superb winding gorge of the River Dunajec. A favourite tourist treat is a trip downstream on a raft piloted by a traditionally dressed mountaineer and entertained by folk singers. One bird-watcher saw buzzard, hobby, black and white storks, great grey shrike, hoopoe, little ringed plover, and rock thrush on one of these trips. The highest point is the Trzy Korony (Three crowns) peak, at 2,500 feet well below the tree line, and the avifauna lacks the high Alpine element found in the Tatras. Nevertheless rock thrush and wall creeper are found with the two eagles, golden and lesser spotted, and three species of woodpecker. Both redwing and fieldfare breed and nutcrackers and crossbills are found in the extensive pine forests. A large part of the area was declared a national park in 1954 though protected since 1921.

SUMMER: black stork, golden eagle, lesser spotted eagle, eagle owl, black grouse, hazel hen, nutcracker, three-toed woodpecker, white-backed wood-pecker, grey-headed woodpecker, rock thrush, fieldfare, redwing, wall creeper, marsh warbler, crossbill.

Szczawnica is the base for exploration and the Orlica chalet is a good place to stay. There are tourist chalets in Kroscienko, and a small 'Orbis' hotel in Czorsztyn. Access to the area is by bus from Kraków and Zakopane. Permits from Dyreckcja Pieninskiego Parku Narodowego, Króscienko, ul. Jagiel-lónska 5/6, pow. Nowy Targ, woj Kraków.


## SŁOWIŃSKI NATIONAL PARK

The outstanding coastal area between Leba and Rowami, a distance of 30 km, was declared a National Park in the autumn of 1966 covering 45,000 acres. The huge mobile dune system here reaches over 100 feet in height and is noted for its rich flora. There are also two large lakes, Lebsko 18,000 acres and Gardno 6,200 acres, and several smaller waters including Lake Dolgie between the two. Both of the major waters have large areas of marshes particularly on the south-western side and both are shallow and extensively overgrown with emergent vegetation. There are vast reed beds and the marshes are particularly difficult to penetrate. Only the strip of dunes separate them from the Baltic and there are narrow exits to the sea. Poles are wont to claim this area as the most beautiful dune scenery in Europe and certainly from the bird point of view it is outstanding. Eagle owl and white-tailed eagle breed and hen harriers are said to be common. Amongst the hordes of wildfowl are greylag, tufted, pochard, and gadwall, with a heavy passage of sawbills, long-tailed duck, and goldeneye. The reeds and marshes hold crane, Savi's warbler, blue-throat, and black-tailed godwit, and stone curlews breed on the sandy wastes. The concentration of migrants in both spring and autumn along this coast brings large numbers of waders and wildfowl to the marshes and lakes. This is undoubtedly a very fine area and it is encouraging that such a valuable site has been made a National Park.

SUMMER: great crested grebe, pochard, tufted duck, gadwall, greylag goose, mute swan, crane, white-tailed eagle, hen harrier, black-tailed godwit(?), stone curlew, long-eared owl, eagle owl, red-breasted flycatcher, bluethroat, Savi's warbler(?).

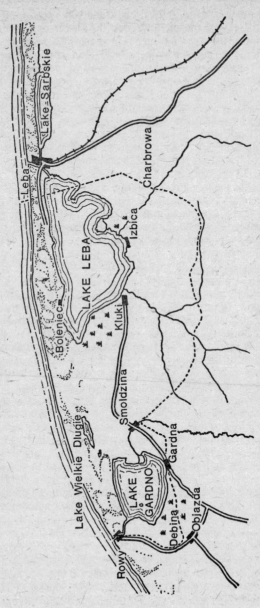

BALTIC

Lake-Sarbskie

Leba

Charbrowa

Boleniec

LAKE LEBA

Izbica

Kluki

Smoldzina

Lake Wielkie Dlugie

LAKE GARDNO

Gardna

Debina

Rowy

Objazda

The Słowiński National Park lies within the dotted line on the Polish Baltic coast. Though of interest throughout the year, in autumn the area is a major migration post.

AUTUMN: goldeneye, long-tailed duck, merganser, goosander, shelduck.

Though a National Park a large part of the area including the two largest lakes can easily be explored from roads and tracks and indeed along the shore. Leba, where there is a tourist information centre and a camp site, is the best place to stay. It is adjacent to the outlet of Lake Lebsko and within motoring distance of the other good spots. There are a number of marshland villages on the inland side of the lakes but accommodation would probably be a problem. The Director of the National Park is at Leba Al. Wojska Polskiego 9, woj Gdańsk. The best route to Leba is by train or bus from Gdansk, Gdyni, or Koszalina.

## TATRZANSKI NATIONAL PARK

The Polish Tatras lie on the Czechoslovak border in the extreme south of the country and are best reached from Kraków. They are part of the Carpathian chain and consist for the most part of granite giving rise to a dramatic peak and valley landscape. Mount Rysy, about 6,250 feet, is the highest peak though there are others in Czechoslovakia that are higher. The scenery is spectacular with gorges and a network of streams and lakes, pine clad hillsides, and Alpine meadows. Like most mountainous areas the Tatras are best treated as vertical ecological zones as most of the birds are widespread in their particular habitats. Below 3,000 feet there is mainly mixed forest, while above this up to 3,750 feet is the coniferous zone which continues with smaller trees up to 4,500 feet. Alpine meadows and grasses then take over and gradually merge into the open rock areas of the tops.

The National Park covers 55,000 acres and was created in 1954. The adjacent Czech Tatra National Park was created in 1948 but was enlarged at the same time as the creation of the Polish Park. Sixty people are employed in the Park half of whom are guards. Though the mammals including ibex, bear, wolf, lynx, and marmot are a major interest, the birds of the area are an attraction in their own right. Golden and lesser spotted eagles breed as do an excellent collection of owls including eagle, Ural, and Tengmalm's. Black stork nest along the Cicha Woda and Bialka rivers and various grouse species can be found in the pines and open country above, while the classic and exquisite rarity, the wall-creeper, is resident in the Park. 230 species have been recorded.

SUMMER: black stork, golden eagle, lesser spotted eagle, red kite, peregrine, hobby, long-eared owl, eagle owl, Ural owl, Tengmalm's owl, black grouse, capercaillie, hazel hen, nutcracker, three-toed woodpecker, rock thrush, wall creeper, willow tit, Alpine accentor, crossbill.

Zakopane is the stepping off point for the Park and lies 90 km south of Kraków. There are over a million and a half visitors each year and most of the area can be explored. Permits to visit the protected area can be obtained from Dyrekcja (Director) Tatrzanskiego Parku Narodowego, Zakopane, ul. Chalubinskiego 42a. There is a good selection of hotels in Zakopane, including two 'Orbis' pensions, and twenty mountain refuges and chalets higher up in the Park. These all lie on marked tourist tracks and several can be reached by car. They provide quite luxurious headquarters for exploration and are within walking distance of each other.

## WARSAW

There are two outstanding ornithological sites within striking distance of central Warsaw. Some 10 km to the west is the

1. **Puszcza Kampinoska:** a complex of mixed lowland forests between the rivers Vistula and Bzury. The area was formerly the course of the Vistula and a large tract of marshes remains. The forests are frequently very damp but there are drier areas, and in some places open cultivated fields. There are also peat bogs, and the whole area is famous as exhibiting a mosaic of landforms. Some of the most interesting parts form the Kampinoski National Park covering 50,000 acres, and are the home of elk and a wide variety of interesting birds. Though so near the largest city in the country, Kampinoska is not just convenient, it is first rate. Short-toed eagle, red and black kites, peregrine and hobby, and probably hen harrier are among the raptors and black stork and crane are among other 'suburban' birds. The forest of Leśna podkowa, part of Skuly forest, is a good spot for many species.

SUMMER: black stork, short-toed eagle, red kite, black kite, peregrine, hobby, hen harrier, crane, stone curlew, short-eared owl, capercaillie, white-backed woodpecker, hoopoe, golden oriole, woodchat shrike, lesser grey shrike, bluethroat, barred warbler, thrush nightingale.

There are 'buses from Warsaw along the southern side of the Puszca route 17 and some of the area can be explored from this. For access to the Park, contact Dyrekcja (Director) Kampinoskiego Parku Narodowego Izabelin, pow. Pruszhów, woj. Warszawa. Information can be obtained from Stacji Badawczej Instytutu Ekologicznego PAN in Dziekanowie.

2. **Zegrze Lake:** immediately north of Warsaw, the Bug and Narew rivers were dammed below their confluence in 1962. The resulting lowland is surrounded by swamplands and an excellent area for migrating wildfowl. Unfortunately the area has not been studied and there is little information as to breeding birds. But one can imagine that a wetland of this magnitude in this part of Europe would soon attract a wealth of interesting species.

SUMMER: unknown but probably rewarding.
AUTUMN: wildfowl.
Leave Warsaw northwards on route 11.

## WOLIN ISLAND

This large inhabited island lies in the mouth of the River Oder on Poland's western boundary, between the fresh lake Szczecinski and the Baltic Sea. It covers 125,000 acres and is a gently undulating land reaching a maximum height of 350 feet. Though very sandy there are some quite high cliffs along the coast. Sandy ridges are covered with conifers and there are large areas of meadows, peat bogs, and a total of 1,750 acres of lake. Primitive mixed forests cover considerable areas and in many places these are flooded and marshy. In the middle of the island the Wolin National Park was established in 1960 covering 12,000 acres. One of its principle objects was the protection of the breeding white-tailed eagles. Other probable breeders include lesser spotted eagle, osprey, and honey buzzard, though there is no doubt about the breeding of black kite and eagle owl.

Lying on the southern Baltic coast, Wolin is an excellent place for migrants and collects an interesting range of waders and wildfowl. Both wild swans, both scoter, eider and goldeneye winter, and the latter may well breed. Kentish plovers pass through and so do Caspian terns.

SUMMER: goldeneye(?), mute swan, lesser spotted eagle(?), osprey(?), honey buzzard(?), white-tailed eagle, black kite, peregrine, eagle owl.

AUTUMN: long-tailed duck, scoter, velvet scoter, eider, whooper swan, Bewick's swan, Kentish plover, Caspian tern.

There are trains and buses to the island, which is a seaside resort, from Szczecin. Tourist information available in Dziwnowie, Swinoujsciu and Miedzyzdroje, and the latter boats two 'Orbis' pensions and a camp site. Visitors should try to cover the marshes in the south-west as well as the lakes, forests and other habitats. Permits for the National Park are obtainable from Dyrekcja (Director) Wolinskiego Parku Narodowego, Miedzyzdroje, A1. Niepodleglosci 3, woj. Szczecin.

# Portugal

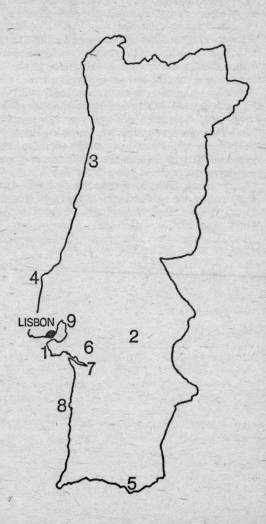

SOCIEDADA PORTUGUESA DE ORNITOLOGIA,
Seccâo de Zodogia, Faeuldade Ciências, Porto.

READ: *The Birds of Portugal* (1924) by W. Tait.

## LAGOA DE ALBUFEIRA

Though superficially an interesting-looking wetland this lagoon, situated next to the sea and joined at high tide by an artificial cut, is apparently useless for birds. In summer it is the resort of water-skiers and skin-divers, and in spring at least though undisturbed it held nothing when recently prospected. The marshy inland appendix boasted a purple heron, white stork, and a moorhen but hardly enough to merit international consideration. Nevertheless the surroundings are very attractive with fields of hay, olive groves, stone pines, huge pine forests, scrub and open dunes with an attractive flora. There are a wealth of birds including buzzard, rare in western Portugal, plus the great spotted cuckoo and azure-winged magpie that are more generally associated with the Alentejo. Warblers include Bonelli's, orphean, and Sardinian, and Scop's owl can be heard.

SUMMER: white stork, purple heron, buzzard, stone curlew, little owl, Scop's owl, great spotted cuckoo, great grey shrike, woodchat shrike, azure-winged magpie, bee-eater, hoopoe, Sardinian warbler, orphean warbler, Bonelli's warbler, fan-tailed warbler, cirl bunting.

The Lagoa can be reached on rough tracks southwards from a minor road off the N10. At the head of the marsh there is a large colony of bee-eaters adjacent to the road. This is probably the best bird-watching within the distance of Lisbon.

## ALENTEJO

The Alentejo is a working agricultural landscape with vast wheatfields, cork oak plantations, and rolling rocky hills. It is an arid land with cactus in the hedges though in spring the flowers, and particularly the yellow lupins, give a misleading picture of fertility. The plains stretch all the way from Montemore-o-Novo to the Spanish frontier and are progressively more interesting the nearer you get to the border. Elvas to Badajoz is the most exciting part of the Alentejo and contains most of the typical birds of this habitat. The great bustard is the outstanding bird and it is often seen from the main road. Andalucian hemipodes are another speciality though they are much less likely to be seen. There are only two areas of water, a small lake near Borba and the Caia river that forms the border. They are particularly important and therefore worth watching in summer when the Alentejo is unbearably hot.

SUMMER: white stork, little egret, great bustard, little bustard, Andalucian hemipode, hoopoe, crested lark, thekla lark, golden oriole, great grey shrike, woodchat shrike, black-eared wheatear.

To view this area, merely drive across the N4 and stop at likely spots. Much better is to make a base at Elvas and explore along the roads that run in all directions. In Elvas there is the hotel, the Pousada de Santa Lucia which is of the usual excellent standard. There is also a camp site. Évora, to the west, is worth a visit and has lesser kestrels on the cathedral.

## AVEIRO

Aveiro lies at the mouths of several rivers, the most important of which are the Rio Vouga and Rio Agueda. The rivers have been forced by the build-up of the dune beach to find a common exit to the sea and this they have done via an intricate lagoon system. The town itself lies on the landward side of the lagoons and the surrounding land is flat with what were formerly rice fields. Aveiro is reminiscent of Venice with its buildings ranged along canal banks and the life of the town revolves around the lagoons and sea.

The lagoons are reed fringed and cover an area that together with the surrounding marshes amounts to 45,000 acres. Almost anywhere is good for birds, but the following places are known to be very good:

1.  **The northern arm:** good for warblers particularly fan-tailed, and for black kites which are numerous throughout the area. This part can be seen to advantage along the Ovar–San Jacinto road which can be reached via the new Bestida–Torreira bridge. The Pousada da Ria lies along this sandspit and all the bedrooms have a terrace overlooking the lagoons, so you can combine ornithology and your early morning tea (coffee?). The spit and hotel can also be reached by ferry from Aveiro.

2.  **The main marsh area** lies to the north of Aveiro and east of the main lagoon. This has been extensively reclaimed and drainage ditches make access frustratingly awkward. Nevertheless the area is worth exploring with cattle and little egrets and other herons, marsh harrier and black kite and various warblers. The best way to explore this region is by boat which can be hired in Aveiro. There are, however, many tracks leading on to the marsh and these do provide access.

3.  **Salt pans** lie between Aveiro and the coast along the Barra road from which many can be seen. Others can be approached on foot from this road. Egrets are common here and Kentish plover and black-winged stilt are numerous. There is a heavy wader passage and many interesting species can be seen.

4.  **Saltmarsh areas** are less important than the others. The major one lies north of the Aveiro–Barra road just before the bridge across the main lagoon. Birds include waders, gulls, and terns.

SUMMER: white stork, little egret, cattle egret, marsh harrier, black kite, Kentish plover, little ringed plover, black-winged stilt, avocet, fan-tailed warbler.

PASSAGE: flamingo, waders.

Apart from the Pousada da Ria there are several other hotels in Aveiro and camp sites at Ovar, Torreira, and San Jacinto.

## BERLENGA ISLANDS

Berlenga lies a few km off the Portuguese west coast north of Lisbon, and its rugged shoreline is a beautiful haunt of seabirds. There is a cold upwelling here that is rich in marine life and that consequently attracts large numbers of feeding birds. It is, however, as a breeding haunt that the islands are famous and in particular for nesting Cory's shearwaters in the north-east. Other breeders include guillemot, shag, and various species of gull. Blue rock thrush and rock sparrow are both common. Migrant passerines are often noted at the lighthouse in autumn but pride of place at this season goes to Sabine's gull, numbers of which regularly occur offshore. Other interesting seabirds include Balearic shearwater, Wilson's petrel, all four skuas, and phalaropes.

SUMMER: Cory's shearwater, shag, guillemot, blue rock thrush, black redstart, rock sparrow.

AUTUMN: Cory's shearwater, Manx shearwater, Balearic shearwater, Wilson's petrel, gannet, Sabine's gull, great skua, Arctic skua, pomarine skua, long-tailed skua, phalaropes, passerine migrants.

Berlenga Island is reached by daily boat (in season) from Peniche, fare 10s return, no booking needed. The Pousada de São João Baptista is an hotel perched like a fortress on an offshore rock linked to the island by a short causeway. If camping, it is advisable to take all water and food, except fish, from the mainland.

With the known autumn concentrations of migrants in the Cape St Vincent area this island seems to be one of the most outstanding sites for a bird observatory in Europe. Seabirds offshore merely adds to its importance and attraction.

## FARO

Faro is the largest and most important town on the Algarve coast. It lies behind a huge complex of sand bars and islands that stretches away eastwards beyond Tavira. It is the build up of sand along this coast that has enclosed the lagoons that are the major ornithological attraction of the area. There is a maze of islands and peninsulas of varying sizes and with varying amounts of cover. The water is saline and the whole area dominated by tides. Passage is particularly attractive with really large numbers of waders of a wide variety of species. Regulars include black-winged stilt, avocet, godwits, wood sandpiper, curlew sandpiper, little stint, and most other species that one could expect to see entering and leaving north-west Africa. In addition there is a good selection of breeding birds including marsh and Montagu's harriers on the marshes inland, both kites and lesser kestrel. Pratincole breed on the parched areas and little bitterns are found in some places, but really the breeding birds have not been thoroughly investigated.

SUMMER: white stork, little bittern, red kite, black kite, buzzard, lesser kestrel, Kentish plover, pratincole, azure-winged magpie.

PASSAGE: grey plover, turnstone, whimbrel, black-tailed godwit, green sandpiper, wood sandpiper, curlew sandpiper, greenshank, ruff, little stint, sanderling, black-winged stilt, avocet, terns, gulls.

Several tracks leave Faro southwards and it is quite possible to drive out amongst the lagoons and see many birds from a car. Indeed, cars make an excellent hide for photography here. Explore the marsh behind the town and the pine woods to east and west for azure-winged magpies. There is a camp site and several good hotels.

## MARATECA

Between the plains of the Alentejo and the estuaries of the Tagus and Sado and yet physically part of the Alentejo is an area of rolling countryside with cork oaks and pines along the N10. This sandy area is park-like and only interrupted here and there by agriculture. It is an excellent area for most of the species typical of the Alentejo, plus a number of woodland birds. It is a particularly favourite haunt of white stork and up to a dozen nests can be found in a single tree. Azure-winged magpies are numerous and hoopoe, various shrikes, and turtle dove find this mixture of habitats ideal. It is, however, too far west for great bustards, but little bustards can be found in the more open parts.

SUMMER: white stork, cattle egret, little bustard, hoopoe, golden oriole, great grey shrike, woodchat shrike, azure-winged magpie, wryneck, crested lark, thekla lark, black-eared wheatear, orphean warbler, serin, hawfinch.

Drive along the N10 on a circular tour from Lisbon via the Salazar Bridge and Vila Franca de Xira. The main area is between Marateca and Porto Alto. The cross-roads at Marateca overlook a colony of white storks and with rice fields nearby there is a constant movement of these birds overhead. Try to stop anywhere along the road where pines and corks are found together.

## SADO ESTUARY

It is perhaps strange that the two most important wetlands in Portugal should lie within a few km of each other. The Tagus and Sado are both workable in a day and to stay on the Setúbal peninsula between them is an excellent way of seeing many of the best birds in the country. The Sado is not well known though the habitats of open shore, alkaline marshes, salines, lagoons, and large areas of rice fields are rich in birds. Certainly 400 pairs of white storks breed and there are colonies of herring gulls, terns, and avocets and black-winged stilts. There are three major areas that need exploring. In the north between the fishing port of Setúbal and Marateca is a large area of marshes and salt pans intersected by many creeks and with shoals in the river. Pines here hold great spotted cuckoo. Across the river and immediately to the south is another similar area bound on the western side by the large sand-dune beach generally referred to as Tróia. Behind the beach to the south is the village of Comporta with interesting marshes and storks in the village. Higher up the river on both banks below Alcacer do Sal are a further series of salt pans. Alcacer itself is surrounded by open pine woods and cork oak forests that are excellent for birds including azure-winged magpie and the old citadel has a colony of storks.

SUMMER: white stork, little egret, cattle egret, marsh harrier, black kite, avocet, black-winged stilt, terns, hoopoe, great grey shrike, woodchat shrike, azure-winged magpie.

PASSAGE; WINTER: waders.

The coastal road eastwards beside the railway from Setúbal runs out to the marshes and salines on the northern bank and waders concentrate here at high tide. From Alcacer in the higher estuary it is possible to explore along the river bank salines in one direction and amongst the irrigated rice crops in the other. Comporta is reached by leaving the N120 at Grandola on a mixture of tracks and auto-routes. There is the hotel Estalagem Herdade do Barrosinha in Alcacer.

## SINES

Sines is a pretty coastal town on a peninsula in south-western Portugal. To the south are the rugged cliffs that stretch almost without interruption to Cape St Vincent, while northwards there is a vast beach that is uninterrupted to Tróia near Setúbal. The rocky shore holds blue rock thrush and black redstart, with tawny pipit, black-eared wheatear, and Sardinian warbler on the open tops. To the north of the town the pines are alive with serins and there are great grey and woodchat shrikes, larks, and a pretty steady passage of seabirds. 17 km to the north are two lagoons:

1. Lagoa de Santo André.
2. Lagoa de Melides.

Both are separated from the sea by only the coastal dunes though both have a narrow channel to it through which small boats can pass at high tide. Their open sandy shores hold egrets, fair numbers of waders and there are always interesting gulls and terns, like gull-billed, to be seen. Kentish plover breed alongside the short-toed larks. Oddities like scoter, spoonbill, and goodness knows what else turn up. Inland, and between the two lagoons that are only a short distance apart, is a sandy waste of pines, olive groves, and poor crops. It holds stone curlew, great spotted cuckoo, orphean warbler, shrikes, and several colonies of bee-eaters, one along the road to Melides. This lagoon has more emergent vegetation and the reeds hold Cetti's warbler, with Bonelli's warbler nearby. Both waters are attractive, with a vast unspoilt beach adjacent, and ideal for migration-time holidays.

SUMMER: little egret, Kentish plover, stone curlew, great spotted cuckoo, great grey shrike, woodchat shrike, hoopoe, bee-eater, crested lark, short-toed lark, orphean warbler, Sardinian warbler, Cetti's warbler, fan-tailed warbler.

AUTUMN: seabirds, waders.

SPRING: gannet, spoonbill, little stint, sanderling, little ringed plover, Kentish plover, gull-billed tern, Sandwich tern.

Sines is easy to reach westwards off route 120 at Santiago do Cacém. The lagoons also have to be reached via Santiago but both have good roads, so it is possible to do Melides in the morning and St André in the afternoon because of the light – but beware of being cut off by the tides. There is good accommodation at Sines and Santiago.


## TAGUS ESTUARY

Between the two lowest bridged crossing places of the Tagus at Vila Franca de Xira and the great new Salazar Bridge in Lisbon itself, lies the 40 km estuary of Portugal's largest river. To the north and west it is bounded by the country's largest city and a range of low hills. In contrast, to the south and east is a flat lowland area insected by river channels but now largely drained and traditionally used for rearing fighting bulls. This lowland can be conveniently divided into two major parts.

In the north opposite Vila Franca and between the Tagus and its tributary, the Rio Samora, is Lezerias Land. This is the bull-breeding area of flat drained grasslands, but there has been an extension of irrigation and various annual crops are now raised. There are several creeks running deep into the meadows and in some places there are small lagoons with reed beds. Only a few eucalyptus trees break the horizon. Amongst a rich avifauna, cattle and little egrets, and white storks are regularly seen, two species of harrier are quite common, black kites are numerous, and small birds include bee-eater, roller, great grey shrike, short-toed lark, and vast numbers of waders at high tide. There are pratincoles in spring. South of the Rio Samora the land is more cultivated and less marshy with olive groves, vineyards, and pine woods. Though these are worth exploring it is the tributary river valleys that hold the greatest attractions. In their higher parts they have been turned into rice fields while along the Tagus itself are large areas of salt pans. The valley of the Rio das Enguias east of Alcochete is the best example. Avocet and black-winged stilt are the birds of the salines, though passage periods bring hordes of waders. The rice fields are generally unproductive though the marshy edges have a good variety of smaller birds. The Salinas west of Alcochete are also worth exploring.

The area is not well known and species lists, sites, and counts at all times of the year would be welcome.

SUMMER: white stork, bittern, cattle egret, little egret, purple heron, marsh harrier, Montagu's harrier, black kite, Kentish plover, avocet, black-winged stilt, pratincole, hoopoe, roller, bee-eater, crested lark, great grey shrike, rock sparrow.

PASSAGE: grey plover, little ringed plover, Kentish plover, little stint, curlew sandpiper, whimbrel, black-tailed godwit.

The Lezerias Land can be reached by crossing the bridge from Vila Franca de Xira and leaving the N10 to the south to Ponta da Erva; also it is possible to go westwards on a major track to the river. Do not venture onto the fields – there are fighting bulls! The southern area of rice fields and salines between Barreiro and Alcochete can be explored on a decent network of roads and there is a road up the western side of the excellent valley of Enguias. Exploration is unrestricted.

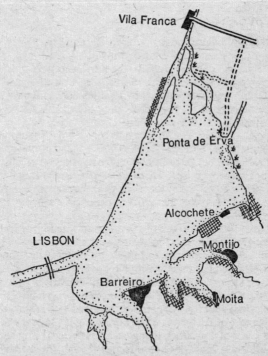

Tagus estuary – the cross-hatching represents the major areas of salinas which are the most important high tide roosts of waders. The road to Ponta de Erva is excellent.

# Romania

1 Băneasa and Lake Oltina
2 Călărași
3 Danube Delta
4 Danube Floods between
    Giurgiu and Oltenița

5 Ditrău
6 Dobroudja Hills
7 Satchinez

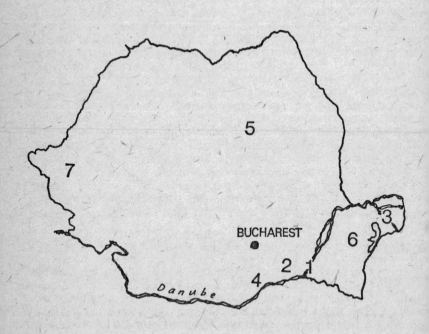

READ: *Systema Avium Romaniae* (1959) by G. D. Vasiliu, Alauda supplement.

## BĂNEASA AND LAKE OLTINA

This area on the southern bank of the Danube is typical of the agricultural land of the Dobroudja. The small village of Băneasa is surrounded by fields of wheat and maize, with steppe-like pastures, and areas of forest. To the east are the calcerous outcrops called *canaras*, a curiously eroded rock face with pillars that hold breeding Egyptian vultures and eagle owls. To the north, alongside the Danube, lies Lake Oltina which is some 8 km long and a noted haunt of waterbirds. The whole is good for birds and with an excellent variety of habitats in a confined area one can see a cross section of the birds of this part of south-east Europe without travelling at all.

Starting in the north Lake Oltina has reeds and a growth of willows and salix that harbours herons including purple and squacco, and the glossy ibis that one tends to take for granted in the lower Danube but which is otherwise virtually unknown in Europe. White pelicans are also frequently seen but do not breed. The fields and woods with the range of hills are the haunt of several raptors, though none can be said to be common. They include lesser spotted, white-tailed, and short-toed eagles, saker and honey buzzard, as well as the vulture. The area also shelters a wealth of smaller birds including olivaceous warbler, three species of shrike, Spanish sparrow, and one of Europe's peripheral birds, the pied wheatear, that breeds in the coastal regions of Romania and Bulgaria and nowhere else on the sub-continent.

SUMMER: white pelican, purple heron, squacco heron, little bittern, glossy ibis, garganey, honey buzzard, lesser spotted eagle, white-tailed eagle, Egyptian vulture, hen harrier, marsh harrier, short-toed eagle, saker falcon, goshawk, eagle owl, alpine swift, thrush nightingale, firecrest, bee-eater, hoopoe, lesser grey shrike, great grey shrike, icterine warbler, olivaceous warbler, pied wheatear, ortolan bunting, Spanish sparrow.

Băneasa lies on route 3, 100 km west of Constanţa, with Lake Oltina 8 km to the north. The *canaras* are to the east of the village. Exploration of the triangle between the Danube and the Bulgarian border should prove fruitful, and most of the birds should be seen without tramping over fields.

## CĂLĂRAŞI

There is a tendency to think of Romania as the Carpathians, the Danube Delta and not much else. In fact there are a number of other areas of outstanding ornithological interest that would be treasured by many less fortunate countries. The Danube floods twice each year and covers a vast area that remains marshy to varying extents throughout the year. On the Romanian side this is particularly extensive and there are some large lakes and strings of lakes that remain when the floods subside. It is, of course, impossible to divide this huge stretch of excellent bird-watching into manageable areas especially as there is little information available about many of the lakes, particularly those furthest from the sea. Yet if we are thinking in terms of conservation the whole area of the lower Danube valley must be considered, and we must look very carefully at any plan to construct reservoirs higher up the river with the inevitable control of flooding that this will involve. If we are trying to set out the best and most important ornithological sites in Europe we must include a large part of these marshes.

Here we are concerned with the area immediately west of Călăraşi, which is 127 km east of Bucharest on route 3, including the large Lake Călăraşi and its subsidiary waters. The lake itself is 15 km long but is so heavily overgrown that many maps show it in two halves. In the southern part particularly, extensive reed beds and growths of carex have created an impenetrable jungle. As the land dries out there is more salix, with willows and poplars along the river banks in the extreme south.

Interesting birds in the river bank forest include barred warbler, golden oriole, and penduline tit. It is, however, the salix and phragmites zone that holds the most interesting birds of the area, the herons. There are nine colonies of these birds in the southern half of the lake, four of which are on the subsidiary Lakes Melcu and Rotundu to the south-east. The most numerous bird is the glossy ibis, but there are also little egret, night heron, and squacco heron in these mixed colonies, and the 1,000 nest colony at Lake Derfu boasts 150 pairs of spoonbill, not a common bird in this region. Purple heron and little bittern are more scattered but are present in good numbers. Dalmatian pelicans are often present, pygmy cormorants breed, and there is a wealth of smaller birds including three marsh terns in the carex zone, and black-necked grebe, Savi's, moustached, and great reed warblers amongst the reeds.

SUMMER: black-necked grebe, Dalmatian pelican, pygmy cormorant, purple heron, squacco heron, night heron, little egret, glossy ibis, spoonbill, little bittern, black tern, white-winged black tern, whiskered tern, golden oriole, hoopoe, penduline tit, barred warbler, Savi's warbler, moustached warbler, great reed warbler.

There are roads to north-west and south-west out of Călăraşi providing good starting points for exploration. The one to the south-west towards Silistra in Bulgaria (no bridge or ferry) is particularly convenient and a walk westwards into the area along the banks of the Danube should produce most of the more exciting species. Lakes Melcu and Rotundu with the heronries lie very near this road. Route 3 from Bucharest leads directly to Călăraşi.

## DANUBE DELTA

The Danube carries more water than any other European river and runs 3,000 km from its origins in the Black Forest to its mouth on the Black Sea. Every year it brings down an estimated hundred million tons of silt that piles up at the mouth and is extending the delta at the incredibly rapid rate of 410 feet per year. Ninety kilometres from its mouth it splits into three channels, the Chilia, Sulina, and St Gheorghe which enclose nearly 3,000 sq km of reed-beds, swamps and lakes, intersected by innumerable smaller channels and backwaters. To the south, and separated from the St Gheorghe channel by a similar delta area of 1,500 sq km lie the large open waters of Lakes Razelm and Sinoe. Though these are connected to the sea they are included in this account together with the Delta proper. Though the Danube Delta is larger than the Camargue and Coto Donãna put together, the ornithological problems posed by such a vast area are to a considerable extent eased by the broad uniformity of the area. Over 95 per cent consists of reeds and lakes and though outstanding for birds of these interesting and declining habitats, the numbers of waders and most passerines is small. The growth of the delta is so fast that many former beaches have been left high and dry many kilometres from the sea. Several have extensive areas of deciduous woodland notably the largest island of Lutea between the Chilia and Sulina. This island has a village with its own church complete with white stork and an oak wood with a scattering of white poplar, ash, willow, and elm that cannot be more than 150 years old. These woods provide nest sites for a variety of raptors that frequent the marshes including honey buzzard, black kite, hobby, and lesser spotted and white-tailed eagles, as well as a variety of birds like golden oriole, icterine warbler, olivaceous warbler, thrush nightingale, and red-breasted flycatcher that are otherwise not found in the delta.

The build up of sandy beaches and islands is paralleled along the river courses themselves by the build-up of natural embankments. These 'dry-land' river margins which are flooded twice yearly are heavily overgrown with the sallow woods that are such a feature of the delta landscape and which add a grey-green touch to the monotonous yellow-brown reed beds. Typical birds found here include roller, hoopoe, hooded crow, kingfisher, river warbler and collared flycatcher, with black kite and marsh harrier constantly present and in view.

The reed beds often grow on a floating blanket of vegetation and being up to 16 feet in height are the dominant feature of the area. Here and there firmer land allows sallows to grow and these are favoured as breeding sites by the vast numbers of herons. Unlike the Coto Donãna and the Camargue, the mass of Danube lakes are fresh and hold a rich and varied population of fish; 47 species of fish are regularly found in the delta including three species of sturgeon. Easily the commonest bird is the glossy ibis. There are some 20 large mixed heronries varying from 10,000 nests downwards and in each there are probably more ibises than all other species put together. They are frequently seen flying over and it is impossible to move about in the delta without being constantly aware of their presence. This situation is in sharp contrast to the universal decline of this bird over the rest of Europe. Next in order of abundance are night and squacco herons and then rather fewer little egrets. The latter are, of course, the most numerous heron in the Coto and Camargue. The spoonbill is generally rather scarce as is the great white heron though the latter is frequently seen about the delta and its breeding haunts need not (and should not) be disturbed. Grey heron, purple heron, bittern and little bittern, all breed but are rather local or secretive and numbers are difficult to estimate.

The most outstanding birds are the pelicans both European species of which breed. The white pelican breeds at few other places in Europe and the Dalmatian pelican is otherwise only locally distributed in the Balkan peninsula. Last century the Dalmatian was the commonest but a catastrophic decline has reduced the population to less than 500 pairs and it is now outnumbered by the white with perhaps 2,000 pairs. The vast majority of the birds breed in the special reserve at Uzlina village though there are smaller colonies at Buhaiova and Zadoane. The situation varies annually and like terns the birds can abandon one site in favour of another without apparent reason. Though these magnificent birds were almost exterminated during the war they have now recovered and seem to be steadily increasing.

Also to be found amongst the reeds and lakes are good populations of greylag geese and various species of duck including white-headed duck. Over the lakes large numbers of marsh terns of three species can be seen while there is an interesting selection of gulls and terns to be found breeding on the coastal lagoons. These include gull-billed and Caspian terns, and slender-billed and Mediterranean gulls. Another bird found only on the saline lagoons to the south of the delta proper is the ruddy shelduck. This is one of the few European breeding sites but even here the reserve island of Popina in Lake Razelm is regularly used by shepherds. Waders are generally scarce in the delta but are found on these lagoons including avocet, black-winged stilt and pratincole.

SUMMER: pygmy cormorant, white pelican, Dalmatian pelican, purple heron, little egret, great white heron, squacco heron, night heron, spoonbill, glossy ibis, ferruginous duck, white-headed duck, ruddy shelduck, mute swan, lesser spotted eagle, white-tailed eagle, red-footed falcon, pratincole, slender-billed gull, Mediterranean gull, white-winged black tern, whiskered tern, gull-billed tern, Caspian tern, roller, calandra lark, short-toed lark, penduline tit, thrush nightingale, river warbler, Savi's warbler, moustached warbler, great reed warbler, olivaceous warbler, collared flycatcher, red-breasted flycatcher, lesser grey shrike.

AUTUMN: incredible passage of cranes, geese, and other species.

How does one summarize the inexhaustible possibilities of exploration in an area of nearly 6,000 sq km? Look at a map, choose an area, and explore it thoroughly and come back next year to do some more. At even a cursory glance the lagoons on the northern shore where Lakes Razelm and Sinoe join the sea look very likely places, and one part of the delta seems to be very much like any other. However, for most people the delta is a once and for all trip in which they will want to see as much as possible, and they must clearly aim to see a cross section of the habitats. Cruising down the channels and exploring a few backwaters amongst the reeds and lakes should produce most of the herons and other water birds. There is a two-day cruise from Tulcea to

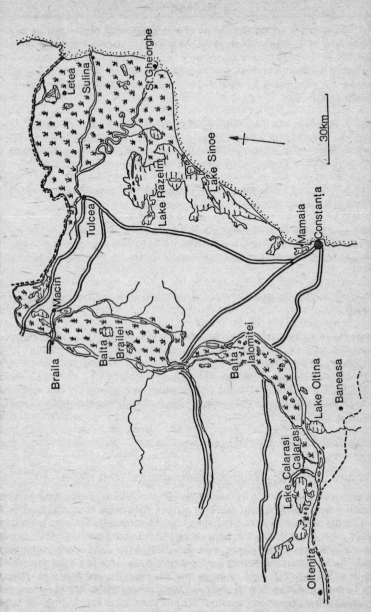

The Danube Delta and flood plain – the most important area for birds in Romania. Many of the marshes are being drained for agriculture and the situation changes from year to year.

Maliuc, the new village on the Sulina channel, that can be booked at any tourist bureau in Romania. Outings by rowing boat can be arranged through the hotel.

Accredited ornithologists may apply to the Romanian Academy of Sciences, Bucharest, for permission to visit the various reserve and sanctuary areas. These are as follows:

1.  **Rosca–Buhaiova–Hrecisca Reserve:** this covers 45,000 acres of the inland delta north of the Matita lake and depression. This has pelicans, herons, and glossy ibis colonies. Babitele on the eastern side of the Chilia sandbank and Lake Merheiul Mare form a buffer zone to the main part of the reserve.

2.  **Letea–Hasmacul Mare Reserve:** this covers 1,700 acres of marine sandbank and oak forests with the woodland species already described.

3.  **Perisor–Zataone Reserve:** this covers 35,000 acres of dunes, dune slacks, and lakes along the coast. This is the major haunt of mute swans and also has good numbers of herons. In autumn there are thousands of cranes and geese here.

4.  **Periteasca–Leahova Reserve:** this covers 10,000 acres of the Razelm–Sinoe lake area.

5.  There are an additional 20,000 acres of smaller special reserves including:
    a.  Popina Island in Lake Razelm for ruddy shelduck.
    b.  Uzlina and Lake Iacub at Crisan for pelicans and herons.
    c.  Golovita for great white heron and spoonbill.
    d.  Histria for Shelduck, here reaching a southern outpost.
    e.  Murighiol and Plopul (Beibugeac) where the salt marshes hold avocet and stilt.

6.  There is also a research station at Braila.

One of the best ways of seeing the delta is to join one of the parties organized specifically for naturalists. Half of the time is spent on a floating hotel (more like a cheap pension) which is towed around the delta and which stops at some of the best ornithological spots for guided tours of the reserves. Though there is little opportunity for individual exploration this is probably the cheapest way of seeing this outstanding area.

For those whose ambitions run to more intensive work an expedition approach is the only way. Permission to visit reserves should be sought well in advance and travel arrangements for cars and boats made locally. Tulcea is the natural place to start. Constanta, on the Black Sea coast, is an international airport.

## DANUBE FLOODS BETWEEN GIURGIU AND OLTENIŢA

The importance of the flood area of the lower Danube is outlined briefly under Călăraşi. The area between Giurgiu and Olteniţa is under water twice each year. Just below Giurgiu the river divides and the minor northern arm feeds a series of lakes and marshes including Lake Greaca which is 17 km long. In spite of these permanent lakes and marshes agriculture continues outside of the flood periods and the crops form a home for the numerous corncrakes. The main zone for birds lies in the south between the open water and the river where reed beds slowly give way to salix and willow. Herons are numerous and white storks are extremely common. Purple heron, little egret, night heron, and squacco heron all breed, the latter being particularly numerous around Prundu and Chirnogi. Glossy ibis frequently flight in to feed and pygmy cormorants are regular if rare breeders. Duck include ferruginous, and common, black and whiskered terns breed, the latter have become abundant since first breeding in 1952.

Because of increasing drainage at Lake Greaca the government are planning efficient protection of the Comana Forest and Lake Mostistea, both of which should be visited.

The reed beds hold great reed warbler and marsh harriers, the latter being said to be abundant, and the surrounding land contains a wealth of interesting species including bee-eater, golden oriole, lesser grey shrike, and ortolan bunting. Though never numerous the variety of raptors here is as good as anywhere in Romania and includes both spotted and lesser spotted, and white-tailed eagles.

SUMMER: pygmy cormorant, white stork, purple heron, little egret, night heron, squacco heron, little bittern, glossy ibis, teal, garganey, ferruginous duck, greylag goose, red-footed falcon, saker falcon, spotted eagle, lesser spotted eagle, white-tailed eagle, marsh harrier, common tern, black tern, whiskered tern, corncrake, spotted crake, little crake, golden oriole, bee-eater, lesser grey shrike, red-backed shrike, crested lark, sedge warbler, great reed warbler, ortolan bunting.

This extremely attractive area lies just over 50 km south of Bucharest and makes an excellent day out, though obviously worth a week or more. It is, however, a rich and still comparatively little known area that would undoubtedly repay investigation. There are cheap trains to Olteniţa from Bucharest.

## DITRĂU

Ditrău is a small village in the central Carpathians between Bacău and Tirgu Mures on route 12. The surrounding hills rise to the 6,000 feet mark though the countryside is basically open and rolling, with deep valleys cut by rather insignificant-looking streams. The woodlands are mainly coniferous and apparently semi-natural and hold a good population of nutcrackers. Other birds include sombre tit. Though Ditrău is principally known as the type locality for ditroite it has been visited by some bird-watchers who bring back reports of a variety of raptors, for which Romania is not terribly well off. These include golden and lesser spotted eagles, honey buzzard, and several falcons. The open areas of decaying woodland and bogs, as well as agricultural land hold crested lark, hoopoe, and black redstart. This area is not well known – you certainly will not find other foreigners – but seems to have promise for someone looking for fresh ground to break.

SUMMER: lesser-spotted eagle, golden eagle, honey buzzard, falcons, hoopoe, nutcracker, sombre tit, crested lark, black redstart.

Ditrău can be reached on route 12, but is also accessible by train to those who want to see the Carpathians and the Danube Delta in a single holiday.

## DOBROUDJA HILLS

In spite of the Carpathians Romania is not a particularly good country for raptors. The state has a very sensible attitude towards conservation and the establishment of reserves but birds of prey are still classified as 'harmful' and destroyed. Even the Danube Delta itself is not the raptor paradise one would imagine. Nevertheless the range of wooded hills immediately south of the river between Galati and Tulcea is one of the best places for these birds. The hills rise to 1,400 feet, are well wooded but with some crags, and slope gently down towards the sea and the Dobroudjan steppe. The best area lies between the Danube and the River Taita continued westwards from where it cuts northwards into the hills. It has been known as a haunt of raptors for a considerable time and as a result the smaller birds have been largely neglected. This is surely not due to their absence or lack of interest. Even the present situation regarding the raptors is not clear and any information on the avifauna of this area would be most welcome. Certainly there is a variety of eagles including imperial, white-tailed, and lesser spotted. Falcons include hobby and the magnificent saker, and there are also goshawks, buzzards, and black kites. Whether the griffon and black vultures that formerly bred on the crags and the pallid harrier are still to be found in spite of persecution is unknown.

SUMMER: black kite, goshawk, buzzard, lesser spotted eagle, imperial eagle, white-tailed eagle, pallid harrier(?), griffon vulture(?), black vulture(?), saker, hobby, red-footed falcon.

There are decent roads to the north and south of the range, several passable tracks across, and some useful cul de sacs into the hills. Tulcea is an excellent base for this area and for the Danube Delta, and visitors with a car should have little difficulty exploring. The following spots are known to be worth visiting from west to east.
1. Mts Greci for saker.
2. The forests of Cocoş and Valea Teilor for most of the other raptors and whatever passerines.

3. The steppe and marshland area between Nalbant and Isvoare for falcons and typical Dobroudja species.

The international airport at Constanţa is the obvious starting point.

## SATCHINEZ

In the extreme west of Romania the land drops from the heights of the Carpathians to the steppes of the Hungarian plain. Here the tributaries of the River Tisa meandered over the level ground slowly finding their way to the main river and ultimately to the Danube. Seasonal floods, oxbow lakes, pools and backwaters all created a marsh landscape that was systematically drained during the eighteenth century. Reed beds which contained glossy ibis and spoonbill till 1914 have given way to vast fields of cereals, and the sedge thickets and primeval oak forests have disappeared. Only in the area around Satchinez, 25 km north-west of Timişoara, has any area of marsh remained. The pools and marshes here were declared a Monument of Nature in 1942 and 100 acres now form the Satchinez Bird Reserve. The area is mainly noted as a breeding haunt of herons but when these birds moved in 1961, further areas north of Satchinez were incorporated to maintain protection. The species involved are purple heron, night heron, little egret, squacco heron, and little bittern and are mainly found at Rîtul Dutin and Rîtul Mărăşeşti. The reserve also harbours a range of other species that are rare in this part of the country including greylag, ferruginous duck, marsh harrier, and white-winged black tern. The pond surrounds are the haunt of penduline tit, bluethroat, and an interesting collection of warblers including reed, marsh, and Savi's warblers. The surrounding drained area is one of the best in Romania for great bustard.

SUMMER: purple heron, little egret, squacco heron, night heron, little bittern, white stork, greylag goose, ferruginous duck, marsh harrier, white-winged black tern, great bustard, penduline tit, bluethroat, Savi's warbler, reed warbler, marsh warbler.

Leave Timişoara northwards on route 69 and fork left to Sînandrei, and Satchinez just outside the town. The main marsh and pools lie south of the village and are a reserve, though in fact the reserve covers a very small part of the area and most of the birds can also be seen outside it. Timişoara is connected by air and train to other major Romanian cities.

# Spain

1 Southern Andalucia
2 Andorra
3 Badajoz
4 Coto Donãna
5 Ebro Delta
6 Estartit and La Escala
7 Sierra Guadarrama
8 Huelva

9 Majorca
10 Pamplona
11 Pyrenées
12 Ronda
13 Silos
14 Sierra Nevada
15 River Tiétar at Candeleda

SOCIEDAD ESPAÑOLA DE ORNITOLOGIA,
Castellana 84 (Museo Nacional de Ciencias Naturales), Madrid 6.

READ: *Prontuario de la avifauna Española* (*incluyendo aves de Portugal, Baleares, y Canarias*) (1955) by F. Bernis in *Ardeola*.

## SOUTHERN ANDALUCIA

Too often when southern Spain is thought of, the thinking goes no further than the Coto Donãna. While the Coto remained private and therefore accessible only to a privileged few, most ornithologists were forced to search around its edges; even so, it acted as a sort of unattainable paradise. With its declaration as a reserve the Coto has theoretically been opened up to all, though the number of visitors has been so great that there are now considerable restrictions. Yet wonderful as the Coto is, the immediate area has an equally fine range of birds with the added advantage of a good road system for ease of travel, and is thus more suited to those who prefer a modicum of comfort. In particular the Andalucian hemipode, Audouin's gull, eagle owl, ruddy shelduck, red-rumped swallow, and black wheatear are found exclusively outside the Coto.

In the extreme south around Barbate there are a number of good places. Cape Trafalgar holds an interesting cliff breeding colony of cattle and little egrets. The Laguna de la Janda was once an outstanding area but has been reduced by drainage though herons and stilts are still common. The area holds the usual Andalucian species such as griffon and Egyptian vultures, black kite, hoopoe, spotless starling, woodchat shrike, Sardinian, rufous and olivaceous warblers, and has the only breeding little swifts in Europe in the Sierra de la Plata. These birds were first proved to breed in 1966 in disused red-rumped swallow's nests.

To the north there are a number of good places like the salt pans at Cadiz with stilt, little egret, lesser short-toed lark, and a host of waders at migration times. The area at the mouth of the Guadalquivir around Sanlucar de Barrameda has marshes and pine woods and is especially noted for large numbers of black kites that feed on dead fish along the river. A nice touch of home is provided for British bird-watchers by the sewage farm at Jerez de la Frontera where stilts breed. The cliff-top town of Arcos de la Frontera provides an excellent vantage point for watching lesser kestrels and griffon vultures land on the cliffs below. One of the most outstanding 'ticks' of the area is to be enjoyed on the Rock of Gibraltar, the Barbary partridge is found nowhere else on the European mainland. Watching the migration of raptors and storks at Tarifa is often dramatic but the serious student would be well advised to cross the Straits to watch from the African side in autumn.

SUMMER: little egret, cattle egret, red-crested pochard, ruddy shelduck, Egyptian vulture, black vulture, griffon vulture, golden eagle, Bonelli's eagle, booted eagle, black kite, lesser kestrel, Barbary partridge, Andalucian hemipode, quail, great bustard, Kentish plover, avocet, black-winged stilt, stone curlew, Audouin's gull, black-bellied sandgrouse, pin-tailed sandgrouse, eagle owl, red-necked nightjar. Alpine swift, little swift, bee-eater, hoopoe, short-toed lark, lesser short-toed lark, thekla lark, red-rumped swallow, chough, azure-winged magpie, rock thrush, blue rock thrush, black wheatear, black-eared wheatear, Cetti's warbler, moustached warbler, melodious warbler, olivaceous warbler, orphean warbler, Sardinian warbler, rufous warbler, fan-tailed warbler, woodchat shrike, spotless starling, serin rock bunting, rock sparrow.

There is a considerable variety of accommodation available mainly on the coast. The western resorts of the Costa del Sol cater for thousands of tourists though the Atlantic coast, recently called the Costa de Luz, is probably more interesting for birds. Those without a car could choose one of the villages between Chiclana and Tarifa. The major centres to be visited are as follows:

1. Laguna de la Janda, Cape Trafalgar, and the Sierra de la Plata.
2. Cadiz salt pans.
3. Guadalquivir mouth and pine woods at Sanlucar de Barrameda.
4. Cliffs at Arcos de la Frontera.
5. Gibraltar for barbary partridge.
6. Migration of hawks and storks at Tarifa or Tangier.

There are several international airports nearby.

## ANDORRA

The Valleys of Andorra, as this small principality is correctly known, lie in the heart of the Pyrénées forming a triangle between Spain and France. The total area of 450 sq km is exactly the right size for an ornithological holiday of exploration. Most of Andorra is above 3,000 feet and to enjoy the maximum number of species trips should be made preferably southwards into Spain and the Valley of the Segre. The highest peak Pla de l'Estany rises to over 9,000 feet.

Below the peaks there are woods of conifers, with deciduous trees and sallows lower down. The valleys have streams and meadows that are the haunt of numerous grey wagtails and dippers. A single major road passes through Andorra and there is a bus service from France at Latour-de-Carol railway station near Puigcerda right through the principality to Sant Julia de Loria. There are three minor roads and several tracks that enable the whole area to be fully worked. Birds include Egyptian and griffon vultures and a wealth of small birds including the obscure (to identify) pallid swift which breeds in the tunnel along the Ordino road. Alpine accentor, rock sparrow, rock bunting and both choughs are found high up, and the valleys have many warblers including Bonelli's, melodious, and subalpine. Crag martins hawk overhead and golden eagles sail majestically around the buttresses.

SUMMER: Egyptian vulture, griffon vulture, golden eagle, Alpine chough,

chough, golden oriole, pallid swift, crag martin, Alpine accentor, lesser grey shrike, dipper, black redstart, black-eared wheatear, Bonelli's warbler, melodious warbler, subalpine warbler, cirl bunting, rock bunting, rock sparrow, crossbill, serin.

Andorra is reached southwards from Foix in France or northwards from Ripoll in Spain. Puigcerda, the Spanish frontier town, has a railway and there are buses from Latour-de-Carol. There are over sixty hotels in Andorra, many camp sites, and duty free living. Ordino is an excellent place to start birdwatching.

## BADAJOZ

Badajoz lies next to the Portugese frontier on the River Guadiana in western Spain.

1.  **Badajoz irrigations:** to the east of the town there are large areas of irrigation fed by canals from the main river. In particular the Canal de Montijo is an excellent spot for birds as it draws most of the birds of this arid neighbourhood to drink. To one side of the Canal there are dry arid grasslands with no water in summer and on the other side are miles of luxurious green crops. The mixture of arid and wetland birds makes exciting bird-watching and an area worth exploring. The dry grasslands hold the diminishing great bustard, though this area of Spain and Portugal is one of the bird's strongholds. Little bustard are also found with typical 'dry' species like sandgrouse and crested and thekla larks. On the other side, along the canals and amongst the crops and woodland are black and white storks, hoopoe, bee-eater, roller and kingfisher. Bluethroat have been noted here and though proof of breeding is lacking this would represent an extension southwards of the isolated pocket of this species in central Iberia.

SUMMER: white stork, black stork, lesser kestrel, great bustard, little bustard, sandgrouse, quail, thekla lark, crested lark, roller, bee-eater, hoopoe, spotless starling, bluethroat.

Though this excellent area extends for miles it is difficult to find without a detailed map such as the Vegas Bajas, Plan de Badajoz insert in the Firestone Hispania Number 7. Access, which is unrestricted, is along the canal side maintenance road.

2.  **Rio Burdalo and Rio Guadiana:** the arid land east of Merida has only the partly dry river valleys of these rivers as a water supply. The valleys are good for waders like black-winged stilt and various sandpipers on passage, and most of the birds of the surrounding land come here to drink. These include arid species like pratincole and black-eared wheatear, and a whole range of the commoner birds of this part of Spain such as red-rumped swallow, melodious warbler, and black kite.

SUMMER: black kite, black-winged stilt, pratincole, red-rumped swallow, spotless starling, yellow wagtail, tawny pipit, black-eared wheatear, melodious warbler, ortolan bunting.

Explore any of the river valleys on foot starting from near Medellin east of Merida.

3.  **Rio Zapaton:** lies to the north of Badajoz and near Don Benito and is a shallow but fast flowing river in an otherwise very arid region. The river bed is gravel with some islands and backwaters and with a growth of rushes along the banks. It is an excellent area with night heron, little ringed plover, white storks, and stilt along the river, and black-eared wheatear, crested lark and pratincole in the drier spots. The range of intermediate birds includes woodchat and great grey shrikes, spotless starling, and red kite. The cattle egret is the outstanding bird of the area.

SUMMER: night heron, cattle egret, white stork, pochard, red kite, black-winged stilt, little ringed plover, pratincole, spotless starling, great grey shrike, woodchat shrike, corncrake, crested lark, black-eared wheatear.

Explore along the river banks near Don Benito.

## COTO DONÃNA

The River Guadalquivir enters the Atlantic between Huelva and Cadiz some fifty miles south of Seville in southern Andalucia. Below Coria it flows through the marismas which are its delta and which it floods during the rainy season starting in October. Unlike most deltas the Guadalquivir has only one outlet to the sea because of the huge sand-bar that stretches from the Rio Tinto to the mouth at Sanlucar and which holds some of the highest dunes in Europe. It is the south-eastern strip of this dune coast that forms the Coto Donãna proper. Though the Coto Donãna Reserve covers this area and an adjacent section of the marismas it is in reality only part of a larger region that is exceptionally rich in birds. For our purposes this section will cover only that part of the Guadalquivir basin to the north of the river which has to be approached from the Seville–Huelva road and thus includes the Spanish government reserve at Las Nuevas. Other areas like the pine woods and salt marshes at Sanlucar de Barrameda are included under Southern Andalucia.

A section across the Coto reveals the following main habitats:

1.  The beach is straight and sandy and interrupted only by the medieval stone towers built to guard the shore against the Barbary pirates and which sometimes hold breeding peregrines. Otherwise only the occasional Kentish plover and Caspian tern breed.

2.  The dunes run parallel with the coast with slacks between them. Some have a covering of marram and other vegetation but most are mobile sand and are spreading inland. The hollows hold scrub with some pines and form important refuges for migrants especially in spring. Only stone curlew and thekla lark breed here but it is a favourite hunting ground of short-toed and imperial eagles.

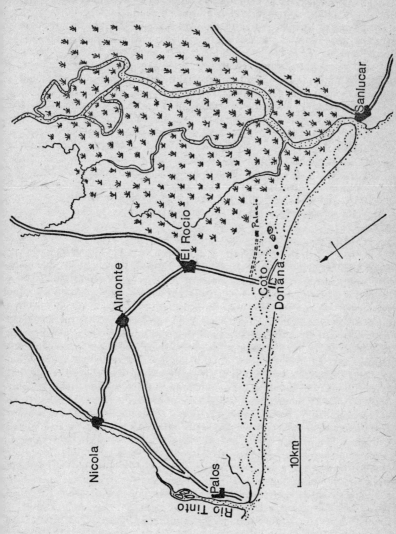

The Coto Donãna Reserve is approached via El Rocío and the road that leads to the coast and a fast-developing beach resort. Permits must be obtained in advance to venture on to the reserve track which leads to the Palacio.

Sanlucar

El Rocío

Coto
Donãna

Palacio

Almonte

Nicola

Palos

Rio Tinto

10km

3.   Woods of stone pine grow on the landward side of the dunes and are in some places disappearing under the advancing sand. Some junipers grow with the pines and replace them to the west while to the east the pines are larger and form more of a forest. There is a rich breeding avifauna including imperial and booted eagles, red and black kites, azure-winged magpie, great grey and woodchat shrikes, great spotted cuckoo, red-necked nightjar, orphean, Sardinian and Dartford warblers, and an exciting array of mammals including mongoose and wild boar.

4.   The parkland is basically halimium thicket with scattered cork oaks which does not, in spite of its being waist to head height, present any barrier. There are, however, gorse thickets here and there that are quite a different story, and low depressions have a growth of tree heath. The basic birds of the area are stone curlew, red-necked nightjar and Sardinian and Dartford warblers, while the cork oaks hold herons, white stork, imperial and booted eagles, both kites, great spotted cuckoo, golden oriole, and great grey and woodchat shrikes. The heronry in this zone is at Algaida.

5.   The grassland borders the marismas and holds species like quail and Savi's and fan-tailed warblers. It is the favourite zone for birds of prey.

6.   The marismas consist of cracked clay with a growth of glasswort for most of the year, interrupted about 1 km from the edge of the Coto and running parallel to it by the Madre de las Marismas which is the channel bringing fresh water to the marismas. The channel has a strong growth of reeds and is flooded for most of the year and thus attracts a great variety of wildlife. Here and there in the marismas are vetas, little islands which remain dry throughout the year, and which have an extensive covering of suaeda, grasses and thistles. These islands hold important colonies of waders and terns including Kentish plover, avocet, black-winged stilt, pratincole, slender-billed gull and gull-billed tern, as well as marbled duck, pintail, pin-tailed sandgrouse, bee-eater, and short-toed lark. The open salicornia zone of the marismas hold Montagu's harrier, sandgrouse and calandra and short-toed larks, while the reeds along the channel have purple and night herons, spoon-bill, purple gallinule, and great reed warbler. The intermediate wet zone of rushes holds grebes, red-crested pochard, ferruginous duck, white-headed duck, marsh harrier, Baillon's crake, crested coot, and black and whiskered terns.

7.   The lagoons stretch in a chain across the Coto to the south-west of the

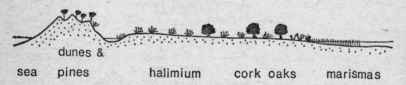

sea     pines         halimium      cork oaks     marismas

Section through Coto Donãna (adapted from Mountfort).

Palacio de Donãna. The largest is Santa Olalla and this together with the tiny Sopeton seldom dry up. Purple heron, marbled duck, red-crested pochard, white-headed duck, and crested coot breed.

8.  The buildings and agriculture are of little importance though the spotless starling is found.

SUMMER: purple heron, little egret, squacco heron, cattle egret, night heron, little bittern, white stork, spoonbill, flamingo, marbled duck, red-crested pochard, ferruginous duck, white-headed duck, Egyptian vulture, griffon vulture, black vulture, golden eagle, imperial eagle, booted eagle, red kite, black kite, short-toed eagle, lesser kestrel, Baillon's crake, purple gallinule, crested coot, avocet, black-winged stilt, pratincole, slender-billed gull, black tern, whiskered tern, gull-billed tern, black-bellied sandgrouse, pin-tailed sandgrouse, great spotted cuckoo, Scop's owl, red-necked nightjar, bee-eater hoopoe, calandra lark, short-toed lark, lesser-short toed lark, thekla lark, golden oriole, azure-winged magpie, Cetti's warbler, Savi's warbler, great reed warbler, melodious warbler, orphean warbler, Sardinian warbler, subalpine warbler, spectacled warbler, Dartford warbler, fan-tailed warbler, tawny pipit, great grey shrike, woodchat shrike, spotless starling, serin.

The reserve is open to visitors but access is still awkward and an expedition atmosphere and preparation are a necessity. Leave the Seville–Huelva road southwards at Almonte to El Rocio. From El Rocio to the Palacio de Donãna access is along a recently constructed track leaving the road from El Rocio to the coast just before it reaches the sea and the freshly constructed flats and villa development. At El Rocio, cattle egrets are common and many species can be seen along the river, and the pines along the Almonte road hold a wealth of raptors.

Visitors must bring all their own food. Camping is permitted only at authorised places and there is sometimes a possibility of obtaining lodging at the Palacio. Transport within the reserve can sometimes be arranged. All arrangements and permits must be obtained in advance from the Director, Dr Jose A. Valverde, Estacion Biologica de Donãna, Paraquay 1, Sevilla, Spain. Please mention the number of people involved, the proposed dates of visiting, and any other relevant details.

# EBRO DELTA

The Ebro is one of Europe's great rivers and has built up a huge delta area at its mouth that is excellent for birds. Yet no similar area of Europe has been so neglected by bird-watchers. The Camargue to the north is larger and has a number of species, notably the flamingo, found in very few other places. The Coto Donãna to the south benefits from its geographical position adjacent to Africa and is thus the furthest north for a number of species. Both have drawn attention away from the Ebro.

The Ebro reaches the Mediterranean between Barcelona and Valencia near Amposta. Commercial development along this coast of Spain has turned the former fishing villages into international holiday paradises with hotels, swimming pools, etc, and the delta area is probably the largest unspoilt area on the Spanish Mediterranean. Certainly the coastlines on either side are lined by tourist resorts. The delta proper covers 550 sq km and consists of large lagoons of varying degrees of salinity, with smaller lagoons near the sea used for the commercial production of salt. Some lagoons have dense reed beds partly overgrown with scrub while inland, in the fresher zone, there are extensive rice fields and salicornia and suedia covered plains that are seasonally flooded.

The salines are the breeding haunt of the most interesting birds of the delta. Avocet and black-winged stilt breed here with the terns that are the best documented birds of the area. There are 500 pairs of little tern at Punta de Fangal and with smaller numbers at Punta de la Banya, and colonies of common terns, as well as black-headed gullery. The latter is a recent addition to Spain's breeding birds. Gull-billed terns breed at Punta de Fangal, and whiskered terns are common especially on Canal Vell lagoon. The other noteworthy bird group are the herons and though there is a heronry in the south, the colony of purple herons amongst the reed beds at Buda Island contains about 400 nests and makes this species the dominant heron. Out of season but regular visitors are flamingos, and the glossy ibis has been noted. Red-crested pochard breed and marsh harriers are numerous.

The delta is a very important migration and wintering area for duck.

SUMMER: purple heron, little bittern, little egret, marsh harrier, red-crested pochard, avocet, black-winged stilt, Kentish plover, black-headed gull, herring gull, whiskered tern, gull-billed tern, common tern, little tern, roseate tern, Sandwich tern, Cetti's warbler, Savi's warbler, fan-tailed warbler.

The best headquarters is Amposta on the coastal route N340, but most visitors prefer to stay at one of the adjacent coastal resorts rather than this inland town. San Carlos de la Rápita to the south is convenient, has hotels and three camp sites. The three areas already mentioned, Punta de Fangal, Punta de la Banya, and Buda Island are well worth exploring as are La Encanizada, La Tancada, and Canal Vell. Buda is preserved as a private shoot but access can usually be obtained locally outside of the hunting season. The nearby mountains rise to 4,700 feet and should prove interesting.


## ESTARTIT AND LA ESCALA

The rocky and beautiful Costa Brava of north-eastern Spain is broken by only two rivers of any consequence. The mouths of the Rio Fluvia and Rio Ter reach the Mediterranean near La Escala and Estartit and provide the only wetland areas between the French border and Barcelona. Both are low lying heavily cultivated plains with areas of rice and some reed marsh in the wetter parts. Amongst a wide variety of species, fan-tailed, Cetti's and Savi's warblers are reasonably numerous and Bonelli's eagles and black kites are frequently seen. Little egrets and purple herons are noted on the rice fields, and the marshy lagoon behind the beach south of Estartit holds passage waders and gulls.

The rocky coast between La Escala and Estartit is covered with maquis, with an extensive forest of stone pines on the rising ground inland. Agriculture is confined to the low lying parts and is fighting a losing battle with the lucrative tourist trade. The neglected olive groves and vineyards are good places to see many birds that are more characteristic of the maquis and the forest. Species along the coast include blue rock thrush, black-eared wheatear and three species of swift, and outstandingly a small number of Marmora's warblers.

Seabirds have been noted offshore and Eleanora's falcons are seen frequently enough to make one wonder whether they breed locally.

SUMMER: little egret, purple heron, little bittern, peregrine, lesser kestrel, black kite, marsh harrier, Bonelli's eagle, Kentish plover, Scop's owl, bee-eater, hoopoe, thekla lark, crested lark, short-toed lark, blue rock thrush, swift, Alpine swift, pallid swift, red-rumped swallow, tawny pipit, lesser grey shrike, woodchat shrike, great spotted cuckoo, penduline tit, black wheatear, black-eared wheatear, Savi's warbler, Cetti's warbler, fan-tailed warbler, great reed warbler, moustached warbler, orphean warbler, spectacled warbler, Sardinian warbler, subalpine warbler, Dartford warbler, Marmora's warbler, melodious warbler, olivaceous warbler, Spanish sparrow, rock sparrow, serin.

Either La Escala or Estartit make an ideal base though most bird watchers have used the latter. Ensure visits to:

1. The coast between Estartit and the mouth of the Rio Ter.
2. The pine forest along the road to Sobrestany or southwards from Riels south of La Escala.
3. The Coastline between La Escala and Estartit to Roca Fordada especially south of Playa Mongo.
4. Roman ruins at Ampurias and surrounding fields.
5. Marsh and rice fields north and west of Ampurias.
6. San Pedro Pescador and eastwards along Rio Fluvia.
7. Rice fields at Pals.
8. Mountain area between Rosas and Cadaques for red-rumped swallow.

Travel is by air or train to Barcelona, train to Gerona or Figueras, bus to Estartit or La Escala.

## SIERRA GUADARRAMA

This mountain range lies within 60 km of the centre of Madrid and represents the ideal area for the casual bird-watcher to take a quick trip up into the high Sierras and see some of the most exciting birds in Europe. It is, however, not only convenient to central Madrid but also one of the best areas in the whole country. Rising to over 8,000 feet at Peñalara it is outstanding for birds of prey and is noted as one of the major strongholds of the black vulture. Much of the area is covered by fine pine forests and dense maquis scrub harbouring a

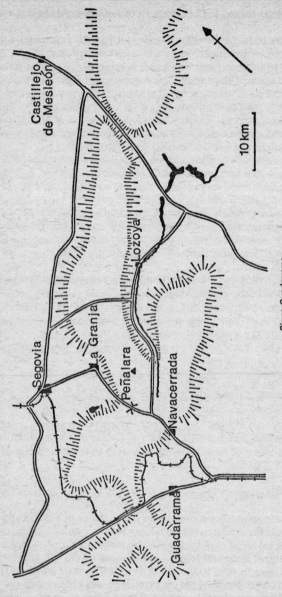

Sierra Guadarrama.

wealth of small birds including Dartford, subalpine and melodious warblers. Great grey shrikes are common and the higher areas hold rock thrushes, rock sparrows and crag martins. Open areas of gum-cistus bushes and broom lower down, have crested, calandra, and short-toed larks and white storks are very numerous in the villages. Up to five nests have been counted on a single church tower in the village of Guadarrama.

These must take an ornithological second place to the raptors of the area. Griffon and black vultures are present in about equal numbers and eagles include golden, imperial, Bonelli's and booted. The latter are even described as common. Both black and red kites are common and honey buzzards are present in good numbers and goshawk are frequently found in the forest. Hobbys are numerous and this excellent collection of predators is completed by peregrines, kestrels, lesser kestrels and the occasional hen harrier.

SUMMER: white stork, griffon vulture, black vulture, golden eagle, imperial eagle, Bonelli's eagle, booted eagle, black kite, red kite, buzzard, honey buzzard, goshawk, lesser kestrel, hobby, peregrine, crag martin, great grey shrike, woodchat shrike, rock thrush, crested lark, calandra lark, hoopoe, roller, bee-eater, golden oriole, firecrest, Dartford warbler, subalpine warbler, melodious warbler, Bonelli's warbler, citril finch, cirl bunting, rock bunting, rock sparrow, serin.

There are many roads to and through the area and probably none better than the main N601 between Madrid and Segovia. On the north side of the 5,800 foot pass of Navacerrada there are excellent pine forests for most of the raptors of the area. Rock bunting are quite common here, and the country lower down around La Granja with its lush gardens holds most of the more interesting passerine species as well as lesser kestrels. Most of the larks seem commoner on the southern side of the range and the high top at Peñalara is good for rock thrush, crag martin, and citril finch.

There is a good range of accommodation particularly in Segovia, but also in La Granja, and the villages to the south. The Lozoya Valley in the middle of the range looks very appealing and the Hostelia del Paular near the monastery of the same name could prove an idyllic setting for a thorough exploration. The area is easy to reach from Madrid.

## HUELVA

The town of Huelva lies at the mouth of the Rio Tinto immediately west of the Coto Donãna and anyone visiting either should not miss the other. Not, of course, that Huelva in any way compares with the Coto but it is easier to get to and to find accommodation, and the birds are very exciting. The estuary itself is mainly red mud and frequented by huge numbers of migrant waders and by lesser numbers of breeding birds. There are several lagoons with reeds that in some places amount to reed beds where they hold Savi's, great reed, and other warblers. The usual southern Andalucian herons are found at the estuary and lagoons alike, and two species of harrier and black kite are quite common and can be seen almost anywhere in the area. La Rábida near the mouth of the Rio Tinto has a statue of Columbus which is not only a good tourist spot but also a likely area for scrub warblers like the Sardinian, spotless starling, and harriers. Also on the eastern bank is Palos de la Frontera which has large areas of beautiful pine woods holding all the usual Andalucian species including azure-winged magpie and great spotted cuckoo. The road between Huelva and Seville is bound to produce the exotic rufous warbler.

SUMMER: purple heron, little bittern, night heron, little egret, cattle egret, spoonbill, ferruginous duck, black kite, marsh harrier, Montagu's harrier, azure-winged magpie, great spotted cuckoo, woodchat shrike, spotless starling, Savi's warbler, great reed warbler, Sardinian warbler, subalpine warbler, rufous warbler.

The area around the rivers within walking distance of Huelva is worth exploring and it is a simple drive to the eastern shore and Palos and La Rábida. Birds can be found throughout the area and the Coto and Seville (where the Cathedral has lesser kestrels) are not too distant for day trips.


## MAJORCA

Majorca is the largest and most populated of the Balearic Isles which lie off the Mediterranean coast of Spain. Recent years have seen the islands turned into a holiday paradise to be compared only with the Costa Brava and Costa del Sol on the mainland. The airport at Palma is in direct contact with most European capitals and there is a good network of roads to most other parts of the island. In spite of the tourist development Majorca is one of the best and most accessible places to watch birds in south-west Europe. In many places especially along the north-west coast, the cliffs and rocky shorelines are of outstanding beauty and hold interesting birds including blue rock thrush, peregrine, various eagles and vultures, and outstandingly Eleanora's falcon. In the north-east near Alcudia lies the marsh of Albufera covering some 10 square miles of reeds, dykes, and marshes intersected by rough tracks and separated from the sea by a line of dunes. An English firm attempted to drain the marsh earlier this century but went bankrupt in the process. There is a mile-long lagoon next to the road providing excellent watching from cars, but unfortunately the whole area is threatened with drainage, and development as a tourist attraction to be called the City of the Lakes. Birds of the marsh include purple heron, little egret, little bittern, frequent feeding parties of Eleanora's falcons, marsh harrier, osprey, red kite, and a wealth of warblers including fan-tailed, great reed, Cetti's and moustached. Black-winged stilts are found here and on the salt pans near Campos called Salinas de Levante. The latter also hold little egret, gull-billed tern, Kentish plover and passage waders, and Audouin's and Mediterranean gulls. Up to 25 Audouin's gulls have been noted in Palma Harbour and clearly it is a good idea to have a close look at any gull here. Large areas of the island are covered with macchia sheltering a resident population of Dartford, Sardinian and Marmora's warblers. A likely spot for these is near the lighthouse at Porto Colom where there are also rock sparrow and blue rock thrush. In the upland area of Mount Galatzos and indeed all along the north-west coast the variety of raptors includes booted and Bonelli's eagles, and black and Egyptian vultures. The best place is Escorca half way along the mountain road where black vulture and crag martin are near certainties.

SUMMER: Balearic shearwater, Cory's shearwater, purple heron, little egret, squacco heron, little bittern, marsh harrier, osprey, peregrine, Eleanora's falcon, red kite, booted eagle, Bonelli's eagle, black vulture, Egyptian vulture, spotted crake, Kentish plover, black-winged stilt, Audouin's gull, Scop's owl, hoopoe, shrike, crag martin, short-toed lark, thekla lark, blue rock thrush, tawny pipit, fan-tailed warbler, great reed warbler, Cetti's warbler, moustached warbler, Marmora's warbler, Sardinian warbler, serin, crossbill, cirl bunting.

SPRING: red-footed falcon, whiskered tern, gull-billed tern, white-winged black tern, black tern, little stint, Temminck's stint, marsh sandpiper, avocet.

Though almost any part of Majorca produces interesting birds the visitor will be particularly anxious to visit the northern part of the island and would be well advised to make Alcudia his centre.

The following areas should be covered:

1. Sea cliffs at Formentor and northwards along the lighthouse road to Cape Formentor for Cory's and Manx shearwaters, and Audouin's gull.
2. Salt pans at Salinas de Levante near Campos. Ask permission at the factory and take the track down the east side of the pans to the stone pines and beach.
3. La Albufera de Alcudia marsh and reed bed; find the cement factory in the middle of the marsh. Undoubtedly one of the finest places to watch birds anywhere. The gathering of Eleanora's falcons to feed on beetles in the evening at the lagoon south of Alcudia is worth travelling to Majorca for alone.
4. Mount Galatzos, take the road out of Capdella and continue on the rough track.
5. The Pollensa–Calobra road for raptors.

Palma de Mallora is an international airport. Bicycles can be hired at 5s 0d per day.


## PAMPLONA

Pamplona is famous for its festival when bulls run through the streets and the local boys run before them. It lies inland from San Sebastian beyond the foothills of the Pyrénées in Navarre. The bare cultivated plain around the town is almost treeless and the largest areas of woodland are the ilex forests on the low Sierras. Some of the best habitats are the town gardens which hold the abundant serin and golden oriole. The few streams have poplars, sallows, and willows but these are not extensive save on the Ebro 80 km to the south.

Typical birds of the open plain dominate and ortolan bunting, crested lark, short-toed lark, tawny pipit are all widespread. Rock sparrows are found in the stony gullies on the small hills and on the stone work of the bridges. Cetti's warblers haunt the streams with melodious warbler wherever there is more luxuriant vegetation. Black kite and griffon vultures are occasionally seen overhead. The Hermanas Gorge, about 15 km north-west of Pamplona on route 4 is a particularly good place for vultures.

SUMMER: griffon vulture, black kite, hoopoe, golden oriole, Calandra lark, crested lark, short-toed lark, tawny pipit, woodchat shrike, red-backed shrike, Bonelli's warbler, Cetti's warbler, melodious warbler, ortolan bunting, rock sparrow, serin.

Pamplona is not an outstanding area though it is typical of this part of Spain and being on many tourist itineraries is more likely to be visited than some of the more remote areas. There are three camp sites and many hotels to choose from.


# PYRÉNÉES

The Ordesa National Park was created in 1918, rises to over 8,000 feet, and is basically a single mountain valley of 5,000 acres. It lies close to the French frontier and is separated from the excellent and similar area of Gavarnie to the north by the massif of Mount Perdido (10,997 feet). The valley is wooded with streams and fields, and an impressive array of cliffs and buttresses that are the haunt of many of the rare mammals for which the Park is famous. These include chamois, brown bear, and Pyrenean ibex. Outstanding amongst the birds is the lammergeier, a pair of which frequent the valley making it the most reliable publishable spot in Europe for this species. Other interesting birds include Alpine chough, goshawk, and peregrine.

Further south the valleys of the Aragon and Gallego are wide and beautiful with rugged hillsides and huge outcrops of rock. Though surprisingly little known, the bird populations here are rich and varied. Lammergeiers are still likely to be seen and Egyptian and griffon vultures are numerous. Though black and red kites are the most numerous raptors there are three species of eagles to keep the identification experts on their toes. Other predators include Montagu's harrier and peregrine, with Scop's and eagle owls. There are three species of wheatear here – the black being exceptional so far north and right on the edge of its range – and a whole array of other small birds.

SUMMER: lammergeier, griffon vulture, Egyptian vulture, booted eagle, Bonelli's eagle, short-toed eagle, black kite, red kite, Montagu's harrier, peregrine, goshawk, Scop's owl, eagle owl, Alpine chough, chough, Alpine swift, great grey shrike, hoopoe, wheatear, black-eared wheatear, black wheatear, rock thrush.

The nearest large town is Huesca though Jaca is not much smaller and is far nearer. For visitors coming from the north the two routes southwards from Pau over the Puerto del Somport and Puerto el Portalet are the best with interesting birds all the way. The Portalet route is the minor one but is more convenient for Ordesa (but it is shut until mid-June. There are many tourists in the area and a growing wealth of hotels. There is a hotel at Sallent high up in the Gallego valley new and visited by naturalists, and the National Park has a Refugio open from June to October, and a small private hotel as far into the valley, as you can go by car. There are also camping sites inside the Park. Do not spend all the time available at high altitude. Many birds, booted eagle for example, are only found lower down.

## RONDA

Andalucia is full of wonderful places to watch birds and though the Coto Donãna and Sierra Nevada are better known, the area around Ronda has several attractions of its own. Ronda itself lies in the Sierra de Ronda and the gorge of the Rio Grande cuts straight through the centre of the town, the two parts of which are joined by bridges. This was the last stronghold of Andalucian bandits. The views from the bridges are superb and enhanced for the bird-watcher by the presence along the cliffs of black and griffon vultures. Other specialities of the area include Alpine swift, crag martin, blue rock thrush, rock bunting, and lesser kestrel. The roads in all directions from Ronda are mountainous and excellent for birds of prey, though the remote track going eastwards from the C339 south of the town to Bosque de Pinsapos could be well worth a detour.

To the north lies the saline lagoon at Fuentepiedra and Lantejuela over 1,600 feet above sea level and surrounded by an area of salt marsh. The lake holds marbled teal and red-crested pochard, and is a winter haunt of duck.

To the east of Ronda lies the Pantano del Conde de Guadalhorce which has some areas of woodland holding most of the species one would expect to find in southern Spain.

SUMMER: marbled teal, red-crested pochard, gadwall, griffon vulture, black vulture, lesser kestrel, Alpine swift, crag martin, black wheatear, azure-winged magpie, hoopoe, blue rock thrush, rock bunting.

Ronda is easy to reach off the coastal E26 along the Costa del Sol via the C339. It is thus in close contact with the tourist transport facilities and accommodation of that coast and particularly with Marbella. The nearest airports are Gibraltar and Malaga. The bottom of the gorge and the river can be reached by an underground staircase made by the Moors for use when the town was besieged. Fuentepiedra is north of Antequera on the N334.

## SILOS

High up in the Sierras south of Burgos is the Monasterio de Santo Domingo de Silos looking down on the village of Silos itself at 6,000 feet. The garden of the Benedictine monastery holds a wealth of small birds including melodious warbler and spotless starling, while the buildings themselves are the haunt of rock bunting, and storks breed on the bell tower. The beautiful valley floor has water-meadows, with the Spanish race of the yellow wagtail, interrupted by rows of poplars holding woodchat, oriole, and serin. The pine clad hillsides have the exotic azure-winged magpie and roller, and above the tree-line there are rock thrush and black wheatear. High above the valley breeding among the crags are griffon and Egyptian vultures, Alpine swift, crag martin and chough. Other birds occurring in the area are eagle owl, red-necked nightjar, and the wall creeper which should not be in this part of Spain at all. The area is beautiful and right off the beaten track enabling an excellent bird area to be explored at leisure.

SUMMER: white stork, griffon vulture, Egyptian vulture, lesser kestrel, eagle owl, golden oriole, roller, azure-winged magpie, chough, Alpine swift, crag martin, woodchat shrike, spotless starling, wall creeper, red-necked nightjar, short-toed tree creeper, rock thrush, black redstart, black wheatear, melodious warbler, crested tit, cirl bunting, rock bunting, rock sparrow, serin.

Leave Burgos southwards on route 1 but fork left on to route 234 at Sarracín. Follow this to Hacinas then turn right to Santo Domingo de Silos.

## SIERRA NEVADA

The Sierra Nevada lies in the south of Spain, and reaches over 11,000 feet within 40 km of the Mediterranean. The nearest big town is Granada to the north-west and both the mountains and the Alhambra should be on the itinerary of any visitor. The woods and gardens of Generalife hold interesting birds including serin, and melodious and Sardinian warblers, but it is in the high sierras that the main attractions lie. Egyptian and griffon vultures are common and the area remains one of the last strongholds of the lammergeier. Golden eagles, lesser kestrels, and choughs haunt the crags together with Alpine swifts and crag martins. On the lower slopes rock buntings and black wheatears are found, while the valleys hold most of the more usual Andalucian species, including woodchat shrike, hoopoe, Sardinian and subalpine warblers, azure-winged magpie, roller, and serin.

SUMMER: griffon vulture, Egyptian vulture, lammergeier, golden eagle, peregrine, lesser kestrel, chough, Alpine swift, crag martin, black wheatear, woodchat shrike, azure-winged magpie, roller, hoopoe, Sardinian warbler, subalpine warbler, melodious warbler, serin, rock bunting.

The Sierra Nevada lies between Granada and Almeria, though the best area is in the west and Granada the best starting point. For those without transport a railway runs up to Maitena and one can then walk up to one of the high hotels or refugios. For car drivers there is an excellent road from Granada up to the Pico Velera. Before it reaches the summit a smaller road leaves to the right and this later forks into two rough tracks, the left hand of which leads down to Lanjarou making an excellent round tour from Granada. The whole area has been opened up for tourists with several hotels very high up to cater for skiers. The Parador de Sierra Nevada is an excellent state inn hotel, though there are several albergues at an even higher level. There are also a series of mountain huts for walkers making a walking holiday of exploration a straight-forward matter for those who know about mountains.

## RIVER TIÉTAR AT CANDELEDA

The River Tiétar is a tributary of the Tagus rising in the foothills of the Sierra de Gredos. Candeleda lies on a rather beautiful stretch of route 501 overlooking the valley, and dominated by the peak of Almanzor to the north. The area is 130 km west of Madrid and situated at 1,200 feet. The mountains behind are covered with pines and junipers with open areas near the top, and cistus bushes and scrub below. Though not as well known as the Sierra Guadarrama similar species of birds can be found with the usual wealth of raptors including griffon and black vultures and both kites. The firecrest, crested tit, and crossbill are found amongst the pines with rock bunting and serin in the more open parts.

The river, which is the central feature of the area has a lush growth of alders, poplars, oaks, and elms along its bank, and these are the haunt of many birds including golden oriole, azure-winged magpie, spotless starling, Cetti's warbler, several colonies of bee-eaters and the odd pair of common sandpipers. The surrounding land of the valley floor has gum-cistus and ilex trees with hoopoe, woodchat and some interesting warblers including rufous warbler. There are red-necked nightjars, black-eared wheatears, and the very common thekla lark. Downstream is the canal feeding lake Pantano del Rosarito.

SUMMER: griffon vulture, black vulture, red kite, black kite, common sandpiper, stone curlew, quail, azure-winged magpie, golden oriole, hoopoe, beeeater, woodchat shrike, red-necked nightjar, thekla lark, spotless starling, black-eared wheatear, firecrest, orphean warbler, Dartford warbler, Cetti's warbler, rufous warbler, crossbill, rock bunting.

The road southwards from Candeleda to the Tiétar is a good start to this area which is not greatly frequented. There are little if any tourist comforts. Route 501 leaves the E4, 11 km west of Madrid and is a far more interesting if slower route westwards.

# Sweden

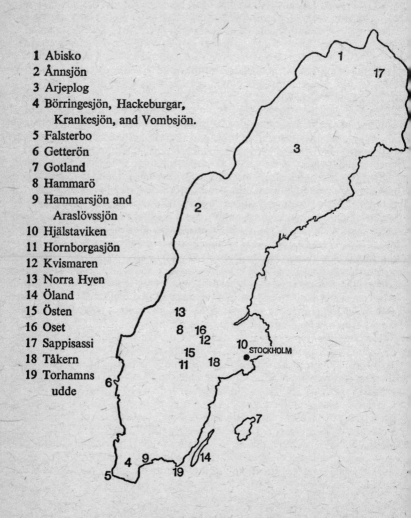

SVERIGES ORNITOLOGISKA FÖRENING,
Östermalmsgatan 65, Stockholm Ö.

SVENSKA NATURSKYDDSFÖRENINGEN,
Riddargaten 9, Stockholm.

READ: *Våra Fåglar i Norden* (1959–63), by K. Curry-Lindahl (covers all four Scandinavian countries); *Forteckning över Sveriges Fåglar* (1962) by Sveriges Ornitologiska Förening. See Denmark.

## ABISKO

This area of Swedish Lapland is one of the most famous and yet remote of all the areas mentioned in this book. It lies north of the 68° parallel 170 km north of the Arctic Circle near the Norwegian border, and can be approached only by foot or rail. Fortunately the rich iron ore deposits of the Kiruna neighbourhood must be carried westwards by rail during the winter when the Gulf of Bothnia is closed by ice and this has opened up Abisko to tourists and naturalists who would otherwise have had to walk. It is thus an ideal spot for those without cars.

The area is outstandingly beautiful with the large Lake Torneträsk and mountains rising steeply from the shore. In the distance is the 'Lap Gate' a prominent raised U-shaped valley. The high tops are basically tundra giving way to birch scrub on the mountain sides and marshes around the lake-edge with meres and tarns. The tundra belt holds rough-legged buzzard, long-tailed skua, ptarmigan, Lapland bunting, dotterel, and snow bunting, while the woods abound with willow warblers. Rather scarcer in this habitat but worth the searching are Arctic warblers, while red-spotted bluethroats are comparatively common. The marshes and meres are probably the most attractive habitats with red-necked phalarope, Temmincks' stint, whimbrel and wood sandpiper. Stated simply, Abisko holds most of the species one would expect to find in the Arctic area of Europe.

The Swedish tourist organisations have appreciated the specialist needs of visitors to the area and have established a number of tourist hotels. The STF also maintain a number of mountain huts (*kåte*) equipped with simple sleeping and cooking facilities and a limited supply of food. These make long walks a possibility and further information can be obtained from the STF.

SUMMER: black-throated diver, red-throated diver, long-tailed duck, scaup, gyr falcon, golden eagle, white-tailed eagle, rough-legged buzzard, Temminck's stint, purple sandpiper, red-necked phalarope, ruff, whimbrel, wood sandpiper, dotterel, golden plover, long-tailed skua, ptarmigan, three-toed woodpecker, redwing, fieldfare, wheatear, bluethroat, Arctic warbler, willow warbler, sedge warbler, great grey shrike, brambling, mealy redpoll, Lapland bunting.

The whole of the Abisko area is worth exploring and will produce birds though a cross section of the habitats must be examined. The following walks are therefore merely a guiding sample.

1. Kaisepakte Station southwards into the hills to Pessidalen for mountain species.
2. Abisko north-eastwards along the lake shore for waders.
3. Abisko Turiststation southwards along the Abiskojokk valley for woodland birds near the Turiststation and raptors further into the hills.
4. Abisko Turiststation westwards along the footpath to Bjorkliden, easy going to look for Arctic warblers near the Bjorkliden end of the railway tunnel.
5. Abisko Turiststation over the hills to Låktajåkke for mountain species and red-necked phalaropes at the end.

Access to Abisko is only by railway from Kiruna and Stockholm or from Narvik in Norway. Motorists should leave their cars at Kiruna (parking arrangements are made at the station) and then travel by train not forgetting to scan the platforms for bluethroats. The Abisko Turiststation is the largest, there are others at Låktajåkke and Bjorkliden, and provides accommodation of varying degrees of luxury and price. Cheaper and more modest accommodation is available at Abisko Lägerby in Abisko village which is 1½ km east of the Turiststation where there is also a camp site.

The Turiststation acts as an information centre for visiting naturalists and the latest information can usually be obtained by chatting to the 'experts' who have been there 2–3 days. Exact locations of nests is unlikely to be revealed and nests found should not be disturbed. Kiruna has an airport with flights to Stockholm.

## ÅNNSJÖN

Ånnsjön is a 25,000-acre lake lying south of the E75 near the Norwegian frontier west of Östersund. It lies in the coniferous belt, with substantial hills rising on three sides the nearest of which Snasahögarna reaches over 4,500 feet. Over half of the lake is shallow water, surrounded by lagoons, marshes, and bog, and a superb example of an inland delta. Conditions are ideal for marsh birds and large numbers of waders can be seen. These include whimbrel, red-necked phalarope, ruff, Temminck's stint, and broad-billed sandpiper. Duck are also numerous and breeding species include wigeon and two species of scoter. Two species of diver also breed, and to round off the collection one can add hen harrier and crane. Surely this must be one of the best unfrequented bird spots anywhere in Europe, especially when one adds the birds of the high tops like dotterel, ptarmigan, and Lapland and snow buntings on Snasahögarna. Ånnsjön is also good for migrants.

SUMMER: black-throated diver, red-throated diver, wigeon, pintail, scaup, scoter, velvet scoter, hen harrier, crane, ptarmigan, dotterel, whimbrel, red-necked phalarope, Temminck's stint, ruff, broad-billed sandpiper, greenshank, Lapland bunting, snow bunting.

Follow the E75 from its origins at Sundsvall through Österund to Ånn. In the next few kilometres there are three minor roads leading southwards to the lake. The last of these from Enafors goes to Handöl which is a good base for lake and mountain. This area is remote and novices should not venture too far without the mountain requisites.

## ARJEPLOG

The town lies in the south of Swedish Lapland 45 km south of the Arctic Circle on the shore of the huge Hornavan Lake. Other lakes lie on almost all sides of the town and form one of the most important habitats. Quaking bogs are numerous, while the rest of the area is covered with mature coniferous woodland. The lakes hold black-throated diver, goldeneye, scaup, and smew are a local speciality. This is an isolated pocket of this species, the main breeding area being in Northern Finland. Whimbrel can be found along the shores though most waders are found on the bogs. These are essentially lakes covered with a thick mat of vegetation and can be very alarming to walk over at first. Provided, however, that one avoids the area of thin vegetation they are generally wet but safe. Wood sandpipers are common and spotted redshank and jack snipe also breed. The woodlands are extensive but interesting species include Siberian jay, Siberian tit, and waxwing, the latter being thinly distributed and best looked for in the damper woodland areas.

SUMMER: black-throated diver, smew, scaup, goldeneye, rough-legged buzzard, whimbrel, jack snipe, spotted redshank, greenshank, wood sandpiper, waxwing, Siberian jay, Siberian tit, great grey shrike.

Arjeplog is a good centre for the surrounding area with roads leading in all directions. Birds can be found almost anywhere but the lakes and woodland at Stensund 10 km east are particularly rewarding. An outing westwards towards the village of Laisvall 30 km away is also recommended. Though not a large town Arjeplog has a number of hotels and a youth hostel. There is general access to the countryside with comparatively little agricultural land. Leave the Baltic coast road the E4 at Skellefteå which is 860 km north of Stockholm.

## BÖRRINGESJÖN, HACKEBERGAR, KRANKESJÖN, AND VOMBSJÖN

Skåne is the southernmost province of Sweden and holds a number of species of more southerly distribution that occur nowhere else or rarely in the country. The best known of these are red kite and golden oriole, both of which are found in the area of the lakes.

1. **Börringesjön**: 5 km east of Svedala which is east of Malmö, and is surrounded by woodland. The northern end has a marshy area which holds

breeding black tern. The woods hold buzzard, red kite, golden oriole and thrush nightingale, an exceptional collection for Sweden. During passage periods the lake is a major staging post for wildfowl and several species of raptors.

SUMMER: buzzard, red kite, black tern, golden oriole, thrush nightingale, hawfinch.

SPRING: bean goose, swans, duck, crane, raptors.

AUTUMN: buzzard, honey buzzard, rough-legged buzzard, black kite, crane.

Take route 11 from Malmö, turn south at Börringekloster and view the lake.

2. **Hackebergar (Dalby Söderskog National Park):** 89 acres of mature beech wood adjacent to Dalby church. It is a typical area of south Swedish woodland with thrush nightingale, barred warbler, but no rarities.

SUMMER: thrush nightingale, barred warbler, hawfinch.

Continuing from Börringesjön on route 11 turn northwards on minor roads to Dalby.

3. **Krankesjön:** 15 km east of Lund. It is an exceptional marshy lake with extensive reed beds and is mainly known as a breeding haunt of many south Sweden rarities. These include bittern, marsh harrier, and black tern, and in certain years great reed warbler. Spring passage is noted for wildfowl.

SUMMER: red-necked grebe, bittern, marsh harrier, black tern, great reed warbler.

SPRING: bean goose, swans, duck.

Continuing from Dalby take minor roads to Silvåkra. The lake can be reached on foot either at the south-western corner, or from Silvåkra village south-east, or along the north side.

4. **Vombsjön:** 4 km east of Krankesjön and best known for its surrounding meadows which hold breeding black-tailed godwits. On passage and in winter this is a superb spot for geese, particularly bean, but also white-fronts. Two species of eagle regularly winter, and cranes stop here in September.

SUMMER: black-tailed godwit.

AUTUMN: geese, crane.

WINTER: bean goose, white-fronted goose, golden eagle, white-tailed eagle, rough-legged buzzard.

Continuing from Krankesjön and from Silvåkra village go south for ½ km and turn east to Vomb. Turn north for 1 km to the lake. The tour outlined here is ideal for the visitor to Falsterbo, but is worthwhile for its own sake to anyone in southern Sweden.


## FALSTERBO

The peninsular of Falsterbo lies at the south-western corner of Sweden and it is this geographical situation rather than any special habitat that has made the area world famous as a migration watch point. The two coastlines of Sweden come together like a funnel in the province of Skåne, and Falsterbo collects all the diurnal migrants that are looking for a continuation of their overland route southwards. Raptors in particular are concentrated here in vast numbers. Though admittedly lacking the variety of the Bosphorous the numbers here are certainly larger. Mainly due to the pioneering studies of Dr Gustaf Rudebeck a Bird Observatory was started in 1949 and a research station completed in 1955.

The coastline is low and sandy with a line of dunes backed by a golf course in the middle of which is a small hillock which makes an admirable watch point. Beyond this are woods of pine, aspen and beech. Thousands of small migrants are found here with wagtails, chats, flycatchers and warblers, forming the bulk of the passage, though there are regular numbers of crossbills, tawny pipits, and red-breasted flycatchers. Nutcrackers are regularly seen and almost any rarity can turn up.

It is, however, for the passage of birds of prey best seen at Ljungen that Falsterbo will attract most visitors with early September being the best time for honey buzzard and October for common and rough-legged buzzards.

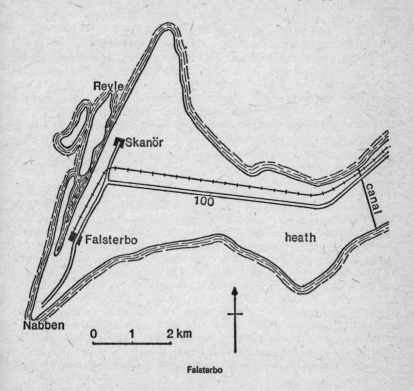

Falsterbo

Though it is an exceptional day when over nine thousand common buzzards can be counted, a thousand a day is by no means infrequent. Such days are usually fine with a south-west wind. Other species regularly noted in numbers include osprey, hobby, merlin, peregrine, red kite, and marsh and hen harriers, while the latter part of the season usually brings an exciting sprinkling of white-tailed eagles and the odd spotted eagle.

To the north lies the area of heath and marsh of Skanörs revlar. The sand-pit and pools here regularly hold an excellent variety of waders including good numbers of spotted redshank, and Temminck's and little stints while avocet and Kentish plover breed. This is a regular haunt of broad-billed sandpiper. Even further north between Skanör and the mainland lies a sandy bay that holds terns and skuas including the rare Caspian tern, and a gathering of several thousand mute swans.

SUMMER: avocet, Kentish plover, golden oriole.

AUTUMN: divers, mute swan, Caspian tern, honey buzzard, buzzard, rough-legged buzzard, osprey, hen harrier, marsh harrier, sparrowhawk, white-tailed eagle, peregrine, hobby, spotted redshank, Temminck's stint, little stint, broad-billed sandpiper, black woodpecker, tawny pipit, red-breasted fly-catcher, nutcracker, rarities, vagrants.

SPRING: avocet, spotted redshank, whimbrel, migrants.

The Fågelstation can accommodate a limited number of visitors who intend to help with observatory work which is mainly counting migrants and trapping and ringing. The overnight fee is modest and places should be booked well in advance with Gunnar Roos, Osbygatan 16a, Malmö, Sweden. For those who enjoy their bird-watching in smaller doses there is accommodation at the Strandhotelet, at the local youth hostel, and a nearby camp site.

The area can be reached from Copenhagen by the frequent ferry to Malmö. Falsterbo is 34 km by road or rail.


## GETTERÖN

Getterön is a peninsula just to the north-west of Varberg on the south-western coast of Sweden. It has a shallow muddy shore, that always attracts large numbers of passage waders and duck, backed by wet meadows with areas of reed and sedge. The peninsula itself boasts a ringing station and bird-tower that gives excellent views over the area. During the summer bird-watching other than from the tower platform is prohibited. About 100 pairs of avocets and some black-tailed godwits breed, and osprey, marsh harrier and peregrine can generally be seen. Regular summer and autumn visitors are little gull, black tern, and red-necked phalarope but the area is also known for the rare vagrants that have a habit of turning up here. Recent examples are black-winged stilt, marsh sandpiper, great white heron, and Dalmatian pelican.

SUMMER, osprey, marsh harrier, peregrine avocet, black-tailed godwit.

AUTUMN: red-necked phalarope, little gull, black tern, waders, rarities.

In the centre of Varberg watch for signs to Getterön. Follow the road towards Östra Hamngatan and Getterövägen, continuing to the sanctuary with its bird-tower (also shown by a road sign) on the north shore. The platform at the top is always open but the room below is as a rule open only at week-ends. On other days a key can be obtained at the police station in Varberg. There is no overnight accommodation. During the breeding season (1 April–31 July) no watching other than from the tower is permitted.

## GOTLAND

Gotland is the largest of the Baltic islands. It is 130 km long and 50 km wide and has the mildest climate in Scandinavia. The influence of the sea can also be seen in the ruggedness of the limestone cliffs, caves and stacks that are the dominating feature of the shoreline. Off the west coast are the two islands of Stora and Lilla Karlsö where the limestone has been eroded into ledges favoured by breeding seabirds. To the north of Gotland the adjacent island of Fårö is a military security zone and foreigners are not allowed access. This is unfortunate for bird-watchers as the island is the only Swedish breeding site of the roller. Nevertheless there are many other attractions and several species are right on the northern fringe of their range. The collared flycatcher, for instance, is found nowhere further north in the world.

1. **Allekvia äng:** a small deciduous wood with large areas of open grassland. It is an interesting place because of the mixture of southern and northern species that meet here including collared flycatcher (more than ten pairs) and redwing.

SUMMER: thrush nightingale, collared flycatcher, icterine warbler, redwing.

Take route 147 from Visby and turn right (signposted Dalhem) after 3 km. In 6 km there is a small green sign on the right hand side of the road that shows the way to Allekvia äng.

2. **Lina myr:** a marshland area with a growth of reeds surrounded by large wet meadows. It holds an excellent collection of regular breeding birds that includes ruff and black-tailed godwit, but in some years river warbler, great reed warbler, and marsh warbler occur.

SUMMER: ruff, black-tailed godwit, thrush nightingale, icterine warbler, marsh warbler, great reed warbler, river warbler(?).

Take route 147 eastwards from Visby and turn right after 35 km on to route 146. After 10 km turn right for 1½ km and fork right. Pass the bridge over the Gothemsån and after 1½ km turn left on to a road which goes straight down to to the marsh.

3. **Gothems Storsund:** an attractive lake set in a coniferous wood. There is a bird tower on the southern shore giving views over the lake which has emergent vegetation and attracts a wide variety of interesting marsh birds. The most outstanding are crane and greylag goose but there are also osprey, Caspian tern and little gull. Casual non-breeding visitors include white-tailed

eagle and great reed warbler. The surrounding woodland holds black woodpecker, goshawk, and green sandpiper which can often be seen near the bird-
tower.

SUMMER: greylag goose, crane, osprey, goshawk, green sandpiper, Caspian
tern, black tern, little gull, black woodpecker, great reed warbler(?).

PASSAGE: white-tailed eagle.

Leave Visby eastwards on route 147 and turn right after 35 km on to route
146. After 12 km pass Gothem church and in 1½ km is the road to Botvaldevik.
Soon afterwards there is a small track going off to the left to a car park.
The bird-tower can be seen from here.

4. **Stockviken:** a shallow marshy lake with fringe vegetation and wet
meadows. There is a bird-tower to the east of the lake which gives excellent
views. Though the breeding marshbirds are the main attraction and include
greylag goose and avocet the area is noted for the number and variety of
rarities that turn up, probably due to its strategic position in the south of the
island. Vagrants have included blue-checked bee-eater, little bittern, greater
flamingo and black stork.

SUMMER: greylag goose, ruff, avocet, Caspian tern.

PASSAGE: rarities.

From Burgsvik in the south of Gotland take the last road eastwards on the
south side of village and fork right after 2 km. Continue 3 km southwards to
the Stockville signpost and in 2 km the bird-tower can be seen to the right.

5. **Stora Karlsö and Lilla Karlsö:** Sweden's only seabird colonies. The latter
is a nature reserve of the Svenska Naturskyddsföreningen covering 375 acres
of sheep pasture. Both lie a few km off the west coast south of Klintehamn
and hold breeding auks. A regular passage of passerines often includes
greenish warbler and scarlet grosbeak, and the red-breasted flycatcher is a
regular summer visitor.

SUMMER: guillemot, black guillemot, razorbill, red-breasted flycatcher.

PASSAGE: bluethroat, red-breasted flycatcher, barred warbler, greenish
warbler, scarlet grosbeak.

The boat *Grisslan* sails daily at 10:00 from Klintehamn and returns in the
afternoon.

There are daily ferries (a 4–5 hour crossing) from the mainland towns of
Sodertälje, Nynäshamn, Västervik, and Oskarshamn to Visby and in some
cases Kappelshamn and Klintehamn. Gotland is only an hour by air from
Stockholm. Because of the mild climate, interesting buildings, and beautiful
scenery, the island is a favourite holiday resort and there is plenty of accommodation.

# HAMMARÖ

Hammarö Bird Station lies at the northern end of the huge Lake Vänern 15
km south of Karlstad, and is based at Skagen lighthouse. There are two pine

clad islands offshore and some skerries. Migration concentration points are inevitably thought of as islands or peninsulae jutting out into the sea, but Vänern, which is 130 km long and half as wide, forms an effective barrier to birds coming from the north in autumn. In particular the bird station has a habit of collecting numbers of grey-headed and white-backed woodpeckers, species which are generally considered to be more or less resident. It is also known as a good place for irruptive species such as waxwing, all the crossbills, and northern tits, some years in exceptionally high numbers. There is always a very strong passage of thrushes, pipits, chaffinches and bramblings and the honey buzzard is the dominant raptor. There is quite a good collection of breeding birds including three grouse, black woodpecker, and duck.

SUMMER: goldeneye, goosander, black grouse, capercaillie, hazel hen, black woodpecker, brambling.

AUTUMN: honey buzzard, grey-headed woodpecker, white-backed woodpecker, waxwing, crossbill. Leave Karlstad southwards to Takene which is well signposted. From there three small roads run further. The middlemost leads to the bird station though the last 500 metres to the lighthouse is on foot. Overnight accommodation is available; apply in advance to Ulf Ottoson, Mossgatan 39, Karlstad. The Norra Hyen area is also near Karlstad.

## HAMMARSJÖN AND ARASLÖVSSJÖN ·

These two lakes lie south and north of Kristianstad respectively, in the east of Skåne in southern Sweden. Both lakes have a wealth of vegetation and surrounding meadows that are excellent for breeding birds. The Håslövs ängar immediately north-east of Hammarsjön are carefully protected to enable the numerous black-tailed godwit and ruff to breed. Other breeding birds in the area include black tern, marsh harrier, spotted crake, and several species of duck. During migration periods the lakes are excellent for wildfowl and Caspian terns occur with some regularity.

SUMMER: pintail, garganey, marsh harrier, black-tailed godwit, ruff, spotted crake, corncrake.

AUTUMN: duck, geese, swans, Caspian tern.

1. Hammarsjön lies immediately south of Kristianstad and the northern shore is the most accessible. The meadows of Håslövs ängar are best reached from the village of Gustaf Adolf 4 km east of Kristianstad. They are carefully protected.

2. Araslövssjön is immediately north of Kristianstad and is generally accessible except for the eastern shore which due to military training is open only at week-ends.

## HJÄLSTAVIKEN

Hjälstaviken was originally part of the large Ekolsund Bay of Lake Mälaren but is now almost a separate lake. It lies just north of route E18 between

Stockholm and Enköping and can easily be seen from the road. Almost the whole lake is covered by reed beds and sedge and the birds are typical of these habitats. Slavonian grebe, bittern and marsh harrier breed and three species of crake are seen almost annually. The adjacent woodland holds honey buzzard, hobby, and osprey. There are many waders on the muddy areas during passage periods including Temminck's stint, while September regularly brings a few bluethroats and red-throated pipits.

SUMMER: Slavonian grebe, bittern, marsh harrier, honey buzzard, hobby, osprey, water rail, spotted crake, little crake, Baillon's crake, red-backed shrike, icterine warbler.

AUTUMN: greenshank, wood sandpiper, green sandpiper, Temminck's stint, ruff, bluethroat, red-throated pipit.

Hjälstaviken lies just north of the E18 60 km from Stockholm and 20 km from Enköping. There is a car park for visitors on the small road south-east of the lake. Excellent views can be obtained from the hill Kvarnberget east of the lake. During the period 15 March–15 July visitors must keep to the path marked with yellow paint which goes round the lake shore.

## HORNBORGASJÖN

Hornborgasjön lies south of route 49 between Skara and Skövde and was until 1900 Sweden's richest bird lake. Attempts had been made to drain it in 1803, 1850, and 1870 but all resulted in failure and at the turn of the century it still covered over 25 sq km. Further attempts were started in 1902 and continued for the next 60 years resulting in a total loss in excess of a quarter of a million pounds. The results of these attempts was to create a vast reed bed and willow carr giving sanctuary to many birds. Recently the lake has been partly restored improving the habitats available and making the lake once more one of the best in the country from an ornithological viewpoint. Huge reed beds remain and these hold a large population of marsh harriers, plus a wide variety of other species including bittern, black-necked and Slavonian grebes. Hen harriers and hobbys also breed here.

In April the largest gathering of cranes in Sweden takes place to the south-west of the marsh between Bjurum and Dagnäs along route 47 between the towns of Skara and Falköping. Early in the morning thousands of cranes can sometimes be seen here. It is prohibited to leave the roads and car parks at this time of the year. At other times the best place is Fågeludden on the east side. There is a bird tower here which is always open giving excellent views over the marsh. Apart from cranes this is also an excellent place for duck especially in spring, and there is a strong likelihood of an encounter with elks.

SUMMER: black-necked grebe, Slavonian grebe, pintail, bittern, marsh harrier, hen harrier, hobby, water rail, spotted crake, long-eared owl, short-eared owl, red-backed shrike, grasshopper warbler.

SPRING: duck, crane.

View the cranes in April from route 47 but do not leave the road or car parks. For Fågeludden follow the road on the east side of Hornborgasjön. Just over 1 km north of Broddetorp church turn west on a track signposted Fågeludden. At the car park continue on foot for 600 metres to the bird tower. There is also a small refuge for those who wish to stay overnight; apply to the farmer at the nearby farm, Mr Gillis Larsson, Kärragården, Broddetorp. Jönköping is the nearest large town of any consequence but places such as Skara, Skövde and Falköping would undoubtedly offer accommodation.

## KVISMAREN

Kvismaren is a vast area of over 1,800 acres consisting of two drained lakes, the eastern one of which, Östrasjön, has now been partly restored. The principal habitats are marsh and fen with enormous reed beds broken by two canals. The area, which is very beautiful if you like the romance of reed beds and pine trees, is worth visiting at any time of the year. In winter there are always golden eagle and goshawk, and passage brings many wildfowl, and waders like ruff and wood sandpiper. During the summer Kvismaren is one of the outstanding wetland sites in southern Sweden with most species of duck, marsh and hen harriers, bittern, spotted crake, and in some years little and Baillon's crakes to really confuse the issue. There are black-tailed godwit and a variety of warblers including in certain years the river warbler which is extremely rare in Sweden. The surrounding fields and copses are worth exploring with honey buzzard, quail, and ortolan bunting.

SUMMER: Slavonian grebe, duck, marsh harrier, hen harrier, honey buzzard, hobby, bittern, spotted crake, little crake, Baillon's crake, water rail, black-tailed godwit, long-eared owl, short-eared owl, quail, wryneck, grasshopper warbler, river warbler, icterine warbler, ortolan bunting.

PASSAGE: duck, wood sandpiper, ruff, greenshank.

WINTER: golden eagle, goshawk.

From Örebro follow route 207 for 15 km then turn right on a minor road signposted 'Norrbyås 4'. From Norrbyås village continue for 3 km to a bridge over the Kvismare Canal. It is a good idea to climb the hill Öby Kulle just north of the canal and close to the road to get an idea of the lie of the land. Continue on foot along the bank starting at Öby Kulle which goes along the lake to the east. Most water birds are likely to be seen here. There is also a bird station, Kvismare fågelstation, which is 1 km south-east of Norrbyås. This offers overnight accommodation; apply to Kent Larsson, Ekängsgatan 39, Örebro.

The Oset area is also near Örebro.

## NORRA HYEN

Norra Hyen is 17 km north of Karlstad and an exceptionally rich and convenient lake for bird-watchers. Its shallow edges are heavily overgrown with reeds that in some places form large reed beds. There are areas of damp meadow, open fields, and coniferous woodland nearby. The breeding birds include bittern and marsh harrier here breeding on the same latitude as Fair Isle, together with other marsh species such as spotted crake and occasionally grasshopper warbler. Ospreys are seen daily and some cranes spend the summer here. Regular migrants in spring and autumn include red-throated pipit and Lapland bunting.

SUMMER: bittern, osprey, marsh harrier, water rail, corncrake, spotted crake, crane, grasshopper warbler(?), ortolan bunting.

PASSAGE: whooper swan, smew, red-throated pipit, Lapland bunting.

Leave Karlstad northwards on route 61. The lake is by the road after 17 km.

## ÖLAND

Öland is an island in the Baltic separated from the Swedish mainland by only a few kilometres of water. It is 137 km long but only 16 km wide and runs from north to south parallel with the mainland coast. The west has a range of limestone cliffs and the land gradually falls away to the shallow east coast which has large beds of seaweed in several places. Öland is a land of woods, including one of the largest deciduous forests in Sweden, of dry stone walls and meadows, of commons with junipers, and of marshes with windmills. The *alvar* is a characteristic heath on a limestone plateau, and is the steppe-like habitat of the golden plover. Öland's birds are rather special and include a number of species that are not common in Sweden. Kentish plover, avocet (10 colonies), collared flycatcher, and red-breasted flycatcher (the latter found at only one other site in the country) are the outstanding specialities. Scandinavia's northernmost colony of Sandwich terns is found at Nabbelund in the north, while turnstones breed on offshore islands, and a wealth of smaller birds here reach one of their furthest points north-east. These include thrush nightingale, barred warbler, and icterine warbler.

1. **Ottenby:** the bird observatory at the southernmost point of Öland and one of the best places in Sweden for studying migration. In particular the passage of Arctic waders in spring and August is outstanding. The latter part of the autumn is dominated by passerines and ringing totals have exceeded a thousand birds per day. Duck are numerous and the passage of raptors can be exciting though never as heavy as at Falsterbo. Breeding birds are unusually good for an observatory area and include ruff, avocet, and in some years scarlet grosbeak. In the deciduous wood Ottenby lund north of the observatory there are breeding golden oriole, red-breasted flycatcher, and the very numerous icterine warbler.

SUMMER: ruff, avocet, Caspian tern, short-eared owl, golden oriole, red-breasted flycatcher, icterine warbler, barred warbler, scarlet grosbeak.

AUTUMN: duck, raptors, passerines.

It is possible to stay at the bird observatory; apply in advance to Ragnar

Edberg, Järnvägsparken 9, Oxelösund. There is a recommended guest house 20 km north of Ottenby; write to Thyra Andersoons pensionat, Degerhamn.

**2. Mellby Ör:** a small island connected to the east coast of Öland. Though known primarily as a breeding haunt of avocet it is an excellent place in other ways especially the southern tip for passage waders.

SUMMER: avocet.

AUTUMN: ruff, knot, curlew sandpiper, sanderling.

Take the track eastwards in the village of Mellby.

**3. Kapelludden:** on the east coast opposite Borgholm, the only town on Öland. The meadows along the shore are an excellent place for migrating waders and duck, and greylag geese breed here.

SUMMER: greylag goose.

AUTUMN: ruff, knot, curlew sandpiper, sanderling.

Take the road to the east at Bredsätra church.

**4. Södviken:** a shallow sandy shore backed by meadows on the east coast in the north of Öland. It is an excellent area for breeding marsh birds including avocet, black-tailed godwit, and in some years Kentish plover, here reaching about its furthest north in the world. Södviken is also a resting place for many migrating duck.

SUMMER: shelduck, Kentish plover(?), ruff, avocet, black-tailed godwit, Arctic tern.

AUTUMN: duck.

Take the road eastwards at Föra church to Husvalla, or the road at Gamla Gästgivaregården in Södvik to the innermost western part of Södviken.

**5. Betgärde träsk:** a reed covered marshland area 15 km north of Borgholm and 4 km east of Stacketorp beside the road running along the east coast of Öland. Breeding marsh birds can be seen.

SUMMER: marsh harrier, little gull, black tern.

There is a bird-tower in the south-western part of the marsh hidden in a pine copse.

**6. Möckelmossen:** a shallow lake in the southern part of Alvaret 8 km east of Resmo church. Its surrounding marshes and emergent vegetation are the breeding ground of Slavonian grebe and black-tailed godwit.

**7. Beijershamn:** a muddy reed-covered area on the shore north of the old pier to the south of Färjestaden. It holds colonies of breeding terns, barred warbler and in some years marsh warbler, and turnstone. It is an excellent spot for resting duck and waders.

SUMMER: turnstone, Arctic tern, little tern, barred warbler, marsh warbler.

AUTUMN: duck, waders.

Leave Färjestaden, where the ferries from Kalmar land, and follow route 136 southwards. Turn west at Vickleby church.

The major ferry to Öland is from Kalmar to Färjestaden but there are two regular services from Oskarshamn to Grankullavik and Byxelkrok. There are a few hotels in Degerhamn, Mörbylånga, Färjestaden, and Borgholm, several boarding-houses, and a great many good camping sites. Information is available from the tourist offices at Färjestaden and Borgholm harbours.

## ÖSTEN

Östen is a comparatively small lake lying between the two huge lakes of Vättern and Vänern in central Sweden. It is shallow edged with extensive areas of reed and sedge and the River Tidan runs through the middle. As a result of this moving water Östen rarely freezes over completely and numbers of duck winter. The lake is known as one of the best places in Sweden for visiting swans and geese in spring and maximum numbers are 1,600 whoopers, 2,200 geese (mainly bean but also greylags, white-fronts, and barnacles) and 5,000–6,000 duck. The best time for this passage is late March and April. Östen, however, is not to be overlooked in summer or at other times of the year; breeding birds include marsh harrier, bittern, duck and grebes, and there is always a good return passage.

SUMMER: bittern, marsh harrier, water rail, spotted crake.

SPRING: bean goose, white-fronted goose, barnacle goose, whooper swan, duck.

AUTUMN; WINTER: duck.

Leave Skövde northwards and take the track 400 metres south of Odensaker church and follow it for 1½ km. There is a bird tower on the south-western side of the lake.

## OSET

Oset is a bird sanctuary situated just to the east of Örebro in the central Swedish province of Närke. There is a large range of habitats including the western part of the lake Hjälmaren with small deciduous copses along its shores, the marshy outflow of the River Svartån with reed beds and sedges, a sewage farm, and a large area of meadows. The passage periods are outstanding and thirty-four species of waders have been recorded. Amongst the regulars are ruff, green and wood sandpipers, and spotted redshank; Caspian terns can regularly be seen in July and August. Autumn always brings a few bluethroats, and red-throated pipits are often quite numerous. Breeding birds are good too with bittern and marsh harrier in the reed beds, and lesser spotted woodpecker and icterine warbler in the copses. There are always a few fishing ospreys to be seen.

SUMMER: bittern, osprey, marsh harrier, little ringed plover, lesser spotted woodpecker, icterine warbler.

PASSAGE: duck, ruff, green sandpiper, wood sandpiper, spotted redshank, greenshank, bluethroat, red-throated pipit.

From the main street in Örebro take the Engelbrektsgatan road (just south of River Svartån) for 800 metres, then take the road to Sturegatan on the left and after a few hundred metres take the Skebäcksvagen road for 2 km. At the end of this is a former rubbish tip and a small car park. Cross the tip and follow the path along the shore. A small platform is erected south of the estuary. It is prohibited to go further than the platform during the breeding season. There is also a bird-tower just across the small bay from the platform. This is normally kept locked but keys can be borrowed from Jan Philipson, Tengvallsgatan 5, Örebro.

Kvismaren is also near Örebro.

## SAPPISASSI

This area lies 120 km north of the Arctic Circle and 45 km east of the industrial town of Kiruna. It is, however, much lower than Abisko and its consequent richer vegetation holds a significantly different avifauna. The three dominant Lapland habitats are found. The vast area of marshes to the east of the village hold breeding cranes and whooper swans, while bean geese breed in the damp forests. Waders however are dominant, with spotted redshank and broad-billed sandpiper the most interesting species. Alongside the road and separating it from the marshes is a narrow belt of woodland while the lower slopes of the hill to the north are covered with conifers. Pine grosbeak and Siberian tit are the most exciting species but the area is little known and visitors should be able to break new ground. Climbing the hill of Ounistunturi (not to be confused with the Ounastunturi National Park 100 km east across the Finnish border) gives excellent views over the surrounding woods and marshes.

Caution should be exercised when walking over the quaking bogs that are a feature of the marshes. In particular the areas around the occasional small lakes are to be avoided but with waterproof footwear and a little care there is no danger.

SUMMER: crane, whooper swan, bean goose, osprey, spotted redshank, wood sandpiper, broad-billed sandpiper, hazel hen, Siberian tit, pine grosbeak, ortolan bunting.

The area lies on route 396, the Vittangi–Karesuando road, 20 km north of Vittangi. There is a ferry immediately north of Vittangi which is a good place for osprey and ortolans. Vittangi is the best place for accommodation though it is not a large town and hotels are few and small. Sappisassi itself is only a few cottages. Kiruna and Gällivare offer a wider range of accommodation but are a considerable distance away. Incidentally, the latter is within striking distance of the biggest peat bog in Sweden to the north of Jutsarova which holds most of the Arctic wildfowl and waders including whooper swan and broad-billed sandpiper. Travel is by road, or train to Kiruna from Stockholm.

## TÅKERN

Tåkern is one of the best known bird resorts in central Sweden. It lies immediately to the east of the huge lake Vättern 20 km west of Mjölby, and consists of 12,500 acres of shallow water nowhere deeper than 6 feet, and a further 2,500 acres of marshes. The latter vary from open mud to vast dense reed beds which hold a particularly large population of marsh harriers. Other breeding water birds include bittern, Slavonian and red-necked grebes, spotted crake, crane, and most species of duck. Many species of wader pass through in spring and autumn and often large numbers are present for weeks on end in autumn. Ospreys breed and are always to be seen. There is a bird station to the south of the lake where there is a tower, and there is another tower at Stra-Herrestad in the north.

SUMMER: Slavonian grebe, red-necked grebe, bittern, duck, marsh harrier, hobby, osprey, water rail, spotted crake, crane, long-eared owl, grasshopper warbler, icterine warbler.

SPRING: bean goose, waders.

Leave route E4 northward between Odeshög and Mjölby at either Rök or Kullen; Glänås is reached in 4 km, then follow the signs to the bird station. There are buses six times a day from Mjölby railway station to Kullen and Rök. Overnight accommodation during May–September must be booked in advance with Göran Bergengren, Dalgårdsgatan 12, Boxholm.

## TORHAMNS UDDE

This bird station lies at the south-eastern most point of the Swedish mainland, 33 km from Karlskrona, and consists of flat meadows and a shallow shore. There are also a few bushes and small copses one of which holds a Heligoland trap. The birds of Torhamns udde are good because of its geographical position rather than any particularly attractive habitat. Thus it is to be compared with Falsterbo in Skåne and Ottenby in Öland as a migration watch place, though it does boast six species of tern in summer including Caspian. Spring brings barnacle and brent geese and movements of passerines. In autumn there is a heavy passage of geese, duck, and birds of prey, notably rough-legged buzzard and osprey, and waders and passerines. Many roughlegs stay in winter and there are usually a few white-tailed eagles about at this time.

SUMMER: Caspian tern, common tern, Arctic tern, Sandwich tern(?), barred warbler(?).

SPRING: barnacle goose, brent goose, passerines.

AUTUMN: geese, duck, rough-legged buzzard, osprey, waders, passerines.

WINTER: long-tailed duck, white-tailed eagle, rough-legged buzzard.

Leave Karlskrona eastwards along route 15 to Jämjö church in 33 km. Turn right to Torhamn church, and take the track 3 km to the point – most people risk their car springs. There is a daily bus service from Karlskrona to Tor-hamn church. Access to the point is generally unrestricted though it is sometimes used for military training. For spartan accommodation apply in advance to Gunnar Stromberg, Nya Skeppsbrogatan 1, Karlskrona.

# Switzerland

1 Col de Bretolet
2 Chavornay Clay-pits
3 Grindelwald

4 Lac Leman
5 Lac de Neuchâtel
6 Mont Tendre

SCHWEIZERISCHE VOGELWARTE SEMPACH,
Postkono 60 2316

READ: *Die Brutvögel der Schweiz* (1962) by U. N. Glutz von Blotzheim: *Verzeichnis der Schweizerischen Vogelarten* (1959), by E. Sutter *et al* in Orn. Beob. Vol 56, pp 69–93.

## COL DE BRETOLET

The Col de Bretolet lies on the French border at a height of 9,000 feet and is the most important migration watch point in the whole of the Alpine chain. There is a bird observatory at the top of the Col, which is south of Lac Leman near Champéry, and which does not boast a road. The pine clad hillsides hold crested tit and black woodpecker and on the bare open areas higher up there are Alpine choughs and Alpine accentors. The lower valleys hold crag martins. But visitors come to Bretolet to watch the dramatic migration of birds across this pass. Raptors can be exciting and buzzard, honey buzzard, and marsh harrier should all be seen, together with a sprinkling of kites and various falcons. Passage of smaller birds and particularly of hirundines is quite fantastic with a constant procession of birds passing a few inches from the ground, and amounting to many thousands in a single day. Later there are equally huge movements of finches.

SUMMER: Alpine chough, Alpine accentor, black woodpecker, crested tit.

AUTUMN: buzzard, honey buzzard, red kite, marsh harrier, falcons, swallow, sand martin, chaffinch.

The observatory has very limited accommodation and this is rightly reserved for those enthusiasts who intend to actively contribute to the work of the station, i.e. counting and ringing birds. Those interested should contact Observatoire Ornithologique Alpin de Col de Bretolet, Champéry, Valais; or Station Ornithologique de Sempach, Postkono 60–2316. The col is reached by mountain railway from Aigle to Champéry and then by a hard walk up the mountain track past the Swiss national rifle range. It is possible to get up and down in a day from Champéry where there are many hotels.

## CHAVORNAY CLAY-PITS

These abandoned clay-pits which once served the Chavornay brick-works lie between Lac Leman and the Lac de Neuchâtel. They vary in depth but some are shallow enough to have allowed a growth of emergent vegetation and there are now considerable areas of reeds, scrub, willows, and a small broad-leaved wood. Two of the deeper pits and their dense surrounding vegetation constitute a reserve but the most rewarding area, a shallow pit with muddy edges, grass and willow fringe, and subject to seasonal flooding, is not protected and is still occasionally shot over. It has a rubbish dump in one corner. Though excellent at all times of the year and holding breeding little bittern and great

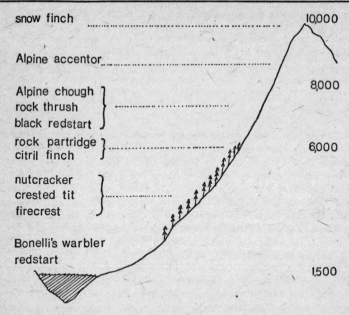

Section through the Swiss Alps, showing the vertical distribution of the commoner Alpine birds. The distribution of most birds in this and other mountainous countries is influenced more by altitude than any other factor. Thus it is more important to explore a single area thoroughly than move from place to place in search of different birds.

reed warbler, it is especially good at migration periods. Most species of European herons and waders pass through, including little egret, night heron, numerous Temminck's stint, regular marsh sandpiper, and red-necked phalarope. Other species include crakes (Baillon's may breed), raptors, and passerines like bluethroat and penduline tit.

SUMMER: hobby, black kite, buzzard, little bittern, great reed warbler.

AUTUMN: little egret, night heron, honey buzzard, osprey, harriers, Temminck's stint, wood sandpiper, green sandpiper, marsh sandpiper, red-necked phalarope, bluethroat, penduline tit.

Leave the Chavornay–Orbe road northwards 2 km west of Chavornay village on a concrete track. The whole area lies 11 km south of Yverdon at the south end of the Lac de Neuchâtel which is also worth visiting for grebes, waders, and terns.

## GRINDELWALD

Grindelwald is a skiing resort in the Bernese Oberland and the place where summer tourists peer through binoculars at the antics of climbers on the

North Face of the adjacent Eiger. It is an exceedingly convenient base for exploring a typical Alpine area and with railways rising fantastically to the Jungfraujoch at 11,300 feet through the heart of the Eiger even those not fond of walking can enjoy the most elusive of mountain birds. The village has two holiday seasons, mid-December to mid-April and June to September. In spring and autumn most hotels are shut and mountain transport does not run. A visit from June onwards produces an excellent variety of birds from the meadowland shrikes and redstarts, up through the pine forest birds like grey-headed woodpecker and nutcracker with citril finch where the pines end, and on to the Alpine choughs in their droves at say Jungfraujoch. Snow finch, Alpine accentor, Alpine swift, and fieldfare are all likely to be seen, and wall creepers occur in the vicinity of the railway station amongst other places.

SUMMER: Alpine swift, nutcracker, Alpine chough, grey-headed woodpecker, wall creeper, Alpine accentor, ring ousel, fieldfare, water pipit, redstart, red-backed shrike, black redstart, citril finch, snow finch.

From the 3,400 feet at which Grindelwald lies there are railways to Kleine Scheidegg (6,700 feet), and then to Wengen and Lauterbrunnen in the next valley. Also from Kleine Scheidegg there is the Jungfraujoch railway through the Eiger that is better for views than birds, though Alpine choughs haunt the top. There is also a chair lift in the other direction to First (7,300 feet). Transport up and walk down bird-watching *en route* is the usual technique. Plenty of accommodation exists but motorists should ensure that their choice of hotel has garage or parking space.

# LAC LEMAN

The eastern end of Lac Leman (Lake Geneva) has a variety of habitats that provide a good cross section of the birds of the whole country. Lying at 1,250 feet the lake itself is a haunt of grebes and duck and is particularly important in winter. In the south-east where the Rhône enters the lake a sizeable delta area has been created with large reed beds, pools, and scrub, and holding little bittern, great reed and marsh warblers and an important population of wintering and migrating duck and waders. The latter include 'maritime' species like knot. The beech woods hold golden oriole, and black kites are everywhere. This area, part of which is a reserve, is called Les Grangettes and is threatened by the proposed development of a new airport. Above Montreux, Alpine meadows, carpeted with wild flowers in spring, give way to pine forests with nutcracker, grey-headed woodpecker, and crested tit, and above this at Rochers-de-Naye are Alpine accentor, Alpine chough, wall creeper, and other usual high altitude species. Black redstart and serin are found in Lausanne and golden oriole in the woods nearby, while black kites are common along the lake edges. There is a good chance of a golden eagle here, and the goldeneye seen on the lake in summer do in fact breed.

SUMMER: little bittern, goldeneye, golden eagle, black kite, golden oriole, nutcracker, Alpine chough, grey-headed woodpecker, Alpine accentor, wall creeper, great grey shrike, woodchat shrike, rock thrush, firecrest, black redstart, crested tit, great reed warbler, marsh warbler, Bonelli's warbler, snow finch, citril finch, serin.

AUTUMN: bar-tailed godwit, turnstone, knot, wood sandpiper, little stint.

Montreux is an excellent headquarters with the mountain railway as an aid to access to the high tops for Alpine species. The best area of the Rhône delta lies east of both arms of the river at Les Grangettes where there is a camp site nearby. The area between the Vieux Rhône and the Grand Canal is also good. Leave route 9 westwards 3 km south of Villeneuve, where there are numerous paths along the shore, canal, river, and through the woods.


## LAC DE NEUCHÂTEL

At the northern end of Lake Neuchâtel is a marshy zone about 500 metres wide and extending for some 40 km along the lake shore. It is the most important wetland in Switzerland. The open shallows are excellent for waders particularly on passage and the adjacent marshes are also very attractive. The large reed beds hold little bittern, purple heron, and great reed warbler, and are a favoured haunt of marsh harriers on passage. Black kites are always to be seen here as on every other Swiss lake. The surrounding woodland contains pied flycatcher and Bonelli's warbler with crested tit on the higher slopes, but unfortunately there is no high (6,000 feet) peak adjacent and those who are in search of high Alpine species as well will have to go through Berne to the Oberland (see Grindelwald).

There is a small reserve at Le Fanel, covering part of the marsh and an area of woodland, that is noted for the longest annual list of migrants in French-speaking Switzerland. It boasts two watch towers.

SUMMER: black-necked grebe, little bittern, purple heron, shoveler, tufted duck, pochard, black kite, pied flycatcher, crested tit, Bonelli's warbler.

PASSAGE: duck, raptors, waders.

The shore from Neuchâtel right round the eastern end and south to Portalban is worth exploring, but the Fanel reserve can always be relied on to produce something of interest. Access requires gumboots, and permits from the Société Romande pour l'Étude et la Protection des Oiseaux, c/o Paul Géroudet, Avénue de Champel 37, 1206 Geneva. Most birds, however, can be seen from public footpaths along the embankment of the canalised River Broye where it enters the lake. These turn off westwards from the road between Campelin and Cudrefin 16½ km south-east of Neuchâtel. There are camp sites and hotels in many places.


## MONT TENDRE

Mont Tendre is the second highest summit of the limestone south-west Swiss Jura, and much less frequented than the slightly higher Dole, though the peak itself is sometimes thronged at summer seek-ends. The flora is superb and the birds are good too. The summit ridge holds typical species like black redstart, ring ousel and the occasional raptor, and as the open ground gives way to the extensive coniferous forest there are citril finch and nutcracker. The forest itself is full of crested tits, goldcrests and firecrests, grey-headed woodpeckers, and periodically crossbills. Rather harder to find but present are capercaillie, black woodpecker, and Tengmalm's owl, while honey buzzards are sometimes seen overhead.

SUMMER: honey buzzard, capercaillie, black woodpecker, grey-headed woodpecker, Tengmalm's owl, nutcracker, black redstart, ring ousel, crested tit, goldcrest, firecrest, crossbill, citril finch.

Leave the Le Pont–Morges road southwards at the Col du Mollendruz along a motorable track. It is a good move to descend by footpaths to Montricher village or to continue along the summit ridge to the Col du Marchairuz. Both of these alternatives are excellent for birds but involve the organisation of return transport.

# Turkey

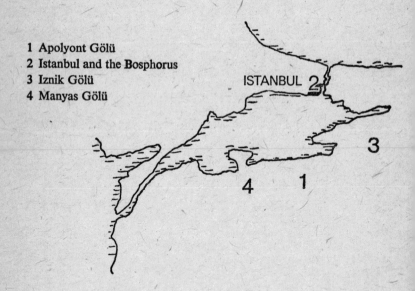

1 Apolyont Gölü
2 Istanbul and the Bosphorus
3 Iznik Gölü
4 Manyas Gölü

ISTANBUL 2

3

4    1

ORNITHOLOGICAL SOCIETY OF TURKEY,
c/o RSPB, The Lodge, Sandy, Beds., UK.

## APOLYONT GÖLÜ

As it is necessary to cross the Bosphorous in order to enjoy the most spectacular migrations in Europe, and as the many people who do inevitably decide to make a dash for one or more of the famous Turkish wetland areas, Lakes Manyas, Iznik, and Apolyont are included in this guide.

Lake Apolyont lies south of the Sea of Marmara to the east of Lake Manyas in a very attractive setting. The village of the same name stands on one of the six lake islands and is an incredibly beautiful mixture of pink and red buildings and bright green trees. Though lush in spring, by late summer the ground becomes parched and dry. The lake is shallow with large reed-fringed mudflats particularly along the south-western shore. Here there are sand banks with large colonies of black-winged stilt and spur-winged plover. The village boasts a colony of whiskered terns on the adjacent water lily beds, and lesser kestrel, and bee-eater and black-headed bunting. White and Dalmatian pelicans, and various herons frequent the shores on passage, and the mud flats are excellent at this time when a wide variety of waders occurs.

SUMMER: black-necked grebe, white-tailed eagle, lesser kestrel, whiskered tern, spur-winged plover, black-winged stilt, Kentish plover, rock nuthatch, Rüppell's warbler, olivaceous warbler.

AUTUMN: pelicans, herons, marsh harrier, falcons, ruff, greenshank, little stint, green sandpiper, avocet, pratincole.

Apolyont lies to the south of the major road just west of Bursa, where there are many hotels. To the north of the town is an area of rice paddies that sometimes holds herons and glossy ibis.

## ISTANBUL AND THE BOSPHORUS

The migration of raptors and storks is largely dependent upon thermals of rising warm air. In such circumstances the birds will soar high on one thermal before gliding in the required direction of travel in search of the next. As thermals occur only over land, birds that soar on migration avoid long sea crossings, which in Europe means that storks and raptors concentrate at the narrow crossings at either end of the Mediterranean. Gibraltar has recently received some attention and is obviously a first rate place but the Bosphorus, between the Mediterranean and the Black Sea, is famous for its dramatic migrations. The main period of passage is from late August, when honey buzzards reach peak numbers, till early October. Birds vary according to the actual period of watching but generally mid-September is the best time for variety with up to eighteen different species of birds of prey seen in a single day. A recent expedition counted for the whole autumn period, some 27 species of birds of prey and amassed the following totals; white stork 207,000;

black stork 6,200; buzzard 13,000; honey buzzard 9,000; lesser spotted eagle 4,300; spotted eagle about 20; short-toed eagle 1,200; booted eagle 250; black kite 2,500; Levantine sparrowhawk 5,000; Egyptian vulture 360; griffon vulture 120. These figures give some idea of the most likely species to be seen but others include imperial eagle, long-legged buzzard (very rare), goshawk, red kite, harriers, and falcons. All of these are also likely to be seen on spring passage which is best at the end of March and beginning of April.

Though these migrants are the major attraction there are others, including the passage of a wide range of other species. Yelkouan shearwaters occur on the Bosphorus, and Istanbul itself boasts black kites over the open street markets while palm doves scavenge amongst the market debris.

PASSAGE: yelkouan shearwater, white stork, black stork, lesser spotted eagle, spotted eagle, short-toed eagle, booted eagle, imperial eagle, buzzard, honey buzzard, griffon vulture, Egyptian vulture, Levantine sparrowhawk, black kite, red kite, hobby, lesser kestrel, crane.

In the autumn migrants keep to the south of the Bosphorus passing over Istanbul. During the crossing, height is lost and on the Asian side the birds are lower and easier to see. The best vantage point is the Kuçuck Çamliça which is the smallest of the two hills opposite Istanbul. There is a frequent and cheap ferry across the straits. In spring the route is much less definite but there is a concentration to the north of Bujukdere and with the right weather actually along the Black Sea coast. Unfortunately this area is unattainable for military reasons and the hill to the north of Bujukdere is the best in the circumstances. It can be excellent. There is a wealth of accommodation in Istanbul.

## IZNIK GÖLÜ

Iznik Lake is the most eastern of the three lakes in Asiatic Turkey included in this guide, and thus is more convenient to the Bosphorus. It is also the largest of the three. There are extensive reed beds with breeding purple heron, little bittern, and the various warblers such as great reed and Savi's. There is also a heronry with night and squacco herons, as well as a strong colony of the ruddy shelduck that is becoming so scarce in Europe. The surrounding farmland and oak scrub by this lake as well as Manyas and Apolyont holds blacked-headed bunting, olivaceous and rufous warblers, great spotted cuckoo and masked shrike.

Passage brings all of the herons, terns and waders that are found at the other lakes and possibly more of the species that can be seen crossing the Bosphorus.

SUMMER: purple heron, night heron, squacco heron, little bittern, ruddy shelduck, great spotted cuckoo, masked shrike, Savi's warbler, great reed warbler, rufous warbler, olivaceous warbler, black-headed bunting.

Iznik Gölü lies north-east of Bursa and is of straightforward access.

## MANYAS GÖLÜ

Lake Manyas lies south of the Sea of Marmara, to the west of Lake Apolyont, and is the site of Turkey's first bird reserve known as Kuş Çenneti (Bird Paradise). The reserve, which lies on the north-eastern shore, covers 125 acres and was created in 1959, though it had previously been protected privately. The shallow water and reed fringed edges provide excellent feeding for a variety of herons about 1,700 pairs of which breed. These include grey and night herons, little egret, and spoonbill, with little bittern and purple heron amongst the reeds. The wood, on which the reserve is based, also holds colonies of pygmy cormorant. Great reed and Savi's warbler haunt the reed beds and roller, Scops owl, and penduline tit haunt the woods, while the agricultural land beyond has bee-eaters in profusion, and black-headed bunting.

Migration of water birds here is outstanding with flocks of up to 2,000 white pelicans and large numbers of glossy ibis and squacco heron. Other species like terns, garganey and ferruginous duck are frequently numerous.

SUMMER: white stork, pygmy cormorant, night heron, little egret, spoonbill, purple heron, little bittern, lesser kestrel, Kentish plover, spur-winged plover, Scop's owl, roller, bee-eater, penduline tit, black-headed bunting, Spanish sparrow.

PASSAGE: white pelican, glossy ibis, squacco heron, ferruginous duck, Caspian tern, white-winged black tern.

Manyas is reached by the ferry across the Bosphorus at Istanbul and then by a major road that passes along the north side of Apolyont. Turn right past here towards Bandirma and Lake Manyas. There is the Özdil Otel at Bandirma, and the Park Otel and Motel Denizkent at Gönen to the west. Many people camp wild near the lake shores. The Kuş Çenneti reserve is well signposted at the lake shore.

# Yugoslavia

1 Baranja (the Danube-
   Drava confluence)
2 Carska Bara
3 Dojransko Jezero
4 Fruska Gora
5 Metković

6 Obedska Bara
7 Plitvico Jezero
8 Lake Prespa
9 Skadarsko Jezero
10 Titov Veles

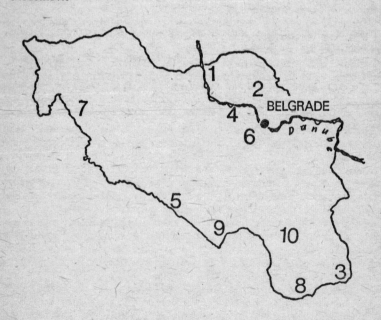

ORNITOLOŠKI ZAVOD,
Zagreb, Ilirski trg 9/2

READ: *Ornithogeographia Serbia* (1950) by S. D. Matvejev (in Serbian with minimal French summary).

## BARANJA (the Danube–Drava confluence)

The marshes, floods, peatbogs, backwaters, and lakes that are such a feature of the Drava as it flows along the Hungarian border and particularly of the Danube in the southern part of its course through that country are brought together at the confluence in a maze of oxbows and counter-oxbows. This area is one of the most important wetlands in southern Europe and can be compared with the Obedska Bara as an ornithological site in Yugoslavia. To the north of the Drava are a series of huge oxbows, several with quite sizeable islands, and just north-east of Osijek lies the magnificent reserve of Kopački Rit. This is a complex of ponds, reed beds, marshy meadows, peatbogs, and flooded forests of outstanding ornithological interest with grebes, pygmy cormorant, purple heron, great white heron, little bittern, greylag goose, and a wide variety of other waterbirds.

The Danube too has a wealth of oxbows on both banks but the more important areas are the backwater ponds that still take some of the flow of the river. They form an intricate and almost unbelievable pattern. The pond reserve at Veliki Rit covers 1,250 acres on the east bank of the Danube at the confluence, while to the north near Bački Monoštor is the reserve of Crna Bara. These Danube marshes (and not only the reserves) are the haunt of some very rare birds including black stork, great white heron, glossy ibis, and white-tailed eagle, as well as a wealth of other species.

The whole of the complex is a mixture of marshes, lakes, agricultural land and forests; large areas are, of course, covered by the rivers in flood twice each year.

SUMMER: grebes, pygmy cormorant, black stork, white stork, little egret, purple heron, great white heron, glossy ibis, little bittern, greylag goose, ferruginous duck, white-tailed eagle, marsh harrier, spotted crake, penduline tit, hoopoe, lesser grey shrike, Savi's warbler, great reed warbler.

Osijek is the obvious headquarters with the rich Kopački Rit reserve just across the Drava. The whole area can be explored by car. The east bank of the Danube is reached by the car ferry at Batina in the north and the new bridge at Erdut to the east. Permits for Kopački Rit can be obtained from Republički Zavod za Zaštitu Prirode SRH, Zagreb, Ilica 44/1.

To the north-east and separate from this major area lies Lake Ludas, which is near Stanišić and against the Hungarian border. This is a shallow water with huge reed beds and is noted for grebes, herons, rails, gulls, and duck including white-headed duck.

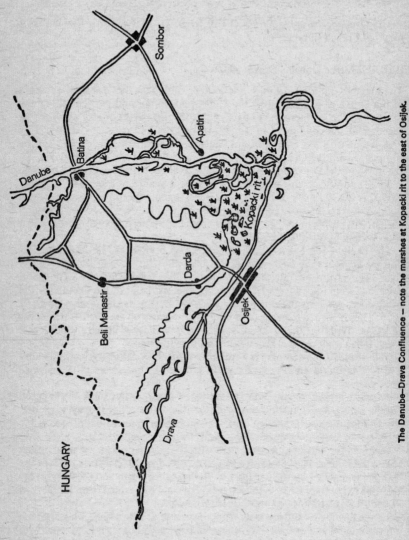

The Danube–Drava Confluence — note the marshes at Kopacki rit to the east of Osijek.

## CARSKA BARA

Carska Bara is an important marsh area north of Belgrade near Zrenjanin that though protected is threatened by the construction of the new Danube–Tisa–Danube Canal. Though quite small it lies in the centre of a quite extensive wetland area that includes the marshes of Perleska Bara and Tiganjica. The breeding population is outstanding and includes 50 pairs of purple heron, little egret, squacco heron, 300–400 pairs of night heron, both bitterns, a few glossy ibises, and 10 pairs of spoonbill. The great white heron occasionally breeds and there is the largest colony, over 200 pairs, of pygmy cormorants in the country, and two pairs of white-tailed eagles. This superb collection of birds is not, however, the only attraction of the area. To the south at the Danube–Tisa Confluence is the flood region of Koviljski Rit which though heavily shot over by the inhabitants of Novi Sad still holds breeding little egrets and a few glossy ibises, and some 20 pairs of pygmy cormorants. It is also a noted gathering ground of storks, and 60 plus black and 150 white storks can be found in autumn.

SUMMER: garganey, pygmy cormorant, purple heron, great white heron, squacco heron, night heron, little bittern, bittern, glossy ibis, white-tailed eagle.

AUTUMN: black stork, white stork, herons.

Carska Bara lies at the centre of the wetland complex between the Tisa, the Bergej Canal, and the fishponds at Ečka south of Zrenjanin. Koviljski Rit lies north of the Danube just east of Novi Sad. Both areas can be reached comfortably from Belgrade in a day.

## DOJRANSKO JEZERO

Dojransko Lake lies in Macedonia and is cut cleanly in half by the Greek border, though the only two villages of any importance lie on the western Yugoslav shore. It is a shallow lake with large reed beds that hold a wide variety of breeding and wintering birds. Dojransko has found its way into the tourist guide books on its ornithological merit too. The local fishermen practice a unique method of harvesting this rich water by using grebes and ducks to herd the fish into the shallows. The headquarters of this fishery is at Stari Dojran, a small village with a population of a hundred. Breeding birds on this 10,500 acre lake are exciting and include great white heron, purple heron, white pelican, and white-headed duck.

The lake is the winter quarters of many grebes, duck, and herons, and there are nearly always some pelicans present throughout the year. The surrounding land with fruit trees has been little explored.

SUMMER: white pelican, great white heron, purple heron, white-headed duck, Savi's warbler, subalpine warbler.

AUTUMN: grebes, duck, herons, pelicans.

Leave the E5 motorway at Valandovo to Stari Dojran. There are two hotels, the Polin and Dojransko Ezero, and a camp site. Boat trips can be arranged easily here. Photography is not allowed within 15 km of Yugoslavia's borders.

## FRUSKA GORA

Fruska Gora is a range of hills to the north-west of Belgrade and immediately
south of Novi Sad. They are not outstandingly high reaching a maximum
height of 1,768 feet, nor are the habitats, mainly beech forest with a sprinkling
of oaks, very exciting. The wealth of birds of Fruska Gora is due to its position
immediately adjacent to the floods and marshes of the Danube to the north,
and Sava to the south. This is the only range of hills near this rich wetland
complex and is thus a favourite breeding haunt of birds that hunt over the
marshes, In 1960, 55,000 acres were declared a National Park with full public
access and various tourist installations. Breeding raptors include golden,
imperial, and white-tailed eagles, black kite, and saker falcon. Of course, the
larger birds are nowhere common but they can be seen soaring about the
main ridge. The smaller birds of the hills include woodpeckers, collared
flycatcher and ortolan bunting, and both storks are regularly noted.

SUMMER: black stork, white stork, golden eagle, imperial eagle, white-tailed
eagle, buzzard, black kite, saker falcon, little owl, golden oriole, lesser grey
shrike, collared flycatcher, hawfinch, ortolan bunting, bee-eater.

From Sremska Mitrovica on the Sava it is only 30 km by road to the Danube
right across the middle of the hills. The main road south from Novi Sad
towards Ruma crosses the hills and there are several minor roads, including
one to the highest point, off to the west. There is a camp site and the hotels
Park, Putnik, and Vojvodina at Novi Sad, and the area is not far from Belgrade. The marshes with huge reed beds along the Danube to the south-east
of Novi Sad are well worth exploring. They hold squacco heron and lesser
grey shrike, and presumably many other herons and marsh species, and can
be seen from the main road E5.

## METKOVIĆ

Metković is situated in the lower Neretva River 95 km north-west of Dubrovnik and 15 km from the sea. Below Gabela the river flows across a marshy
valley floor though it has been extensively canalised near its mouth. The
area of marsh is constantly being reduced by drainage, but the dykes amongst
the water meadows are lined with reeds, and the two large lakes of Deransko
Jezero and Hutovo Blato are not threatened. The latter was declared a reserve
in 1954 covering 8,500 acres, 750 acres of which are totally protected. The surrounding hills rise to 1,750 feet and add a large number of birds to the area's
list which at present numbers about 300 species. The following habitats can
be distinguished and visitors should try to explore them all:

1. Mountains: the open areas above the tree line have some quite extensive
and impressive cliffs. The scrub zone below the tops, and the pine and cypress
woods on the lower slopes are all worth exploring.

2. **Lowlands:** the most important marshes are the reserves at Hutovo Blato and Deransko Jezero, and the nearby odd lakes and ponds. Then there are water-meadows intersected by drainage ditches with a fringe of reeds, and agricultural cultivated areas mainly devoted to maize, vines, and figs. The riverain scrub along the banks of the Neretva consists mainly of salix and poplars. There are also woods and finally the estuary itself to explore.

The whole of the lowland area is liable to winter flooding.

The first and most dramatic area visited by bird-watchers is the Deransko Jezero which holds a wealth of herons of which squacco is the commonest, but purple and night herons, little egret, and both bitterns also breed. Other birds of this area include pygmy cormorant, Cetti's and great reed warblers, as well as excellent numbers of waders and black terns on passage. The hills, of which Rujnica is the best explored, hold rock partridge on the lower slopes and blue rock thrush, rock nuthatch, and Alpine chough higher up. Species like the two vultures, white-tailed eagle (said to breed), short-toed eagle (the commonest raptor), and lanner falcon can be seen almost anywhere. The area also holds several other interesting birds like eagle owl, olivaceous and olive-tree warblers (the latter reaching its furthest north and evidently expanding its range), and bee-eater.

SUMMER: pygmy cormorant, purple heron, little egret, squacco heron, night heron, little bittern, bittern, ferruginous duck, Egyptian vulture, griffon vulture, white-tailed eagle, marsh harrier, short-toed eagle, lanner falcon, rock partridge, quail, Scop's owl, eagle owl, Alpine swift, bee-eater, hoopoe, crested lark, tawny pipit, lesser grey shrike, blue rock thrush, black-eared wheatear, Cetti's warbler, great reed warbler, olivaceous warbler, olive-tree warbler, orphean warbler, Sardinian warbler, subalpine warbler, sombre tit, rock nuthatch, black-headed bunting, ortolan bunting, golden oriole, Alpine chough.

WINTER: white-headed duck.

This area is excellent for a single centre holiday of exploration based on Metković where the Hotel Narona is recommended. Access to most of the countryside is unrestricted though permission must be obtained to visit Hutovo Blato reserve. Contact Professor I. Gluscevic of the local grammar school. One can, however, drive to Karaotok at the centre of the reserve where there is a shelter and an ornithological museum. Metković can be reached by bus and train from Dubrovnik.

## OBEDSKA BARA

The Reserve of Obedska Bara which was created in 1951 covers 1,800 acres to the west of Belgrade and is the richest ornithological area in Yugoslavia. It lies between the Danube and the Sava and is part of a larger and more varied area that is dominated by the regular flooding of the latter river. This occurs in spring and autumn and creates areas of marshland that sometimes persist throughout the year. Of the many permanent backwaters and oxbow

lakes the Obedska Bara is the best known. It is a horseshoe of marsh 12 km
long and 400–700 metres wide near Kupinova holding a series of ponds tha
are heavily overgrown with reeds and sedge. The woods of the area lie alon
the left bank of the Sava and form seven distinct copses separated by mainl
boggy cultivated land. They are mainly ash and blackbeam, the latter bein
protected from flooding by a dyke. The wood at the Kupinova bend of th
Sava is called Kupinski, and this is bounded on the north by the Obedsk
Bara and to the south by the floods. It is intersected by several channels an
these remain flooded boglands throughout the year. The whole of thi
Kupinski–Obedska Bara region is extremely broken with pools, clearings
meadows, and a variety of woodland types. There are also higher wood
outside the flooded areas in the Matijevica region, and at Kadionica an
Darz for example. These have fig trees and a mixture of oaks, ash, elm, an
hornbeam. The final habitat is the agricultural area which is largely compose
of small fields of wheat and maize with some fallow land. The habitats the
are:

1. Flooded woodlands as at Kupinski.
2. Dry woodlands as at Matijevica.
3. Swamps and marshes like Obedska Bara.
4. Cultivated fields.
5. Inhabited areas.

Naturally such a vast and varied area will boast a rich avifauna and thoug
it is surprisingly little visited by foreign ornithologists there is no doubt tha
Obedska Bara is one of Europe's top bird spots. As it is only 40 km from
Belgrade there cannot be many places more conveniently situated. Bird
include imperial and white-tailed eagles, both storks, four grebes, pygm
cormorant and a superb variety of herons including great white heron an
glossy ibis, though the former is only a doubtful breeder. Amongst the smalle
birds penduline tit, lesser grey shrike, and an abundance of 'reedy' warbler
are the most interesting.

SUMMER: the following species can be found in the various habitats:

**1. Flooded woodland:** black stork, imperial eagle, buzzard, black kite, long
eared owl, wryneck, golden oriole, icterine warbler, lesser grey shrike, red
backed shrike.

**2. Dry woodland:** white stork, hobby, golden oriole, hooded crow, lesse
grey shrike.

**3. Swamps:** red-necked grebe, black-necked grebe, pygmy cormorant
purple heron, little egret, great white heron(?), squacco heron, night heron
little bittern, bittern, spoonbill, glossy ibis(?), ferruginous duck, greylag
goose(?), marsh harrier, spotted crake, penduline tit, Savi's warbler, grea
reed warbler, icterine warbler.

**4.  Cultivation:** hobby, quail, hoopoe, crested lark, golden oriole, lesser grey shrike, red-backed shrike.

**5.  Villages:** white stork, collared dove, barn owl, hoopoe, Syrian woodpecker, golden oriole, lesser grey shrike.

The following species are also often seen in the area and possibly breed: lesser spotted eagle, red kite, honey buzzard, Montagu's harrier, red-footed falcon, black-tailed godwit (here reaching furthest south), little gull, whiskered tern, bee-eater.

Only a small part of this magnificent area is a reserve and there is unrestricted access to large parts. The best areas to visit in order to see a cross section of the habitats are the flooded woodland at Kupinski, the dry woodland of Kadionica which lies between the Stone road and the Obedska Bara on the northern part of the swamp, and the villages of Kupinovo and Obrež which lie south and north respectively of the floods. Obedska Bara lies between Belgrade and Sabac and can be reached by leaving the E94 southwards. Permits to visit the reserve must be obtained in advance from Republički Zavod za Zaštitu Prirode SRS, Beograd, Studentski trg 5.

## PLITVICO JEZERO

This area is one of Yugoslavia's favourite inland holiday resorts. It consist of sixteen lakes set in a mountainous region 140 km south-west of Zagreb, between the Kapela and Plješevica massifs. The surrounds are covered with pine forests and these are the main ornithological interest, though the waterfalls between the lakes reflecting different colours from green to blue are the major tourist attraction. The woods contain no less than eight European woodpeckers, and at the current rate of expansion it should not be long before one can add the Syrian woodpecker to the list. Most of the other birds in the area are comparatively commonplace species with the notable exception of the Ural owl. This magnificent bird has an outpost in the mountains of Yugoslavia.

SUMMER: Ural owl, lesser-spotted woodpecker, middle-spotted woodpecker, great-spotted woodpecker, three-toed woodpecker, white-backed woodpecker, black woodpecker, green woodpecker(?), grey-headed woodpecker, crested tit, firecrest.

The whole of this area, which was declared a National Park in 1946, is of open access up to the 3,000 feet and over tops. There is a camp site next to Lake Kozjak, and the first-class Plitvice Hotel. Buses run regularly from Zagreb, and there is a bus connection to the station at Vrhovine.

## LAKE PRESPA

Lake Prespa lies in the very south of Yugoslavia at the point where the country borders Greece and Albania. It is a mountainous region and the lake itself lies at 2,980 feet and is 122 feet deep, facts which do not suggest a good bird area. The Galicia mountains separate Prespa from Lake Ohrid which is larger, 938 feet deep, and a haunt of cormorants, while to the east Prespa is dominated by the 8,500 foot Mount Pellister. The major habitats are the bare rocky mountain tops, then a zone of bushes, thickets and scrub, large oak woods from 5,000 feet downwards, and the agricultural land surrounding the lake. In spite of the height an excellent variety of aquatic species can be seen and both white and Dalmatian pelicans are regular visitors. Other non-breeding but regular visitors include great white heron, spoonbill, and marsh harrier. Purple and squacco herons, and little egret breed and white storks are numerous. There are, for instance, often eight nests at Perovo. The surrounding agricultural land typically holds quail, olivaceous warbler, black-headed bunting, and nightingales are exceptionally numerous. The oak woods are the haunt of buzzard, nightjar, sombre tit and Bonelli's warbler, and where they thin out the thicket zone and bare rock area have rock partridge, black-eared wheatear and the ubiquitous red-backed shrike. The top of Mount Pellister has Alpine accentor.

The lake is a good place for spring migration of waders and terns. The black tern is a common migrant and white-winged black a regular. Autumn passage has been little studied here.

SUMMER: white pelican, Dalmatian pelican, purple heron, little egret, great white heron, squacco heron, white stork, spoonbill, ferruginous duck, marsh harrier, pratincole, gull-billed tern, quail, Syrian woodpecker, crested lark, golden oriole, rock nuthatch, Alpine accentor, nightingale, Cetti's warbler, marsh warbler, olivaceous warbler, Bonelli's warbler, lesser grey shrike, red-backed shrike, black-headed bunting, ortolan bunting.

This is a good holiday place with camp sites at several places and hotels at Oteševo and Carino. The oak woods near the former area hold most of the typical birds. There are no restrictions on access but visitors should not approach the Albanian border too closely. Prespa is conveniently approached in summer via the seasonal airport at Ohrid.


## SKADARSKO JEZERO

Lake Scutari lies at the south-western corner of Yugoslavia in Montenegro and is crossed by the frontier with Albania. It is a huge water covering 100,000 acres, the majority of which is Yugoslav. Several of its feeder rivers, notably the Morača, have formed deltas on the northern shore and a string of marshes runs from the border to beyond the bridge at Virpazar. This area is a maze of lagoons, reed beds, and grasslands and is regularly flooded. The outstanding bird is the white pelican, 25 pairs of which breed regularly, but there is a wide range of other species along this shore including pygmy cormorant, little egret, purple heron and little bittern. During passage periods and in winter the area holds up to 10,000 white-fronted geese, and thousands of dabbling and diving duck. There is also a heavy passage of herons, rails, gulls, and waders.

To the west on the beautiful Montenegrian coast is Petrovac. It is little different to any other part of this coast but has been ornithologically explored and is probably typical of the area. The rocky headlands separate sandy beaches and inland the rugged mountains are clothed with pines on the lower slopes. Typical birds in and around the village are subalpine warbler, olivaceous warbler, and black-headed bunting, the three commonest species. There are also a few olive-tree warblers and a good deal of migration in mid or late May when species include the odd red-footed falcon and Levant sparrow-hawk.

SUMMER: white pelican, pygmy cormorant, little egret, purple heron, little bittern, red-footed falcon, Levant sparrowhawk, marsh harrier, woodchat shrike, red-rumped swallow, subalpine warbler, olivaceous warbler, olive-tree warbler, Spanish sparrow, black-headed bunting.

Lake Scutari is easily reached from Titograd which has an airport. There are several roads across the marshes from the north including the main road to Petrovac. It is only 58 km to this resort and it could form a good base for an exploration of both areas by car. The Villas Oliva is a series of modern flatlets set in an olive grove and they are usually booked as part of a package air holiday. There is a camp site neaby.

The road north of Titograd, route 2, is a well known haunt of wall creeper.

# TITOV VELES

There are three areas of outstanding ornithological interest within a short distance of this southern Yugoslavian town which forms an admirable base for the area:

1. **Babuna Gorge:** formed by the river of that name flowing eastwards from the Solunska massif across the Babuna plateau before joining the River Vardar. Titov Veles is only 4 km to the north and the Yugoslav motorway E5 runs along the Vardar valley. The gorge itself is precipitous with 300 foot cliffs dropping straight down to the river bed. There are some caves near the highest point on the surrounding hills. The latter are dry with a sparse covering of grass and scrub. The river has a few trees along its bank after leaving the gorge, and the Vardar has a luxuriant growth of trees and bushes that add considerably to the variety of birds to be seen here. These include hoopoe, roller, golden oriole, white-backed and Syrian woodpeckers, and penduline tit all nesting within a few yards of each other. However, it is the gorge itself which is the premier attraction with a good collection of raptors. Regular visitors include griffon and Egyptian vultures, golden and booted eagles, long-legged buzzard, red-footed falcon, and lesser kestrel. Over 200 of the latter have been seen in the evening probably flying to a roost near Negotino. Flying around with these birds are a mass of smaller species including Alpine swift, red-rumped swallow, and crag martin. The hillsides hold rock partridge,

the quite common rock nuthatch, rock and blue rock thrushes, and a variety of warblers including the localised olive-tree and olivaceous warblers. Black-headed, ortolan and Cretzschmar's buntings are all found.

SUMMER: griffon vulture, Egyptian vulture, golden eagle, long-legged buzzard, peregrine, lesser kestrel, Alpine swift, red-rumped swallow, crag martin, rock partridge, rock nuthatch, hoopoe, roller, golden oriole, white-backed woodpecker, Syrian woodpecker, penduline tit, sombre tit, rock thrush, blue rock thrush, short-toed lark, black-eared wheatear, tawny pipit, Sardinian warbler, orphean warbler, olive-tree warbler, olivaceous warbler, icterine warbler, black-headed bunting, ortolan bunting, Cretzschmar's bunting.

PASSAGE: black stork, booted eagle, red-footed falcon, lanner falcon.

Leave Titov Veles southwards on the motorway E5 and stop after 4 km where there is an obvious white farmhouse on the right just before the road crosses the Babuna River. There is a well marked track to a farm and a fork that in 2 km leads by foot to the gorge. Sit at the gorge entrance or on the hills above it. Explore the whole area thoroughly not forgetting the trees beside the Vardar on the far side of the motorway.

Several groups have camped 'wild' here but there is a camp site and the Hotel Internation in Titov Veles.

2. **Derven:** an unmapped place on the Titov Veles–Prilep road consisting of a round obvious monastery and a restaurant. The hillsides rising to the west are dry and covered with scrubby bushes. Hoopoe, rock bunting and rock partridge are found on the 1 km ascent to the top. Here one looks down into a gorge that will probably become as well known to bird-watchers as the Babuna Gorge to the north-east. Egyptian and griffon vultures and lammergeier can be seen and eagle owls are present. Long-legged buzzards have been seen as has the localised isabelline wheatear.

SUMMER: long-legged buzzard, griffon vulture, Egyptian vulture, lammergeier, eagle owl, hoopoe, rock partridge, rock nuthatch, woodchat shrike, isabelline wheatear, rock bunting.

The route 500 is very poor and the best route from Titov Veles is south along the motorway to its junction with route 19 at Gradsko. Then westwards to Prilep and north on route 500 for 10 km to Derven. Watch for round monastery on right and climb hill on the opposite side of the road.

3. **Katlanovo:** to the north of the village of that name near the motorway between Skopje and Titov Veles is an area of ponds, marshes, peatlands and submerged plains in the valley of the River Vardar. In particular the central lake which is ½ km across, shallow and mainly reed-covered is excellent. In 1965 there was just a little open water, and in 1967 serious drainage works were in progress. Nevertheless the area should be good for a while yet and there is always the hope that the project might fail. The aridity of the surrounding scrubby hillsides is in strong contrast to the willow-fringed lake though to the south there is a mixed plantation of young trees. Birds in this miniature

bird haunt include little egret and little bittern, pygmy cormorant, ferruginous duck, black tern, and a good collection of small birds including icterine warbler and the unexciting thick-billed reed bunting. Raptors have included short-toed eagle.

SUMMER: black-necked grebe, pygmy cormorant, little egret, little bittern, ferruginous duck, short-toed eagle, lesser kestrel, water rail, black tern, golden oriole, kingfisher, icterine warbler, thick-billed reed bunting.

This area, though being drained, is so convenient to visit by bird-watchers bent on seeing the Babuna Gorge or Greece that it is hoped that some will stop and have a look round and watch the progress of what was one of the eight most important wetlands in Yugoslavia.

Leave the motorway at Skopje if coming from the north and take the old Skopje–Titov Veles road. The lake is nearby just before Katlanovo. This route is no longer than the E5 but slightly slower and more interesting.

# Index of Places

## John Gooders
## How to Watch Birds  95p

Concise, comprehensive and practical – the essential handbook of how, when and where to watch birds. Advice is given on equipment and reference books; details of clubs and societies; suggestions for record-keeping and more advanced field-study; bird photography and sound recording.

Illustrated throughout with charts, maps and diagrams, *How to Watch Birds* explains where and when to find summer and winter visitors, the migrants and the rarities.

## Where to Watch Birds  £1.50

Wherever you go in England, Scotland and Wales there's a wealth of bird life to watch – geese at Slimbridge on the Severn, puffins at Bempton Cliffs, buzzards in Snowdonia, or Arctic terns on Tiree . . .

*Where to Watch Birds* is a complete guide to the best sites – how to get there and what to expect at what time of year – with map references for every site and pages of maps.

## Tony Soper
## Wildlife Begins at Home  75p

'The casual approach of reluctant gardeners may encourage wild life more than garden enthusiasts' manicured lawns and flower beds. As woodland disappears the garden is becoming an important refuge for bird and insect life'  DAILY TELEGRAPH

'Informal yet informative' WILDLIFE

## Greet Buchner and Fieke Hoohgvelt
## Nature On Your Side

Pests in the garden or home? This fascinating handbook tells you how to get rid of garden and household pests *without* using expensive and often harmful pesticides and aerosols. Nature's own very effective deterrents for aphids, slugs and snails, rats and mice, wasps and fleas, cockroaches and rabbits. Plus special chapters on compost-making and 'biodynamic' gardening. A most original and useful handbook for every home-maker and gardener.

## Roger Phillips
## Wild Flowers of Britain £3.95

A unique encyclopedia of the flowers of the countryside in which over 1,000 wild flowers are illustrated in beautiful full-colour photographs set out in the sequence of the seasons and accompanied by comprehensive descriptions.

## Brian G. Furner
## Food Crops from your Garden or Allotment 60p

This easy-to-read handbook makes raising fruit and vegetables simple, economical and satisfying. One of today's foremost horticulturists clearly sets out information on types of soil . . . fertilizers and compost . . . watering . . . pest control . . . exotic vegetables for entertaining . . . home freezing . . .

You will be able to grow your own delicious crops and enjoy the flavour of the best and tastiest fruit and vegetables that even market produce cannot equal.

## The Kitchen Garden 60p

A comprehensive guide to providing your family with healthy, nourishing food all the year round.

Here is sound, practical advice by a well-known vegetable specialist – on planning your garden space; how to dig; fertilizing the soil; what to sow. There is a monthly time-table of essential jobs, and many labour-saving hints are given.

'Splendid value' HOME GARDENER

## C. E. Lucas Phillips
## The Small Garden 95p

The classic book on general gardening, it contains everything the amateur gardener needs to know. Layout and design . . . soil cultivation . . . greenhouse management . . . diseases and remedies . . . the year's work.

'One of the best general books on gardening' COUNTRY LIFE

'So much useful information . . . can take its place among the best professional textbooks' HOUSE AND GARDEN

## J. H. B. Peel
## Along The Roman Roads of Britain 95p

'Watling Street takes him from Dover to Wroxeter ; Sarn Helen East conducts him into Welsh mountains ; Dere Street from York to the Wall and over the Border ; Peddars Way into East Anglia ; and a final journey along the Foss Way into the West Country. With his strong sense of history, easy flow of narrative, and wide knowledge of what will repay a digression en route, he is a rewarding companion on each of these excursions' TIMES LITERARY SUPPLEMENT

## G. R. Crosher
## Along the Cotswold Ways £1.25

Takes the modern traveller in the footsteps of the Iron Age, Roman and Saxon settlers, the medieval monks and traders, salt-carriers, wool merchants and Welsh drovers — who travelled the ancient Ways for more than fifty centuries. 'From Chipping Campden to Dryham, from Burford to Cheltenham, scarcely a village is missed . . . soundly informative about history, landscape and architecture . . .' COUNTRY LIFE

## Barry Williams
## Camping

A complete guide to one of the fastest growing pastimes for the holidaymaker and everyone who loves the open county. Written by the editor of *Camping* magazine, here is an authoritative handbook essential for the novice and very useful for even the most experienced camper.

## Ken Welsh
## Hitch-Hiker's Guide To Europe 80p

'Very useful information to any travellers who like to get about at low cost . . . Hitch-hikers will adopt it as their travelling bible but it's amusing and informative for those who fancy more traditional ways' BBC

This invaluable guide covers the whole of Europe and gives advice on what to take, routes, eating, sleeping and local transport together with currency hints, useful phrases and information on working abroad.

'An absolute necessity' UCL STUDENT NEWSPAPER

## Alan Young
# Modern Sea Angling 70p

When first published this book was immediately acclaimed an outstanding work of practical instruction for sea anglers. It has since been thoroughly revised to include modern improvements in technique and equipment and an up-to-date coverage of angling facilities around the coast.

# Sea Angling for Beginners 50p

Sea angling remains basically the problem of getting the fish to take a baited hook – by following the author's expert advice the new fisherman will avoid much disappointment. The book deals in a practical way with all the many aspects of fishing – what fish you may catch, what are the best baits to use, and there is a full coverage of tackle and techniques.

## Kenneth Seaman
# Canal Fishing 60p

Traditional methods and tackles are critically examined, and there is advice on bait selection and preparation. There are chapters on angling – for well-known species as well as the more unusual ones – match fishing techniques and the problems of canal maintenance.

## Kenneth Mansfield
# Trout Fishing 70p

Seven articles about all aspects of trout fishing, written by acknowledged experts, and edited to eliminate any duplication of coverage. Supplemented by an appendix on tackle and knots, they make up nearly three hundred pages of solid, no-nonsense advice and help for all trout fishermen.

## Basil Dalton
## **The Complete Patience Book** 60p

You may be alone . . . but you'll never be lonely when you discover
the pleasure of patience. You'll find hours of absorbing but relaxing
activity in this complete guide to a fascinating pastime . . . An authority
on card games, the late Basil Dalton was an expert on Patience. Here, in
one volume, are the results of his years of interest in the subject. Some
are easy, some are more difficult — all provide a unique form of mental
exercise and entertainment.

## Oswald Jacoby & John R. Crawford
## **The Backgammon Book** £1.25

A complete, up-to-date, step-by-step guide on how to play backgammon
for love or money — and win. Written by two world champions and
illustrated with large, precise diagrams, this essential guide ranges from
the crucial opening moves to the finer points of the middle and end games.

In addition to probability tables, etiquette and the official rules of the
International Backgammon Association, there are chapters on the
history of the game, how to run a tournament and how to play chouette
(backgammon for more than two people) plus a useful glossary.

## Jack Nicklaus with Ken Bowden
## **Golf My Way** £2.50

'An absorbing analysis of his method and approach to the game,
covering every aspect in remarkable detail . . . a work unapproached by
any great player since Hogan and Cotton dissected their swings in
books' GUARDIAN

'One of the most comprehensive and best-produced golf books to
appear in recent years' GOLF WORLD